Human-Machine Symbiosis: Trust Reconstruction and Risk Governance in the Era of Generative AI

Zhan Haibao

Translated by Tu Jiajin

CHICAGO ACADEMIC PRESS

Human-Machine Symbiosis: Trust Reconstruction and Risk Governance in the Era of Generative AI
Author: Zhan Haibao
Translator: Tu Jiajin
Language: English
Word Count (for space of all pages): 370 thousand words
Publisher: Chicago Academic Press
Number of Pages: 414
ISBN: 978-1-965890-75-2

Publishing	Chicago Academic Press
	5923 N Artesian Ave
	Chicago IL 60659
Email	contact@chicagoacademicpress.com
Website	http://chicagoacademicpress.com/
Book Size	6X9 inches
First Edition	

About the Translator

TU Jiajin, Ph.D. (Foreign Linguistics and Applied Linguistics, Shanghai International Studies University, 2011), is a professor at Fujian University of Technology (FJUT) in China. He serves as the Director of the Master of Translation and Interpreting (MTI) program and the Center for Translation and International Communication Studies of FJUT. From 2014 to 2015, he was sponsored by the China Scholarship Council to undertake visiting research at Northwestern University in the United States. His scholarly interests include rhetoric, rhetoric and translation, argumentation, discourse analysis and technical communication. He has as a PI completed several ministerial-/provincial-level research projects in these fields.

Translator's Note

This translation is part of a broader initiative to bring contemporary Chinese scholarship to the international audience, with a particular focus on the crucial domain of AI governance. While China's rapid and brilliant advancements in generative AI are increasingly recognized globally, its sustained commitment and significant contributions to shaping global AI governance are less visible, yet equally important.

These contributions are multifaceted, including both state-led efforts, such as the Global AI Governance Initiative proposed in 2023, joint release of AI Global Governance Action Plan at 2025 WAIC, active participation in multilateral frameworks like the UN's Global Digital Compact, and a vibrant, emerging discourse among the nation's scholars. Professor Zhan Haibao's recent monograph, *Human-Machine Symbiosis*, stands as a landmark and latest contribution to this scholarly conversation of AI governance. It exemplifies the depth of contemporary Chinese thought on the ethical and societal futures of AI. We hope our translation of this work is not merely to disseminate ideas, but more importantly, to foster a deeper dialogue, translating and transforming shared values and principles into a foundation for collaborative global action.

This scholarly translation is a collaborative undertaking. I extend my sincere gratitude to my MTI student, Liu Huilin, who pre-edited the Chinese version and produced the initial drafts of translation of the first six chapters. I translated the preface and the remaining chapters, and revised comprehensively and post-edited the entire manuscript. The ultimate responsibility for the final text is my own.

This project would not have been possible without the generous permission of Professor Zhan to translate his work, nor without the timely and invaluable support of the YGYM for its publication.

Preface

In the information age, the emergence of artificial intelligence (AI) technologies, particularly generative AI, is profoundly reshaping the communication landscape and trust mechanisms within human society. This book examines the transformative changes characterizing the current era, with a particular emphasis on the evolution of digital trust, the emergence of intelligent risks, and their implications for the order of communication. As a revolutionary technology, generative AI is fundamentally disrupting traditional modes of information production and dissemination through its powerful content generation capabilities. While this transformation brings unprecedented opportunities, it also raises profound questions about trust, risk, and social order. As such, exploring the construction of digital trust and the management of intelligent risks is crucial for maintaining social stability and promoting healthy technological development.

The motivation for writing this book stems from my deep concern with the transformation of communication order in the era of generative AI. As AI technologies rapidly advance, digital trust is increasingly replacing the traditional forms of interpersonal trust and institutional trust and becoming a central issue. This transformation not only affects the daily lives of individuals, but also fundamentally reshapes the operational fabric of the society. Consequently, there is an urgent need for comprehensive research into intelligent risk, given its particularity and complexity as a new form of risk.

This book is divided into three parts, systematically elaborating on digital trust, intelligent risks, and their interactions in the era of generative AI. The first part focuses on digital trust, and starting from the historical evolution of trust, explores its connotation, construction mechanism, and the influencing factors. The second part examines intelligent risks, and analyzes the evolution of risk forms, the various risks engendered by generative AI and their governance strategies. The third part, in an effort to address intelligent risks, studies the reconstruction path of digital trust from two perspectives: technological construction and social cultivation.

This book is innovative in the following aspects. First, it systematically and holistically explores digital trust and intelligent risk, the two closely related but often separately discussed issues, thus providing a new perspective for understanding the communication order in the era of generative AI. This integrated framework not only helps to comprehensively grasp the impact of AI technology on society, but also provides a theoretical basis for formulating comprehensive management strategies. Second, it proposes a multidimensional trust evaluation framework specifically designed for generative AI systems which can serve as both a theoretical basis and practical guidance for quantitatively evaluating their trustworthiness. This groundbreaking framework systematically integrates technical, ethical, and social dimensions, hence enabling more comprehensive and accurate assessments of AI systems' trustworthiness, and provides new ideas for enhancing their social acceptance. Third, it delves into the formation mechanism and calibration strategies of trust bias in generative AI, offering new ideas for improving human-machine collaboration efficiency. By analyzing the sources and impacts of trust bias, this book not only reveals potential problems in AI trust-building processes, but also proposes specific and feasible strategies for correcting these biases. Additionally, it innovatively proposes a digital trust reconstruction mechanism based on hard trust and soft trust, providing a systematic solution to address intelligent risks and reshape communication order. This balanced approach emphasizes both technological optimization and the importance of socio-cultural factors, charting a clear pathway for establishing a comprehensive and sustainable digital trust ecosystem.

This book aims to provide a comprehensive, in-depth, and cutting-edge perspective for academia, industry, and policy makers, so as to promote the building of digital trust and effective governance of intelligent risks in the era of generative AI, and ultimately foster a positive interaction between AI technology and social development. Through in-depth exploration of digital trust and intelligent risks, it not only deepens the understanding in related fields, but also provides theoretical and practical inspiration for building a new communication order in the era of generative AI.

Zhan Haibao

June, 2024

Contents

PART I Digital Trust in the Era of Generative AI

Chapter One The Evolution of Trust: From Interpersonal Trust and Institutional Trust to Digital Trust

The evolution of social trust from interpersonal trust and institutional trust to digital trust reflects profound transformations in social structures and interaction patterns driven by technological advancement and social change. In traditional societies, interpersonal trust served as the foundation of social interactions. It was rooted in direct human contact and deep emotional bonds. Its core lay in the intuitive evaluation of individual character and behavior. As societies progressed and social activities grew more complex, direct contact between individuals has decreased. Especially after the industrial revolution, the social division of labor has been refined, thus institutional trust has become the key to the operation of modern society. For example, people trust general social systems and institutions—such as government, legal system, education and medical care—by their evaluation of system functionality, stability and efficiency. During this phase, the construction of trust relies more on the reasonableness of institutional design, legal norms, and organizational structure. With the rapid development of the Internet and digital technology in the 21st century, digital trust has become a new form of trust. The trust in this stage is not just about trust between people or in systems, but extends to trust in digital platforms, network services, and algorithms. Digital trust is characterized by its multidimensional foundations, including technological security and reliability, information transparency, data privacy protection, and user experience satisfaction, etc. While technological innovation enables new possibilities for constructing digital trust, it simultaneously introduces challenges such as data breaches, privacy violations, and information distortion. This requires our society to improve laws and regulations, ethical norms, and public digital literacy while developing technology, so as to jointly build a stable and reliable digital trust system. Therefore, the evolution from interpersonal trust, institutional trust to digital trust not only mirrors the change of social interaction mode, but also reflects the profound transformation of social governance structure, technological development and cultural values. Throughout this evolution, trust, as an important component of social capital, undergoes changes in form and mechanism that result from social progress and serve in turn as key drivers of continued advancement.

Section 1 Interpersonal Trust: Emotional Bonds of Intimate Relationship Building

In traditional agricultural societies, interpersonal trust has particular significance and impact. In this social structure that is linked by land, and based on blood relations and geographic proximity, interpersonal trust serves not only as the foundation of social interaction, but also as the core of community cohesion and social order. This trust is built on close connections in face-to-face interactions, deeply rooted in shared life experiences, similar values, and social norms passed down from generation to generation. In such environments, people's understanding and mutual trust go beyond mere verbal communication. Through long-term interaction, collective labor, and mutual support in daily life, a deep and almost self-evident trust relationship naturally emerges. This trust based on interpersonal relationships provides an effective social coordination mechanism for traditional agricultural societies, enabling them to maintain stability and harmony in resource-constrained environments. In this regard, interpersonal trust represents both an expression of interdependence among individuals and a crucial form of social capital that sustain the functioning of traditional agricultural societies. Its existence and preservation play an irreplaceable role in promoting cooperation within the community, maintaining social order, and transmitting social norms. Therefore, a deeper understanding and appreciation of interpersonal trust is of great academic and practical significance for grasping the social structure and cultural characteristics of traditional agricultural society, as well as understanding the evolution of trust mechanisms in human society.

1. Interpretation of Connotation: The Essential Nature and Key Elements of Interpersonal Trust

In traditional agricultural societies, interpersonal trust occupies a central position in social communication, and its formation and maintenance mainly rely on direct interpersonal interactions and deep social bonds. Characterized by smaller population sizes, tightly-knit social networks, and relative social insularity, these societies foster frequent and profound connections between individuals. Therefore, shared life experiences and common value systems form the bedrock of trust.[1] In such a social context, interpersonal trust has its unique features. Compared with institutional trust in modern society and digital trust in digital society, it relies more on direct contact and emotional contact between individuals.

Another defining characteristic of interpersonal trust in traditional agricultural societies is its emotional foundation. In such a society, people's lifestyles are relatively simple, the social division of labor is not too complex, and most of them are closely connected to people's daily lives. Consequently, common life experiences have led to the formation of deep emotional bonds among the people. Relationships within families, kinship groups, and neighborhoods are grounded not merely in economic exchanges

1 ZHANG, Qing, GUO, Shengnan. Interpersonal trust, legal trust, and digital trust: the spectrum and evolution of social trust[J]. Journal of Harbin Institute of Technology (Social Sciences Edition), 2021, 23 (6): 51-57.

but primarily in mutual support and collective lived experiences.[1] This emotionally-anchored trust goes beyond simple transactions and profit calculations, being fundamentally rooted in people's deep belief in each other's honesty, integrity, and kindness. For example, mutual assistance between neighbors, mutual support during natural disasters and difficult times, and other trust practices based on mutual assistance are important cornerstones of traditional social stability.

Another defining characteristic of interpersonal trust lies in its reliance on word-of-mouth and reputation. In agricultural societies with relatively limited information dissemination, individual behavior and reputation quickly spread within small communities, serving as crucial criteria for others to evaluate their credibility. Through daily interactions and social activities, people observe and evaluate others' conduct to determine whether someone deserves trust. Honest and trustworthy individuals enjoy a good reputation in the community, while dishonest or unreliable behavior is quickly known to community members, leading to social exclusion or punishment. This reputation-based trust mechanism greatly enhances the social order and the harmony of social relationships.

Furthermore, interpersonal trust in agricultural societies also manifests a respect for tradition and customs. Traditional customs play a role in regulating individual behavior and decision-making in agricultural societies, and the customs and norms formed over time have become the foundation of mutual trust among people. Individuals who adhere to traditional customs and social norms are perceived as more reliable and trustworthy. This form of trust extends beyond direct personal interactions, being deeply rooted in a shared commitment to cultural values and collective identity. For

---

1 ZHU, Qiujin, ZHANG, Fan, ZHONG, Nian. Kinship is paramount, but kinship and virtue are still important: the influence of closeness and personal orientation on interpersonal trust[J]. Psychological Science, 2021, 44 (6): 1461-1468.

instance, in many traditional societies, integrity is regarded as a virtue, and those who abide by social norms and traditional customs are considered trustworthy partners.

In traditional agricultural societies, these characteristics of interpersonal trust collectively constitute its connotative core, reflecting the closeness of interpersonal relationships and the importance of emotions in such societies. Compared with modern society, this trust mechanism based on direct interpersonal contact, emotional bonds, reputation, and respect for tradition and customs plays an irreplaceable role in maintaining social order and promoting social harmony. Despite ongoing evolution in the forms and mechanisms of trust amid social changes, interpersonal trust formed in traditional agricultural societies remains an important perspective for understanding social relationships and building trust.

2. Logic of Trust Building: Socio-Psychological Mechanisms for the Formation and Consolidation of Interpersonal Trust

The construction mechanism of interpersonal trust is a complex socio-psychological process involving multiple levels of interaction across individual psychological traits, sociocultural environments, historical experiences, and specific contexts of interpersonal engagement. In traditional agricultural societies, this process proves particularly pronounced, as the intensity of interpersonal relationships and the unique nature of social structures exert profound influences on trust formation. The following analysis aims to explore in depth the different dimensions of interpersonal trust construction mechanisms, and to reveal the logic and driving forces behind them.

The building of interpersonal trust first relies on direct interaction between individuals. In this interaction, trust is seen as an expectation based on mutual understanding and emotion, which is gradually built and strengthened through continuous social interaction.[1] Direct interpersonal contact provides a platform where individuals can showcase their integrity, reliability, and goodwill, while also observing and evaluating the behavior and trustworthiness of others. Through this interaction, trust gradually forms between individuals. Such trust transcends mere affirmation of present behaviors, extending to positive anticipations of future conduct.

In the process of building interpersonal trust, the socio-cultural environment assumes a crucial role. Social culture provides a shared set of values and behavioral norms that largely define how people interact and what behaviors are considered trustworthy. In traditional agricultural societies, the socio-cultural environment often emphasizes the importance of community cohesion, interdependence, and traditional values. This cultural milieu encourages individuals to place greater emphasis on integrity, responsibility, and contribution to the community in their daily interactions, thereby facilitating the establishment and maintenance of enduring social trust. Cultural traditions and social customs act as a bridging and linking role in this process, not only guiding individual behavior, but also shaping their understanding and expectations of trust.

Historical experience constitutes another critical factor influencing the building of interpersonal trust. Individuals' accumulated experiences from past interactions profoundly shape their assessments of others' trustworthiness. [2] Positive experiences, such as others fulfilling commitments in the past, demonstrating integrity and reliability, can enhance trust; instead, negative experiences, such as deception and betrayal,

---

1 YAO, Xiaodong, QIN, Yaxun. The cognitive emotional integration view of interpersonal trust restoration[J]. Modern Foreign Languages, 2019, 42 (6): 743-754.
2 ZHU, Hong. From "personal trust" to "benefit related": the shift of interpersonal trust—an empirical study on the status of interpersonal trust[J]. Xuehai, 2011 (4): 115-121.

may lead to a loss of trust. In this sense, the construction of trust is a dynamic process that needs to be validated and strengthened through continuous interpersonal interactions. In addition, individuals acquire indirect insights about trust-building through observing and learning from others' trusting or distrusting behaviors within their social environments. This social learning mechanism plays a vital role in transmitting and shaping trust norms across generations.

The building of interpersonal trust also involves a principle of reciprocity, where trust is viewed as a two-way, reciprocal relationship. In this relationship, the giving and receiving of trust are interdependent, and one person's trust in another often expects a reciprocal trust in turn. This reciprocity not only enhances the trust relationship between individuals, but also provides a foundation for the stability and harmony of social relationships. In traditional agricultural societies, the principle of reciprocity holds particular significance in interpersonal trust building due to the interconnectedness of social networks. Mutual support and cooperation among community members are grounded not merely in calculations of personal interest, but, more fundamentally, in a shared commitment to collective well-being and adherence to established social norms.

In short, the construction of interpersonal trust is a multidimensional and dynamic process that involves direct interaction between individuals, socio-cultural environment, historical experience, and the interaction of reciprocity principles. In traditional agricultural societies, this process exhibits specific complexity and uniqueness, profoundly influencing the formation and maintenance of social relationships. By understanding the construction mechanism of interpersonal trust, we can not only better grasp the essence of social relationships, but also provide useful thinking and strategies for promoting social harmony and stability.

Section 2 Institutional Trust: The Institutional Cornerstone of the Operation of Modern Society

Institutional trust in modern society is the dominant form of social trust, which reflects the complex trust relationship between individuals and abstract social systems. With the deepening and specialization of social division of labor, as well as the advancement of information technology and globalization, individuals no longer depend exclusively on direct interpersonal communication for trust building; rather, they increasingly rely on diverse social systems such as government agencies, financial markets, legal systems, healthcare systems, etc.[1] This trust is grounded in the normativity, predictability, and professionalism of the systems. People trust that they can operate according to established rules and serve social members impartially and selflessly. In this process, institutional trust has become the basis for the operation of modern society, thus the transaction cost is reduced, social coordination enhanced, and the stability and development of social order promoted. However, the establishment and maintenance of institutional trust is not spontaneous, but requires the systems themselves to continuously prove their efficiency, transparency and accountability. As modern societies grow increasingly dependent on them, constructing and preserving institutional trust, while ensuring its adaptability and sustainability, constitutes a critical challenge for social governance and progress. Therefore, a deep understanding of the connotation, mechanism and challenges of institutional trust is of vital significance for promoting the harmony and progress of modern society.

---

1 YANG, Yiyin. "We belong to the same community": a case study of trust construction process[J]. Sociological Research, 1999 (2): 40-54.

1. Connotation Analysis: The Core and Prominent Characteristics of Institutional Trust

The evolution of social trust reflects the change of social structure and communication mode, from interpersonal trust based on direct human contact to institutional trust dependent on abstract social system, and then to emerging digital trust. This evolution not only reveals the diversity of trust mechanisms, but also reflects how social organization and technological advancements fundamentally reshape human trust-building paradigms.

In the early days of human society, interpersonal trust was the foundation of social interaction. As societies evolved, especially when entering modern society, the scope of individual social activities has expanded, alongside increasingly specialized labor divisions. Direct interpersonal relationships can no longer cover all areas of social communication. Therefore, institutional trust has become an indispensable form of trust in modern society, defined as individuals' trust in institutional systems (such as government institutions, financial system, legal system, education system, etc.). The trust builds on people's confidence in a system's functional efficacy, operational stability, and behavioral predictability, rather than relying on direct knowledge of individual members within the system. The defining characteristics of institutional trust are manifested in the following dimensions:

First, institutional trust is based on confidence in the overall operational mechanism of a system, which is typically established through its historical performance, public image, and understanding of the internal rules and procedures. For example, citizens' trust in the legal system is founded on their belief that the law will be enforced fairly and justly. Such faith supports the protection of social order and individual rights.

Second, institutional trust has certain predictability. Individual trust in a system is grounded not only in past experience, but also in expectations of the system's future performance. This expectation involves the stability and predictability of the system, that is, its capacity to consistently deliver reliable services over time. For example, investors' trust in financial markets includes expectations of fair enforcement of market rules and effective market oversight, both of which critically affect their investment decisions.

Furthermore, the establishment and maintenance of institutional trust are also affected by information transparency and communication efficiency. In the information age, transparent information flow and effective communication mechanisms prove crucial for maintaining and enhancing public trust in institutions. For instance, a government can improve the transparency and public participation in policy-making by regularly releasing policy implementation reports, conducting public consultations and feedback mechanisms, thereby enhancing public trust in it.

The formation and maintenance of institutional trust is faced with many challenges, including comprehension barriers caused by increasing system complexity, information asymmetry and the spread of false information, as well as the impact of system failures. To address these challenges, system designers and administrators must implement measures such as improving the transparency of system operation, strengthening public communication, and improving the response and repair capabilities of the systems to maintain and enhance institutional trust.

With the further development of society, particularly the rapid evolution of digital technologies, digital trust has emerged as a new form of trust, the trust in emerging technologies such as digital platforms, network services, and algorithms. While distinct from institutional trust, digital trust, like its institutional counterpart, fundamentally relies on the functional efficacy and operational stability of abstract social systems. The evolution of institutional trust reflects the adaptability and diversity of the social trust building mechanism. With the change of social structure and technological environment, the form and mechanism of trust are constantly evolving and adapting.

2. Trust-Building Path: Formation Mechanism and Influencing Factors of Institutional Trust

The formation mechanism of institutional trust constitutes the cornerstone of modern social operation, involving a series of complex social, psychological and political processes, aiming to establish and maintain individual trust in the social systems.[1] These systems, including government, law, education, healthcare, and finance systems, are the core of complex interactions in modern society. Institutional trust is shaped not only by the performance and efficiency of a system or an institution itself, but also by the sociocultural context, historical precedents, and its interactions with the public.

Transparency of social systems is one of the key elements to build institutional trust. It means that the operation, decision-making process, and results of a system are open and accessible to the public.[2] For example, a government can increase the visibility and predictability of its activities through measures such as holding open meetings, implementing transparent decision-making processes, and disclosing public fiscal budgets, thereby enhancing public trust in it. In the financial system, transparency is achieved through public disclosure of investment risks, detailed information

---

1 ANANNY, M., CRAWFORD, K. Seeing without knowing: limitations of the transparency ideal and its application to algorithmic accountability[J]. New Media & Society, 2016, 20 (3): 973-989.

2 MATTEI, M., PLATIKANOVA, P. Enhancing bank transparency: financial reporting quality, fraudulent peers and social capital[J]. Accounting & Finance, 2023, 63 (3): 3419-3454.

on financial products, and regulatory reports from financial institutions. These practices empower investors to make wiser decisions while strengthening public trust in the market.

Accountability mechanisms and responsibility frameworks of the systems also constitute vital components in establishing institutional trust. An effective accountability mechanism ensures that when systemic failures or misconduct occur, responsible parties can be promptly identified and appropriate corrective measures implemented. For example, the legal system ensures fairness and accountability through independent judicial review and legal liability system to strengthen people's trust in it. Similarly, in the healthcare system, the investigation and handling mechanisms for medical accidents, as well as the professional certification of healthcare service providers, are also key factors in building public trust.

The performance and efficiency of social systems are equally crucial for the construction of trust. A system's capacity to effectively and efficiently fulfill its functional mandates and service commitments forms the foundational basis for earning public trust. For example, the education system can establish public trust in it by providing high-quality educational services, ensuring educational equity, and promoting academic achievement. Similarly, the healthcare system can gain the trust of the public by providing reliable and efficient medical services to meet their health needs.

Historical experience and cultural factors also play an important role in the construction of institutional trust. The historical experience of individuals and groups, including their memory and evaluation of a system's past performance, affects their expectations and level of trust in its future behavior. In addition, cultural values and social norms shape people's basic understanding of trust and trustworthiness. These cultural elements may vary across societies and groups, yet collectively exert substantial influence on the formation of institutional trust.

Public participation and feedback mechanism is another crucial aspect of building institutional trust. By involving the public in the decision-making process and providing channels for feedback and suggestions, systems or institutions can enhance the transparency and fairness of their decisions while better aligning with societal needs and expectations. For example, in the process of formulating public policies, a government can increase the acceptance of policies and enhance public trust in it through methods such as public consultation, opinion solicitation, and public hearings.

In conclusion, the construction of institutional trust is a multi-dimensional and dynamic process. It requires the systems or institutions not only to meet the public's expectations regarding performance and efficiency, but also to promote transparency, accountability, public participation and cultural adaptability. Through these comprehensive measures, they can establish a solid foundation of trust among the public, providing support for the stable operation and development of modern society.

Section 3 Digital Trust: A New Form of Trust in the Intelligent Era

Digital trust, as an emerging and unique form of social trust in the digital society, reflects the degree of public reliance on digital platforms, network services, data processing, and algorithms amid rapid advancements in information technology. This trust is distinct from the traditional interpersonal trust and institutional trust, and is the one in both technology and the participants in the digital ecosystem (including service providers, platform operators, content creators, etc.). The formation of digital trust depends on key factors such as technological security, operational transparency, privacy data protection measures, and user satisfaction. With the deepening of digital transformation, digital trust has not only become the cornerstone maintaining the digital economic operation, but also a driving force behind social innovation and technological development. However, building and maintaining digital trust faces numerous challenges, including data breaches, online fraud, and algorithmic bias. Addressing these issues requires multidimensional efforts spanning technology, law, and ethics to enhance public trust in digital environments. Therefore, understanding the essence of digital trust and the challenges it faces has profound significance for promoting the healthy development of the digital society and building a more open, just, and secure cyberspace.

1. Definition Clarification: The Concept and Attributes of Digital Trust

As an emerging form of trust, digital trust has increasingly become the focus of attention with the rapid development of digital technology and the popularity of Internet applications. It refers to an individual or organization's trust in technology platforms, network services, data processing, and online transactions in a digital environment.[1] The core of digital trust lies in the trust subject's dependence on technology and trust in all parties within the digital ecosystem, including service providers, platforms, technologies, and algorithms. In this process, the construction of trust is not only influenced by technological characteristics, but also closely tied to factors such as user experience, information security, privacy protection, and laws and regulations.

One of the significant characteristics of digital trust is its technology-centric nature. The establishment of this trust largely depends

---

1 KELTON, K., FLEISCHMANN, K. R., WALLACE, W. A. Trust in digital information[J]. Journal of the American Society for Information Science and Technology, 2007, 59 (3): 363-374.

on the stability, security, and user friendliness of the technology platform.[1] For example, e-commerce platforms establish and maintain consumer trust by providing safe and secure payment systems, clear transaction processes, and high-quality customer service. Large e-commerce platforms such as Amazon and Alibaba provide a stable and reliable online shopping experience, effectively protecting consumers' transaction security and personal information, thus earning widespread user trust.

Digital trust also heavily relies on the transparency and accessibility of information. In the digital environment, users can easily access a large amount of information, including product reviews, service ratings, and user feedback, which is crucial for building and maintaining trust. For example, travel booking platforms, such as Booking.com or Airbnb, offer user reviews and rating systems that allow potential users to make decisions based on others' experiences and evaluations. This community-based trust mechanism significantly enhances users' trust in the platforms.

Digital trust also involves issues of privacy protection and data security. With the frequent occurrence of data breaches and privacy violations accidents, users are increasingly concerned about the security and privacy rights of their data.[2] Therefore, how to protect user data and prevent data abuse has become a key challenge in building digital trust. For example, the social media platform Facebook once faced a serious public trust crisis after a data breach incident, prompting the company to strengthen privacy protection measures and data security management to regain user trust.

---

1 LI, W. The role of trust and risk in citizens' E-government services adoption: a perspective of the extended utaut model[J]. Sustainability, 2021, 13 (14): 7671.

2 SÖLLNER, M., HOFFMANN, A., LEIMEISTER, J. M. Why different trust relationships matter for information systems users [J]. European Journal of Information Systems, 2016, 25 (3): 274-287.

In addition, laws, regulations, and standards also play an important role in building digital trust. With the advancement of the digital economy, numerous countries and regions have started to formulate and enforce pertinent laws and regulations aimed at regulating the functioning of digital markets and safeguarding consumer rights, such as the General Data Protection Regulation (GDPR) of the European Union (EU). These laws and regulations not only enhance users' trust in digital services, but also promote the formation of a healthy and orderly market environment.

The building of digital trust is also influenced by socio-cultural factors. People's acceptance and trust in technology vary across different social and cultural backgrounds. Some societies may rely more on interpersonal relationships and direct social interactions to establish trust, while in others, people may be more willing to trust technology and systems. Therefore, understanding and respecting the trust building mechanisms of users from different cultural backgrounds is particularly important for cross-border digital platforms.

In short, the content and the characteristics of digital trust reflect the comprehensive effects of multidimensional factors such as technology, information, privacy, law, and culture. In the digital age, building and maintaining digital trust is not only a technological challenge, but also a social and cultural one. To tackle these challenges, efforts from multiple aspects such as technological innovation, regulatory improvement, cultural adaptation, and social education are needed to establish a safe, secure, reliable, transparent, and inclusive digital ecosystem.

2. Formation Mode: A Multidimensional Dynamic Mechanism for Building Digital Trust

In the digital age, building digital trust has become the key to ensuring the healthy development of the digital economy. The construction mechanism of digital trust is not merely related to the development and application of technology, but also involves user experience, data security, privacy protection, improvement of laws and regulations, and comprehensive consideration of social and cultural factors. This section will delve into the construction mechanism of digital trust from multiple dimensions, aiming to provide a comprehensive perspective to understand and address the challenges currently faced.

The reliability and security of technology serve as the cornerstone for building digital trust. At the technical level, strengthening system security and ensuring stable operation of technology are prerequisites for establishing user trust. For example, adopting advanced encryption technology to protect the security of data transmission, using blockchain technology to improve transaction transparency and immutability, and enhancing fraud detection capabilities through machine learning technology are all effective means of building digital trust. Amazon improves the stability and processing power of its e-commerce platform by using cloud computing services, while utilizing machine learning technology to enhance the accuracy of personalized recommendations. These technological applications greatly enhance users' trust in the platforms.

Optimizing user experience is also a key step in building digital trust. A concise and clear user interface, smooth interaction process, and personalized service experience can effectively enhance user satisfaction and trust. In addition, timely and transparent customer service and feedback mechanisms can help users receive effective support when encountering problems, thereby enhancing trust. For example, Spotify[1] has established user trust in its music recommendation algorithms and services by

1 Spotify is a streaming music service platform and known in China as "Shengtian" (声田, field of sound) and "Sheng Po Tian" (声破天, Sound Pierces the Heavens).

providing personalized music recommendations and excellent customer support experiences.

Data security and privacy protection are essential elements of digital trust that cannot be ignored. With the frequent occurrence of data breaches, users are increasingly concerned about the security and privacy of their data. Therefore, digital service providers need to take effective measures to protect user data, such as implementing strict data access controls, providing data encryption services, and conducting regular security audits. Meanwhile, transparent data processing policies and users' ability to control their own data are also keys to enhancing trust. For example, the EU's GDPR requires companies to clearly inform users how their data is collected, used, and stored, giving users greater control over their data and thus enhancing their trust in digital services.

The establishment and improvement of laws, regulations, and industry standards provide institutional guarantees for digital trust. By formulating and implementing laws and regulations on data protection, consumer rights, and cybersecurity, rules and standards can be set for the healthy development of the digital economy. At the same time, the formulation of industry standards also helps to unify technical specifications and service quality, and enhance the trust of the entire industry. For example, the Payment Card Industry Data Security Standard (PCI DSS) provides strict security measures and compliance requirements to protect payment data, fostering user trust in online payments.

Sociocultural factors also play an important role in the construction of digital trust. Users from different cultural backgrounds may have varying levels of acceptance of and trust in digital technology. Therefore, understanding and respecting users' cultural values and habits, and designing services and communication methods that are in line with local cultural characteristics, are particularly important for cross-cultural service platforms. For example, WeChat's success in China, in part, stems from its keen understanding of Chinese users' social habits and cultural preferences; by providing services and features tailored to these nuances, WeChat has cultivated widespread trust and adoption.

The building of digital trust is a multifaceted process that involves multiple dimensions such as technology, regulations, and culture. Facing the increasingly complex digital environment, only by comprehensively considering these factors and adopting effective strategies and measures can we build and maintain user trust in the digital age, and promote the healthy and sustainable development of the digital economy.

Chapter Two Intelligent Trust: Digital Trust in the Generative AI Era

In the era of generative AI, digital trust, particularly AI-centric trust, has become a critical pillar of social operation. With the rapid development and widespread application of generative AI technology, from content creation to decision making, and then to personalized services, AI is redefining the way people interact with technology and reshaping paradigms for information consumption, social interaction, and even economic activities. In this process, users' trust in AI systems affects not only the adoption and application of the technology itself, but also the society's attitude and response to the emerging technologies. The complexity and autonomy of generative AI require users to maintain trust in the behavior and output of AI systems even without direct control and complete understanding of them. This trust is built on cognitive evaluations of AI technological performance, affective bonds between AI systems and their development teams, and trust in the institutional environment that supports AI applications. Furthermore, digital trust in the generative AI era also involves broader social, ethical, legal, and cultural issues. How to ensure the fairness, transparency, and explainability of AI applications, and how to deal with privacy protection and data security issues arising from the applications are key challenges in building and maintaining digital trust. Therefore, digital trust in the era of generative AI serves not only as a catalyst for technological innovation and social progress, but also a cornerstone for maintaining social stability and promoting human well-being. As AI technology assumes an increasingly pivotal role in shaping the future of society, building a robust and sustainable digital trust system, one that ensures broad social support for and active participation in AI development, will be critical for advancing human progress.

Section 1 Exploring the Nature of AI Trust: Contextual Shifts of Trust under Technological-Ethical Risks

The concept of trust in AI is fundamentally grounded in the critical reflection on techno-ethics, human-machine collaboration, and social impact. As emphasized by Weizenbaum in his groundbreaking work *Computer Power and Human Reason*[1], the development of technology must be accompanied by a commitment to human values and social responsibility. The trust in AI is based not only on the evaluation of its technical performance, but also on the assessment of its design principles, ethical standards, and social objectives. Luhmann's viewpoint on trust as a mechanism for simplifying social complexity proposed in *Trust and Power*[2] provides a theoretical basis for our understanding of trust in AI. In the AI domain, this trust manifests as expectations of system capability, benevolent intent, and procedural integrity, and is a prerequisite for users to accept and rely on AI technology. Meanwhile, Floridi's exploration of information ethics in *The Ethics of Information*[3] emphasizes the importance of ensuring transparency, fairness, and accountability in building trust in the technology. Thus, the construction of AI trust is a complex process involving multidimensional technical, ethical, and social factors. It demands that in technological innovation, we should examine AI's social impacts to ensure harmonious alignment between technological development and the preservation of human values as well as collective well-being.

---

1 WEIZENBAUM, J. Computer Power and Human Reason[M]. San Francisco: W. H. Freeman and Company, 1976.
2 LUHMANN, N. Trust and Power[M]. New York: John Wiley & Sons, 2018.
3 FLORIDI, L. The Ethics of Information[M]. Oxford: Oxford University Press, 2013.

1. The Nature of AI Trust: Conceptual Expansion of Trust from the Perspective of Human-Machine Integration

The conceptualization of AI trust evolves from the concepts of technological trust, human-machine trust, and digital trust. It reflects contemporary society's perceptions and expectations of and reliance on this emerging technological domain amid its widespread application. Through in-depth analysis of these foundational trust concepts, we can gain a more comprehensive understanding of the complexity and multidimensional nature of AI trust.[1]

Technological trust, as the cornerstone of AI trust, primarily focuses on users' confidence in a technological system's reliability, security, and effectiveness. This trust is built on the evaluation of technical performance, emphasizing the system's ability to execute tasks according to predefined standards and expectations.[2] In the field of AI, technological trust not only includes the evaluation of algorithm accuracy, but also involves system transparency, explainability, and security of data processing. As AI technologies advance, ensuring both technical efficiency and algorithmic fairness has become a critical challenge in building technical trust.

Human-machine trust further expands the dimensions of trust. It not only includes trust in technology itself, but also encompasses people's trust in the interactions with AI systems. This trust emphasizes interaction intimacy, behavioral naturalness, and system responsiveness in human-machine engagements. The building of human-machine trust requires AI systems to not only understand human needs and intentions, but

---

1 SUN, Liwen, LI, Shaoshuai. Construction and analysis of trust mechanism for artificial intelligence technology under risk scenarios[J]. China Science and Technology Forum, 2022 (1): 150-160.

2 HE, Jiangxin, ZHANG, Pingping. Research on the path from "Algorithm Trust" to "Human Machine Trust"[J]. Dialectical Research, 2020, 36 (11): 81-85.

also provide feedback and response in a way that meets human expectations. Therefore, the design of human-machine interface, the behavioral predictability of AI systems, and the sensitivity to user emotions are all key factors that affect the construction of human-machine trust.

Digital trust, formed within digital ecosystems, integrates elements of technical and human-machine trust while emphasizing user confidence in platforms, service providers, and the broader network environment. The construction of digital trust relies on the transparency of information in the digital environment, the security of online transactions, and the protection of user privacy. In AI applications, digital trust manifests as users' confidence in AI service platforms grounded in the comprehensive evaluations of the quality of AI services, and the transparency and fairness of data processing provided by the platform.

By applying these concepts of trust to the analysis of AI trust, it can be inferred that it is a multidimensional trust system integrating technical trust, human-machine trust, and digital trust. This composite trust system demands not only technical efficiency, security, and reliability in AI technologies but also requires transparent, intimate, and natural interactions between AI systems and users. Concurrently, in digital applications, it is necessary to ensure the credibility of AI service platforms and the integrity of network ecosystems. [1] Therefore, building trust in AI demands a comprehensive and holistic approach, encompassing technological advancements, system design, user experience, and legal and regulatory frameworks, to ensure technological progressiveness, system affinity, and service fairness, thereby fostering widespread user trust and support. Transparent algorithm design, impartial data processing, efficient user

1 MENG, Xiaoxiao. Risk crisis and trust construction in the era of artificial intelligence: an analysis based on risk theory[J]. Journal of Zhengzhou University (Philosophy and Social Sciences Edition), 2020, 53 (5): 120-125.

feedback mechanisms, and comprehensive privacy protection measures are all essential factors in this process.

Generative AI trust, as a vital branch of AI trust, focuses on users' trust in AI systems capable of content generation, innovative problem-solving, and autonomous learning. These types of systems—including natural language processing (NLP) models, image generation algorithms, or music composition AI—challenge traditional trust building paradigms by demanding high accuracy and reliability of technology, and creative outputs aligned with human ethical standards, aesthetic tastes, and social expectations. Therefore, building trust in generative AI not only necessitates precision and security at the technical level, but also requires the generated content to be appropriate, creative, and ethical.

When constructing trust in generative AI, users' trust in the authenticity, originality, and applicability of AI-generated content is particularly crucial.[1] For example, when employing AI for news generation, users need to trust the system to provide factually accurate information; in the field of artistic creation, users seek the outputs of originality and artistic value. These demands necessitate that generative AI systems achieve not only technical sophistication in handling complex data patterns and learning models, but also ethical alignment with human norms and social standards.

In addition, generative AI trust is greatly influenced by the transparency and explainability of AI systems. Given the inherent complexity of generative AI's operational mechanisms and decision-making processes, users often struggle to understand how AI generates specific content or solutions. Therefore, enhancing system transparency—enabling

---

1 KONG, Xiangwei, TANG, Xinze, WANG, Ziming. A review of research on interpretability of artificial intelligence decisions[J]. Systems Engineering Theory and Practice, 2021, 41 (2): 524-536.

users to understand AI's working principles and decision logic—is vital. This includes developing explainable AI models and providing user-friendly explanation tools to help users understand the process and logic of AI generated content.

Ethical data usage and privacy protection are equally crucial in building generative AI trust. Since generative AI systems depend on vast datasets for training and operation, ensuring that the collection, processing, and use of data respect user privacy and comply with ethical standards forms another important aspect of building user trust. This involves not only improvements in technology and management measures, but also compliance with relevant laws and regulations and the assumption of social ethical responsibilities.

2. Technical Competence, Goodwill, and Integrity: The Three-Dimensional Construction of Al Trust

AI trust is a multifaceted construct, reflecting the complexity and diversity inherent in its formation. It encompasses cognitive (evaluative), emotional and behavioral components, and is shaped by characteristics of both the trustor and the trustee (AI), and the factors related to knowledge, institutional systems, calculations, perception and personality. This comprehensive framework captures key elements in the trust building process: from rational evaluation at the cognitive level, and intuition and feelings at the emotional level, to actual dependence at the behavioral level; from the personality and cognition of the trustor to the ability, goodwill and integrity of the trustee; from the enhancing effect of knowledge on trust, and the contribution of institutions, to the sense of security, and the application of calculational methods in evaluating costs and benefits. In addition, the cognitive dimension emphasizes the influence of initial impressions, while the personality dimension highlights the impact of individual differences on trust attitudes. These dimensions work together to form a dynamic interactive trust building mechanism, indicating that AI trust is neither linear nor simplistic, but rather a complex phenomenon shaped by a variety of factors across multiple aspects. Such a holistic understanding enables us to grasp the essence of AI trust, providing guidance for promoting the healthy development of AI technologies and their harmonious integration into social frameworks.

(1) Cognition (Evaluation), Emotion and Behavior

AI trust involves cognition, emotion and behavior, which collectively shape human trust in AI systems. In the era of generative AI, this trust grows increasingly complex and multidimensional, as AI's applications and capabilities expanding rapidly.[1]

At the cognitive level, trust in AI is first manifested as the evaluation of the capabilities and reliability of AI systems. Through their knowledge and usage, users form an understanding of the performance of AI systems, including their speed, accuracy, and performance in processing information and in specific tasks. For example, they may evaluate the safety and reliability of autonomous vehicles based on their performance in complex traffic environments. This cognitive process is often accompanied by a "cognitive leap", where users infer and trust AI's abilities based on limited direct experience; thus the trust goes beyond simple experience and logical reasoning, but becomes a belief in the potential of AI systems.

Emotional trust involves establishing emotional connections between users and AI systems. Although the systems are non-human entities, users can still form an emotional connection while interacting with them. This kind of connection may stem from users' emotional reactions to the

---

1 YANG, R., WIBOWO, S. User trust in artificial intelligence: a comprehensive conceptual framework[J]. Electronic Markets, 2022, 32 (4): 2053-2077.

convenience and personalized experience provided by AI systems, or their appreciation and dependence on AI capabilities. For example, when using voice assistants or chatbots, users may experience intimacy due to AI's "understanding" and "response". This trust at emotional level is quite important in AI, as it affects users' acceptance of and willingness to rely on AI systems.

Behavioral trust is reflected in users' cognitive and emotional connections to the capabilities of AI systems, as well as their expectations and dependencies on the future behavior of the systems. This trust assumes that users believe that the AI systems' future behaviors are predictable and reliable, even if such behaviors are highly complex and uncertain. For example, companies adopt AI for market analysis and decision-making because they trust its analytical capabilities and expect it to deliver accurate market forecasts and actionable decision-making recommendations. This kind of trust in AI behavior means that users are willing to rely, to some extent, on the judgment and actions of AI systems, even if they may bring risks.

Cognitive, emotional, and behavioral trusts interact and complement each other, jointly shaping users' trust experiences with AI systems. Cognitive trust necessitates that users have a comprehensive understanding and accurate evaluation of AI's capabilities; emotional trust requires AI systems to interact with users in a more human-like and empathetic way; behavioral trust is predicated on users' positive expectations of the future performance of AI systems. The relative importance of these three dimensions may vary across different application scenarios, but they together form a multidimensional framework for evaluating AI trust, providing important perspectives for understanding and promoting social acceptance of AI systems.

(2) Trustor and Trustee Characteristics

When discussing the dimensions of AI trust, Mayer's theory offers an important analytical framework and is instructive for a deeper understanding of digital trust in the era of generative AI. He decomposes trust into two dimensions: trustor characteristics and trustee characteristics, which enable us to uncover how users form trust in AI systems.[1]

The trustor characteristics, especially the trust tendency, reflect the predisposition of an individual to trust others or technology. This tendency is shaped by a combination of factors such as an individual's personality, past experiences, and cultural background. For example, a person who frequently uses technology and has positive online interaction experiences may be more likely to trust new AI technologies. However, the inclination to trust alone does not fully explain why a person chooses to trust a particular AI system; this requires taking into account the characteristics of the object of trust, that is, the AI system itself.

The trustee characteristics, including competence, goodwill and integrity, are the key factors affecting the degree to which an AI system is trusted. Competence focuses on the technical capabilities and professional attributes of AI systems in specific tasks or fields; for example, the competence of a language generation AI lies in the accuracy and naturalness of the text it produces. Goodwill involves whether an AI system considers the interests and goodwill of users in its design and operation process, and whether measures are taken to protect users' privacy and data security. Integrity is related to the consistency and reliability of AI systems, including whether AI companies transparently share the working principles and potential deviation risks of the systems.

---

1 AMEEN, N., TARHINI, A., REPPEL, A., et al. Customer experiences in the age of artificial intelligence[J]. Computers in Human Behavior, 2021, 114: 106548.

These characteristics of the trustee are dynamic and interrelated. In the early stages of user interaction with AI systems, integrity may be a key factor in building trust, as users will seek evidence to confirm whether an AI system has followed recognized principles and standards. As interaction proceeds, users may gradually feel the goodwill of AI systems, such as whether it can provide personalized services without infringing on user privacy. Meanwhile, users' understanding of AI system capabilities will also increase over time and with accumulated experience, thereby further influencing the trust formation.

However, it should be noted that although Mayer's model is useful in analyzing specific trust relationships, it may have limitations when applied to a wide range of social trust environments. Especially in emerging fields like generative AI, trust building is not merely a one-way flow, but also includes the interaction and dynamism between users and AI systems. Moreover, with the rapid changes in technology and social environments, the variables in the original models may also need to be updated and adjusted, so as to more accurately describe the actual trust in AI.

In summary, by analyzing the characteristics of trustor and trustee, we can better understand how users form trust based on their cognition, emotion and behavioral response to AI systems in the era of generative AI. This process involves not only evaluating the capabilities of AI technology, but also trusting the values and ethical principles underpinning the AI design, as well as anticipating the future behavior of AI systems.

(3) Personality, Perception, Knowledge, Calculation, and Institution

Gefen's theory can also be used as an analytical framework of AI trust which categorizes the factors affecting trust into five types: personality, perception, knowledge, calculation, and institution. This framework is also of great theoretical value for understanding digital trust in the era of generative AI, in that it can reveal the multidimensional complexity of trust building and its dynamic changes in different contexts.[1]

Personality-based trust or trust tendency refers to an individual's inherent personality trait of trusting others, which is particularly important in the early stages of a trust relationship. For example, users with optimistic personality traits may more readily trust emerging AI applications and be willing to try and accept AI technologies. This trust tendency, as an individual trait, is instructive for predicting how users approach and evaluate AI technologies.

Perception-based trust, on the other hand, is established on the initial impressions of AI technology and is often formed during the early stages of user contact with AI systems. This form of trust is built through users' initial perceptions of the AI system's appearance, functional descriptions, or brand image, without the need for long-term experience accumulation. For example, an AI application with a well-designed user interface and clear functional descriptions may create a sense of trust in users from the very beginning.

Knowledge-based trust involves users' level of understanding of AI technology or service providers. As users interact more with AI systems, their understanding of the working principles, performance limitations, and application scenarios of AI gradually deepens. The accumulation of this knowledge helps to reduce social uncertainty about AI technology and establish deeper levels of trust.[2] For example, users who become familiar with a certain AI recommendation system through continuous use may trust

---

1 GEFEN, D., KARAHANNA, E., STRAUBD, W. Trust and tam in online shopping: an integrated model[J]. MIS Quarterly, 2003, 27 (1): 51.

2 JIA, L., ZHOU, Y., YAO, J., et al. An empirical investigation of trust in AI in a Chinese petrochemical enterprise based on institutional theory[J]. Scientific Reports, 2021, 11 (1): 13564.

it more due to their understanding of the system's capabilities.

Calculation-based trust, rooted in economic principle, is built by evaluating the costs and benefits of establishing trust relationships with AI systems. This form of trust assumes that user behavior is rational and driven by benefit maximization. For example, companies using AI systems for market analysis may be based on a calculation that the efficiency improvements and cost savings brought by AI technology outweigh its potential risks and investments.

Institution-based trust, stemming from users' sense of security toward non-interpersonal structures in specific environments, is closely relevant to AI applications in online environments. This includes trust in legal resources, management systems, and trust in the security signs provided by the website.[1] For example, users may trust an AI service platform for its data encryption and privacy protection statements.

These five dimensions, covering a wide range of factors from individual traits to social and institutional environments, together constitute a complex framework of AI trust. Through this framework, we can gain a more comprehensive understanding of how users form trust in AI technology at different stages and levels, which is significant in advancing its wider applications.

(4) Generative AI Trust

The trust in generative AI occupies a crucial position in current AI research and applications, especially in understanding how users trust and adopt these advanced technologies. Generative AI, with applications such as automatic content generation, speech recognition and conversion, image

---

1 LUKYANENKO, R., MAASS, W. Trust in artificial intelligence: from a foundational trust framework to emerging research opportunities[J]. Electronic Markets, 2022, 32 (4): 1993-2020.

and video editing, poses new challenges and requirements for trust building due to its high complexity and innovation. Generative AI trust is affected by three independent and operable factors: cognition, emotion and institution. These factors reflect the relationship between trustor (user) and trustee (generative AI service), as well as the consideration of micro environment (service itself and service provider) and macro environments (social impact and structural guarantee).

In terms of cognition, generative AI trust focuses on users' understanding and evaluation of AI capabilities, performance, and efficiency. Through direct experience, performance feedback, and demonstrations of generative AI effectiveness, users form perceptions of its functionality and reliability. For example, when using AI for text generation, users' trust may stem from the accuracy, fluency, and alignment of the generated content with their expectations.

The emotional trust involves the emotional connection and response between users and generative AI services. This trust arises from both users' intuitive recognition of AI technology and their positive feelings toward AI service providers. For example, when using AI to create music or work of art, users' trust in it may be enhanced by the emotional resonance and aesthetic satisfaction triggered by AI works.

The institutional trust is built on the social and institutional safeguards that support the construction of user trust, including laws and regulations, industry standards, and platform policies. These institutional factors provide users with a safe and reliable usage environment and reduce perceived risk of generative AI applications. For example, legal provisions for copyright protection of AI generated content can enhance users' trust in the legality and morality of using generative AI services.

McKnight and his cooperators [1] emphasize the interrelationships between these factors rather than treating them solely as sets of related variables. They constitute an aggregation model, indicating that no single factor can fully explain social trust. Generative AI trust may be a linear or nonlinear function of these factors, and each may carry different weights when they function as a whole.

This viewpoint emphasizes the complexity and multidimensionality of building and understanding generative AI trust. It reveals that the process of user trust in generative AI is multifaceted, involving not only the evaluation of AI performance, but also the emotional resonance and trust in social systems that support AI technology. Therefore, to promote the social acceptance and application of generative AI technology, it is essential to consider these factors comprehensively. Only by enhancing the AI transparency, enriching users' emotional experience, and strengthening institutional guarantees, can trust in generative AI be built and solidified.

Section 2 Generative AI Trust Assessment: Quantifying Trust from a Multidimensional Perspective

The assessment of generative AI trust plays a crucial role in promoting its acceptance, user satisfaction, and sustainable development. As generative AI has been widely used across industries—from content creation and design simulation to decision support—its impact on social life grows significantly. Therefore, accurately measuring users' trust in generative AI not only helps to understand their needs and expectations so

1 MCKNIGHT, D. H., CHOUDHURY, V., KACMAR, C. Developing and validating trust measures for E-commerce: an integrative typology[J]. Information Systems Research, 2002, 13 (3): 334-359.

as to optimize and improve the technology, but is also beneficial for its healthy integration with society and winning wider public trust. Trust measurement spans multiple dimensions of user-AI interaction, from technical performance to emotional connection, and from individual experiences to social impacts. These dimensions collectively form a comprehensive evaluation of trust in generative AI. Through this systematic measurement, key factors influencing trust formation can be identified, thereby providing direction for the technology developers and policy makers. This, in turn, fosters the healthy development and social integration of the technology.

Specifically, generative AI trust measurement involves such key factors as understandability, technical capability, reliability, usefulness, individual attachment, granted autonomy, decision trust, and the reputation of research and development (R&D) institutions. Understandability refers to users' comprehension of the working mechanism and decision-making process of AI, which is the foundation for enhancing user trust. Technical capability emphasizes the performance of AI in specific tasks; it directly affects users' trust level. Reliability and usefulness, based on the stability of AI systems and the degree of satisfaction with users' actual needs, reflect the practical foundation of user trust. The attachment and autonomy granted by individuals to generative AI involve emotional bonds and psychological experiences. These dimensions enhance users' emotional investment and positive evaluations of AI. Decision trust and the reputation of R&D institutions are the social and ethical dimensions of trust; they are related to users' trust in the quality of AI decisions and their evaluation of the credibility of its development teams or companies. The comprehensive consideration of these measurement factors offers a multidimensional framework for a deeper understanding and more robust evaluation of trust in generative AI. This is of great significance for managing the healthy development of generative AI, optimizing user experience, and promoting the harmonious coexistence of technology and society.

1. Cognition, Emotion, and Behavior: Multi-level Trust Measurement

The understandability of generative AI, as an important dimension of trust measurement, reflects people's basic needs for transparency and explainability of emerging technologies. As Rousseau et al.[1] emphasize in their pioneering research on trust, trust is built on the clarity and reliability of predicting the trustee's behavior. For generative AI, understandability becomes a bridge, connecting users' basic knowledge and deep trust in the technology. In addition, Floridi's exploration of information ethics in *The Ethics of Information*[2] further reinforces the importance of transparency and user understanding of AI, especially when decision-making processes of the technology directly affect individual lives and social well-being.[3]

Understandability of generative AI essentially refers to users' level of understanding of the working principles of an AI system, as well as their comprehension of its behavior, assistance capabilities, and expected outcomes. This dimension covers not only users' intuitive understanding of the underlying logic of AI technology, but also their observations into how AI systems process data, make decisions, and generate outcomes. For example, when using generative AI for text generation, users' understanding of how AI selects vocabulary and constructs sentences based on input information directly affects their expectations and trust in the quality of the

1 ROUSSEAU, D. M., SITKIN, S. B., BURT, R. S., CAMERER, C. Not so different after all: A cross-discipline view of trust[J]. Academy of Management Review, 1998, 23 (3), 393-404.
2 FLORIDI, L. The Ethics of Information[M]. Oxford: Oxford University Press, 2013.
3 JOBIN, A., IENCA, M. The global landscape of AI ethics guidelines[J]. Nature Machine Intelligence, 2019, 1 (9): 389-399.

generated content.

Specifically, the understandability of generative AI can be elaborated as follows. First, it requires AI systems to present their working mechanisms in a user-friendly manner, enabling non-professional users to grasp the basic logic and operational principles of AI. This may be achieved through various methods such as visualization tools, simplified explanation interfaces, or case demonstrations, aiming to lower the technical threshold and improve users' cognitive skills. Second, the understandability of generative AI emphasizes technical transparency, meaning users can obtain necessary information about the AI decision-making, data sources, and potential biases. This transparency is key to building user trust, especially in application scenarios involving sensitive information processing or critical decision making. Finally, users' anticipation of the outcomes and value that may be obtained from future AI use is also vital. This is not only about the functionality and effectiveness of AI technology, but also about how users can integrate the technology into their daily lives and working practices, as well as how AI can help users achieve personal or organizational goals.

2. Competence, Integrity, and Goodwill: Analysis of the Characteristics of Trustee

The technical capabilities of generative AI constitute a pivotal dimension in trust measurement, with their significance rooted in the systems' ability to deliver high-quality and accurate outcomes. As Lee and See elucidate in their seminal research on trust and automation, users' trust in technological systems predominantly relies on performance evaluations, particularly on the assessments of a system's accuracy and reliability in critical tasks. This perspective finds echo in Shneiderman's research, where he emphasizes that system dependability and operational efficacy form the bedrock of user trust in digital environments. For generative AI, this dimension proves exceptionally critical, as its applications inherently involve complex data processing and content generation, domains where users maintain heightened expectations regarding the precision of outputs and their contextual appropriateness.[1]

The technical capabilities of generative AI primarily refer to the abilities of AI systems to produce accurate and contextually relevant outputs from user-provided input by employing appropriate methods, which include their proficiency in processing input data and generating outputs that are both precise and meaningful within the given context. For example, in NLP applications, a generative AI model needs to understand the users' query intent and generate accurate and useful textual information related to it. In image generation applications, technical capability manifests as the system's capacity to synthesize high-quality visuals that precisely match user descriptions.

The dimension also covers the evaluation of the efficiency of AI system algorithms, that is, how the systems optimize the processing flow to improve the speed and accuracy of task execution. It also includes considerations for the adaptability of AI systems, that is, how the systems process novel or unseen input information and produce reasonable outputs. In addition, it is also related to the robustness of the systems, that is, the systems' capability to maintain the stability of output quality when facing changes or disturbances in inputs.

The technical capabilities of generative AI not only directly influence users' satisfaction with output quality but also shape their trust in the systems' long-term performance stability. When users consistently experience generative AI systems' delivering accurate and useful results

---

1 SHNEIDERMAN, B. Designing trust into online experiences[J]. Communications of the ACM, 2000, 43 (12): 57-59.

across diverse scenarios over time, their trust progressively develops and deepens. Therefore, enhancing generative AI's technical capabilities necessitates not only continuous algorithmic and model optimization but also an in-depth understanding of user needs and application scenarios, ensuring that the AI systems meet user expectations in their applications.

3. Knowledge, Institution, and Calculation: Analysis of Trust Promoting Factors

The reliability of generative AI fundamentally determines whether users can continue to trust the services and outputs provided by AI systems. As Luhmann[1] explains in his theory, trust is essentially an expectation of the future, the stability of which is grounded in historical consistency and predictability. For generative AI, this holds heightened significance. Generative AI systems are often endowed with heightened autonomy and creative capacity, where the predictability and consistency of their behaviors directly correlate with user trust levels.[2]

The reliability of generative AI, specifically, refers to the ability of AI systems to consistently provide their expected outputs and respond in the same way at different times under the same conditions. This dimension includes two aspects: the stability of system output and the consistency of system behavior. For example, a generative AI text editor is expected by users to generate texts with consistent quality and style when processing identical input prompts at different times. Similarly, in image recognition or processing, a generative AI system should yield predictable and uniform results when handling similar visual inputs. Such output consistency forms

---

1 LUHMANN, N. Trust and Power[M]. New York: John Wiley & Sons, 2018: 127-129.
2 MURALIDHAR, D. Thesis summary: operationalizing user-inclusive transparency in artificial intelligence systems[J]. Proceedings of the AAAI Conference on Artificial Intelligence, 2024, 38 (21): 23401-23402.

the foundation for users' trust in the system's capabilities.

Furthermore, the reliability of generative AI also hinges on its ability to consistently maintain its performance and output quality across diverse inputs and contexts. In practical applications, the diversity of user inputs and the complexity of scenarios require generative AI systems to possess sufficient robustness to deliver accurate and consistent outputs even when faced with unseen data or abnormal situations. This robustness constitutes another important dimension for evaluating the reliability of generative AI.

The reliability of generative AI is crucial for building user trust, as users are only willing to rely on AI systems for decision support, content creation, or other applications when convinced of their capacity to provide stable and consistent services. Therefore, to ensure the reliability of generative AI systems, developers need to consider the stability and robustness of the systems when designing and training AI models, and improve their adaptability to various inputs and contexts through continuous testing and optimization.

4. Understandability and Transparency: Key Trust Determinants in Generative AI

The utility of generative AI, as an important measurement of trust, is indicative of users' direct evaluation and expectations of AI system capabilities. In the Technology Acceptance Model (TAM), Davis proposes the concept of perceived usefulness and emphasizes the importance of technology in improving job performance. This concept remains relevant in the era of generative AI, where the utility of AI systems is directly correlated with users' perceptions of their practical value, which, in turn, affects the formation of trust.[1] Venkatesh et al.[2] further study the TAM and verifies its core role in promoting technology adoption and trust building, especially when users expect AI systems to solve specific problems or meet specific needs.

The utility of generative AI essentially concerns the ability of AI systems to provide effective and responsive solutions when users need help. It is embodied not only in the systems' immediate feedback on user requests, but also in the quality and adaptability of the provided solutions. For instance, in the field of medical diagnosis, generative AI can quickly analyze patient data and provide accurate diagnostic recommendations; in the field of customer service, AI chatbots can respond to user queries in real-time, providing relevant information and actionable solutions. The usefulness of these practical applications demonstrates the potential of generative AI in improving work efficiency and optimizing user experience.

Furthermore, the utility of generative AI extends to its applicability across diverse scenarios. AI systems need not only to demonstrate high efficiency in specific fields, but also to be able to provide cross-domain support and adapt to the diverse needs of different users. This requires them to have high flexibility and scalability, and be able to generate customized solutions based on users' specific needs. Additionally, the utility is also reflected in its ability to continuously learn and optimize. Through iterative updates, AI systems can provide more accurate and innovative assistance to meet the growing needs of users.

---

1 LEY T., TAMMETS, K., SARMIENTO-MARQUEZ, E. M., et al. Adopting technology in schools: modelling, measuring and supporting knowledge appropriation[J]. European Journal of Teacher Education, 2021, 45 (4): 548-571.

2 VENKATESH, V., MORRIS, M., DAVIS, G. B., et al. User acceptance of information technology: toward a unified view[J]. MIS Quarterly, 2003, 27 (3): 425.

5. Humanity-Technology Integration: The Emotional Bond between Individual Attachment and Generative AI

Individuals' attachment to generative AI demonstrates the emotional connection between users and AI systems, as well as the degree of alignment with personal preferences, a critical dimension in trust measurement. According to attachment theory, individuals tend to seek and maintain intimate and lasting emotional relationships with key objects. Although this theory originated from interpersonal relationship research, it is equally applicable in the context of user technology interaction.[1] Shneiderman[2] proposes in the discussion of user interface design that improving system usability and personalization can enhance user satisfaction and attachment. In the application of generative AI, users' attachment to AI systems is based not only on their functionality and efficiency, but also on their ability to meet users' unique needs and preferences.

The personalized services and highly customized user experience of generative AI are critical to build user attachment. For instance, applications such as music recommendation systems, content creation tools, and personalized learning programs leverage generative AI to precisely capture users' preferences and behavioral patterns, delivering tailored content that aligns with their expectations. When users perceive that AI systems can meet their individualized needs just like considerate companions, they develop emotional attachment to these systems. Such attachment transcends mere utilization of technological tools and arises

---

1 THOMSON, M., MACINNIS, D. J., PARK, C. W. The ties that bind: measuring the strength of consumers' emotional attachments to brands[J]. Journal of Consumer Psychology, 2005, 15 (1): 77-91.

2 SHNEIDERMAN, B. Designing the User Interface: Strategies for Effective Human-Computer Interaction[M]. New York: Pearson Education India, 1987: 6.

from recognition of the unique value and satisfaction provided by the systems.

Moreover, individual attachment to generative AI develops through habit formation and emotional value accrual during user-system interactions. When users become accustomed to relying on AI systems for daily tasks or decision support, any change in usage habits may cause discomfort or loss. The formation of this attachment not only increases users' trust in AI systems, but also enhances their overall acceptance of AI technology. For example, in the smart home scenario, users may develop an attachment to voice assistants due to their role in simplifying household management and enhancing quality of life. They may find it difficult to dispense with the assistants due to their familiarity with the convenience and comfort brought by them.

6. Coexistence of Empowerment and Control: The Impact of Generative AI on Individual Autonomy

The autonomy empowered by generative AI, as a crucial dimension of trust measurement, highlights users' dominant position and sense of control during human-AI interactions. The importance of this concept is emphasized by self-determination theory (SDT), which maintains that autonomy is a core component of intrinsic human motivation and exerts a significant impact on promoting active engagement and satisfaction. In the application scenarios of generative AI, user autonomy not only relates to their trust in the technology, but also directly affects their effective use and acceptance of it. The self-efficacy theory also emphasizes individuals' confidence in their own abilities when performing tasks, pointing out that the sense of control and self-efficacy are crucial for adopting new technologies and systems.

The autonomy granted to individuals by generative AI is in the sense of control that users have when operating various functions and features of an AI system. It requires that generative AI systems allow users to adjust system settings, select and customize features according to their own needs and preferences to enjoy personalized interactive experiences. For example, the AI systems for content creation should allow users to choose different styles, themes, or parameters based on their purposes to produce outputs that meet their expectations. Similarly, the autonomous learning path selection and progress adjustment functions provided by the AI education applications should be able to enhance users' sense of participation and satisfaction.

In addition, this autonomy also includes the ability of users to predict and control system behavior, that is, users can understand the operating logic of AI systems, predict system reactions, and modulate system behavior based on their own intentions and decisions. This sense of control not only enhances users' trust in the systems, but also promotes deeper cooperation and collaboration between them. As such, it is essential to achieve user autonomy, transparent system design and a user-friendly interactive interface.

7. Judgment of Decision Rationality: The Cognitive Basis of Individual Trust in Generative AI Decision-Making

Individuals' trust in generative AI decision-making, a critical dimension of trust measurement, reflects users' confidence in AI systems' capabilities under conditions of uncertainty. This concept is inspired by the research[1] on organizational trust theory, which believes that trust is based on the cognition of trustee's ability, goodwill and integrity. Trust in the

---

1 BROMME, R., HENDRIKS, F. Trust in Science: Considering Whom to Trust for Knowing What is True[M]. A research agenda for trust. Cheltenham, UK: Edward Elgar Publishing, 2024: 37-49.

decision-making of AI systems becomes especially paramount in complex scenarios, where individuals often rely on external systems or expert judgments.

Individuals' trust in generative AI decision-making also encompasses their willingness to rely on AI systems for decisions despite their incomplete knowledge of the systems' operational mechanisms or inability to fully predict the decision outcomes. This trust is based on users' evaluation of the overall capabilities of the AI systems, as well as their confidence in the systems' professionalism and efficiency in specific tasks. For example, in medical diagnostics, physicians and patients may experience uncertainty regarding AI-generated diagnostic suggestions. However, trust may emerge from the systems' proven capacity in processing vast datasets and recognizing complex pathological patterns, thus leading to eventual acceptance of AI judgments. Similarly, financial investors may rely on generative AI analysis and prediction when facing market volatility and complex data, even if they cannot fully understand the internal mechanisms of AI models.

This dimension also includes users' trust in the applicability and actual effectiveness of decision support provided by AI systems, which demands not only technical precision and reliability but also alignment between the systems' decision-making logic and users' practical needs within specific scenarios. Users' trust in AI decisions will also be affected by system transparency and explainability, namely, by their comprehension of how AI arrives at conclusions. By providing decision rationale, logical paths, and possible outcome predictions, generative AI systems can enhance users' trust.

8. Institutional Reputation Building: Generative AI Developers' Image and User Trust

The credibility of generative AI R&D institutions, also a key dimension of trust measurement, is important because it provides users with a foundation for trusting generative AI technology. Trust functions as a mechanism to simplify social complexity, and institutional reputation, acting as a social signal, can significantly mitigate uncertainty in individual decision-making. This reputation not only represents an institution's technical capabilities and professional standards, but also reflects its commitment to industry standards and ethical norms. As Schaap emphasizes in his research on institutional legitimacy, institutional reputation promotes the formation of social trust by establishing legitimate expectations among external stakeholders regarding institutional behavior.[1]

The credibility of generative AI R&D institutions implies that users' trust in AI systems is not only based on the performance of the technology itself, but also dependent on the reputation of its developer or provider. Users tend to trust AI systems developed by reliable and responsible institutions. This trust stems from confidence in the institutions' adherence to industrial norms, quality control standards, and commitments to consumer rights protection. For example, an AI application developed by a renowned tech company may be perceived as more trustworthy and secure due to the firm's history of innovation and commitment to user privacy.

Furthermore, the reputation of generative AI R&D institutions is dependent too on the evaluations of their compliance with legal regulations and industry norms. Globally, with the strengthening of AI technology regulations, users are increasingly concerned with whether AI products

---

1 SCHAAP, D. Police trust-building strategies: a socio-institutional, comparative approach[J]. Policing and Society, 2020, 31 (3): 304-320.

align with relevant legal requirements and ethical standards. Institutions that demonstrate their products have undergone rigorous review and certification significantly enhance user trust. Likewise, users place greater confidence in institutions that engage in industry standard-setting and assume social responsibilities in AI ethics and sustainable development.

Section 3 Trust Building in Generative AI: The Interaction and Integration of Interpersonal, Institutional, and Technological Trusts

From the perspective of trust transfer, it is both necessary and significant to examine the impact of interpersonal, institutional, and technological trusts on generative AI trust. This perspective posits that trust does not exist in isolation but can be transferred or extended to new entities or domains. For example, interpersonal trust, the foundation of trust between individuals, can be extended to generative AI technology through positive human-machine interaction. Similarly, institutional trust, which refers to confidence in social systems and organizational structures, serves as a prerequisite for establishing trust in generative AI technology. When users believe that social systems can effectively supervise the development of the technology, it is easier for them to establish trust in specific AI systems. Technological trust, especially trust in advanced technologies and systems, is directly related to users' confidence in the capabilities and security of generative AI. This trust transfer mechanism suggests that by strengthening trust in interpersonal interactions, improving the transparency and reliability of social systems, and enhancing the performance and security standards of advanced technologies, users' trust in generative AI can be effectively fostered. Therefore, from the perspective of trust transfer, a deeper understanding of the interaction and transferring among these trusts is significant for building and maintaining users' trust in generative

AI, and is conducive to promoting its healthy development and wider application.

1. Transfer of Interpersonal Trust to AI Trust: The Mediating Effect of Social Interaction Perceptions

Trust, as a core element of human social fabric, is an invisible bond that promotes social collaboration, bridges information gaps, and reduces transaction costs. In modern communication ecology, it affects not only interpersonal interactions, but also broader human-machine engagements. When examining how interpersonal trust influences trust in generative AI, we must first uncover the underlying socio-psychological and communicative mechanisms.

According to trust transfer theory, individuals can transfer trust from familiar domains to unfamiliar ones based on established trust experiences. This transfer is not a simple linear process but relies on intricate cognitive, affective, and behavioral mechanisms. The trust accumulated through interpersonal relationships pertains not merely to specific individuals but also to the internalization and endorsement of social interaction norms, cultural conventions, and behavioral patterns. When encountering novel entities like generative AI, individuals instinctively seek familiar social interaction cues, attempting to position these systems within preexisting trust frameworks. Symbolic interactionism from communication studies offers insights into this process. Under this theoretical framework, people interact with others through symbols, language, and behavior to form common understandings and identities. Generative AI, a completely different entity from traditional media, has a high interactivity and adaptability. It transcends mere information transmission, engaging users in emotional, cultural, and value-based exchanges. Consequently, human-AI interactions not only establish trust at the technical level but also facilitate profound sociocultural and affective communication.

In this interaction, social interaction perceptions play a critical mediating role. It involves how individuals perceive, interpret, and evaluate the depth, quality, and emotional connection of their interactions with AI. High levels of social interaction perception imply that people experience emotional fulfillment, a sense of identity, and a sense of belonging akin to human interactions when engaging with AI. When such perceptions are reinforced, individuals are more likely to transfer trust formed in interpersonal relationships to their interactions with AI. This indicates that the establishment of trust in generative AI is not solely based on technical performance or accuracy but also hinges on the social, emotional, and cultural attributes it embodies. Furthermore, the mediating role of social interaction perceptions underscores the complexity of trust construction in modern communication environments. Trust between humans and AI is not merely rooted in technology and algorithms but also relies on sociocultural symbols, emotional bonds, and value resonance. This poses new challenges for AI designers: how to make AI more socially aware, emotionally intelligent, and culturally sensitive to meet humans' profound needs for social interaction. At the same time, it opens novel research avenues for communication scholars to better understand and facilitate trust relationships between humans and AI, thereby promoting harmonious human-machine coexistence.

In exploring the trust relationships between humans and AI, Social Cognitive Theory has its valuable insights. This theory posits that people's evaluations of external entities—including others and technologies—are shaped by their cognitive structures, which are formed through past experiences, cultural contexts, educational backgrounds, and social interactions. In interpersonal trust, trust formation can be relatively direct and intuitive due to shared contexts and common experiential frameworks.

But when this trust is transferred to the interaction between humans and AI, the complexity of the situation increases significantly, as AI lacks emotions, consciousness, and cultural backgrounds. At this point, people's perceptions of social interaction serve as the bridge connecting the two, acting as the medium for trust transfer. In addition, today's AI is not an isolated, single function tool, but is often embedded in more complex social and technological systems such as social media, online communities, virtual assistants, etc. These environments provide richer backgrounds and contexts for human-AI interaction, while introducing heightened challenges. Given the socially enriched nature of AI interactions, users may inadvertently forget they are engaging with algorithms rather than humans. This can lead to overestimated or underestimated expectations of AI capabilities, resulting in trust deviations. The key is that generative AI has high adaptability and simulation complexity, allowing it to simulate certain interpersonal interaction features such as emotional feedback and social habit imitation in its interactions with people. These features not only enhance individuals' perception of social interaction, but also facilitate the identification of familiar interpersonal clues during their interactions with AI, thereby promoting the transfer of trust. However, at the same time, excessive social interaction simulation may lead to people's excessive dependence and expectations on AI. When AI fails to meet these expectations, users may experience disappointment or distrust. Therefore, balancing AI's social simulation with its actual capabilities—ensuring users correctly understand and assess AI—constitutes a pivotal challenge in human-AI interaction design.

In the context of demanding trust in generative AI, individuals with higher levels of interpersonal trust are more likely to believe in positive external evaluations of new technologies, and thereby to develop trust in generative AI. Conversely, those with lower interpersonal trust may remain skeptical of external evaluations, making them less susceptible to social normative influences. Thus, subjective norm perception acts as a mediating variable, bridging interpersonal trust and the one in generative AI. This phenomenon reveals that technology acceptance and trust formation depend not only on technical attributes or functionalities but also on social and psychological factors. When encountering new technologies, people not only consider their technical performance, but also the social and cultural contexts in which they are embedded, the social norms they conform to, and the external perceptions or evaluations associated with them. This also means that in order to increase the acceptance and trust of technology, relying solely on technological advantages is not enough. It is also necessary to consider how to shape a positive social environment through social communication and social networks. In addition, this mediating role also reveals the importance of social communication in technology acceptance and trust formation. In the information age, the dissemination and sharing of information have become increasingly rapid and widespread. Decision making is not only based on people's own experience and knowledge, but also affected by information and evaluations from various sources. Consequently, how to effectively spread positive information and create a social environment conducive to technology acceptance has become the key to technology promotion and application. By elucidating how social and psychological factors shape trust in generative AI, this mediating mechanism offers inspirations and strategies for the technological promotion and application.

2. Institutional Environment and Individual Risk Perception: The Impact of Institutional Trust on Generative AI Trust

Institutional trust, a kind of trust in social systems, institutions or organizations, exerts broad influence. In interpersonal interactions, institutional trust reflects individuals' recognition and acceptance of social systems, and shapes their behaviors and decisions. In the trust building of generative AI, institutional trust also plays an important role. It is directly relevant to individuals' trust in generative AI by affecting their perceived risks and benefits.

According to the theory of trust transfer, trust can be extended from one entity to another. As such, institutional trust, as a foundational form of trust, can be transferred to generative AI. This shift reveals not only the impact of institutional trust, but also the formation mechanism of generative AI trust. The existence and development of institutional trust has a significant impact on the formation of generative AI trust. The impact is evidenced not only in the direct transfer of trust, but also in individuals' perceptions of the risks and benefits associated with the use of generative AI; these perceptions represent users' direct cognitive evaluations of potential risks and advantages that generative AI may entail. In other words, institutional trust can indirectly influence the development of trust in generative AI by shaping individuals' perceived risks and benefits.

The impact of institutional trust on individuals' perceived risks highlights its significant role in shaping their risk judgments and acceptance. The level of institutional trust influences how they gauge and accept risks, thus affecting their trust in generative AI. The higher the level of institutional trust, the more willing they are to accept risk, and the higher their trust in generative AI. This impact not only reveals the influence of institutional trust on individuals' risk perceptions and risk acceptance, but also underscores the mediating role of risk acceptance in the relationship between institutional trust and trust in generative AI. Similarly, the impact of institutional trust on individuals' perceived benefits highlights its role in shaping their judgments and expectations regarding potential gains. The level of institutional trust directly influences how they evaluate and anticipate benefits, thereby affecting their trust in generative AI. Higher levels of institutional trust are associated with elevated benefit expectations and increased trust in generative AI. These findings not only demonstrate the effect of institutional trust on individuals' benefit assessments and expectations, but also show the mediating role of benefit expectation in the relationship between institutional trust and trust in generative AI.

In the relationships among institutional trust, perceived risk, perceived benefit and trust in generative AI, there exists a complex web of interactions and influences. Institutional trust not only directly influences the formation of trust in generative AI, but also indirectly facilitates the establishment of such trust by shaping individuals' perceived risks and perceived benefits. This complex interplay elucidates the mechanism by which institutional trust affects trust in generative AI, highlighting the mediating roles of perceived risk and perceived benefit. These mediators, in turn, display the intricate relationships among institutional trust, perceived risk, perceived benefit and trust in generative AI. Such findings have both theoretical and practical implications for understanding and optimizing the development of trust in generative AI.

3. Trustworthy Technical Core: Aggregational Trust in Hardware, Software, and Personnel

Generative AI, a prominent subfield of AI that emulates human creativity to produce original content, has a wide range of applications, including the creation of text, music, artwork, designs, and inventions. The level of technological trust in AI is closely linked to the trustworthiness of associated hardware, software, systems, and personnel, as well as to its specific characteristics and applications.

Hardware, as the physical cornerstone of technology, is particularly crucial for generative AI. The training of Generative Adversarial Networks (GANs) requires a large amount of computing resources and storage, high-performance graphics processing units (GPUs), and stable storage systems such as NVMe solid-state drives, so as to provide a solid physical foundation for GANs and ensure the stability and speed of model training. The hardware of generative AI includes not only traditional processors and memory, but also specialized ones for machine learning, such as GPUs and tensor processing units (TPUs), whose performance and stability directly impact the AI's effectiveness. For example, hardware malfunctions may cause an AI system to generate incorrect or nonsensical content. Therefore, users' trust in hardware is the foundation of their trust in generative AI.

In terms of software, the design and optimization of generative AI algorithms are fundamental to ensuring trustworthiness. The software for generative AI includes algorithms for training and generating content, as well as system software for managing and controlling these algorithms. The quality and performance of the software directly affect the effectiveness of generative AI. For example, flawed algorithms may lead an AI system to generate inaccurate or biased content. If the system software is unstable, generative AI may experience operational failures. Therefore, users' trust in software is the key to their trust in generative AI. OpenAI's GPT models, which have gained user trust through continuous iteration and optimization, are a case in point. The stability and predictability of these algorithms convince users that AI-generated content is both creative and reliable.

The trustworthiness of the AI related systems is also very important. The systems not only include hardware and software, but also operating systems and applications that manage and control these hardware and software. The stability and reliability of these systems have a direct impact on the effectiveness of generative AI. For example, if the operating system malfunctions, generative AI may cease to operate; and if the application has defects, it may produce incorrect or nonsensical output. Therefore, users' trust in the systems is the guarantee of their trust in generative AI too.

The trustworthiness of personnel is also crucial for generative AI. Personnel include engineers who develop and maintain hardware, software, and systems, and users who use and evaluate generative AI. Expertise, accountability, and integrity of these individuals directly shape trust in generative AI. For example, engineers lacking sufficient expertise may produce flawed hardware or algorithms, thus compromising system reliability. Users without a strong sense of responsibility might misuse generative AI, leading to the production of inappropriate content. Therefore, users' trust in personnel serves as a foundational pillar for trust in generative AI.

However, why do we trust generative AI's outputs? The trust we place in generative AI's content or decisions hinges on its foundational technological infrastructure. When we know that a generative AI model is built on stable hardware, runs through reliable software and systems, and is maintained by an experienced and responsible team, we are more inclined to trust the content it outputs. In addition, the applications of generative AI have further strengthened our trust in it. In the medical field, generative AI is used to simulate drug molecules and assist in the development of new drugs; in the entertainment industry, it can create music, painting, or writing; in education, it can provide students with customized learning materials. These practical applications offer empirical support for the technological trust in generative AI, making it no longer an abstract technical concept, but a technology that truly serves society and delivers tangible benefits to people.

4. Dynamic Trust Relationship Building: The Tripartite Interaction of Users, Technology and Service

The construction of generative AI trust is, in fact, an evolving process characterized by the expansion of relational trust. In this context, human-AI relationships represent a novel paradigm of trust dynamics, analogous to the development of trust observed in human interpersonal interactions. In the digital environment, this kind of relationship evolves from a binary interaction into a tripartite trust network involving users, technology, and service providers, which must be built over time through iterative interactions. The unique characteristics of generative AI introduce distinct features to this trust-building process. Generative AI can not only simulate human creative thinking and generate new and original content, but also continuously improve the quality and innovation of its generated content through learning and optimization. These capabilities imbue human-AI relationships with a complexity and dynamism akin to human social interactions, rendering the trust-building process more intricate and multifaceted.

In building trust in generative AI, the roles of and interactions among users, technology, and service providers are pivotal determinants. Users' engagement with and evaluation of generative AI directly shape their trust perception toward the technology. The performance and stability of technology determine its trustworthiness. The professionalism and integrity of service providers shape its trust environment. The interactions among and feedback of these three parties constitute the process of building trust in generative AI. For example, users can generate diverse content such as articles, dialogues, and stories by interacting with OpenAI's GPT-3, a typical generative AI model. Throughout this process, users' experiences and evaluations, the performance and stability of the model, and the professionalism and integrity of OpenAI the service provider collectively affect their trust in it.

However, the building of generative AI trust is not simply a technical problem, but also a social one, as the trust formation requires both technological reliability and social recognition. In the digital environment, this recognition emerges from the joint efforts of users, technology, and service providers. Users need to understand and accept generative AI; the AI technology should provide high-quality and stable services; service providers must maintain professionalism and integrity. Only in this way can trust in generative AI be established. However, the trust building also faces other challenges. For instance, the uncertainty, unpredictability, complexity, and opacity of generative AI can all affect user trust. These challenges require us to work together and solve them at multiple levels such as technology, society, and law.

5. Trust Transfer and Refactoring: The Formation Mechanism of Generative AI Trust

As digitalization accelerates, generative AI technologies—ranging from art creation to drug discovery and exemplified by tools like OpenAI's GPT-3 and DeepArt's artwork generator—are increasingly permeating a wide array of domains. In this context, trust-building becomes critical. The formation of trust in generative AI can be conceptualized as a process of technological trust-building, shaped by the transfer and interplay of interpersonal trust and institutional trust.

On the one hand, in interpersonal relationships and social interactions, individuals often establish trust based on the behavior and characteristics of others. For example, interacting with an individual who fulfills promises can foster a greater sense of interpersonal trust, which will strengthen over time and with accumulated experiences. When generative AI technology is used for art creation or text generation, users may transfer trust experiences from interpersonal interactions to machines. On the other hand, institutional trust focuses on the overall institutional structure, mechanism and process, such as the legal, financial or medical systems. This trust is based on the understanding of the systems and the belief in that the systems can operate normally, stably, and predictably. When generative AI technology is involved, institutional trust may be affected by the organization or institution that provides this technology. For example, users are more likely to trust AI models developed by renowned research institutions due to their perceived adherence to rigorous scientific, technical, and ethical standards.

The widespread adoption of generative AI has catalyzed transfer of interpersonal trust and institutional trust in the digital environment. For example, in the medical field, generative AI has been used to assist in drug development and disease diagnosis. Here, patients may transfer their interpersonal trust in doctors to AI systems, believing that the latter can provide accurate diagnostic results. At the same time, they may also transfer their institutional trust in the medical system to the AI technologies, hoping that they have followed all medical and ethical standards in the research and development process. Similarly, there is also a trust transfer in the field of digital art. Art enthusiasts and creators may transfer their interpersonal trust in artists to art AI tools, anticipating that they can produce high-quality works. In addition, they may also trust the art platforms and institutions that use AI technologies based on their institutional trust in the artistic field. But the inherent complexity of generative AI also produces barriers to the transfer in the same environment. In addition, trust transfer between different environments can also be influenced by various factors such as culture, habits, and experiences.

Trust in generative AI arises from multiple interconnected dimensions, involving both the interplay of interpersonal trust and institutional trust, as well as their transfer across diverse environments and channels. Understanding this intricate trust transfer mechanism is of great significance for deepening our understanding of generative AI technology and popularizing its application. To establish robust trust in generative AI, coordinated efforts must span several key dimensions. At the technical level, it is necessary to improve the transparency of generative AI so that users can better understand its working principles; at the social level, effective oversight mechanisms are needed to prevent its misuse and abuse; at the legal level, relevant regulations should be formulated to safeguard user rights and bolster confidence in generative AI applications. Only in this way can we truly achieve deep trust in generative AI and promote the healthy development of the technology in the digital age.

Section 4 Enhancing Trustworthiness Quotient (TQ): A New Dimension of Generative AI's Communicative Influence

When examining generative AI's applications in communication, it is essential to recognize that apart from traditional metrics like IQ and EQ, the concept of trustworthiness quotient (TQ) plays a pivotal role in determining its social acceptance and impact. The intelligence of generative AI is demonstrated in its ability to process and parse large amounts of data and generate meaningful outputs, while its EQ is reflected in its ability to understand and process human emotions. However, unlike traditional AI, generative AI's TQ is particularly important in human-AI interaction and application in communication, because it is directly related to users' trust in and acceptance of AI generated content.

The essence of generative AI lies in its capacity to generate novel content by leveraging extensive datasets, with broad applications across diverse media formats such as text, image, audio, and video. For example, it can draft articles, produce artworks, and synthesize voices. In this process, AI's IQ ensures the relevance and innovation of content, while its EQ guarantees that generated content can resonate emotionally with human audiences. However, both of these are based on the premise that the generated content can be perceived as trustworthy by the audience. This points to the importance of TQ, which encompasses not only the accuracy and authenticity of outputs but also the transparency and fairness of the generation process itself.

In today's society, rampant misinformation and fake news have heightened audiences' sensitivity to the source and authenticity of information. In this context, generative AI must prioritize its TQ. A high-TQ generative AI system not only produces high-quality and highly relevant content, but also ensures that the outputs are grounded in truthful data and unbiased algorithms, free from distortions or misleading intent. For example, a news-generating AI needs to ensure the accuracy of the information it provides when reporting on major events, thereby avoiding unnecessary panic or misunderstanding.

Furthermore, the elevation of a generative AI's TQ hinges on adherence to ethical principles throughout its design and development, particularly transparency, accountability, and explainability. This means that generative AI must prioritize social impact and moral responsibility alongside technical sophistication. For instance, a transparent AI system would allow users to understand its working principles and decision-making process, while a responsible one would promptly correct potential biases or errors and assume responsibility for possible negative impacts.

In addition, generative AI is rapidly extending its applications across diverse fields or scenarios—from creating content for social media and developing personalized educational materials to designing personalized medical treatment plans. To be sure, its IQ and EQ may ensure the content quality and audience engagement, but ultimately, it is its TQ that secures its user trust and widespread adoption. For example, in personalized healthcare applications, AI-generated treatment recommendations or health advice must be both scientifically accurate and ethically defensible, thus requiring a strict alignment with medical ethics and robust safeguards for patient privacy.

Chapter Three Causes and Effects: Research Landscape of AI Trust

The rapid advancement and extensive application of AI have positioned trust as a critical concern in human-machine interactions. The rise of generative AI, in particular, is reshaping human perceptions, emotional responses, and behavioral patterns toward intelligent systems. Amidst the interplay of digital trust and intelligent risks, communication dynamics now exhibit unprecedented complexity and unpredictability. Analyzing the causal mechanisms of AI trust holds profound significance for optimizing human-AI collaboration, reconstructing social trust frameworks, and informing AI governance policies. This chapter investigates trust mechanisms and order restructuring in the generative AI era through a multidimensional lens. Drawing on global research, it examines the key factors shaping trust, uncovers behavioral outcomes associated with trust, and addresses practical challenges and strategies specific to the Chinese context. The objective is to provide theoretical insights and actionable recommendations for demystifying AI trust, mitigating technological risks, and fostering a symbiotic human-AI coexistence.

Section 1 Research Landscape: International Academic Vision of AI Trust

The trust mechanism of AI is a complex, multidimensional, and multi-level construct that involves technological, organizational, contextual, social, and individual factors. These factors are intertwined and jointly shape the trust in human-AI interaction. Trust, a key factor in AI applications, profoundly influences users' cognitive, emotional, and behavioral responses to AI systems. Therefore, a deeper understanding of the causes and effects of trust in AI is of great significance for optimizing human-AI interaction design and improving user experience. This section analyzes such influencing factors of trust in AI as technology, organization, context, society, and individuals. It also examines the trust's transformative effects on user satisfaction, emotional engagement, adoption behaviors, and continued usage, aiming to shed some light on the ethical design and application of AI technologies.

1. Exploration of Causes: A Multidimensional Analysis of Factors Influencing AI Trust

(1) Technical Dimension: Trust Shaping through Service, Information, System, and Design Quality

In examining the trust mechanisms of generative AI in human-machine communication, international literature identifies four core technological factors: service, information, system, and design.

First, as AI technologies proliferate in service domains, studies by Mostafa and Kasamani[1] demonstrate that user trust in AI is shaped by its performance, compatibility, and ease of use. Nasirian and other scholars[2] advocate for analyzing the causes of trust in AI through the lenses of service quality, information quality, and system quality in AI applications. In particular, AI-driven services have elevated user expectations beyond traditional service benchmarks, with users now demanding greater convenience, robust security, faster response, better personalization based on user preferences, and enhanced customer support.[34]

---

1 MOSTAFA, R. B., KASAMANI, T. Antecedents and consequences of chatbot initial trust[J]. European Journal of Marketing, 2022, 56 (6): 1748-1771.

2 NASIRIAN, F., AHMADIAN, M., LEE, O. K. D. AI-based voice assistant systems: evaluating from the interaction and trust perspectives[C]. Proceedings of the Twenty-third Americas Conference on Information Systems. Boston, USA. 2017.

3 NISREEN AMEEN, ALI TARHINI, ALEXANDER REPPEL, et al. Customer experiences in the age of artificial intelligence [J]. Computers in human behavior, 2021, 114: 106548-106548.

Second, Ashfaq and other scholars[1] argue that information quality hinges on the content an AI application delivers to users. Trust in AI applications depends on their ability to provide accurate, authentic, timely, and comprehensive content that supports user tasks.[2] Notably, the issue of automation bias has garnered increasing attention in recent years, particularly when AI technologies exhibit tendencies to unfairly categorize or judge specific user groups.[34]

Third, Nassar[5] proposes that system quality can be evaluated based on the reliability, flexibility, accessibility, and timeliness of its functional characteristics. The trust of users in information systems is related to their security and privacy policies. Anwar and other researchers[6] point out that high-quality systems should strive to protect the confidentiality, integrity, and authenticity of data, while improving the transparency, traceability, and predictability of their processes.

Fourth, from the perspective of design quality, a series of studies have emphasized the importance of perceptional design of AI systems. The appearance of the design and the feel it triggers, such as the color scheme of

---

4 SHERIDAN, T. B. Individual differences in attributes of trust in automation: measurement and application to system design[J]. Frontiers in Psychology, 2019, 10: 1117.

1 ASHFAQ, M., YUN, J., YU, S., et al. I, Chatbot: modeling the determinants of users' satisfaction and continuance intention of AI-powered service agents[J]. Telematics and Informatics, 2020, 54, 101473.

2 AHMADI, V., TUTSCHKU, K. Privacy and trust in cloud-based marketplaces for AI and data resources[C]. Proceedings of the 11th IFIP International Conference on Trust Management. Gothenburg, Sweden. 2017: 223-225.

3 ROBERTS, D. E. Automating inequality: how high-tech tools profile, police, and punish the poor[J]. Harvard law review, 2019, 132 (6): 1695-1728.

4 MAÑERO, J. Review of Virginia eubanks. Automating inequality: how high-tech tools profile, police, and punish the poor[J]. Post Digital Science and Education, 2020, 2 (2): 489-493.

5 NASSAR, M., SALAH, K., UR REHMAN, M. H., et al. Blockchain for explainable and trustworthy artificial intelligence[J]. Wiley Interdisciplinary Reviews: Data Mining and Knowledge Discovery, 2020, 10 (1): e1340.

6 ANWAR, M. Supporting privacy, trust, and personalization in online learning[J]. International Journal of Artificial Intelligence in Education, 2020, 31: 1-15.

the interface, can affect user trust.[1,2] In addition, numerous studies have shown that the human-like or anthropomorphic design of AI can help cultivate users' emotional trust.[3,4] This is related to the theory of social existence, which involves subjective experiences of interacting with real people.

In summary, individual trust in generative AI is a complex and important research field. Understanding the key technological factors that affect user trust is valuable for the further development and application of AI technology.

(2) Organizational Dimension: The Impact of Institutional Reputation, Accountability, and Ethics on Trust

In human-AI interaction, users' trust in AI is also influenced by their trust in relevant organizations. This organization-dependent trust constitutes another critical component of user confidence.[5,6] Therefore, it is essential to understand the organizational factors that influence trust.

First, a large number of studies have focused on the image and

---

1 AMEEN, N., TARHINI, A., REPPEL, A., et al. Customer experiences in the age of artificial intelligence[J]. Computers in Human Behavior, 2021, 114: 106548.
2 FAISAL, C. N., GONZALEZ-RODRIGUEZ, M., FERNANDEZ-LANVIN, D., et al. Web design attributes in building user trust, satisfaction, and loyalty for a high uncertainty avoidance culture[J]. IEEE Transactions on Human-Machine Ssystems, 2016, 47 (6): 847-859.
3 GULATI, S., SOUSA, S., LAMAS, D. Design, development and evaluation of a human-computer trust scale [J]. Behaviour & Information Technology, 2019, 38 (10): 1004-1015.
4 SHI, S., GONG, Y., GURSOY, D. Antecedents of trust and adoption intention toward artificially intelligent recommendation systems in travel planning: a heuristic-systematic model[J]. Journal of Travel Research, 2021, 60 (8): 1714-1734.
5 CHEN, Y. K., WEN, C. R. Impacts of attitudes toward govenment and corporations on public trust in artificial intelligence[J]. Communication Studies, 2021, 72 (1), 115-131.
6 WEI, K., LI, Y., ZHA, Y., et al. Trust, risk and transaction intention in consumer-to-consumer e-marketplaces: an empirical comparison between buyers and sellers perspectives[J]. Industrial Management & Data Systems, 2019, 119 (2): 331-350.

reputation of AI service providers.[1,2] From the perspective of social evaluation, an organization's adherence to social norms and regulations—particularly its performance in social responsibility and digital accountability—has become a key benchmark for assessing its reputation.[3] Elliott's group[4] believe that the social and digital responsibilities demonstrated by organizations, such as adopting environmental protection policies, supporting local communities, treating employees fairly and using ethical data, are particularly critical to their reputation.

In addition, Kaplan's team[5] demonstrates that in e-commerce, organizational reputation exerts a particularly pronounced influence on user trust. This may stem from the perception that reputation reflects genuine customer-centricity. E-commerce providers often leverage brand identity (e.g., organizational names, trademarks, logos) to gain recognition. In this setting, Söllner and other scholars[6] posit that users may rely on brand identity as a proxy for evaluating service quality, thereby placing greater trust in reputable brands during decision-making processes.

---

1 BURDA, D., TEUTEBERG, F. The role of trust and risk perceptions in cloud archiving: results from an empirical study[J]. The Journal of High Technology Management Research, 2014, 25 (2): 172-187.

2 HAMID, N. H. A., AHMAD, M. S., AHMAD, A., et al. Trusting norms: a conceptual norms trust framework for norms adoption in open normative multi-agent systems[C]. Proceedings of the 12th International Conference on Distributed Computing and Artificial Intelligence. 2015: 137-144.

3 JELOVAC, D., LJUBOJEVIC, č., LJUBOJEVIC, L. HPC in business: the impact of corporate digital responsibility on building digital trust and responsible corporate digital governance[J]. Digital Policy, Regulation and Governance, 2022, 24 (6): 485-497.

4 ELLIOTT, K., PRICE, R., SHAW, P., et al. Towards an equitable digital society: artificial intelligence(AI) and corporate digital responsibility (CDR)[J]. Society, 2021, 58 (3): 179-188.

5 KAPLAN, A. D., KESSLER, T. T., BRILL, J. C., et al. Trust in artificial intelligence: meta-analytic findings[J]. Human Factors, 2023, 65 (2): 337-359.

6 SÖLLNER, M., HOFFMANN, A., LEIMEISTER, J. M. Why different trust relationships matter for information systems users [J]. European Journal of Information Systems, 2016, 25 (3): 274-287.

Nordheim's team[1] also point out that the reputation of service providers often spreads among users, hence playing a key role in cultivating trust. Pickering[2] and Weitz[3] emphasize that, to build user trust, organizations must demonstrate integrity in data protection, particularly in preventing data misuse. Therefore, Janssen and other scholars[4] propose that organizations need to develop and maintain relevant policies, principles, and procedures, such as establishing ethics committees, conducting risk assessments, and implementing regular audits.

Alhazmi[5] also emphasizes that users' trust in service providers depends on the provider's professional insights into users' needs and timely and regular communication with them. It is noteworthy that Triberti's team[6] reveals that reputation is often based on the evaluation and recognition of third parties, which means that people's decisions often depend on others' perceptions of the credibility of the organization. In addition, Lapinska and other scholars[7], Li's team[8], and Ryan[9] all demonstrate that AI technology

---

1 NORDHEIM, C. B., FOLSTAD, A., BJORKLI, C. A. An initial model of trust in chatbots for customer service-findings from a questionnaire study[J]. Interacting with Computers, 2019, 31 (3): 317-335.
2 PICKERING, B. Trust, but verify: informed consent, AI technologies, and public health emergencies[J]. Future Internet, 2021, 13 (5): 132.
3 WEITZ, K., SCHILLER, D., SCHLAGOWSKI, R., et al. Do you trust me? Increasing user-trust by integrating virtual agents in explainable AI interaction design[C]. Proceedings of the 19th ACM International Conference on Intelligent Virtual Agents.2019: 7-9.
4 JANSSEN, M., BROUS, P., ESTEVEZ, E., et al. Data governance: Organizing data for trustworthy artificial intelligence[J]. Government Information Quarterly, 2020, 37(3): 101493.
5 ALHAZMI, B. M. Religiosity and customer trust in financial services marketing relationships[J]. Journal of Financial Services Marketing, 2019, 24 (1): 31-43.
6 TRIBERTI, S., DUROSINI, I., CURIGLIANO, G., et al. Is explanation a marketing problem? The quest for trust in artificial intelligence and two conflicting solutions[J]. Public Health Genomics, 2020, 23 (1/2): 2-5.
7 LAPINSKA, J., ESCHER, I., GÓRKA, J., et al. Employees' trust in artificial intelligence in companies: The case of energy and chemical industries in Poland [J]. Energies, 2021, 14 (7): 1942.
8 LI, J., ZHOU, Y., YAO, J., et al. An empirical investigation of trust in AI in a Chinese petrochemical enterprise based on institutional theory[J]. Scientific Reports, 2021, 11 (1): 1-12.

can not only support customer service for an organization, but also be applied to other management functions such as production and manufacturing. This means that employees of a certain organization may also become users of AI technology. In this regard, some researchers have focused on the credibility of AI within organizations. For example, Li's team[1] argues that the commitment of organizational leaders to the application of AI in the organization is a key factor.

In summary, from an organizational perspective, the characteristics of AI service providers play an important role in user trust. Bejger and Elster[2] also emphasize the importance of legally and ethically compliant use of AI technologies. Lobschat and other scholars[3] propose that in order to protect user data, AI service organizations should adopt encryption technology, even if it requires more investment.

(3) Contextual Dimension: Utilitarian and Hedonic Demands in AI Applications

In the building of trust in AI, contextual factors play an indispensable role. First, how organizations deploy AI technologies is affected by contextual variables such as industry-specific requirements.[4] Second, trust dynamics also depend on the nature of tasks for which users employ

---

9 RYAN, M. In AI we trust: Ethics, artificial intelligence, and reliability[J]. Science and Engineering Ethics, 2020, 26 (5): 2749-2767.

1 LI, J., ZHOU, Y., YAO, J., et al. An empirical investigation of trust in AI in a Chinese petrochemical enterprise based on institutional theory[J]. Scientific Reports, 2021, 11 (1): 1-12.

2 BEJGER, S., ELSTER, S. Artificial intelligence in economic decision making: how to assure a trust? [J]. Ekonomia i Prawo-economics and Law, 2020, 19 (3): 411-434.

3 LOBSCHAT, L., MUELLER, B., EGGERS, F., et al. Corporate digital responsibility[J]. Journal of Business Research, 2021, 122: 875-888.

4 ARAUJO, T., HELBERGER, N., KRUIKEMEIER, S., et al. In AI we trust? Perceptions about automated decision-making by artificial intelligence[J]. AI & Society, 2020, 35 (3): 611-623.

different AI applications. [1] Task complexity shapes performance expectations, thereby influencing user trust in AI.[2] Numerous studies adopt the Unified Theory of Acceptance and Use of Technology (UTAUT/UTAUT2) framework to examine how AI attributes affect trust across contexts. This theory posits that acceptance of new technologies hinges on users' perceptions of their utilitarian traits such as perceived usefulness, perceived ease of use and hedonic motivations.[3] Bilgihan[4] further underscores that both utilitarian and hedonic characteristics of products or services are critical in shaping user trust.

From a utilitarian perspective, the key is what value AI applications can provide for users' tasks and rational consumption. Research based on the UTAUT model shows that some utilitarian traits, such as perceived usefulness and ease of use, are key factors in forming user trust in different situations.[5] However, users' perception of utilitarian value may vary depending on the context in which AI is used. Moreover, the utilitarian value of AI is also shaped by the cost of errors or perceived seriousness in different contexts. A higher perceived seriousness makes trust-building more challenging. For example, scenarios involving vehicles or medical expert systems are often considered as critical because they directly impact

---

1 AHN, J., KIM, J., SUNG, Y. The effect of gender stereotypes on artificial intelligence recommendations[J]. Journal of Business Research, 2022, 141: 50-59.
2 FAN, W., LIU, J., ZHU, S., et al. Investigating the impacting factors for the healthcare professionals to adopt artificial intelligence-based medical diagnosis support system (AIMDSS)[J]. Annals of Operations Research, 2020, 294 (1): 567-592.
3 MOUSSAWI, S., KOUFARIS, M., BENBUNAN-FICH, R. How perceptions of intelligence and anthropomorphism affect adoption of personal intelligent agents[J]. Electronic Markets, 2021, 31 (2): 343-364.
4 BILGIHAN, A. Gen Y customer loyalty in online shopping: an integrated model of trust, user experience and branding[J]. Computers in Human Behavior, 2016, 61: 103-113.
5 ZHANG, S., MENG, Z., CHEN, B., et al. Motivation, social emotion, and the acceptance of artificial intelligence virtual assistants-trust-based mediating effects[J]. Frontiers in Psychology, 2021, 12: 168-175.

human safety and health.[1]

From the perspective of hedonism, users' subjective experiences, such as fun and entertainment, also have an important impact on trust.[2] For example, consumers may feel hedonic value from how AI entertains them while providing standard services.[3] In addition, the novelty of AI technology is also related to hedonic experience. As demonstrated by Hasan's group[4] in their study on voice-controlled AI applications, users perceive novelty when the technology provides unique experiences that satisfy their curiosity.

(4) Social Dimension: Normative Pressures and Cultural Differences as Constraints on AI Trust

AI has become inseparable from our daily life, and trust in AI is significantly shaped by social factors. Research in this domain primarily examines how social norms and cultural differences influence user trust in AI.

Firstly, social norms play an important role in individuals' trust in AI. As pointed out by Crigger's team[5] and Fan and other scholars[6], with the

---

1 GUPTA, S., KAMBOJ, S., BAG, S. Role of risks in the development of responsible artificial intelligence in the digital healthcare domain[J]. Information Systems Frontiers, 2021:1-18.
2 BILGIHAN, A. Gen Y customer loyalty in online shopping: an integrated model of trust, user experience and branding[J].Computers in Human Behavior, 2016, 61: 103-113.
3 LOU, C., YUAN, S. Influencer marketing: how message value and credibility affect consumer trust of branded content on social media[J]. Journal of Interactive Advertising, 2019, 19 (1): 58-73.
4 HASAN, R., SHAMS, R., RAHMAN, M. Consumer trust and perceived risk for voice-controlled artificial intelligence: the case of Siri[J]. Journal of Business Research, 2021, 131: 591-597.
5 CRIGGER, E., REINBOLD, K., HANSON, C., et al. Trustworthy augmented intelligence in health care[J].Journal of Medical Systems, 2022, 46 (2): 1-11.
6 FAN, W., LIU, J., ZHU, S., et al. Investigating the impacting factors for the healthcare professionals to adopt artificial intelligence-based medical diagnosis support system (AIMDSS)[J]. Annals of Operations Research, 2020, 294 (1): 567-592.

development of AI technology, people's trust in AI will become increasingly similar to trust in another person. Some AI applications, such as chatbots, have been seen as social actors with human like emotions. Therefore, when interacting with AI, users may apply certain social conventions, such as those governing social etiquette.[1] Moreover, research by Janssen's group[2] and Sheridan[3] find out that users' trust in AI also includes expectations for AI services and their providers to follow social norms, especially when these norms have been transformed into laws and regulations. For example, when legal mandates like user consent for data collection are enforced, individuals are more likely to trust AI.[4]

Another key social factor is culture. Robinson[5] believes that culture can directly influence a people's beliefs, behaviors, and preferences. According to Hallikainen and Laukkanen[6], individualism and collectivism characterize the relationships between individuals within a country or cultural community. In individualistic cultures, people tend to care more about themselves and their immediate families, while collectivism emphasizes the close connections between individuals in society. Therefore, people in collectivist cultures are more likely to trust others, especially to trust their abilities. Meanwhile, uncertainty avoidance reflects how

---

1 GILLATH, O., AI. T., BRANICKY, M. S., et al. Attachment and trust in artificial intelligence[J].Computers in Human Behavior, 2021, 115: 106607.
2 JANSSEN, M., BROUS, P., ESTEVEZ, E., et al. Data governance: organizing data for trustworthy artificial intelligence[J]. Government Information Quarterly, 2020, 37 (3): 101493.
3 SHERIDAN, T. B. Individual differences in attributes of trust in automation: measurement and application to system design[J]. Frontiers in Psychology, 2019, 10: 1117.
4 JELOVAC, D., LJUBOJEVIC, C., LJUBOJEVIC, L. HPC in business: the impact of corporate digital responsibility on building digital trust and responsible corporate digital governance[J]. Digital Policy, Regulation and Governance, 2022, 24 (6): 485-497.
5 ROBINSON, S. C. Trust, transparency, and openness: how inclusion of cultural values shapes Nordic national public policy strategies for artificial intelligence(AI)[J]. Technology in Society, 2020, 63: 101421.
6 HALLIKAINEN, H., LAUKKANEN, T. National culture and consumer trust in e-commerce[J]. International Journal of Information Management, 2018, 38 (1): 97-106.

individuals perceive and respond to threats posed by unclear situations and ambiguity. A high degree of uncertainty avoidance will reduce users' trust.

In addition, other dimensions of culture, such as long-term/short-term orientation, power distance, and masculinization/feminization, also have an impact on individuals' trust in AI. For example, long-term-oriented cultural groups, which prioritize future outcomes, may emphasize long-term trust built on multifaceted foundations such as competence, benevolence, and integrity. Meanwhile, high power distance cultures may place greater trust in leaders' authority and competence regarding AI technology adoption and implementation.

(5) Individual Dimension: Micro Impact of User Experience and Characteristics on AI Trust

When exploring user trust in AI, researchers find out that user trust is also affected by micro-level factors, namely personal background and characteristics.[1] For example, Li and other researchers[2] associate user trust with the time when it is established. Qin's team[3] and Sheridan[4] believe that users' familiarity with technology and past experience will affect their trust tendency. This means that positive past experiences will enhance users' trust in AI technology, while negative past experiences (such as privacy issues)

---

1 SABMANNSHAUSEN, T., BURGGRAF, P., WAGNER, J., et al. Trust in artificial intelligence within production management-an exploration of antecedents[J]. Ergonomics, 2021, 64 (3): 364-384.

2 LI, J., ZHOU, Y., YAO, J., et al. An empirical investigation of trust in AI in a Chinese petrochemical enterprise based on institutional theory[J]. Scientific Reports, 2021, 11 (1): 1-12.

3 QIN, F., LI, K., YAN, J. Understanding user trust in artificial intelligence-based educational systems: evidence from China[J]. British Journal of Educational Technology, 2020, 51 (5): 1693-1710.

4 SHERIDAN, T. B. Individual differences in attributes of trust in automation: measurement and application to system design[J]. Frontiers in Psychology, 2019, 10: 1117.

will weaken their trust in AI technology.[1]

As noted by Bawack's group[2], users' prior interactions with AI constitute experiential knowledge, which is aligned with Kaplan's and other scholars' view[3] that past experiences serve as foundational prerequisites for competence-based trust. This is also related to users' knowledge, abilities, expectations, and expert status. Those who fully understand new technologies already have trust in AI, and thus do not need trust building, while those without knowledge, abilities, or expert status cannot reasonably and fully establish trust. Those individuals without direct experience in AI use may rely on their indirect experience in using other new technologies, especially those provided by the same service provider.[4] Therefore, users' trust in AI can be established based on direct or indirect experience.

Chong and other researchers[5] link the role of prior experience in trust formation with its impact on user emotions, attitudes, confidence, and expectations. Previous negative experiences may heighten user anxiety or caution, making it harder for them to trust AI. The mismatch between user expectations and the actual situation of AI applications may have a negative

---

1 LOBSCHAT, L., MUELLER, B., EGGERS, F., et al. Corporate digital responsibility[J]. Journal of Business Research, 2021, 122: 875-888.
2 BAWACK, R. E., WAMBA, S. F., CARILLO, K. D. A. Exploring the role of personality, trust, and privacy in customer experience performance during voice shopping: Evidence from SEM and fuzzy set qualitative comparative analysis[J]. International Journal of Information Management, 2021, 58: 102309.
3 KAPLAN, A. D., KESSLER, T. T., BRILL, J. C., et al. Trust in artificial intelligence: meta-analytic findings[J]. Human Factors, 2021: 00187208211013988.
4 LANGER, A., FEINGOLD-POLAK, R., MUELLER, O., et al. Trust in socially assistive robots: considerations for use in rehabilitation[J]. Neuroscience & Biobehavioral Reviews, 2019, 104: 231-239.
5 CHONG, L., ZHANG, G., GOUCHER-LAMBERT, K., et al. Human confidence in artificial intelligence and in themselves: The evolution and impact of confidence on adoption of AI advice[J]. Computers in Human Behavior, 2022, 127: 107018.

impact on AI trust.[1] However, Hafizoglu and Sen[2] suggest that prior experience related to AI service providers can only affect initial trust, and their effect on trust diminishes over time.

Factors related to users also include their demographic background and personality traits. Kaplan's team[3] find that demographic factors such as age, education, and gender can affect users' trust in AI, with gender being the most significant, and male users are more likely to trust AI.

2. Exploration of Effects: The Reshaping of User Cognition, Emotion, and Behavior by AI Trust

(1) Emotional Sublimation: Enhancement of AI Satisfaction and Emotional Bonding by Trust

In the widespread application of AI, user trust is crucial. Vasiljeva's team[4] points out that trust can not only promote cognitive changes in users, but also influence their emotions. It alters their perceptions of AI's benefits, fostering a more positive evaluation of its advantages.[5]Therefore, once trust is established, users often find using AI systems more interesting, exciting, comfortable, and educational.

---

1 WIRTZ, B. W., WEYERER, J. C., GEYER, C. Artificial intelligence and the public sector-applications and challenges[J].International Journal of Public Administration, 2019, 42 (7): 596-615.
2 HAFIZOGLU, F. M., SEN, S. The effects of past experience on trust in repeated human-agent teamwork[C]. Proceedings of the 17th International Conference on Autonomous Agents and Multi Agent Systems. Stockholm, Sweden. 2018: 2061-2063.
3 KAPLAN, A. D., KESSLER, T. T., BRILL, J. C., et al. Trust in artificial intelligence: meta-analytic findings[J]. Human Factors, 2021: 00187208211013988.
4 VASILJEVA, T., KREITUSS, I., LULLE, I. Artificial intelligence: the attitude of the public and representatives of various industries [J]. Journal of Risk and Financial Management, 2021, 14 (8): 339.
5 BEDUE, P., FRITZSCHE, A. Can we trust AI? An empirical investigation of trust requirements and guide to successful AI adoption[J]. Journal of Enterprise Information Management, 2021, 35 (2): 530-549.

Vasiljeva's team[1] believes that when users establish or lose trust in a service, their attitude will also change accordingly. Specifically, changes in attitude are related to users' positive or negative reactions toward service providers and the services they provide. When AI service providers demonstrate higher credibility (such as skills, goodwill, and integrity), they tend to have more positive attitudes and emotions, which increases their willingness to use AI.[2]

Ameen and other scholars[3] similarly find out that users' trust in AI has a positive impact on their subsequent experiences. For example, trust can be translated into user satisfaction, which refers to the sense of fulfillment arising from positive interactions with a product or service.[4] In this context, users' trust in new technologies is built on sustained and positive experiences, which are also more likely to enhance their satisfaction.[5]

More importantly, cognitive and emotional changes may further influence user behavior. For instance, when users trust AI and derive positive emotional experiences from it, their usage behaviors are subsequently affected, manifesting in a greater propensity for continued usage or recommendation to others.[6]

---

1 VASILJEVA, T., KREITUSS, I., Lulle, I. Artificial intelligence: the attitude of the public and representatives of various industries[J]. Journal of Risk and Financial Management, 2021, 14 (8): 339.
2 LEE, J. C., CHEN, X. Exploring users' adoption intentions in the evolution of artificial intelligence mobile banking applications the intelligent and anthropomorphic perspectives[J]. International Journal of Bank Marketing, 2022, 40 (4): 631-658.
3 AMEEN, N., TARHINI, A., REPPEL, A., et al. Customer experiences in the age of artificial intelligence[J]. Computers in Human Behavior, 2021, 114: 106548.
4 KIM, E., TADISINA, S. A model of customers' trust in e-businesses: micro-level inter-party trust formation[J]. Journal of Computer Information Systems, 2007, 48 (1): 88-104.
5 HSIAO, K. L., CHEN, C. C. What drives continuance intention to use a food-ordering chatbot? an examination of trust and satisfaction[J]. Library Hitech, 2021.
6 BEDUE, P., FRITZSCHE, A. Can we trust AI? An empirical investigation of trust requirements and guide to successful AI adoption[J]. Journal of Enterprise Information Management, 2021, 35 (2): 530-549.

(2) Behavioral Changes: Trust Building as a Key Driver for the AI Adoption, Use, and Loyalty

In AI applications, user trust serves as a critical catalyst for behavioral change. In recent years, the impact of AI trust on users' intention to adopt or use AI has become a core issue in many studies.[1]

First, research has found a positive correlation between user trust and AI usage in various scenarios. For example, Mostafa and Kasamani[2] find in online customer service environments that initial trust increases users' willingness and participation in using chatbots. Similarly, Chatterjee and Sreenivasulu[3] reveal that user trust has a positive impact on personal information sharing behavior on online platforms. In AI-driven travel services, Park[4] also demonstrates a significant positive impact of trust on user intention. Furthermore, users are more likely to disclose important personal information to AI they trust.[5]

However, it is worth noting that Moussawi's team[6] observes that initial trust (in ability, integrity, and goodwill) had a positive but not significant impact on people's willingness to adopt personal intelligent agents. This study, along with some previous research, has explored the

---

1 FAN, W., LIU, J., ZHU, S., et al. Investigating the impacting factors for the healthcare professionals to adopt artificial intelligence-based medical diagnosis support system (AIMDSS)[J]. Annals of Operations Research, 2020, 294 (1): 567-592.

2 MOSTAFA, R. B., KASAMANI, T. Antecedents and consequences of chatbot initial trust[J]. European Journal of Marketing, 2022, 56 (6): 1748-1771.

3 CHATTERJEE, S., SREENIVASULU, N. Impact of AI regulation and governance on online personal data sharing: from socio-legal, technology and policy perspective[J]. Journal of Science and Technology Policy Management, 2021.

4 PARK, S. Multifaceted trust in tourism service robots[J]. Annals of Tourism Research, 2020, 81: 102888.

5 RAHMAN, M., MING, T. H., BAIGH, T. A, et al. Adoption of artificial intelligence in banking services: an empirical analysis [J]. International Journal of Emerging Markets, 2021.

6 MOUSSAWI, S., KOUFARIS, M., BENBUNAN-FICH, R. How perceptions of intelligence and anthropomorphism affect adoption of personal intelligent agents[J]. Electronic Markets, 2021, 31 (2): 343-364.

initial trust (of adoption intention) in the early stages of AI use, without considering the sustained impact of trust on users' long-term behavior. In addition, Hsiao and Chen[1] indicate that when users perceive fewer physical and psychological risks, their trust propensity can affect their intention to continue using AI. User trust not only increases the willingness to use related applications for the first time but also fosters reuse intentions and loyalty, which has been confirmed in numerous studies.[2][3][4] In addition, Ameen's team[5] also find out that trust is equally applicable in the use of offline technology. Thus, higher trust levels correlate with elevated user expectations for technical service providers and reduced likelihood of switching to alternatives.

Section 2 Exploration in China: Multiple Issues of AI Trust in the Chinese Context

This section will discuss the multifaceted issues of AI trust in China's unique sociocultural landscape. Given its distinct cultural background and sociopolitical realities, the development of AI trust in China exhibits characteristics and challenges divergent from those observed in Western societies. Based on local practice, Chinese scholars have conducted research into such issues on AI trust as theoretical model construction, ethical risk mitigation, and practical pathway exploration, aiming to address

1 HSIAO, K. L., CHEN, C. C. What drives continuance intention to use a food-ordering chatbot? an examination of trust and satisfaction[J]. Library Hitech, 2021.
2 BILGIHAN, A. Gen Y customer loyalty in online shopping: an integrated model of trust, user experience and branding[J].Computers in Human Behavior, 2016, 61: 103-113.
3 BITKINA, O. V., JEONG, H., LEE, B. C., et al. Perceived trust in artificial intelligence technologies: a preliminary study[J]. Human Factors and Ergonomics in Manufacturing & Service Industries, 2020, 30 (4): 282-290.
4 ELBELTAGI, I., AGAG, G. E-retailing ethics and its impact on customer satisfaction and repurchase intention: a cultural and commitment-trust theory perspective[J]. Internet Research, 2016, 26 (1): 288-310.
5 AMEEN, N., TARHINI, A., REPPEL, A., et al. Customer experiences in the age of artificial intelligence[J]. Computers in Human Behavior, 2021, 114: 106548.

trust challenges arising from the rapid proliferation of AI in China. China's localized exploration of AI trust offers novel perspectives for global AI governance and underscores the contributions of Chinese scholarship to advancing AI trust research.

1. Theoretical Model Construction: Local Conceptual Frameworks and Pathway Design for AI Trust

In recent years, the widespread adoption of AI technologies has positioned human-AI trust-building as a critical concern for both academic and industrial communities. As evidenced by the aforementioned international literature review, diverse perspectives on such issues have been thoroughly examined.

Wu's team [1] emphasizes that the widespread application of AI technology in daily life and work has brought many confusions and concerns to users. To address this, they integrate trust metrics into the traditional TAM and analyze its interplay with perceived ease of use, perceived usefulness, and system adoption intentions. This study suggests that trust plays an indispensable role in driving user acceptance of AI. From a more microcosmic perspective, Bao and Zeng[2] explore various problems in the establishment of AI trust in the current society, including complex issues such as how to let AI assume the responsibility of trust. Their work proposes a novel trust-building framework aimed at achieving genuine human-AI mutual trust. Wu[3] compares the public's trust in algorithms and experts, and discusses various factors that affect their trust choices. This

---

1 WU, Jun, ZHANG, Di, LIU, Tao, et al. Research on human acceptance of AI trust and brain cognitive mechanism: empirical research and meta-analysis of neuroscience experiments[J]. Journal of Management Engineering, 2024,38 (1): 60-73.

2 BAO, Aorigele, ZENG, Yi. How is it possible to trust artificial intelligence?[J]. Research on Dialectics of Nature, 2023, 39 (2): 67-73.

3 WU, Xinhui. Under algorithm: digital trust or expert trust?[J]. Learning and Practice, 2022 (12): 28-37.

research provides critical insights into the relationships between algorithmic transparency, determinism, authoritativeness, and public trust. Yu and Yang[1] focus on how blockchain technology can solve the trust crisis between the government and the public, arguing that blockchain's decentralized nature facilitates novel, transparent, and equitable trust mechanisms.

In human-machine interactions, Yu[2] proposes a research perspective on how machine agency shapes trust-building, thereby offering new pathways for trust construction in human-AI collaboration. Li and Du[3] focus on how algorithms can achieve "trust" in people in the field of risk control, and point out the ethical challenges brought about by this change. The relationship between privacy and trust has also been a concern for Wang and Liu[4], who have proposed various strategies to protect personal privacy and rebuild public trust. The concept of community in the literary work *Frankenstein* is quoted by Fan[5] to illustrate the impact of the black box of technology on social trust. Xu and Liu[6] further expand the application of the "trust-knowledge" model, providing a new perspective for risk decision-making. And He and Zhang[7], as well as Li and Zhou[8],

---

1 YU, Shui, YANG, Yang. Blockchain empowers people to resolve conflicts: an analysis based on the perspective of government trust[J]. Jianghai Journal, 2022 (6): 143-150.
2 YU, Xue. Building trust in human-computer interaction based on machine agency[J]. Research on Dialectics of Nature, 2022, 38 (10): 43-49.
3 LI, Yanhua, DU, Haitao. How technology "trusts" people: reflections on intelligent risk control justice from the perspective of algorithm trust[J]. Journal of Hohai University (Philosophy and Social Sciences Edition), 2022, 24 (4): 40-46135.
4 WANG, Changxiao, LIU, Na. Privacy crisis and trust reconstruction in the era of artificial intelligence[J]. Friends of the Editor, 2021 (8): 101-106.
5 FAN, Jin. Can we trust the black box? The ideal of reading community in *Frankenstein*. Foreign Literature Review, 2021 (2): 47-70.
6 XU, Xuanhua, LIU, Shanglong. Risk based emergency decision-making method for large groups based on the "trust knowledge" model in the social network environment[J]. Operations and Management, 2021, 30 (2): 31-38.
7 HE, Jiangxin, ZHANG, Pingping. Research on the path from "Algorithm Trust" to "Human Machine Trust"[J]. Dialectical Research, 2020, 36 (11): 81-85.

have explored the trust mechanism in the Internet age from different perspectives.

2. Ethical Risk Prevention: The Potential Impact of AI Misconduct on Social Trust Systems

As AI continues to penetrate into various fields of our daily lives, trust has gradually become a key factor restricting its development. Among them, AI-related trust risks have become a hot topic in academic research in recent years. All kinds of risks and problems caused by the rapid development of modern technologies, especially those of digital trust brought by new technologies, indicate the urgency and necessity of studying the risk of AI trust.

Yan's research[1] into the construction of AI trust emphasizes that trust is not merely a technical issue but also entails both conceptual and practical challenges. The values of trust should be embedded across all stages of AI development. Guo and Huang[2] concentrate on trust issues in the criminal justice system, noting that public skepticism toward algorithms poses significant trust challenges for AI in this domain. To address this issue, they advocate for enhancing AI's transparency and explainability. In addition, Sun[3] investigates the difficulties of AI trust in the field of education, especially the trust crisis caused by algorithm bias, privacy violations and other issues. He proposes a series of solutions to this, hoping to rebuild trust

---

8 LI, Ling, ZHOU, Yeping. The model, risk and reconstruction of network trust in the intelligent era: starting from the trust crisis caused by live streaming sales [J]. News and Writing, 2020 (9): 21-28.

1 YAN, Hongxiu. The trust molding of responsible artificial intelligence: from concept to practice[J]. Yunnan Social Sciences, 2023 (4) 40-49.

2 GUO, Chunzhen, HUANG, Sihan. Artificial intelligence trust and its construction in criminal justice [J]. Journal of Social Sciences, Jilin University, 2023, 63 (2): 19-34234.

3 SUN, Lihui. The subjectivity trust crisis and avoidance of artificial intelligence in educational decision-making[J]. Research on Electronic Education, 2023, 44 (3): 21-27,43.

relationships through legal and institutional construction.

Li's team[1] explores the relationship between the speed of moral decision-making and trust from a unique perspective, finding that individuals are more inclined to trust intelligent machines capable of rapid ethical judgments. Li[2] through empirical research uncovers government trust risks arising from intelligent technology applications and proposes a risk attribution framework to manage the risks. Sun and Li[3] employ a technological trust perspective to systematically analyze trust-building mechanisms for AI technologies in risk-laden contexts. Their work offers robust theoretical support for understanding and constructing complex human-AI trust relationships.

Meanwhile, Song's group[4] explores how public perceptions of AI ethical risks influence their willingness to engage in the governance of ethical risks in AI. Li[5] analyzes the trust issues in algorithmic decision-making in the context of digital China and proposes strategies to address the social trust crisis related to algorithmic decision-making. Meng[6] from a new risk perspective examines the trust issues in the AI era, and advocates for comprehensive risk management in the face of trust

---

1 LI, Yang, CUI, Peng, WU, Mingzheng. Intelligent machines with fast moral decision-making make people more trustworthy: the mediating role of ability perception[J]. Psychological Science, 2022, 45 (6): 1436-1442.

2 LI, Wenjun. Attribution framework, dimensions, and types of government trust risks caused by intelligent technology: a case study of the collapse of "One Code Pass" in Xi'an [J]. Leadership Science, 2022 (10): 100-104.

3 SUN, Liwen, LI, Shaoshuai. Construction and analysis of trust mechanism for artificial intelligence technology under risk scenarios[J]. China Science and Technology Forum, 2022 (1): 150-160.

4 SONG, Yan, CHEN, Lin, LI, Qin, et al. Perception of ethical risks, trust and public participation in artificial intelligence[J]. Studies in Science of Science, 2022, 40 (7): 1153-1162, 1171.

5 LI, Mengbing. Research on the social trust mechanism of algorithmic decision making under the background of digital China[J]. Theoretical Guide, 2021 (10) 90-95.

6 MENG, Xiaoxiao. Risk crisis and trust construction in the era of artificial intelligence: analysis based on risk theory[J]. Journal of Zhengzhou University (Philosophy and Social Sciences Edition), 2020, 53 (5): 120 - 125.

challenges posed by AI.

3. Practical Pathway Exploration: Industry Applications and Case Studies of AI Trust

To systematically understand pathways for AI trust-building, existing research has conducted in-depth analyses across various domains and perspectives. The diversity of these studies exemplifies the complexity of AI trust mechanisms while revealing their distinct application paradigms in different fields.

The research of Wang and Xu[1] illustrates the challenges faced by academic publishing as AIGC (Artificial Intelligence Generated Content) technologies intervene in knowledge production. Emphasizing the need to reshape trust mechanisms in academic publishing, they propose a collaborative model integrating multiple subjects to address disruptions caused by AIGC, offering insights for other sectors grappling with similar challenges. Yan and Sun[2] explore trust restoration in philanthropy amid digital transformation, identifying opportunities and challenges posed by digital technologies. Their work provides insights for cross-sectoral trust repair. Zhao's research[3] deepens understanding of how digital technologies build trust in cultural domains. Focusing on the digitization of film culture, the study investigates the use of blockchain technology to establish robust machine-mediated trust. Du's study[4] addresses cognitive mismatches

---

1 WANG, Pengtao, XU, Runjie. Research on the reconstruction of academic publishing trust mechanism under AIGC intervention in knowledge production[J]. Library and Information Knowledge, 2023: 1-10.
2 YAN, Ming, SUN, Yinglian. On the restoration mechanism of charitable trust under the background of digital transformation[J]. Social Security Research, 2023 (1): 66-76.
3 ZHAO, Yi. Digital construction of film culture based on blockchain technology and machine trust[J]. Contemporary Film, 2022 (9): 60-71.
4 DU, Yanyong. Do you dislike algorithms or appreciate algorithms? Differences in algorithm cognition and algorithm trust construction in the era of artificial intelligence[J]. Philosophical Analysis, 2022, 13 (3): 151-165.

between humans and algorithms, offering guidelines to align algorithm design with human cognitive patterns, and thereby enhancing algorithm trustworthiness. Yang and Mo[1] focus on the essence of trust in the dissemination of AI and the difference between AI trust and traditional trust, and propose some ways to construct AI trust. Song[2], Chen and Ai[3], and Lu[4] discuss how to use digital technology to establish and enhance trust in AI in different fields such as supply chain, healthcare, and enterprise management. The research by Chen and Wang[5] elaborates on how to use blockchain technology to achieve transparency of government information, thereby enhancing public trust in the government.

4. A Comparative Perspective: Theoretical Analysis and Empirical Validation of Trust Differences between Experts and Algorithms

In the era of rapid information technology advancement, how trust in the technology forms and evolves has emerged as a critical academic inquiry. Especially when both experts and algorithms are the main sources of decision-making, the comparison of the levels of trust placed in each has its academic importance.

---

1 YANG, Xianshun, MO, Li. Research on the trust dimension and mechanism construction of artificial intelligence communication[J]. Academic Research, 2022 (3): 43-50.

2 SONG, Hua. Trust chain: the key to the development of supply chain finance in China[J]. China Circulation Economy, 2022, 36 (3): 14-21.

3 CHEN, Yuchao, AI, Yongming. An effective way to enhance trust in artificial intelligence in the medical field: legislative framework and experience reference in the traditional medical field[J]. Qinghai Social Sciences, 2020 (5): 143-148.

4 LU, Zhen. The enlightenment of algorithm trust based on blockchain technology on building superior subordinate trust relationships[J]. Leadership Science, 2020 (7): 28-30.

5 CHEN, Feifei, WANG, Xuedong. Research on building government trust based on blockchain[J]. E-Government, 2019 (12): 56-64.

Liu and other scholars[1] empirically investigate whether users favor data-driven intelligence or expert knowledge. Their findings reveal that while users exhibit higher cognitive trust in algorithmic outputs, they display stronger affective trust in human experts. This not only reveals the complex attitudes of users toward different sources of trust, but also means that there is still great room for improvement in emotional trust through data intelligence. On the issue of information cocoons, Yu and Fang[2] argue that, different from conventional views and contrary to common perception, algorithmic recommendation systems do not reduce users' information diversity, but enhance their trust in non-algorithmic media sources. Zheng and Yang[3] explore the issue of whether news reporting is better conducted by human journalists or automated algorithms. The study points out that when users evaluate news content, their attention is not simply to whether it is generated by algorithms, but also to the background information such as the publisher, media, and topic of the news. This suggests that improving overall news quality and institutional trustworthiness may outweigh excessive focus on algorithmic technicalities.

In summary, there is still some controversy regarding who is more trustworthy between experts and algorithms. Users have high levels of cognitive trust but low levels of emotional trust in data intelligence algorithms; instead of fostering information cocoons, the use of the algorithms results in more diversified information. The acceptance of robot news is affected by multiple factors, not just by the algorithm itself. Thus,

---

1 LIU, Kunfeng, LI, Yanhong, ZHANG, Xinyuan. A Comparative Empirical Study of Data Intelligence and Expert Knowledge from the Perspective of Trust[J]. Library and Information Work, 2021 (6): 110-117.

2 YU, Guoming, FANG, Keming. Will algorithmic content push lead to information cocoons? ——An empirical analysis based on media diversity and source trust[J]. Shandong Social Sciences, 2020 (11): 170-174.

3 ZHENG, Yue, YANG, Fan. Which is more trustworthy, reporters or algorithms? An analysis of the influencing factors of the credibility of "robot news"[J]. Modern Communication (Journal of Communication University of China), 2019 (6): 63-67.

future research should prioritize such issues as how to enhance users' emotional engagement with data-driven intelligence, and the identification of credibility-enhancing factors for algorithmic news production. These inquiries hold critical implications for reconciling trust disparities between human expertise and machine-driven decision-making.

5. Practical Applications: AI Trust Practices in Chinese Industries

AI technology has been widely applied in fields such as justice, public decision-making, consumer product design, and healthcare, which has sparked in-depth exploration of AI trust mechanisms in China too. These context-specific applications offer rich sources for trust-related research.

Zhao[1] analyzes how AI can reshape judicial trust by focusing on the digital transformation of the judicial system. The transformation of trust involves technological updates, and thus poses a significant challenge to judicial philosophy, thus requiring a new model of work based on human-machine collaboration. Ran et al.[2] delve into AI's role in public decision-making and reveal the public's trust in different types of decisions. Their findings can serve as important references for government decision-making and enable governments to flexibly apply AI technology according to the specific requirements of each decision-making scenario.

Some studies focus on AI trust in consumer markets. Chen and Chen[3] study the design of anthropomorphic intelligent voice products, exploring

1 ZHAO, Yang. Judicial trust and its construction in the era of artificial intelligence[J]. Journal of East China University of Political Science and Law, 2021, 24 (4): 73-82.
2 RAN, Longya, et al. The impact of artificial intelligence participation in public decision-making on public trust[J]. Science and Society, 2022 (1) 103-121.
3 CHEN, Qianqian, CHEN, Yitao. Empirical investigation of human computer trust in intelligent voice products[J]. TechnicalEconomics and Management Research, 2021 (8): 31-35.

how human-like features shape human-AI trust mechanisms. Their work offers insights for the design and market positioning of such products. He[1] elaborates on the potential risks of AI in medical decision-making from the perspective of doctor-patient relationships. This study analyzes the uncertainty of AI systems and the challenges they may bring to doctor-patient trust, and offers valuable suggestions for the future development of medical AI. The research of Yang and Zhai[2] reveals the centrality of information transparency in consumer services. The study points out that trust in AI systems is a key factor driving consumer participation, and information transparency is an important support for AI trust.

Ran et al.[3] explore how chatbots can gain initial public trust and reveal the multiple impacts of AI models' technological features on the trust. Zhang and Zhang[4] formulate an overall and macro framework to improve the trustworthiness of AI systems. Their proposed security framework and mechanism are useful for trustworthy AI development.

Section 3 Global AI Trust Studies: Comparison and Cross-Fertilization

Studies on AI trust, both within and outside China, have notable similarities and differences in research perspectives, content and methodologies. Comparing these studies and identifying their respective

---

1 HE, Li. How artificial intelligence assisted decision-making affects doctor-patient trust[J]. Journal of Medicine and Philosophy, 2023, 44 (7): 32-36.
2 YANG, Zhiyong, ZHAI, Shaoling. Research on the relationship between artificial intelligence information transparency and customer fit in service consumption[J]. Price Theory and Practice, 2022 (4): 193-196.
3 RAN, Longya, et al. The impact of technical characteristics on initial trust of government intelligent chatbots[J]. Intelligence Journal, 2022, 41 (7): 138-144.
4 ZHANG, Linchao, ZHANG, Xinhai. A brief analysis of trusted artificial intelligence systems and security frameworks[J]. Journal of the Chinese Academy of Electronic Sciences, 2019, 14 (12): 1253-1258.

strengths and limitations are valuable for future scholarship, as each body of work offers distinct theoretical contributions and practical explorations in the field. Recognizing the unique values and constraints of each approach is conducive to cross-fertilizing and advancing the research on trust in AI and its applications.

1. Research Review: Theoretical and Practical Contributions of Global AI Trust Studies

At present, scholars outside China have made great achievements in the research of AI trust mechanism in terms of perspectives, topics and methodologies. In terms of research perspectives, they examine extensively and multi-dimensionally technical, organizational, situational and social factors influencing trust in AI. This not only lays a theoretical foundation but also provides important references for the subsequent research. In terms of research topics, they have systematically discussed the building, maintenance and repair path of AI trust. For example, in terms of trust building, they explore the role of factors such as technological transparency and organizational reputation; in terms of maintaining trust, factors such as continuous interaction and user satisfaction have been examined; in terms of trust restoration, methods such as risk disclosure and institutional construction have been investigated. These make the research on AI trust mechanism more comprehensive and complete. In terms of research methods, they have widely used experimental and empirical approaches to verify the role of various influencing factors on trust in AI, making the research more convincing.

Chinese scholars have also made some achievements in the research of AI trust. For example, in terms of research perspectives, they mainly focus on the technical aspects such as the explainability and predictability of algorithm decisions. In terms of research methods, they often engage in theoretical elaboration and model constructions. In general, scholars globally have laid a solid theoretical foundation for the further research into trust in AI.

2. Limitations and Shortcomings: Inadequate Sociocultural Perspectives and Weak Empirical Validation

While scholars globally have made progress in AI trust research, there are still several limitations.

First, the main limitation of the studies outside China is that they generally place too much emphasis on technical factors and lack sufficient examination of social and cultural backgrounds and their impact on the trust. AI technology is not value-neutral, and different social environments can affect public cognition and attitudes. Therefore, further efforts need to invest in the socio-cultural research. Second, these studies are mostly confined to conceptual modeling and theoretical speculation, with insufficient empirical validation and context-specific case studies. This compromises their persuasiveness and practical significance. Therefore, further research needs to strengthen empirical testing and case studies to ensure that theoretical models are applicable. Similarly, the research in China currently focuses too much on the characteristics of technology itself, such as the explainability and predictability of algorithms, while neglecting complex social situational factors. AI technology is not rid of socio-cultural influence, and different application environments will have constraints and impacts on it. Therefore, the Chinese research needs to broaden its perspective and consider the interaction between technology and context. Moreover, the research, like its counterpart outside China, is mostly limited to theoretical exploration and model construction, with scant empirical investigations. This again more or less erodes its scientific validity and practical value. Therefore, the research also needs to strengthen its empirical investigation targeting specific contexts.

At present, scholars outside China have carried out research on AI trust mechanism by examining the impact of technical, organizational, situational and other factors on the trust from multiple perspectives. In contrast, Chinese scholars tend to emphasize technical factors such as explainability and predictability of algorithmic decision-making, while their exploration of other influencing elements remains inadequate.

In summary, the global studies still have gaps in addressing sociocultural dimensions, empirical validation, and contextual variability, which have to be filled by subsequent studies to form a more comprehensive and systematic research paradigm on the trust in AI, and eventually to advance both theoretical understanding and practical applications in this field.

Chapter Four Feasibility and Possibility: The Logic and Rationality of Trustworthy AI

Amidst the rapid advancement of AI technologies, developing trustworthy AI has emerged as a critical imperative. As such, this chapter focuses on the issue of trustworthiness in AI. Previous studies have mostly discussed the credibility of AI through the lens of traditional interpersonal trust models such as affective trust and norm-based trust. However, these approaches tend to isolate AI from human agents. Therefore, from the perspectives of shared goals of human and AI and their respective task orientations, this chapter reexamines the connotation of AI trustworthiness, analyzes its fundamental distinctions from interpersonal trust, and constructs a systematic theoretical framework for understanding the trustworthiness. Multiple forms of trust, such as trust in functional adaptability and trust in stability, are discussed. It is hoped to overcome the limitations of existing interpersonal trust theories and to establish one tailored for the characteristics of AI.

Section 1 Ethical Imperative of Trustworthy AI: Inherent Demand to Serve Human Well-being

Since the release of the EU's Ethical Guidelines for Trustworthy Artificial Intelligence, the concept of trustworthy AI has received global attention.[1] Governments and industries all over the world are devoted to its development and application. However, some scholars question the mainstream view of AI as a trustee, arguing that it is an imprudent categorical error and an extreme statement of anthropocentrism, and should

1 WING, J. M. Trustworthy AI[J]. Communications of the ACM, 2021, 64 (10): 64-71.

not be exaggerated or trusted.[1]

In this context, we must reassess the ethical objectives of trustworthy AI. Both the Stanford HAI initiative and the EU's ethical framework guidelines highlight a crucial principle: technological advancement should serve human welfare,[2] illustrating that technology does not exist in isolation but should be closely integrated with diverse humanly domains such as society, culture, and economy to jointly drive social progress. So, building trustworthy AI requires not just technological innovation, but more importantly, a comprehensive consideration of its impact on human welfare.

However, trustworthiness in technology encompasses not only human trust in technology but also the inherent trustworthiness of the technology itself.[3] This raises a critical question: how can we evaluate and enhance the trustworthiness of technology? This is fundamental to gaining human trust and is a guarantee for the technological ethicality. In other words, only when technology itself possesses a certain level of trustworthiness can it be ultimately popularized and accordingly exert its positive impact.

Currently, with the advancement of technology and social changes, we have entered an era of human-machine integration in which technology has been internalized to be an indispensable part of our daily lives and work. This situation has fostered a new type of relationship between humans and technology, where they are no longer isolated entities but rather community members that are interdependent and mutually influential to some extent.

---

1 YAN, Hongxiu. Trustworthiness: an effective depiction of the future landscape of artificial intelligence ethics[J]. Theoretical Exploration, 2019 (4):38-42, 63.
2 ADAMS, A. Stanford university launches the institute for human-centered artificial intelligence [EB/OL]. [2024-6-30]. https://philosophy.stanford.edu/news/stanford-university-launches-institute-human-centered-artificial-intelligence.
3 MCKNIGHT, D. H., CARTER, M., THATCHER, J. B., et al. Trust in a specific technology[J]. ACM Transactions on Management Information Systems, 2011, 2 (2): 1-25.

This necessitates a re-evaluation of the definition and essence of trustworthiness. Specifically, we need to explore whether the concept retains its original meaning in this new relationship, and if not, how the new one should be defined. Then we can delve into how human and technology are essentially interconnected on ethical level. This new mode of association might transform our understanding of trust and offer a novel perspective to comprehend and evaluate trustworthiness. For instance, in traditional views, we typically consider trust to arise from some form of human interaction or exchange. However, in this new connection, it may rely more heavily on this human-AI interrelation, which is established based on their common goals or task-orientation.

Overall, trustworthiness in new relationships carries a more complex, enriched, and profound meaning. It no longer merely signifies whether an entity (such as an individual or organization) is worthy of reliance or delegation by other entities (such as other individuals or organizations). Instead, it addresses a more profound, global, and fundamental issue: how "I" perceive "you" in current social environment, technological conditions, and cultural background, and how this perception forms stable and enduring relationships that are beneficial to both parties and the development of society as a whole.

Section 2 Absence of Interpersonal Trust: A Critical Reflection on Trustworthy AI

In the era of AI, we need to establish trust not only in humans but also in various AI systems, such as voice assistants and autonomous vehicles. Traditional forms of interpersonal trust, including emotional, normative, and rational ones, emphasize emotional bonds, shared values, and the assessment of others' capabilities. However, these forms of trust encounter challenges when interacting with AI systems. Whether AI can possess genuine emotions or moral judgment has to be seriously reexamined. Despite the perception among some individuals that AI is trustworthy due to its stability, transparency, and predictability, interactions with algorithms and machines fundamentally differ from traditional forms of human trust. As such, we must re-evaluate how to build and maintain trust relationships with AI.

1. Analysis of Trust Forms: A Delineation of Emotional, Normative and Rational Trusts

Interpersonal trust, as the foundation of social interaction, has been extensively studied and conceptually enriched across multiple disciplines such as sociology, psychology, and economics. Interpersonal trust is not a unidimensional construct but rather an intricate weave of multiple factors, among which emotional trust, normative trust, and rational trust are considered the most representative forms.[1] These three forms of trust are enacted by different psychological mechanisms and social environments, and are intertwined to shape the complexity of interpersonal trust.

Emotional trust originates from profound emotional connections and spiritual bonds between individuals, and is based on a sense of closeness, degree of liking, or positive evaluations of others' characters. This form of trust underscores the critical role of emotional factors in social interactions, with emotions as a link to build stable trust relationships through emotional exchange between individuals.[2] It often accumulates or develops in long-term, continuous, and deep interpersonal interactions, relying more on non-verbal behavior and subtle emotional feedback, such as smiles, eye

---

1 DUNNING, D., ANDERSON, J., SCHLÖSSER, T., et al. Trust at zero acquaintance: more a matter of respect than expectation of reward[J]. Journal of Personality and Social Psychology, 2014, 1 (107): 122-141.
2 SIMPSON, T. W. What is trust?[J]. Pacific Philosophical Quarterly, 2012, 93 (4): 550-569.

contact, and physical touch. It holds a significant position in many social relationships, such as parent-child relationships, friendships, and romantic relationships.

Normative trust is derived from social norms and moral standards, emphasizing the constraining role of social norms in interpersonal interactions. This form of trust is grounded in morality and ethics, and established through shared values and codes of conduct.[1] It is typically formed within a specific socio-cultural context and profoundly influenced by mainstream values and moral concepts, which reflects the impact of social structures on individual behavior. For instance, in a social environment that emphasizes honesty and fairness, individuals who adhere to these principles and behave thus are more likely to earn normative trust from others.

Rational trust is established based on benefit and risk assessment.[2] This form of trust emphasizes the decisive role of rational calculation in interpersonal interactions, aiming for a balance of interests and risk control. It is built through information collection, analysis, and judgment, which involves strategic thinking, such as "Should I trust others? What might I gain if I do? What might I lose?" This calculation process requires a significant amount of information input and relies on individuals' information processing capabilities. Rational trust is particularly important in scenarios like business transactions and cooperation agreements.

---

1 NICKEL, P. J. Trust and obligation-ascription[J]. Ethical Theory and Moral Practice, 2007, 10 (3): 309-319.
2 GAMBETTA, D. Can we trust trust?[J]. Trust: Making and Breaking Cooperative Relations, 2000, 13 (2000): 213-237.

2. Heterogeneity in AI: The Dilemma of the Traditional Dimensions of Interpersonal Trust

While trust in AI has garnered much attention in both academic and public spheres, it has also incurred a series of critiques, primarily on emotional trust, normative trust, and rational trust.

Emotional trust is built on emotional interaction and connection. Human interactions, such as those between family members or close friends, are often emotionally bonded. In contrast, although AI applications, like voice assistant Siri or home assistant Alexa, can provide users with instant responses, simulate human language interactions, and even adjust their tone to match the users' emotional states, all of this is based on algorithmic presets rather than genuine emotional interaction.[1] For instance, when a user confides in a smart assistant, the comfort or advice offered, no matter how sincere it may sound, is actually generated by algorithms, thus lacking true empathy or understanding.

Normative trust is constructed on shared recognition of norms, principles, and values. In interpersonal relationships, such as those between business partners, trust may be established out of adherence to industry standards and business ethics. However, when we interact with AI entities, such as autonomous vehicles, even if their behavior demonstrates consideration for human safety, it does not necessarily mean they truly understand or internalize these norms.[2] For example, when an autonomous vehicle reroutes in an emergency to avoid hitting a pedestrian, its decision is solely predicated on programmed safety algorithms rather than genuine

---

1 JOKINEN, J. Emotional user experience: traits, events, and states[J]. International Journal of Human-Computer Studies, 2015 (76): 67-77.
2 MITCHELL, M. On crashing the barrier of meaning in artificial intelligence[J]. AI Magazine, 2020, 2 (41): 86-92.

moral judgment.

Rational trust is typically derived from a calm analysis and evaluation. In human interactions, such as the doctor-patient relationship, patients may trust doctors' treatment advice due to their professional knowledge and experience. Conversely, to be sure, AI systems like medical diagnostic software can perform precise analyses based on big data, but they merely execute algorithms on the existing data without genuine judgmental capabilities.[1] For instance, while certain medical software can accurately diagnose diseases, it lacks the comprehensive ability of a doctor to consider a patient's overall health condition, medical history, and personal circumstances.

3. Shift of Trust Evaluation Criteria: The Necessity of Reassessing the Trustworthiness of AI

Trust, as a social bond since ancient times, has always attracted considerable attention from scholars. When addressing trust in AI, critics often turn excessively to the emotional, normative, and rational differences between intelligent agents and humans, while overlooking a more fundamental dimension—trustworthiness[2]. Trustworthiness, viewed as the mirror image of trust, is a prerequisite for understanding trust. From a dialectical perspective, the relationship between trust and trustworthiness is mutually causal and interdependent. Using interpersonal trust as the sole criterion is evidently too narrow.

Trustworthiness refers to the attribute of an entity, human or otherwise,

---

1 LI, Z., YANG, T., GU, X., et al. Differential diagnosis of fetal large ventricular septal defect and tetralogy of fallot based on big data analysis[J]. Echocardiography, 2020, 4 (37): 620-624.
2 Ibid.

that inspires confidence from others,[1] and it pertains to how an entity demonstrates its capability to be deemed trustworthy. As such, the trustworthiness of AI should be regarded as its unique attribute. Some critics view AI as nonliving and emotionless, thus arguing it should not be trusted. However, they overlook the fact that AI's trustworthiness does not stem from its ability to mimic humans but rather from its stability, transparency, and predictability. For instance, a sophisticated algorithm, despite its lack of emotions, operates with clear logic and high stability, consistently providing users with accurate services. This represents not merely a utilitarian trust but one in the intrinsic characteristics of AI itself. .

Therefore, we must propose new definitions and evaluation criteria for trust in AI. The essence of trust, especially in the complex environment of human-machine interaction, cannot be understood solely from the perspective of interpersonal trust. Traditional theories of interpersonal trust are based on human beings' intrinsic emotions, moral values, and logical reasoning, which have their limitations when assessing the trustworthiness of AI. Trust in AI emphasizes its functionality, performance, and security. For instance, in the rapidly evolving field of blockchain technology, our trust rests in its decentralization and encryption algorithms, rather than the emotions or moral stance of its programmers. This trust is more grounded in the understanding of the technology itself, as well as confidence in its stability, transparency, and security.

Overall, the concepts of trust in AI and interpersonal trust are fundamentally distinct, with each characterized by different evaluation criteria and metrics. Attempting to evaluate AI trust through the three dimensions of interpersonal trust overlooks its uniqueness and thus

---

1 DEVITT, S. K. Trustworthiness of autonomous systems[A]. ABBASS, H. A., SCHOLZ, J., REID, D. (eds.) Foundations of Trusted Autonomy. Cham, Springer, 2018: 161-184.

constrains our comprehensive understanding of this complex concept. To better comprehend and assess the trust, it is essential to transcend traditional frameworks and explore the issue from broader and more profound perspectives.

Section 3 Elucidating AI Trustworthiness: Dual Considerations of Shared Goals and Task Orientation

In trust-related research, the trustworthiness of the trustee undeniably holds a significant position. To delve into this topic, it is essential to deconstruct it from the dual dimensions of common goals and task orientation. The former emphasizes how trust is formed based on the alignment and mutual benefits of objectives, while the latter positions trust as an individual's assessment of another party's capability to accomplish specific tasks. AI, as a unique trustee, exhibits significant differences in behavior patterns compared to traditional entities in many key aspects. Notably, the predictability and stability of AI are largely influenced by its algorithm-driven nature. Therefore, when evaluating the trustworthiness of AI, it is crucial not only to focus on its technical characteristics but also to survey its performance in real-world applications and whether it truly meets the needs and expectations of users. This offers a novel perspective and evaluation criterion for trust assessment in the digital age.

1. Trustee's Attribute Deconstruction: Trustworthiness as a Core Trait of AI

The perspectives of shared goals and task orientation broaden our vision to study the trust building.[1] Seen from shared objectives, trust is not merely dependent on personal traits or moral qualities but is more based on

---

1 YAN, Hongxiu. An effective depiction of the ethical future of trustworthy artificial intelligence[J]. Theoretical Exploration, 2019 (4): 38-42, 63.

the alignment and mutual benefits of goals. For example, two completely unfamiliar organizations might establish a trust relationship because they share a business objective. They do not necessarily need to have a deep understanding of each other's actions, decisions, or motivations; as long as they can mutually observe each other's predictable and stable behavior in pursuing the shared goal, it is sufficient for them to form a pragmatic trust. This trust does not imply that one party believes that the other possesses noble qualities or is unconditionally trustworthy, but rather that the other party is reliable and effective in the pursuit of the common goal.

In task-oriented scenarios, the situation becomes more complex. In such contexts, trust is often based on an individual's (the trustor's) assessment of another's (the trustee's) ability to complete a specific task. This evaluation involves various aspects such as the trustee's skills, knowledge, and experience, and may require a certain degree of foresight and risk-taking. For instance, an individual who needs heart surgery is more likely to entrust the operation to an experienced and highly skilled surgeon. This trust is not solely due to the surgeon's ability to complete the task but also encompasses considerations of his or her overall competence, professional ethics, and potential future scenarios.

In summary, in both scenarios, the trustworthiness of trustee is not solely determined by possessing certain fixed and universally trustworthy attributes. Instead, it is more about a dynamic evaluation and judgment based on specific contexts and task requirements.

2. Trilogy of Trustworthy AI: Functional Adaptation, Interactive Experience, and Transparent Explanation

To assess the trustworthiness of AI, we can examine it from the perspectives of shared goals and task orientation. These perspectives have proved to be productive in the studies of trustworthiness in traditional entities, and, we believe, are equally applicable to AI. However, AI, a unique trustee, exhibits operational mechanisms and behavioral patterns that differ significantly from those of humans or human organizations. Therefore, when evaluating the trustworthiness of AI based on these perspectives, it is essential to make necessary adjustments and expansions.

From the perspective of shared objectives, the trustworthiness of AI primarily hinges on its ability to effectively assist users in achieving specific goals. This effectiveness lies not only in achieving these goals but also in its stability, predictability, and adaptability throughout the process. These factors collectively shape users' assessment of AI's practicality, forming the foundation of pragmatic trust. It is noteworthy that this trust does not rely on users' good knowledge of the internal mechanisms of AI, but is instead based on their direct observation and experiential judgment of AI's behavior.

From a task-oriented perspective, the trustworthiness of AI is largely dependent on its capability and performance in executing specific tasks. This involves various aspects such as its technical proficiency, operational efficiency, and error-handling capabilities, and may require a certain level of foresight and risk tolerance. For instance, in the scenario of autonomous driving, users might choose to trust a self-driving system not only because of its technical ability to drive safely but also due to their confidence in the system's stability and reliability in handling complex future road conditions and ensuring passenger safety. This trust necessitates a certain amount of evaluation and judgment by users and may involve a certain level of risk-taking.

However, when evaluating and establishing trust in AI, the methods and standards used to build trust between humans cannot be directly applied to human-AI interactions. After all, AI is not a sentient being with moral responsibility; its predictability and stability are primarily determined by the algorithms and rules set by its designers, rather than intrinsic moral values or orientations. Therefore, assessing the trustworthiness of AI demands greater attention to the operational effectiveness of its behavioral patterns and whether these outcomes align with users' needs and expectations.

Section 4 The Logic and Form of Trustworthy AI Based on Various Forms of Trust

1. The Logic and Form of Trustworthy AI Based on Shared Goal Trust

In discussions surrounding the trustworthiness of AI, goal-oriented trust is a crucial dimension. This type of trust primarily assesses whether AI can effectively assist users in achieving specific objectives. Its various forms, including trust in functional adaptability, interactive trust, transparency-oriented trust, and co-creation trust, may influence each other, collectively shaping users' overall trust evaluation of AI.

Trust in functional adaptability refers to the trust developed out of the functional performance and adaptive adjustment capabilities of AI. In its applications, AI needs to adjust its functions and behaviors according to user needs and environmental changes to better meet user objectives. For instance, an intelligent voice assistant must understand user voice commands and provide accurate responses while also learning and adapting to the users' language habits and changing needs. If the voice assistant can achieve the tasks, the users are likely to have trust in its functional adaptability. This type of trust is crucial for the adoption and proliferation of AI, as it directly affects whether users are willing to accept and use it, as well as their satisfaction with and loyalty to AI technologies.

Interactive trust is the trust established through the interactive experience between AI and users. During the interaction, the behavior responses, feedback information, and error-handling methods of AI can all impact users' trust. For instance, a smart home system should be designed to accurately and promptly respond to user commands, provide clear and understandable feedback, and effectively address and correct errors as they arise. Achieving this fosters users' interactive trust in the system. This type of trust is significant for improving user experience and satisfaction, and for building long-term user relationships.

Transparency-oriented trust is a type of trust in the transparency and explainability of AI. In many instances, users might not fully grasp the internal workings of AI. However, if AI can offer sufficient transparency and explainability, allowing users to comprehend the reasons and consequences of its actions, they are likely to develop such a form of trust. For instance, an intelligent investment advisor system is intended to explicitly explain the rationale underpinning its investment decisions, as well as the potential risks and returns, hence enabling users to make informed decisions. When the system can do this, the users are likely to have trust in its transparency. This kind of trust is critical for enhancing their confidence and satisfaction in decision-making, as well as safeguarding their interests.

Co-creation trust is established in the collaborative value creation between users and AI. In this dynamic, users are not merely consumers of AI, but also active participants in its innovation and enhancement. By providing feedback, offering suggestions, and engaging in testing, they work alongside AI developers to continuously refine and improve the functionality and performance of AI systems. For instance, intelligent educational platforms can collect and analyze users' learning data to constantly refine and optimize their teaching strategies and content, thereby better meeting users' learning needs. Throughout this process, users may develop co-creation trust in the platforms. This type of trust is essential for fostering user engagement, enhancing the innovative capacity of AI, and establishing enduring user relationships.

2. The Logic and Form of Trustworthy AI Based on Task-Oriented Trust

Task-oriented trust, also a key dimension in the studies of trust in AI, is primarily dependent on AI's capability and performance in executing specific tasks. Its various forms, such as evolutionary trust, extensibility trust, and trust in environmental adaptability, may interact with each other, jointly contributing to users' overall trust evaluation of AI.

Evolutionary trust is a form of trust established on the learning capabilities and adaptive performance of AI. In its applications, AI must possess a certain degree of learning and evolutionary ability to adapt to changing tasks and complexities. For instance, an intelligent medical diagnostic system is engineered to continually enhance its diagnostic accuracy and disease prediction capabilities by leveraging large-scale medical datasets. Successful realization of this is likely to foster evolving trust among users. This form of trust is important for enhancing user satisfaction and driving technological advancements of AI.

Extensibility trust is a form of trust derived from the scalability and adaptability demonstrated by AI. In practical scenarios, AI must possess a certain degree of scalability and flexibility to handle the diversity and uncertainty of tasks. For instance, an intelligent logistics management system should be able to dynamically adjust its routing and scheduling strategies based on various factors such as the type, quantity, and destination of goods. Once this is realized, users will form trust in the system's extensibility. This trust is valuable for strengthening user convenience and increasing the scope and efficiency of AI applications.

Trust in environmental adaptability is a form of trust developed out of the adaptability and robustness of AI in varying environments. In those scenarios, AI systems must display a certain level of adaptability and robustness to cope with environmental changes and disturbances. For instance, autonomous driving systems are expected to maintain stability and safety across diverse road conditions and weather scenarios. When an autonomous driving system demonstrates this capability, users are likely to develop trust in its environmental adaptability. This type of trust is indispensable for solidifying users' sense of security and for bolstering the reliability and stability of AI technologies.

Section 5 Rationality Analysis of Trust in AI

In exploring the mechanisms for building trust in AI, the dimensions of shared goals and task orientation play a crucial role in understanding the logic and form of its internal trust formation. Trust based on shared goals emphasizes how AI aligns with users to achieve common goals, thereby providing robust support for them to accomplish specific objectives. This dimension comprises multiple components such as trust in functional adaptability, interactive trust, transparency-oriented trust, and co-creation trust. Each form of trust is closely related to AI's performance in specific scenarios and influences users' perceptions of its trustworthiness. Task-oriented trust is primarily about AI's performance and capabilities in completing assigned tasks. This dimension includes key elements such as evolutionary trust, extensibility trust, and trust in environmental adaptability, aiming to reveal how AI gains user trust through continuous learning, adaptive adjustments, and robust responses. An in-depth analysis of these two dimensions not only facilitates a systematic understanding of AI's trust-building strategies but also provides valuable references for research and practice in related fields, hence enabling a more precise grasp of user trust needs and expectations in the design, development, and optimization of AI.

1. The Rationality of Trust in AI Based on Shared Goal Trust

In today's rapid advancement of AI technologies, generative AI has demonstrated its significant potential and value across various domains. This value transcends a mere unidirectional technological showcase and is fundamentally rooted in the trust established between users and AI to achieve common objectives. Specifically, we can explore the rationale behind this trust from several dimensions.

The synergy validates the rationale behind work efficiency trust. One of the core competencies of generative AI is its ability to create new, unprecedented content. For example, DeepArt is an application that can transform user photos into the style of famous painters, allowing users and systems to collaboratively create unique artworks and demonstrating exceptional efficiency. Similarly, the GPT models can collaborate with users to quickly generate high-quality texts suitable for various scenarios, such as article writing, code generation, and music composition. This collaborative creation not only improves the efficiency but also provides users with greater satisfaction, thereby making the trust in generative AI's work efficiency more justifiable.

Self-optimization underscores the rationale for trust in service quality. A notable feature of generative AI is its continuous self-learning and optimization capabilities. For instance, OpenAI's DALL·E project demonstrates how large language models (LLMs) can generate a variety of unique images through training and iteration. With each user interaction and feedback, the system gains a deeper understanding of user needs and preferences, and accordingly optimizes itself. This ongoing self-evolution ensures that generative AI consistently leads in service quality, and hence solidifies users' trust in its service.

The sharing of responsibility enhances the rationality of trust in risk-taking. Generative AI provides users with unprecedented creative tools, but it also introduces risks related to content copyright and ethical issues. However, some advanced generative AI applications have started to address these concerns. For instance, certain LLMs automatically check for potential copyright infringements when generating content, or issue warnings when users create content that might lead to ethical disputes. This mechanism of shared responsibility not only reduces user risk but also strengthens users' trust in generative AI risk management. When it can collaboratively face and resolve issues with users, this trust relationship naturally becomes more robust and justified.

2. The Rationality of Trust in AI Based on Task-Oriented Trust

Task-oriented trust is primarily built on the close relationship between the practical capabilities of AI and its outputs. The answer to why individuals are inclined to use generative AI for task completion often lies in its ability to consistently, accurately, and efficiently achieve the desired outcomes. Furthermore, this trust is also closely linked to its adaptability, robustness, and error recovery capabilities.

The successful completion of tasks demonstrates the rationality of trust in execution capabilities. For instance, the GPT models are extensively utilized across various text generation tasks, ranging from simple Q&A to complex code generation. In most scenarios, the models exhibit outstanding execution capabilities. In the realm of code generation, projects like GitHub's Copilot assist developers by automatically generating code snippets, thus significantly enhancing programming efficiency. This precise and efficient execution capability largely substantiates the trust in the execution capabilities of generative AI. This trust is not only based on its technical implementation but also on the substantial value it does bring to users in practical applications.

The formidable adaptability and robustness underscore the rationale for trust in stability. The strength of generative AI rests not only in its generative capabilities but, more importantly, in its adaptability and robustness. For instance, generative AI applications in artistic creation can produce artworks in various styles based on user instructions and feedback. This adaptability ensures that they can deliver stable, high-quality services across diverse requirements and environments. Additionally, generative AI models exhibit significant robustness when confronted with attacks or noise interference, such as accurately generating text even when the input contains misleading information. This robustness further enhances trust in the stability of generative AI, enabling it to function reliably across various scenarios.

The error recovery and self-healing capabilities reinforce the rationale for trust in continuity. Even the most advanced generative AI models can make mistakes or encounter tasks that are challenging to handle. However, a significant advantage of these models is their rapid error correction and self-healing abilities. For instance, when the output of generative AI, such as a musical composition or text, does not meet user expectations, the models can quickly adjust and generate new versions. Furthermore, some generative AI models possess real-time learning capabilities, allowing them to learn from previous mistakes and ensure they are not repeated. This rapid error correction and continuous self-healing capabilities guarantee generative AI's service continuity, and strengthen users' trust in its service reliability; and the users in turn will position it as a dependable collaborator.

Chapter Five Cognitive Frameworks: Individual Factors Influencing Trust in Generative AI

In building trust in generative AI, psychological traits, attitudes, experiences, expectations, and socio-cultural backgrounds collectively weave a complex and intricate network of influences. These factors entail cognitive psychology, social psychology and even cultural studies and ethics, forming a multidimensional system that affects trust in generative AI. Psychological traits such as technological familiarity, innovative tendency, risk tolerance, and concerns about security and privacy play a central role in determining individuals' acceptance and trust in AI. These traits shape the trust by influencing emotional attitudes and cognitive evaluations. Simultaneously, individuals' prior experiences and future expectations constitute a crucial foundation for trust perception, where positive AI interactions can significantly enhance trust, while negative experiences may erode it. The consistency between expectations and actual experiences becomes a decisive factor in the strength of trust. Furthermore, the socio-cultural background of individuals also affects trust-building. Different cultural values and social norms subtly influence attitudes and levels of trust in AI. The overall attitude toward technological advancement, the social acceptance of innovation, and the consensus on technology ethics within cultural contexts all play vital roles in shaping individuals' trust in generative AI. Thus, it is evident that individual factors in the construction of generative AI trust are both essential and multidimensional. Through the intertwined interplay of psychological cognition, experiential memory, and cultural values, these factors collectively determine the degree of trust individuals place in generative AI. This process not only reflects the complexity of technology acceptance but also mirrors the psychological reactions and cultural expectations of humanity toward future technology.

Section 1 Psychological Traits and Attitudes: The Intrinsic Foundation of Trust in AI

Psychological traits and attitudes are essential in shaping trust in generative AI. Factors such as technological familiarity, innovativeness, risk acceptance, concerns about security and privacy, and emotional attitudes toward technology form the psychological foundation for trusting generative AI. Technological familiarity determines individuals' understanding of AI's functions and potential, thereby influencing the formation of trust. Individuals' innovativeness reflects their acceptance and adaptability to new technologies, and is conducive to their exploration and trust-building in AI technologies. Risk tolerance reveals a person's psychological capacity to handle potential uncertainties and risks associated with AI, with higher risk tolerance typically correlating with higher levels of trust. Concerns about security and privacy indicate their level of caution when trusting AI technologies, highlighting the conditional nature of trust. Furthermore, individuals' emotional attitude toward technology, such as feelings of pleasure or anxiety, directly impacts the emotional dimension of trust, thereby modulating both quality and depth of interactions with AI technologies. These psychological traits and attitudinal factors constitute a complex influencing network of trust in generative AI. They are relevant not just to the users' trust building, but also to the design, promotion, and social integration of AI technologies, as well as to a harmonious coexistence between technological advancements and human values.

1. Proficiency in Technology: Cognitive Foundation of Understanding the Potential and Limitations of AI

The crucial role of technological familiarity in shaping trust in generative AI can be explained by cognitive psychology and the TAM.[1] According to the theory of self-efficacy, people's confidence in their ability to use and master new technologies is a key factor influencing their technology acceptance and trust.[2] In the trust in generative AI, this confidence often stems from a deep understanding and familiarity with the principles, functions, and potential of the technology. Technological familiarity not only enhances their recognition of the potential value of AI technology but also reduces fears and uncertainties about its potential risks, thereby facilitating the formation of trust.

Technological familiarity also influences people's perception of the predictability of AI behavior, thereby affecting their level of trust.[3] According to trust theory, trust is an individual's expectation of the future behavior of others, which largely depends on their belief in behavioral consistency. Greater technological familiarity enhances individuals' perception of the predictability and consistency of AI system behavior; as such, those with higher technological familiarity are more inclined to trust AI. For instance, individuals familiar with AI technology can understand how AI systems make decisions based on specific data or algorithms, thus enabling them to more rationally assess the causes and reliability when there are deviations in the recommendations or results provided by AI.

The impact of technological familiarity on trust in generative AI is also evident in people's understanding of the development and future

---

1 ZHANG, Le, LI, Senlin. Knowledge, understanding, and trust: mechanisms of individual trust in artificial intelligence[J]. Sociological Review, 2023, 11 (3): 59-83.
2 ZHU, Guang, LI, Fengjing, SHEN, Yumeng, et al. A Study on the willingness to read privacy policies on social media: a perspective based on the TAM Model and self-efficacy theory [J]. Modern Information, 2022, 42 (1): 150-166.
3 QIN, Dan, ZHANG, Yan. An empirical study on teachers' acceptance of Web 2.0 technology from the perspective of the Technology Acceptance Model (TAM)[J]. Journal of Xinyang Normal University (Philosophy and Social Sciences Edition), 2016, 36 (2): 69-74.

applications of AI technology. Those with a better understanding of AI are better equipped to accurately assess the potential and limitations of AI applications in specific fields, thus forming a more objective and comprehensive understanding of the effectiveness and applicability of AI technology. This understanding is not only based on the evaluation of current technological performance but also involves insights and expectations regarding future trends in AI development, hence fundamentally influencing people's trust in and acceptance of AI technology.

Moreover, technological familiarity is closely related to human curiosity and the motivation to learn. According to the self-determination theory, exploration and learning are vital components of intrinsic motivation, driving individuals to seek new knowledge and understand the world around them. Technological familiarity serves not only as a foundation for exploration, but also as a curiosity about the new opportunities and applications enabled by AI. As individuals become more familiar with AI technology, their understanding of it evolves, which in turn further enhances their trust in it.

However, the impact of technological familiarity on trust is a double-edged sword. In certain situations, excessive familiarity may lead individuals to overlook potential risks associated with technology, especially when their understanding of AI technologies remains superficial. Therefore, it is crucial to enhance the public's in-depth understanding of generative AI. Education and frank communication play a vital role in this process. By providing knowledge about how AI operates and how to interact with it safely and effectively, we can help establish a more informed foundation of trust.

2. Innovative Tendency: The Intrinsic Motivation to Embrace and Explore AI Technology

The impact of individual innovativeness on trust in generative AI is multidimensional and complex. It involves the acceptance of technology and has its psychological, social, and even philosophical rationale. It is thus essential to delve into how individual innovativeness influences trust in and acceptance of generative AI, and uncover its underlying logic and mechanisms.[1]

Individual innovativeness, as a significant concept in psychology, refers to the degree to which individuals are willing to accept and experiment with novel ideas and new technologies.[2] This psychological trait enables one to exhibit greater openness and adaptability when confronted with change and uncertainty. It has become one of the critical factors influencing trust in generative AI.

Generative AI, as a cutting-edge technology, has developed rapidly and is widely applied, permeating almost every aspect of daily life, from content creation to decision support. For individuals with high levels of innovativeness, their curiosity and desire to explore new technologies drive them to engage with and experiment with generative AI at an earlier stage[3]. This earlier exposure and hands-on experience create opportunities for them to learn and adapt to new technologies, and facilitate their understanding of the workings and potential of AI and their trust in the technology.

---

1 CHOUNG, H., DAVID, P., ROSS, A. Trust in AI and its role in the acceptance of AI technologies[J]. International Journal of Human-Computer Interaction, 2023, 39 (9): 1727-1739.

2 DAVIS, F. D., BAGOZZI, R. P., WARSHAW, P. R. User acceptance of computer technology: a comparison of two theoretical models[J]. Management Science, 1989, 35 (8): 982-1003.

3 MOGAJI, E., VIGLIA, G., SRIVASTAVA, P., et al. Is it the end of the technology acceptance model in the era of generative artificial intelligence?[J]. International Journal of Contemporary Hospitality Management, 2024, 36 (10): 3324-3339.

For instance, those who are open to new technologies might be among the first to experiment with AI-generated art or text. Through such interactions, they come to know the capabilities and limitations of AI, as well as its potential applications in creative tasks. This experience not only enhances their understanding of AI, but may also alter their perceptions and appreciation of AI-produced works, thereby deepening their trust in generative AI.

Furthermore, individual innovativeness is also related to psychological self-efficacy, which refers to individuals' confidence in successfully using new technologies. When people believe they can effectively utilize generative AI, their level of trust naturally increases. This self-efficacy not only stems from intrinsic beliefs but is also influenced by the positive feedback they receive during their interaction with AI. Positive user experiences can further enhance trust, thereby creating a virtuous cycle.

From the perspective of social psychology, individuals with innovative traits often assume the role of pathbreakers within a community. Their behaviors and attitudes can influence those around them by functioning as a kind of social proof: when people around witness these pioneers successfully utilizing the new technologies, their uncertainties and doubts about the technology are diminished and their overall acceptance and trust increased. This phenomenon is particularly evident in social networks and professional communities, where the positive feedback and successful experiences of innovative individuals can be effectively disseminated, thereby encouraging more to try and trust AI technology.

From a philosophical perspective, individual innovativeness represents a fundamental driving force behind humanity's relentless pursuit of knowledge and technology. This pursuit not only serves as the wellspring of technological advancement but also as a crucial means for individuals and society to adapt to change and achieve self-transcendence. In this process, the establishment of trust in generative AI is grounded not only in the performance and outcomes of the technology itself, but also in the trust in human innovation and the value of progress.

3. Willingness to Take Risks: Psychological Adjustment in the Face of AI Uncertainty

Risk tolerance, as a psychological characteristic measuring an individual's toleration for potential losses, plays a decisive role in building trust in generative AI.[1] In this rapidly developing technological field, risks coexist with opportunities. It influences people's attitude toward new technology and profoundly shapes the manner and depth of their interactions with it.[2] This part will analyze how risk tolerance shapes trust in generative AI from psychological, sociological and philosophical perspectives.

In the application of generative AI, risks are primarily manifested in such aspects as data security, privacy protection, content accuracy, and bias. Individuals with high risk tolerance are more likely to adopt an open attitude toward these potential uncertainties and negative outcomes. This psychological readiness makes them more inclined to accept and trust generative AI. Conversely, individuals with low risk tolerance may hesitate due to concerns about potential risks, leading to a conservative or skeptical stance toward the technology.[3]

---

1 CHOUNG, H., DAVID, P., ROSS, A. Trust in AI and its role in the acceptance of AI technologies[J]. International Journal of Human-Computer Interaction, 2023, 39 (9): 1727-1739.

2 MENG, Xiaoxiao. Risk crisis and trust Construction in the Era of artificial intelligence: an analysis based on risk theory[J]. Journal of Zhengzhou University (Philosophy and Social Sciences Edition), 2020, 53 (5): 120-125.

3 GUO, Jianan, CHEN, Wanying. Security risks and prevention strategies of generative artificial intelligence technology[J]. Science and Technology Think Tank, 2023 (11): 42-52.

From a psychological perspective, risk acceptance is directly related to individual cognitive biases and perceived risk. People's perception of risk is often influenced by their prior information, level of knowledge, and personal experiences. For instance, individuals who have learned about cases of AI data misuse through media reports may harbor doubts about the safety of AI technology. Conversely, those with successful experiences using AI may have a more trusting attitude toward the technology. These psychological and cognitive differences directly affect one's acceptance of and trust in new technologies.

From a sociological perspective, there is an alternative way to understand how risk tolerance influences trust in AI. Social constructionism posits that people's perceptions of risk are shaped through their social interactions and cultural contexts. In certain societies and cultures, innovation and technological advancement are highly valued, and risk is seen as an essential pathway to growth and development. Individuals in such environments may naturally exhibit higher levels of risk tolerance. In contrast, in societies that prioritize stability and security, individuals may be more sensitive to the risks associated with new technologies, thereby adopting a more cautious stance toward generative AI.

Philosophically, risk tolerance indicates human beings' fundamental attitudes toward knowledge, existence, and the future. Existentialist philosophy emphasizes the importance of individual freedom and choice, maintaining that confronting uncertainty and risk is a fundamental condition of human existence. Within this framework, risk tolerance reflects the attitude and response to life's unpredictability. Those willing to embrace risk may perceive generative AI as offering limitless possibilities and opportunities for innovation, rather than merely potential threats.

For instance, utilizing generative AI in medical diagnosis and treatment evidently carries risks, such as inaccuracies in diagnosis or treatment recommendations. However, physicians with a high risk tolerance may be more inclined to explore the potential benefits these new technologies may offer, such as enhanced diagnostic efficiency and accuracy. This exploratory attitude could ultimately foster trust in and acceptance of AI technologies.

Theoretically, the impact of risk tolerance extends well beyond TAMs. It encompasses how individuals seek meaning in an ever-evolving technological landscape, how they make decisions amidst uncertainties, and how they strike a balance between risks and opportunities. This is not merely a psychological and behavioral issue, but also a significant social, cultural, and even philosophical topic.

4. Data Security Awareness: Privacy in Building Trust in AI

In the digital era, concerns about security and privacy have become particularly salient, especially as generative AI technology rapidly develops and is widely applied. These concerns are not merely technical issues, but consequentially related to individuals and society, as well as ethics and philosophy. They directly affect individuals' trust in generative AI, which in turn influences the acceptance and scope of its application. The following discussion will explore how security and privacy concerns shape trust in generative AI from multiple perspectives, while also illustrating the complexity and profound significance of this impact through examples and theoretical elaborations.

From a psychological perspective, safety and privacy are human beings' fundamental needs. According to Maslow's hierarchy of needs, the need for safety is considered basic, second only to physiological one. In the context of generative AI, worries about data security and privacy are essentially instinctive responses of self-protection. When people feel that their personal information might be misused or accessed without authorization, their sense of trust is challenged, leading to resistance and skepticism toward technology. For instance, if an AI application predicates its service on access to personal health records or financial information, users are likely to refuse to use it if they do not trust its security and privacy protection measures.[1]

From a sociological perspective, the theory of social trust emphasizes that trust serves as the foundation of social interaction. In a digital society, with the widespread leakage of personal data, security and privacy have become critical elements in building social trust. The application of generative AI often involves extensive data processing and analysis. If the public lacks confidence in the data handling and protection mechanisms, their trust in the technology may be compromised.[2] As such, concerns about security and privacy are not merely technical issues but also pertain to social trust and social cohesion.

Ethically and philosophically, concerns about security and privacy prompt discussions on human dignity, autonomy, and freedom. Information ethics posits that the protection of personal data is not merely an issue of safeguarding information but also a matter of preserving individual dignity and autonomy. The application of generative AI technology, such as personalized advertising and content recommendations, enhances the efficiency and personalization of services. However, it simultaneously increases the risk of infringing on personal privacy. Fundamentally, individuals' trust in AI hinges on whether they believe it can respect and

---

1 WANG, Yan, YE, Ming. The conflict and balance between personal data sharing and privacy protection in the age of artificial intelligence[J].Theoretical Journal, 2019 (1): 99-106.

2 WANG, Changxiao, LIU, Na. The privacy crisis and trust reconstruction in the age of artificial intelligence[J]. Editors' Friend, 2021 (8):101-106.

protect their fundamental rights and dignity.

For example, the application of generative AI in the medical field can offer personalized treatment recommendations based on individual health data. However, without stringent data protection measures, the leakage of this sensitive information is likely to trigger serious privacy concerns, thereby undermining patients' trust in this technology. In such a scenario, the benefits of the technology are offset by its potential ethical risks, highlighting the critical importance of safeguarding security and privacy in technological advancement.

From both technical and policy-making perspectives, the key to addressing security and privacy concerns lies in establishing effective data protection mechanisms and transparent policy guidelines. This includes employing encryption technology to safeguard data security, implementing stringent data access controls, and providing users with control over their own data.[1] Furthermore, policymakers and technology developers need to collaborate in formulating ethical guidelines for the application of technology to ensure personal privacy and build public trust in generative AI.[2]

5. Emotional Attachment in Technology: Emotional Factors Influencing Trust in AI

Emotions have a profound impact on the construction of trust in generative AI. In human-AI interaction, they determine how individuals perceive and evaluate AI, and thus their potential to develop trust in it. This

---

1 OSENI, A., MOUSTAFA, N. JANICKE, H., et al. Security and privacy for artificial intelligence: opportunities and challenges[J].ARXIV PREPRINT ARXIV: 2102.04661, 2021.

2 CHEN, Yufei, SHEN, Chao, WANG, Qian, et al. Security and privacy risks of artificial intelligence systems[J]. Journal of Computer Research and Development, 2019, 56 (10): 2135-2150.

influence is again multiple-dimensional and complex, having its psychological, social, ethical, and philosophical roots. The following discussion will explore how emotional elements affect trust in generative AI from various perspectives, providing specific examples to analyze the intrinsic logic and mechanisms of this relationship.

From a psychological perspective, the emotional factors encompass the emotional responses to AI technology, such as affection, fear, comfort, or discomfort. These emotional responses directly influence cognitive processes, thereby affecting the formation of trust. For instance, when individuals experience positive emotions toward a particular AI technology, such as fondness and reliance on an AI-driven virtual assistant, they are more inclined to trust the technology and are willing to accept its decisions and recommendations. Conversely, if one feels fearful or uneasy about the technology, such as worrying about robots potentially replacing human, these negative emotions may hinder the establishment of trust in AI.

Seen from social psychology, emotional resonance or socio-emotional tendencies within a group significantly influence group members' trust in generative AI. They are often affected by the emotional responses of those around them. If a society generally holds a positive attitude toward AI technology, this favorable social sentiment can enhance its members' trust in AI. For instance, positive discussions and sharing about AI technology on social media can increase public goodwill toward and trust in it. Conversely, widespread negative reporting and adverse emotions intensify public skepticism and resistance, thereby reducing trust in the technology.

From the perspectives of ethics and philosophy, emotions are linked to human morals and values, and reflect people's ethical considerations of the potential impacts of AI technology. Emotions toward AI technology often represent their intuitive responses to the social changes and ethical implications it may bring. For instance, the fear of AI technology may stem from concerns about future human-machine relationships, privacy invasion, and the loss of decision-making autonomy. Such emotional responses reflect human beings' deep ethical concerns and can fundamentally affect the building of trust in generative AI.

Specifically, the role of emotions in AI applications can be demonstrated through several aspects. In the medical field, patients' trust in AI-based diagnostic tools largely depends on their emotional acceptance of the technology. If patients feel fearful or distrustful of the technology, they may refuse to use it, even if it can objectively provide accurate diagnostic information. In the educational domain, students' emotional responses toward AI teaching assistants, such as friendliness and warmth, can enhance the trust and interaction in the learning process.

In addition, the emotional responses are closely linked to individual experiences and backgrounds. People's historical experiences, cultural backgrounds, and personal values can influence their responses to AI technology. For instance, in cultures that highly value interpersonal interaction and social connection, people may have reservations about AI applications that could potentially weaken these relationships. Conversely, in cultures that prioritize efficiency and technological innovation, people may exhibit more positive emotional responses toward the same applications.

Section 2 Accumulation of Individual Experience: The Cognitive Basis of Trust Building

Experience and expectation are also crucial in shaping trust in generative AI. Experience directly affects individuals' attitudes toward and trust in new technologies, while expectation congruency serves as an essential mechanism for maintaining and deepening the trust. Specifically, positive experiences, such as successful AI interactions or expected outcomes being achieved, can significantly enhance individuals' trust in AI technology, as these experiences provide empirical evidence demonstrating its reliability and effectiveness. Conversely, negative experiences, such as encountered technical failures or unmet expectations, can erode trust, indicating potential deficiencies or unpredictability in AI technology. Moreover, expectation congruency, the degree to which AI's performance aligns with individual expectations, is critical for trust formation. When its actual performance meets or exceeds expectations, trust levels are elevated. Conversely, a gap between actual experience and expectations, even minor mismatch, can negatively impact trust. This trust-building mechanism based on experience and expectation highlights the role of psychological expectation in the trust building, revealing the psychological dynamics influencing trust in generative AI. It also points to potential pathways for enhancing AI trust through the management and optimization of user experience (UX) and expectation.

1. Differences in Interactive Experiences: The Role of AI Usage Experience in Shaping Trust

The crucial role played by prior experiences in shaping individuals' trust in generative AI has already been recognized in the fields of psychology and behavioral sciences, and acknowledged in human-AI interaction studies and the TAM. People's experiences, whether positive or negative, profoundly influence their attitudes, expectations, and levels of trust toward new technologies. By analyzing the mechanisms through which prior experiences exert their influence, we can gain a better understanding of how individuals develop trust in generative AI and how managing and optimizing these experiences can enhance trust.

From the perspective of cognitive psychology, the influence of prior experience on the process of trust can be understood as an experiential learning process. When individuals achieve positive outcomes from past interactions, they develop an expectation that future interactions will yield similarly favorable results. This positive experiential feedback loop can enhance their trust in AI technology. For instance, the successful experiences that individuals receive accurate and timely information and assistance from an AI-driven personal assistant can deepen their trust in the capability and reliability of AI.

Conversely, negative experiences, such as data breaches, erroneous recommendations, or malfunctioning AI systems, can result in a sharp decline in trust. Such experiences leave a lasting impression on individuals, leading them to question the capabilities and safety of AI. In psychology, this phenomenon is referred to as negativity bias, where individuals tend to give more weight to negative information, which is particularly evident in the formation of trust in AI.

Furthermore, research in sociology and social psychology indicates that prior experiences influence people's sense of trust through social comparison and group dynamics. They form trust in AI not only through direct experiences but also by observing and evaluating the experiences and reactions of those around them. In this process, social proof plays a significant role. When individuals witness others successfully utilizing AI technologies, they may develop trust in AI due to the influence of social proof, even if they themselves have not had direct positive experiences.

From a philosophical standpoint, the influence of prior experiences on trust in generative AI touches on the core issues of epistemology and existentialism. Knowledge is derived not only from abstract logical reasoning but also from concrete experiences and practices. In this sense, one's trust in AI is built upon direct perception and interaction with the world, which forms the foundation for understanding and evaluating technology. Moreover, existentialism emphasizes the value of individual freedom and subjective experience. From this perspective, the trust in AI technology has to be invested with the feelings and gains of personal experiences.

For instance, the positive experiences of patients and their family members who benefit directly or indirectly from AI's high accuracy in medical diagnostics not only enhance their trust in the specific AI application, but may also extend that trust into any other generative AI technologies. Conversely, the negative experiences of autonomous driving accidents caused by the malfunctioning AI systems can provoke widespread panic and distrust among the public, even though these technological failures are exceptionally rare.

2. Expectation Congruency: The Alignment between AI Performance and Individual Expectation

Expectation congruency also affects trust building in generative AI. This concept, originated from fundamental principles in psychology and sociology, refers to the consistency between individuals' expectation of an event or behavior and the actual outcome. Expectation congruency related to generative AI specifically denotes the degree of alignment between individuals' expectation about its functions, output, and behavior and its actual performance. When AI's actual performance meets the expectation, trust is established and reinforced. Conversely, discrepancy between expectation and actual experience may weaken or even undermine the trust. The following discussion will delve into various dimensions of how expectation congruency influences trust in generative AI with examples.

From the perspective of cognitive psychology, the influence of expectation congruency on trust building involves individuals' cognitive evaluation mechanism. When individuals use AI systems, they form specific expectations of the technology based on prior knowledge, experiences, and information acquired from social and cultural contexts. These expectations serve as a benchmark for evaluating AI performance. When the actual performance of AI aligns with these expectations, the brain generates a positive cognitive feedback, thereby enhancing trust in AI. For instance, when individuals' actual experiences are consistent with their expectations of an AI chatbot to provide quick and accurate responses, their trust in the technology will be subsequently reinforced.

From the perspective of behavioral science, expectation congruency is also related to the behavioral intentions and usage decisions. In the TAM, the intention to use AI is influenced by the expectation assessment of the technology's performance. When an AI system consistently meets or functions beyond the expectations, the users' satisfaction and their long-term trust and loyalty toward the system are enhanced. This long-term trust is crucial for the popularity of AI technology. For instance, when a company introduces an AI decision support system, the employees' expectations may be on improving work efficiency and decision quality. If the system demonstrates consistent performance, their trust will gradually develop, making them more likely to rely on the system in a prolonged time.

Social psychology offers another perspective on how expectation congruency influences trust, highlighting the roles of social interaction and group expectations. In social interactions, people's expectations are formed not just based on their personal experiences, but also by the expectations and evaluations of those around them. When the actual performance of AI systems lives up to the expectations of the majority within a group, the resulting positive social proof can significantly enhance the rest's trust in AI. For instance, in the social media, if most users share positive experiences of their interactions with AI systems, the other users will be encouraged to adjust their expectations and develop a higher level of trust in their interactions with the AI systems.

In addition, the importance of technological transparency and communication cannot be overlooked. Developers and providers can set reasonable expectations through communication and adjust users' expectations through ongoing dialogue and feedback, which is crucial for maintaining and enhancing trust. This necessitates that in the design and marketing of AI technology, apart from innovation and efficiency, user experience and expectation management should be equally emphasized.

Section 3 Sociocultural Context: The External Domain of Trust Building

Individuals' social and cultural backgrounds also exert a significant and lasting impact on trust in generative AI; they indirectly shape the levels of trust by informing individuals' values, beliefs, expectations and basic attitudes toward the technology. Social factors, such as education level, socioeconomic status, and frequency of technological exposure, constitute a specific cognitive framework and experiential basis for individuals, and work jointly to influence their assessment and acceptance of technological possibilities. At the same time, cultural backgrounds, including traditional beliefs, social norms and historical experience, profoundly affect individuals' views on the potential value and risks of AI technology. In some cultures, the general optimism about technology and emphasis on innovation may facilitate the rapid trust in and acceptance of the technology, while in other cultures, the deep concern about the interference of technology in human life may lead to cautious reactions or even resistance to AI. These socio-cultural factors point to the complexity of trust building and the importance of understanding and respecting cultural diversity in promoting trust in and acceptance of AI technology worldwide. Such an in-depth understanding of the diversity of social and cultural backgrounds can better the design and popularization of AI technology, and foster greater trust across different social and cultural contexts.

1. Social Influence: The Impact of Social Background on Trust in AI

Social backgrounds function decisively in shaping people's trust in generative AI. It operates through various channels and mechanisms, integrating factors such as social environment, cultural background, social networks, and public opinion, all of which collectively influence the trust-building. This section will delve into how social background affects trust in generative AI from different disciplinary perspectives, unveiling its complex mechanisms and implications.

From the perspective of social psychology, social backgrounds primarily affect individuals through three mechanisms: compliance, identification, and internalization.[1] Compliance occurs when individuals outwardly accept group opinions to gain a sense of belonging or to avoid conflict. Although this influence alters behavior, it does not necessarily affect beliefs. Identification occurs when individuals are influenced by their association with members of a valued group, resulting in a stronger impact on their attitudes and beliefs. Internalization represents the most profound level of social influence, where individuals adopt certain beliefs and attitudes because they recognize the intrinsic value and significance of the information. All the three social influence mechanisms are at play. For instance, open expression of their trust in a particular AI application by renowned technology critics or opinion leaders may influence their followers' trust in the technology through the mechanisms of identification and internalization.

The sociological perspective emphasizes the impact of social

---

1 CIALDINIR, B., GOLDSTEINN, J. Social influence compliance and conformity[J]. Annu. Rev. Psychol., 2004, 55: 591-621.

structures and cultural contexts on the trust. Social structures, such as family, educational institutions, workplaces, and social networks, provide channels and contexts for individuals to engage with generative AI.[1] Cultural contexts, including societal attitudes toward technology, values, and the acceptance of technology, profoundly influence the expectation and trust in AI. For instance, in cultures that highly value innovation and technological advancement, individuals may be more inclined to trust and accept generative AI technology. Conversely, in cultures where technological skepticism is more prevalent, trust in AI is relatively lower.

From the perspective of communication studies, media coverage and public opinion are significant social factors influencing trust in generative AI. The manner in which the media reports on successful cases, failures, or ethical controversies related to AI technologies directly affects public perception and trust in these technologies. Positive coverage can enhance public trust and acceptance of AI, whereas negative reporting may incite public fear and aversion. Furthermore, as a crucial channel for information dissemination, social media accelerates the spread of social impact through individual sharing and discussion, leading to a more diverse and complex public perception of AI.

From a philosophical perspective, we gain a profound understanding of the underlying logic of social impact, particularly in discussions surrounding knowledge formation, ethical judgment, and free will. Social impact, in the process of forming individual trust in AI, involves not only the reception and processing of information but also how individuals develop an understanding of truth and morality through social interactions. Furthermore, social impact pertains to the exercise of individual free will, specifically how individuals maintain independent thinking and

---

1 DANG, Baobao, ZHOU, Yutian. Mechanisms and promotion strategies of group trust from the perspective of social interaction[J]. Gansu Theory Journal, 2022 (4):119-128.

autonomous decision-making under social influence. This is crucial for establishing AI trust based on rational and ethical considerations.

2. Cultural Values: Potential Constraints of Cultural Background on Trust in AI

Cultural backgrounds profoundly shape individuals' trust in generative AI. This impact is not only evident in the attitudes toward and acceptance of AI technology itself, but also profoundly affects the understanding of the values, ethical standards, and modes of interaction with human life that the technology embodies. This part will explore how cultural backgrounds influence trust in generative AI from an interdisciplinary perspective by drawing on the studies in sociology, anthropology, psychology, and philosophy.

From a sociological perspective, cultural backgrounds shape individuals' values and belief systems, which in turn significantly influence their attitudes and levels of trust toward emerging technologies. For instance, in cultures that prioritize collective interests and social harmony, people may be more concerned with the broader societal implications of generative AI technology, such as its potential to promote fairness or strengthen social cohesion. In contrast, cultures that emphasize individualism and personal fulfillment may lead individuals to focus on how AI technology can enhance personal capabilities and deliver customized services.

From an anthropological perspective, cultural diversity is crucial for understanding and embracing AI technology. People's perceptions of robots and AI differ significantly across cultures. For example, the longstanding tradition of anime and robotics in Japanese culture has fostered a public that is generally more receptive to interactions with robots and AI, often perceiving them as friendly assistants or companions. In contrast, other cultures may exhibit lower levels of trust in AI, driven by concerns about excessive dependence on technology or apprehensions regarding the potential for machines to replace human employment.

From a psychological perspective, cultures affect the internal mechanisms through which individuals develop trust in AI. Cultural backgrounds shape individuals' cognitive frameworks and psychological expectations, thereby influencing how they interpret AI behavior and ultimately affecting the formation of trust. For instance, in certain cultures, people might primarily perceive AI as a tool or system, with trust contingent upon its performance and reliability. Conversely, in other cultures, individuals are more inclined to anthropomorphize AI, grounding their trust in a humanized interpretation of AI's "intentions" and "actions."

From a philosophical standpoint, cultural backgrounds also shape individuals' understanding and evaluation of the ethics and values underlying AI technology. Different cultures may hold distinct views on issues such as machine autonomy, human-machine relationships, and the implications of technology for personal freedom and moral choices. For instance, some cultures might prioritize the ethical responsibilities associated with technology and the preservation of human dignity, whereas others might emphasize the role of technological innovation in driving economic development and social advancement. These diverse ethical perspectives and value orientations affect individuals' trust in generative AI and their willingness to accept and adopt the technological applications.

For instance, in the domain of healthcare, cultural differences in perceptions of health, illness, and treatment can lead to significant variations in trust toward the healthcare AI applications. In certain cultures, traditional medicine and interpersonal care remain predominant, leading to skepticism toward AI-driven healthcare services. Conversely, other cultures may exhibit greater trust in the capabilities of AI technology, with individuals more willing to accept AI-based diagnostic and treatment recommendations.

Chapter Six Technological Creeds: Intelligent Machine Factors Influencing Trust in Generative AI

In building trust in generative AI, technical capability and performance, security and ethics, and user interaction and adaptability are the major technological factors or "technological creeds". These creeds are the fundamental guidelines that generative AI must adhere to for achieving high levels of automation and intelligence and ensuring a harmonious coexistence between technological development and human values. The enhancement of technical capability and performance not only demonstrates the ability of generative AI to handle complex problems and data but also serves as the cornerstone for earning user trust. A high-performance AI system showcases its problem-solving capability through precise and efficient outputs, thereby providing reliable services to users. However, the improvement of technical capability does not occur in vacuum, but within the frameworks of security and ethics. Security involves the ability of AI systems to protect user data from breaches and their resilience against external threats, while ethics is about whether the AI systems' decision-making process is fair and respectful of user privacy and rights. This necessitates that generative AI adhere to principles of transparency, responsibility, and fairness throughout its design and application, ensuring that technological advancement does not come at the expense of fundamental human ethics and morals. User interaction and adaptability emphasize the quality of interaction between AI systems and users and the systems' ability to adapt to diverse user needs. AI systems with high user adaptability can adjust themselves based on user feedback and behavior, thereby providing more personalized and expected services. This not only enhances the user experience but also deepens user understanding and trust in the systems through continuous interaction and learning. Such trust is dynamic and is strengthened as AI systems demonstrate adaptability, sensitivity, and responsiveness in the applications. These three technological creeds or factors underscore the art of balance in the development of generative AI: while pursuing technological breakthroughs and performance optimization, it is essential to maintain the bottom line of security and ethics and remain sensitive and adaptable to user needs and cultural diversity. This balance is not only a necessary condition for technological development but also the key to gaining widespread public acceptance and trust in generative AI. Only by respecting human values and social norms can generative AI achieve widespread application and enact profound transformation across various fields, ultimately promoting the overall well-being and progress of human society.

Section 1 Technical Capability and Performance: A Multidimensional Foundation of Trust

Technical capability and performance play a crucial role in building trust in generative AI through the integration of model transparency and explainability, performance and accuracy, robustness and predictability, as well as updating and self-learning capabilities. First, transparency and explainability provide users with insights into the AI decision-making process, enabling them to understand the operational logic and underlying principles of AI, which is a prerequisite for trust. Second, performance and accuracy are directly related to the reliability of AI systems; high-performance and high-accuracy systems can effectively complete tasks and reduce errors, thereby gaining user trust. Third, robustness and predictability ensure the stability of AI systems when faced with various inputs and environmental changes, thus enhancing users' expectations of system consistency and reliability. Finally, updating and self-learning capabilities demonstrate the adaptability and progressiveness of AI systems, allowing them to self-optimize in response to new data or environmental changes, a continuous evolution of AI indispensable to maintain the systems' technological advancement. These factors collectively form the technical foundation of trust in generative AI. By ensuring high transparency, reliability, stability, and the ability to continuously improve and adapt, they provide users with ample reasons to trust AI systems, which is crucial for promoting the widespread application and societal acceptance of AI technology.

1. Transparency and Explainability: The Trust Window into AI Decision-Making

Before delving into how the transparency and explainability of generative AI affect user trust, it is essential to first understand the complexity and multidimensionality of "trust" within the realm of human-AI interaction. The trust is perceived as confidence in both the reliability and predictability of technology and the ethicality and accountability of the developers of AI technology. As such, transparency and explainability emerge as critical pillars in building such trust.

Transparency in AI systems generally refers to the openness regarding their operational principles, decision-making logic, and data processing procedures.[1] Explainability, on the other hand, refers to providing sufficient information to enable individuals to comprehend the decision-making processes of AI systems. These two factors directly affect users'

1 RIBEIRO, M. T., SINGH, S., GUESTRIN, C. "Why should I trust you?" Explaining the predictions of any classifier[C]. In Proceedings of the 22nd ACM SIGKDD International Conference on Knowledge Discovery and Data Mining. 2016: 1135-1144.

understanding, evaluation, and ultimately, their trust in AI systems.[1]

In the field of generative AI, transparency entails that developers and researchers disclose their model architectures, the sources of their training data, and the specific processes involved in training the models. For instance, when a generative AI model is employed to create news articles, transparently disclosing the data sources it references and how it learns from these data can assist users in evaluating the credibility of the generated content. Such transparency not only aids in identifying and mitigating biases but also enhances user confidence in the quality of the generated outcomes.

Furthermore, a lack of transparency can lead users to question the reliability and fairness of AI systems, particularly when there is potential bias in decision-making processes. For instance, if a generative AI system is employed to screen resumes during interviews and its training data is predominantly based on non-diverse samples, it is highly likely to result in unfair screening outcomes. Opaque systems make it difficult to identify and rectify such biases, thereby undermining user trust in AI systems.

Explainability is another crucial factor in enhancing trust. Explainable AI systems can clearly articulate to users the reasoning behind the decision-making process and the results they generates. This ability to explain is particularly important in complex decision-making scenarios, such as medical diagnosis or financial risk assessment.[2] In these contexts, users need not only to know the AI systems' decisions but, more importantly, to understand the logic and rationale behind the

---

1 LI, B., QI, P., LIU, B., et al. Trustworthy AI: from principles to practices[J].ACM Computing Surveys, 2023, 55 (9): 1-46.

2 BAKER, S., XIANG, W. Explainable AI is responsible AI: how explainability creates trustworthy and socially responsible artificial intelligence[J]. arXiv Preprint arXiv: 2312.01555, 2023.

decision-making. For instance, AI systems designed to assist in medical diagnosis can significantly enhance the trust of doctors and patients if they can support their recommended diagnosis along with diagnostic and academic evidence.

However, the challenge of enhancing explainability lies in the fact that many advanced AI models today, particularly deep learning models, operate with mechanisms so complex that even their developers find it difficult to fully elucidate their decision-making processes. Nevertheless, the development of explainability tools and methods, such as feature importance scoring and decision tree visualization, can help bridge this gap. These tools offer insights into AI's decision-making process, which, while not entirely transparent, are sufficient to increase user understanding and trust.

The integration of transparency and explainability is crucial for the acceptance of and trust in generative AI. By ensuring that the design and operational processes of AI systems are open and transparent, and by providing clear and comprehensible explanations of decisions, developers can solidify users' trust. This involves technological improvements and establishing a bridge of communication between humans and machines, thereby ensuring that technological advancements serve the broader interests of society rather than becoming the impediments.

Ultimately, the pursuit of transparency and explainability is not merely a technical challenge but also a moral commitment. It requires developers to consider the impact of their innovations on human society, ensuring that the advancement of AI not only fosters technological progress but also strengthens human trust in these advanced technologies. Only when users can understand and trust the workings of AI systems can we fully harness the potential of AI to drive societal advancement.

2. Performance and Accuracy: The Cornerstone of Trust in Optimizing Technical Parameters

When discussing how the performance and accuracy of generative AI affect user trust, we must first recognize that these attributes are not merely technical parameters, but are intricately embedded within a complex network of technological and social interactions. Within this network, the social acceptance of technology, ethical considerations, and practical value intertwine to collectively shape user trust in generative AI.

Performance and accuracy are two critical dimensions for evaluating the capabilities of generative AI, directly influencing whether AI systems can execute tasks accurately and produce high-quality outputs. Performance refers to the efficiency and speed with which the systems perform tasks, while accuracy is about the correctness and reliability of the outputs. The significance of these dimensions may vary across different application scenarios, but together they form the foundation for users to assess the trustworthiness of AI systems.

From a philosophical perspective, performance and accuracy reflect the relationship between generative AI technology and human values. Trust in the technology is not solely based on its capabilities but also on how well it aligns with human goals, expectations, and values. Generative AI systems with high performance and accuracy are not merely addressing users' needs on a technical level, but also responding to their deeper expectations of reliability, efficiency, and ethical correctness.

For instance, the application of generative AI in the medical field involves analyzing vast amounts of medical imaging data to assist in disease diagnosis. The performance and accuracy of such AI systems are directly linked to the precision of diagnoses and the health of patients. In this context, high accuracy not only demonstrates the advancement of technology but also reflects a commitment to patient safety. Therefore, the AI systems' high performance and accuracy in these high-risk domains enhance both work efficiency and trust among users, as they demonstrate a commitment to respecting human life and recognizing its intrinsic value.

In the creative industries, the application of generative AI, such as in the automatic generation of music, artwork, or writing, signifies a shift where performance and accuracy are interpreted as expressions of creativity and cultural sensitivity. In these fields, accuracy may no longer be solely associated with being "correct or not," but rather with the ability to produce outputs that are engaging, emotionally resonant, and culturally valuable.[1] In this context, the establishment of trust is based not only on the technical capabilities but also on the technology's understanding and respect for the values of human culture and creativity.

Furthermore, the performance and accuracy also demonstrate the adaptability and flexibility of generative AI. In rapidly changing environments and demands, AI systems with consistently high performance and accuracy exhibit an ability to adapt and learn from new situations. This adaptability and flexibility are not only hallmarks of technological innovation but also form the foundation for building long-term user trust. The user trust is built not only on the systems' current performance and accuracy, but also on the expectation of their sustained and stable performance in the future.[2]

However, the pursuit of performance and accuracy also entails ethical and social responsibilities. As AI systems are continuously optimized for

---

1 YIN, M., WORTMAN VAUGHAN, J., WALLACH, H. Understanding the effect of accuracy on trust in machine leaning models[C]. Proceedings of the 2019 Chi Conference on Human Factors in Computing Systems. 2019: 1-12.

2 TOREINI, E., AITKEN, M., COOPAMOOTOO, K., et al. The relationship between trust in AI and trustworthy machine learning technologies[C]. Proceedings of the 2020 Conference on Fairness, Accountability, and Transparency. 2020: 272-283.

higher performance and accuracy, issues such as data privacy, algorithmic bias, and technological misuse must be taken into account. These challenges are not merely technical but also ethically related to the responsible use of generative AI technology. As such, the quest for performance and accuracy should not be detached from a thoughtful consideration of social impact.[1]

3. Robustness and Predictability: Pillars of Trust for Ensuring Stable System Operation

When discussing the impact of the robustness and predictability of generative AI on user trust, we must first examine these concepts from both technological and philosophical perspectives. Robustness and predictability are technical attributes indispensable in the interaction between generative AI and human society, embodying both technological reliability and social acceptability.

Robustness refers to the ability of generative AI to maintain its performance and accuracy in the face of minor variations in input data or in non-ideal environments. This characteristic is crucial for building user trust, as it directly relates to AI systems' reliability and practicality. Robust AI systems can handle various anomalies, including noisy data, unseen input types, and even deliberate interference, such as adversarial attacks.[2] For instance, in NLP applications, robust generative AI models can understand and appropriately respond to queries containing slangs, typos, or grammatical errors. This capability makes the models more applicable to real-world scenarios, thereby enhancing user trust in their outputs.

Predictability refers to the ability of generative AI to provide

---

1 CHEN, Yongwei. Beyond ChatGPT: opportunities, risks, and challenges of generative AI[J]. Journal of Shandong University (Philosophy and Social Sciences Edition), 2023 (3):127-143.

2 SU, Jizhu. Robustness Evaluation of Convolutional Neural Network Models Based on Prediction Uncertainty[D]. Beijing: Beijing Jiaotong University, 2021.

consistent outputs in similar or repetitive situations. This not only indicates the stability of AI systems but also pertains to whether users can form reasonable expectations based on past experiences and the systems' performance. In many application scenarios, such as automatic generation of legal documents, medical diagnostic support, or personalized content recommendation, the establishment of user trust is partly based on their ability to predict system behavior. If a system exhibits inconsistency under similar conditions, it will hardly gain user trust because a lack of predictability prevents users from forming stable expectations.

From the perspectives of philosophy and sociology, robustness and predictability reflect the mutual adaptability between generative AI technology and human society. Robust and predictable AI systems demonstrate a profound understanding of human environments and social behavior patterns, enabling the technology to integrate more effectively into society and serve human needs. Moreover, these two characteristics also embody AI's transparency and reliability, thereby enhancing users' trust in the values and objectives underlying the technology.

In practice, enhancing the robustness and predictability of generative AI involves complex technical challenges, including but not limited to improving data processing methods, optimizing model architectures, and introducing adversarial training. Through these approaches, developers can reduce AI models' sensitivity to anomalous inputs, ensuring consistent performance across various operational environments. For instance, adversarial training allows the models to be tested against deliberately misleading inputs, thereby enhancing their ability to respond effectively in real-world scenarios.

However, enhancing robustness and predictability is not without its costs. In certain instances, an excessive focus on these two objectives might compromise AI systems' flexibility and creativity. [1] For example, a generative AI model that overly emphasizes predictability may produce content that is too conservative or lacks innovation, rather than offering genuinely valuable new insights or ideas. Therefore, developers need to find a balance between robustness, predictability, and innovation when designing generative AI.[2]

In a broader social and cultural context, the pursuit of robustness and predictability has sparked debates about technological control and autonomy. On the one hand, users expect generative AI to deliver reliable and predictable outputs; on the other hand, excessive control and preset configurations may constrain the technology's potential and its contributions to society. Therefore, it is a critical issue in technological development to design AI systems that meet societal needs while maintaining flexibility and innovation.

4. Updating and Self-Learning Capabilities: The Driving Force of Trust in Adapting to Environmental Changes

The model updating and self-learning capabilities of generative AI are also essential in building user trust. These capabilities not only reflect the progress and adaptability of AI technology but also touch upon deeper philosophical and ethical issues in human-AI interaction, including the sustainability and autonomy of technology, and respect for human values.

First, the models' updating capability underscores the ability of generative AI systems to self-optimize and improve based on new data, user

---

1 DHULIAWALA, S., ZOUHAR, V., EL-ASSADY, M., et al. A diachronic perspective on user trust in AI under uncertainty[J]. arXiv Preprint arXiv: 2310.13544, 2023.
2 PAPENMEIER, A., KERN, D., ENGLEBIENNE, G., et al. It's complicated: the relationship between user trust, model accuracy and explanations in AI[J]. ACM Transactions on Computer-Human Interaction (TOCHI), 2022, 29 (4): 1-33.

feedback, or changes in the environment. This dynamic adaptability is crucial for the long-term effectiveness and reliability of generative AI. For instance, a generative AI model used for content recommendation that can regularly update itself to comprehend the latest user preferences and content trends will consistently provide relevant and engaging recommendations, thereby enhancing user trust and satisfaction. Conversely, a static model that cannot do that will quickly become obsolete, failing to meet user needs and resulting in a loss of trust.

Furthermore, the self-learning capability of AI models, which allows them to learn and adapt from new data without human intervention, exemplifies the advancement and intelligence of generative AI. This self-learning ability not only enables AI systems to handle complex and unknown tasks but also signifies that they can learn from mistakes and self-correct, thereby improving future performance. For instance, in the field of natural language generation, an AI model with self-learning capability can enhance its language model by continually being exposed to new texts, thereby producing more natural and accurate ones. Users witnessing the process of AI systems self-improving over time will greatly enhance their trust in the systems' capabilities.

From a philosophical perspective, the updating of AI models and their self-learning capability touch upon the balance between the autonomy of technological development and human control. On the one hand, these capabilities reflect a high degree of autonomy in AI technology, showcasing its potential to independently optimize and learn based on inherent algorithmic logic, without reliance on human designers and users. On the other hand, this technological autonomy raises concerns about the controllability, predictability, and ethical responsibility of AI. For instance, if an AI system engages in self-learning without proper oversight, it may develop biased, unfair, or even harmful behavioral patterns.

Thus, ensuring the transparency and controllability of model updates and self-learning processes is crucial for building user trust. Users need to be guaranteed that even when AI systems possess advanced autonomous learning capability, their learning processes remain within the ethical and social boundaries. This necessitates that developers incorporate appropriate oversight mechanisms when designing AI systems, ensuring that the learning and updating processes of AI not only reflect technological advancements but also adhere to the ethical standards of human society.

In addition, AI models' updating and self-learning capabilities raise issues concerning intellectual property and data privacy. As AI systems evolve by continuously learning from new data, they might encounter sensitive information or content protected by copyright. Therefore, the developers and users must maintain transparency regarding the sources, usage, and sharing of data, ensuring that AI systems' learning processes abide by relevant legal and ethical standards.

Section 2 Security and Ethics: The Ethical Core of a Trust Framework

The dimensions of security and ethics, comprising AI model security and privacy protection, adherence to moral and legal standards, and the reputation and integrity of the developers, are also critically relevant to shaping trust in generative AI technology. Emphasizing security and privacy protection ensures the secure handling of user data and strict safeguarding of personal privacy, which directly influences the level of user confidence in utilizing AI systems. Building on this foundation, adherence to ethical and legal standards is not only a fulfillment of social responsibility but also fundamental to sustaining the development of AI technology. It reflects respect for human rights, fairness, and transparency in the development and application of the technology. Furthermore, the reputation and integrity of the developers serve as a social guarantee for trust-building, indicating the consistency of past behaviors and the reliability of future commitments, which are critical for users in assessing the trustworthiness of AI technology. In sum, security and ethics are important dimensions to evaluate trust building in generative AI technology. This not only indicates the importance of intrinsic security and ethical responsibility of the technology, but also reflects societal expectations and demands of its healthy and sustainable development and broad social acceptance.

1. Security and Privacy Protection: The Trust Defense Line in Data Security Management

In today's digital era, with the rapid development and widespread application of generative AI technology, the security and privacy protection of AI models have become critical concerns for the public, developers, and regulatory bodies. They pertain not only to the methods of handling technology and data, but also to technology ethics, social responsibility, and the philosophical exploration of human-machine relationships. They also play a decisive role in establishing and maintaining user trust in generative AI.

In the first place, security pertains to safeguarding generative AI systems from external attacks and internal vulnerabilities, ensuring the integrity, availability, and confidentiality of the systems. [1] Privacy protection involves safeguarding personal data during the processes of collection, processing, and storage, ensuring that users' personal information is not accessed, used, or disclosed without authorization. These two aspects are complementary, collectively forming the foundation of user trust.

---

1 OSENI, A., MOUSTAFA, N., JANICKE, H., et al. Security and privacy for artificial intelligence: Opportunities and challenges[J]. arXiv Preprint arXiv: 2102.04661, 2021.

In terms of security, generative AI systems face various potential threats, including but not limited to data tampering, model theft, and adversarial attacks. Adversarial attacks are particularly noteworthy, as attackers interfere with the normal operation of AI models by using carefully crafted input data, thereby leading the models to produce erroneous outputs.[1] For instance, in image recognition systems, minor yet meticulously designed modifications to input images can cause AI models to incorrectly identify an object as an entirely unrelated one. Such attacks not only pose a threat to the systems' security but also directly affect users' trust in their accuracy and reliability.

In terms of privacy protection, the application of generative AI typically involves processing a substantial amount of personal data, including but not limited to personal preferences, behavioral records, and biometric information.[2] The sensitivity of this data necessitates that AI systems implement stringent data protection measures to prevent data breach and misuse. For instance, a generative AI system used for personalized recommendation, if not handling user data properly, might lead to the exposure of users' purchase history and browsing habits, thereby infringing on user privacy and undermining user trust.

Moreover, the security and privacy protection of AI models are not merely technical issues; they also reflect respect for individuals and social responsibility. The advancement of technology should not come at the expense of individual rights and social values. Therefore, in the development of generative AI, it is imperative to integrate ethical principles

---

1 MADRY, A., MAKELOV, A., SCHMIDT, L., et al. Towards deep learning models resistant to adversarial attacks[J]. arXiv Preprint arXiv: 1706.06083, 2017.
2 ABADI, M., CHU, A., GOODFELLOW, I., et al. Deep learning with differential privacy[C]. Proceedings of the 2016 ACM SIGSAC Conference on Computer and Communications Security. 2016: 308-318.

and humanistic concerns into the technical design, ensuring that technological progress serves the well-being of humanity rather than posing a threat to it.

Furthermore, security and privacy protection are also relevant to the transparency and accountability of generative AI technology. Transparency necessitates that developers clearly inform users about how AI systems handle data and what security and privacy protection measures have been implemented. Accountability requires that in the event of security incidents or privacy breaches, it is possible to trace the responsible parties and take appropriate remedial actions. Transparency and accountability thus are crucial for earning user trust.

To achieve these objectives, a concerted effort is required across technological, legal, and social dimensions. Technologically, methods such as encryption, anonymization, and adversarial training can be employed to enhance system security and privacy protection capabilities. Legally, it is essential to establish an appropriate legal framework and regulatory mechanisms to ensure that the development and application of generative AI abide by ethical standards and legal requirements. Socially, it is necessary to raise public awareness about the importance of AI security and privacy protection, fostering cooperation and dialogue across various sectors to collectively promote the healthy development of generative AI technology.

2. Ethical and Legal Compliance: The Trust Foundation of Ethical Conduct and Value Alignment

With the widespread application of generative AI technology, the ethical and legal compliance of AI models has become a critical factor in determining their credibility and sustainable development. This issue is concerned not only with the specific technical operations but also with the interaction and balance between technological development and conformity to social values. The core of ethical and legal compliance lies in ensuring that the development, deployment, and application of generative AI conform to both legal regulations and ethical principles, particularly in protecting privacy, ensuring data security, and avoiding bias and discrimination.

First, the application of generative AI involves several ethical considerations. Ethical compliance reflects the developers' and users' concerns with the technology's impact, including but not limited to fairness, accountability, transparency, and explainability. For instance, an important ethical consideration is how to ensure that the outputs of generative AI, whether in text generation, image recognition, or decision support, do not reflect or exacerbate existing social biases. A specific case is the use of AI in human resource management for resume screening, where biased training data regarding gender or race could lead to unfair hiring processes. Therefore, developers need to take measures to identify and correct these biases, such as employing diverse datasets for training or developing algorithms to detect and mitigate the emergence of biases.

Second, conformity to legal regulations is equally crucial for building trust in generative AI. Legal frameworks provide clear boundaries and guidelines for the development and application of AI. For instance, data protection laws, such as the EU's GDPR, establish norms for handling personal data, aiming to safeguard user privacy. Compliance with these laws is not only essential for avoiding legal risks and financial losses but also serves as a foundation for gaining user trust and social acceptance. For example, a generative AI application that complies with GDPR must ensure transparency and user control when processing user data, which can significantly enhance user trust in the application.

The challenge to ethical and legal compliance comes from the fact that the rapid development of generative AI often defies the existing legal frameworks, while ethical standards vary across different cultures and societies. This necessitates that policymakers, developers, and users collaboratively explore optimal practices within the bounds of the law that align with ethical principles through ongoing dialogue and reflection. Furthermore, as technology advances and its applications expand, existing legal and ethical frameworks must be continually updated to address new challenges and demands.

In practice, enhancing the ethical and legal compliance of generative AI can be achieved through various measures, including but not limited to: promoting interdisciplinary research that integrates knowledge and methodologies from fields such as ethics, law, and computer science; establishing ethical review mechanisms to ensure that every step of AI projects, from design to deployment, adheres to ethical standards; developing transparent and explainable AI systems that allow users and regulators to understand the decision-making processes of AI; and engaging in international cooperation to jointly formulate cross-border ethical guidelines and legal standards.

3. Reputation and Integrity of AI Developers: Institutional Trust Underpinned by Social Endorsement

The reputation and integrity of AI development organizations are equally crucial in establishing and maintaining user trust in generative AI. This impact is not solely based on the organizations' historical performance and market reputation but is also deeply connected to their adherence to ethical standards, transparency, sense of responsibility, and social commitment. The reputation and integrity of AI developers have become key indicators for users in evaluating the reliability, safety, security, and ethicality of the AI technologies they develop.

The reputation of a R&D organization reflects its recognition and influence both within and outside the industry. It is typically founded on the organization's historical achievements, technological innovation capabilities, product quality, and customer service. For instance, a company that has long been committed to developing high-quality AI solutions, actively responds to user feedback, and enjoys a good reputation within the industry is more likely to earn user trust for its newly launched generative AI products. Users often hold positive expectations for the organization's future products and services based on its past performance and reputation.

The integrity of an organization is directly linked to the ethicality and legality of its business practices. Organizations with high integrity not only comply with laws and regulations but also proactively implement measures to ensure the ethicality of their technologies. This includes adopting stricter measures in data processing and privacy protection than legally required or actively identifying and mitigating biases in algorithm design. Such submission to ethical principles demonstrates the organizations' sense of responsibility and thus solidifies the trust from users.

In addition, the assumption of social responsibility by R&D organizations is a critical factor in shaping their reputation and integrity. By engaging in social welfare activities, supporting science education, and promoting technological equity, they demonstrate their contributions to society. These actions embody their values and positively influence users and the public. The social commitment enhances the organizations' public image and reinforces their position as responsible actors in the technological field, thereby increasing user trust in their generative AI technologies.[1]

---

1 LU, Si. Basis and pathways for corporate social responsibility governance in generative artificial intelligence[J]. China Business Economics, 2023, 37 (12): 100-112.

However, establishing reputation and integrity is not achieved overnight; it requires long-term and continuous efforts. Once trust is lost, rebuilding it could be a lengthy and challenging process. Therefore, R&D organizations need to maintain their reputation and integrity through ongoing dialogue and consistent transparency and accountability. For instance, by disclosing information about technical principles, data processing methods, and AI decision-making logic, organizations can enhance their transparency and foster open communication with users. Additionally, by regularly publishing technical and ethical reviews, they can demonstrate to the public their stringent adherence to quality and ethical standards.

Some organizations build and maintain their reputation and integrity by establishing ethics committees, participating in the development of industry standards, and publicly sharing research outcomes and cases of failure. These practices not only enhance the public image of the organizations themselves, but also contribute to the healthy development of the entire AI industry, fostering trust and acceptance of generative AI technology both within and outside the industry.

Section 3 User Interaction and Adaptability: Key Pathways to Cultivating Trust

The dimension of user interaction and adaptability, through the integration of personalization, customization, emotional intelligence, and social adaptability, has a crucial impact on establishing trust in generative AI. The capabilities of personalization and customization enable AI systems to provide tailored solutions based on the unique needs and preferences of users, thereby significantly enhancing user experience and satisfaction. This targeted service not only demonstrates the high flexibility and intelligence of AI systems but also makes users feel that their needs are understood and valued, thereby building trust. Simultaneously, the introduction of emotional intelligence allows AI to recognize and respond to users' emotional states, providing a more humanized interaction experience. This capability positions AI systems not merely as tools but as "partners" that can comprehend user emotions and offer appropriate feedback. Moreover, social adaptability emphasizes the ability of AI systems to be applied across different cultural and social contexts, reflecting respect for and adaptation to diversity, which further deepens user trust in the systems. Therefore, personalization and customization, emotional intelligence, and social adaptability collectively constitute the dimension of user interaction and adaptability. This not only reflects the advanced development of generative AI technology but, more importantly, establishes a trustworthy and reliable image of generative AI in users' minds by meeting their deep-seated needs and expectations. These are key factors in promoting the widespread application and social acceptance of AI technology.

1. Personalization and Customization: The Trust Bond Fulfilling Users' Unique Needs

In this increasingly digitalized world, personalization and customization have emerged as significant trends in the development of generative AI technologies. The essence of these technologies lies in their ability to deeply understand user needs and preferences, thereby offering tailored content, products, or services to enhance user experience and satisfaction. The personalization and customization capabilities of AI models not only demonstrate the high flexibility and intelligence of AI technology but also play a crucial role in building user trust in generative AI.

First, personalization and customization reflect generative AI's comprehension of the unique needs of users. The traditional "one-size-fits-all" service model, with all of its users receiving the same content and services, often overlooks their differences. In contrast, personalized AI systems can provide tailored responses and services based on users' historical behaviors, preferences, and even emotional states. For instance, recommendation systems analyze users' browsing history, purchase records, and feedback ratings to suggest products or content they might find interesting. This personalized service not only enhances user satisfaction but also builds trust in the systems' ability to "understand" them.

Second, personalization and customization enhance users' sense of engagement and control. Users can adjust the behavior of AI systems according to their own needs and preferences. This interactivity and controllability are crucial factors in building trust. In the field of education, personalized learning systems can provide customized learning materials and teaching plans based on students' learning pace, interests, and proficiency levels. This not only improves their learning efficiency but also makes them feel that the systems are designed to meet their unique needs. This perception strengthens their trust in the systems, making them more willing to accept and use the technology.

Third, personalization and customization rely heavily on extensive data collection and analysis, which inherently involves the protection of user privacy. Therefore, in designing personalized AI systems, striking a balance between providing personalized services and safeguarding user privacy emerges as a critical issue. AI R&D organizations must ensure the transparent handling of user data and implement stringent data protection measures. When users are convinced that their data is being used securely and appropriately, their confidence in AI systems significantly increases. Conversely, any incidents of privacy breaches can undermine user trust in the systems, thereby affecting their long-term acceptance.

In addition, personalization and customization trigger ethical and social responsibility concerns, particularly about the potential exacerbation of social divides and the creation of information bubbles. When generative AI systems provide personalized content, it is essential for them to implement mechanisms that prevent the delivery of information exclusively aligned with users' existing preferences, as this limits users' exposure to diverse perspectives. Consequently, AI developers must strive to optimize personalized experiences while ensuring that recommendation systems promote diversity and balance in the information presented.

2. Emotional Intelligence and Social Adaptability: Trust Catalysts in Humanized Interaction Experiences

Emotional intelligence and social adaptability are also crucial for generative AI's development, as they directly influence users' trust in and acceptance of it. Emotional intelligence refers to AI systems' ability to recognize, understand, process, and simulate human emotions. Social adaptability, on the other hand, denotes the capability of AI systems to effectively communicate and interact across diverse socio-cultural contexts, adapting to human social norms and cultural differences. These two dimensions not only demonstrate the sophistication and complexity of AI technology but more importantly, reflect the profound interaction and integration between the technology and human society.

First, the enhancement of emotional intelligence enables AI systems to become more "human-like," allowing them to better understand and respond to users' emotions and needs. In fields such as customer service, education, and healthcare, AI systems with emotional intelligence can offer more personalized and empathetic services. For instance, in mental health applications, a chatbot capable of recognizing users' emotions and providing corresponding emotional support can alleviate users' psychological stress to some extent and even guide them to seek professional help in emergencies. This emotional connection and understanding facilitate users' trust in AI systems, as users perceive these systems not merely as cold, hard codes and algorithms, but as "partners" who can "understand" and "care" for them.

Second, social adaptability emphasizes the applicability and sensitivity of AI systems within diverse socio-cultural environments. Cultural differences may lead to significant variations in the interpretation and response to certain behaviors. Therefore, AI systems must be capable of recognizing and adapting to these differences to facilitate effective cross-cultural communication. For instance, a social robot may need to employ different greeting methods, expression habits, and communication strategies depending on the cultural context. AI systems that can adjust to these differences are more likely to be accepted and trusted by users from various cultural backgrounds, as this adaptability demonstrates respect for the cultural values and social norms of the users.

The development of emotional intelligence and social adaptability also faces ethical and technical challenges. From an ethical perspective, careful consideration is needed to ensure transparency, fairness, and non-discrimination in AI systems when dealing with emotional and cultural differences. Moreover, when these systems simulate human emotions and cultural adaptability, they must avoid causing misunderstandings or dependencies, particularly in areas involving children and mental health. From a technical standpoint, developing such systems requires in-depth interdisciplinary research, including fields such as psychology, sociology, anthropology, and computer science, as well as extensive field testing and user feedback to ensure the systems behave in a natural and appropriate manner.

In addition, the impact of emotional intelligence and social adaptability on trust in generative AI is also evident in its ability to foster deeper and more enduring user relationships. When users feel understood and respected, they are more likely to engage with AI systems over the long term and recommend them to others. This positive feedback loop is crucial for the social acceptance and commercial success of AI technology.

Chapter Seven Environmental Attunement: Contextual Factors Influencing Trust in Generative AI

Task and social contexts constitute the key environmental factors influencing trust in generative AI. These factors remind us that the formation of trust in generative AI involves a critical process of "environmental attunement." The attunement is a complex interaction of human expectations, technological performance, and sociocultural background. Task context involves the type, difficulty, urgency, and specific scenario of task execution, while social context includes the level of social acceptance, the comprehensiveness of relevant laws and regulations, and the standardization of industry norms. Together, these contextual factors shape users' cognitive frameworks regarding generative AI, thereby affecting their level of trust. Within the task context, users' trust in AI is influenced by task type; creative tasks and analytical tasks involve different trust-building mechanisms. Task difficulty and urgency directly affect users' expectations of AI output—tasks with higher difficulty and urgency demand greater accuracy and faster response from AI systems. The routine or professional nature of the task scenario determines users' tolerance for AI errors, with significantly higher fault tolerance in everyday scenarios compared to professional ones. In terms of social context, social acceptance reflects the public's psychological readiness and cultural adaptability to the widespread adoption of AI technologies. High social acceptance facilitates the formation of trust. Comprehensive legal and regulatory frameworks provide ethical and legal guidelines for AI applications, enhancing users' sense of security and trust. The standardization of industry norms ensures technological consistency and reliability, reducing information asymmetry in the market and further strengthening trust. Environmental attunement plays a crucial role in this process, requiring that AI technologies not only meet users' functional needs at the technical level but also align with users' values and ethical standards at the sociocultural level. This attunement process is dynamic, necessitating the collective involvement of AI developers, policymakers, sociologists, and end users. Through ongoing communication and feedback, a harmonious symbiosis between technology and environment can be achieved. Therefore, environmental attunement is not merely a theoretical construct but also a practical principle guiding the development of generative AI technologies. Its aim is to promote the healthy development and social integration of generative AI through the understanding and integration of diverse human-AI interaction contexts, ultimately realizing the harmonious advancement of technology and human society.

Section 1 Task Context: The Multidimensional Impact of Contextual Factors on Trust in AI

The task context encompasses task type, task difficulty, task urgency, and task scenario, all of which exert a decisive influence on the construction of user trust in generative AI. Task type determines users' baseline expectations of AI systems' capabilities. For instance, life-critical tasks (such as medical diagnosis) demand a much higher level of trust in AI compared to routine, low-risk ones (such as music recommendation). Task difficulty and urgency affect users' trust in AI systems' responsiveness and decision-making accuracy under complex circumstances. In high-difficulty and high-urgency tasks, users' reliance on AI increases, thereby raising the threshold for trust in its performance. Moreover, the specific environment and contextual conditions of the task scenario (i.e., emergency rescue in dynamically changing environments) require AI systems not only to comprehend complex situations but also to adapt to environmental changes, demonstrating a high degree of adaptability and flexibility. These factors collectively shape users' overall assessment and level of trust in AI systems' capabilities. In different task contexts, the process of building user trust in AI is dynamic, influenced by system performance, users' emotional states, as well as sociocultural backgrounds. Therefore, a thorough understanding of the impact of task context on AI trust is essential for the design, evaluation, and optimization of generative AI systems. This understanding is key to ensuring that AI technology can meet user needs and gain widespread acceptance.

1. Differences in Task Types: Distinct Trust Requirements for Creative, Analytical, and Executive Tasks

Before delving into how task type influences the trustworthiness of generative AI, it is essential to first recognize its multidimensionality and impact on the formation of trust in AI systems. The trust placed in generative AI, which is capable of generating novel content, is significantly affected by the nature of the tasks it undertakes. This influence is reflected in users' expectations regarding the reliability, accuracy, and applicability of AI-generated outputs.

Task types can generally be categorized into creative tasks, analytical tasks, and executive tasks. Each type of task imposes different demands on generative AI and shapes distinct trust formation mechanisms. Creative tasks, such as the production of artworks or text generation, require AI systems to possess a high degree of innovation and deep comprehension capability. Users' trust in these tasks largely depends on the creativity and originality demonstrated by AI systems. However, due to the highly subjective nature of creative tasks, users tend to be more tolerant of outcome diversity, which, to a certain extent, reduces the stringency of accuracy requirements.[1]

In contrast, analytical tasks such as data analysis and pattern recognition demand a high degree of accuracy and logical rigor. In these scenarios, the trustworthiness of generative AI is directly linked to the reliability and precision of its outputs. Users' trust in AI systems is predicated on the demonstrated capabilities of these systems in data processing and logical reasoning. The objectivity required in analytical tasks means that any deviation or error can lead to a significant decline in trust.[2]

For executive tasks such as automated process execution or decision support, the emphasis lies on the efficiency and consistency of AI systems. In these contexts, user trust in generative AI depends on the systems' stability and the predictability of their outputs. When AI demonstrates high efficiency and a low error rate in performing such tasks, users' trust levels correspondingly increase. However, any operational failure or inconsistency can negatively impact trust.[3]

The following provides a more detailed explanation through specific examples. Suppose a generative AI system is employed to produce news reports. In this creative task, users may prioritize originality and novelty over accuracy. In contrast, if the same system is utilized for medical diagnosis, an analytical task, accuracy and reliability become the primary considerations for user trust. Furthermore, when the system is applied to

---

1 MANN, B., RYDER, N., SUBBIAH, M., et al. Language models are few-shot learners[J]. arXiv Preprint arXiv: 2005.14165, 2020.
2 SUN, Zaoyi, XU, Weijing, CHEN, Sitian, et al. Algorithm or expert? The impact of task type on human-machine trust and value perception[J]. Packaging Engineering, 2023, 44 (20): 12, 18-24, 87.
3 XU, Ping. Research on Trust Systems Based on Multi-Dimensional Trust Vectors and a Two-Layer Reputation Model in Multi-Agent Distributed Collaborative Environments[D]. Hangzhou: Zhejiang University, 2008.

logistics management, which is an operational task, efficiency and stability emerge as the key criteria for evaluating its trustworthiness.

In addition, the type of task also influences users' tolerance toward errors generated by generative AI. In everyday life scenarios, such as when AI is used for music or movie recommendations, users may exhibit greater tolerance for recommendations that are not perfectly matched, as these tasks are perceived as low-risk and highly subjective. However, in professional or high-stakes contexts—such as legal analysis or financial planning—users' tolerance for errors decreases significantly, given that the consequences of mistakes in these domains can be severe.

Therefore, task type influences users' expectations regarding the capabilities of AI systems, thereby affecting the level of trust. Different types of tasks impose varying demands on accuracy, creativity, efficiency, and stability, all of which are directly linked to users' trust in generative AI. Consequently, understanding the impact of task type on trust formation is crucial for the design, development, and deployment of generative AI systems, ensuring that they meet user expectations and establish the requisite trust.

2. Task Complexity: The Critical Role of AI Performance in Trust Building under Challenging Tasks

The impact of task difficulty on trust in generative AI is a multi-level and multidimensional issue, involving domains such as technology, psychology, and social ethics. In examining this issue, it is essential to first define the concept of task difficulty. Of generative AI, task difficulty typically refers to the high demands placed on technical complexity, the quality and quantity of required data, as well as the expected precision and innovativeness of the outcomes.

The core of generative AI systems lies in learning and emulating human creative processes to produce entirely new outputs that appear to be human-generated. As task complexity increases, the technical demands on AI systems rise accordingly. This not only encompasses the capacity to process large volumes of high-quality data, but also requires the ability to comprehend and innovate upon complex patterns. With the escalation of task difficulty, the uncertainty and likelihood of failure encountered by generative AI systems in handling these tasks also increase, which directly impacts user trust in these systems.

In low-difficulty tasks, such as generating template-based reports or simple image editing, users tend to establish trust in generative AI more rapidly. This is because such tasks generally involve relatively fixed patterns and limited variables, allowing AI systems to perform with high consistency and accuracy. For example, AI systems can accurately generate weather forecasts based on meteorological data or adjust the brightness and contrast of photos according to straightforward user instructions. In these scenarios, users can intuitively assess AI systems' performance, and the outcomes typically align with their expectations, thus facilitating the development of trust.

However, as task complexity increases—such as requiring AI to compose a novel or conduct complex medical diagnoses—the associated uncertainty and demands for innovation rise significantly. In these high-difficulty tasks, AI systems must demonstrate a profound understanding of human language, emotions, or domain-specific expertise, and possess the capability to innovate and make decisions without explicit instructions. Users generally hold high expectations for these advanced tasks, but they are also more vigilant regarding potential errors or inaccuracies produced by AI systems. Consequently, even if AI performs exceptionally well in certain high-difficulty tasks, users' trust in it may be undermined by concerns over technological failures.

For example, while AI may demonstrate remarkable accuracy in medical diagnostics, the inherent complexity of medical decision-making and the exceptionally high standards for precision mean that even minor errors or misjudgments can result in severe consequences, thereby undermining users' trust in AI systems. Similarly, although AI-generated artworks may achieve a high level of technical proficiency, the subjective nature of art and the depth of emotional expression may elude AI systems, which in turn affects users' trust in their creative capability.

Moreover, task difficulty is closely related to user expectation management. In high-difficulty tasks, if AI systems' performance fails to meet users' high expectations, user trust may decline even if the actual performance is already outstanding.[1] Conversely, if users have low expectations for AI's ability to complete high-difficulty tasks, user trust may increase significantly even if it only meets or slightly exceeds these expectations.

Therefore, managing user expectations and clearly communicating the capabilities and limitations of generative AI systems are crucial for establishing and maintaining user trust in AI. This not only requires technical developers and researchers to enhance the technological sophistication of AI systems, but also demands the adoption of transparent and educational approaches in user interface and interaction design. Such approaches should assist users in understanding the operational mechanisms of AI systems, their inherent limitations, and the potential challenges that may arise when handling tasks of varying complexity.

In summary, task complexity is a critical dimension influencing trust in

---

1 CHOUNG, H., DAVID, P., ROSS, A. Trust in AI and its role in the acceptance of AI technologies[J]. International Journal of Human-Computer Interaction, 2023, 39 (9): 1727-1739.

generative AI, encompassing not only technological challenges but also the intricate interplay of user psychology and social ethics. In the design and deployment of generative AI systems, a thorough understanding of how task complexity impacts user trust, the implementation of strategies to manage user expectations, and the enhancement of system transparency and explainability are essential for developing and sustaining user trust.

3. Variations in Task Urgency: Dynamic Adaptation of Trust Building under Time Pressure

Task urgency refers to the time constraints associated with task completion, and it constitutes a critical dimension in evaluating the trustworthiness of generative AI. The influence of task urgency on trust in generative AI is multifaceted, encompassing aspects of psychology, sociology, and technological implementation. To understand how task urgency impacts trust in generative AI, it is necessary to delve into human perceptions of time, decision-making psychology under emergency conditions, and the performance variations of technological systems under different levels of time pressure.

First, the urgency of the task directly influences users' expectations of generative AI systems. When time constraints are relatively relaxed, users may expect AI systems to conduct more in-depth analyses and produce higher-quality outputs. For instance, when generating creative proposals for a project with ample time, users may anticipate that AI systems will provide multiple solutions, each thoroughly considered and incorporating innovative elements. In such scenarios, the systems' meticulousness and creativity become critical factors in establishing trust in AI.

In contrast, under time constraints, users' primary expectations may shift toward speed and efficiency. In urgent situations—such as the rapid dissemination of information during natural disasters or making investment decisions amid abrupt market fluctuations—users are more inclined to trust AI systems that can swiftly provide solutions or recommendations, even if these solutions may not be optimal. Within this context, the response speed and reliability of generative AI become central criteria in the assessment of trust.

Second, increased task urgency amplifies users' psychological dependence on AI systems. Under high-pressure and time-constrained conditions, human decision-makers are susceptible to cognitive overload, which can degrade the quality of their decisions. In such scenarios, generative AI systems function as assistive tools whose capabilities are perceived as transcending human limitations, offering rapid and rational decision support. Consequently, the performance of AI systems in emergency situations directly influences user trust. AI systems with efficient processing and accurate decision support under urgent circumstances can instantly win trust from the users.

However, the urgency of tasks also imposes stringent demands on the performance of generative AI. In time-sensitive scenarios, even minor errors made by AI systems can be magnified, as these mistakes may directly impact the outcomes of critical decision-making processes. For instance, in rapid stock trading or emergency medical diagnosis powered by AI, even slight delays or issues with accuracy can lead to significant financial losses or health risks. Therefore, the stability and reliability of AI systems, as well as their performance under high-pressure conditions, are crucial for building and maintaining trust.

In addition, the impact of task urgency on trust is also related to users' knowledge and understanding of AI system performance. A deep comprehension of how AI systems operate, their limitations, and potential performance variability can help users establish reasonable expectations, thereby enabling more informed decision-making when confronted with urgent tasks. Education and transparency play a critical role in this process, as they contribute to the development of a user base that better understands AI capabilities, ultimately fostering appropriate trust in AI under varying levels of task urgency.

Therefore, task urgency influences users' trust in generative AI from multiple dimensions: by shaping users' expectations of AI system performance, intensifying psychological reliance on AI decision support, and subjecting AI performance to more stringent scrutiny. In the design and deployment of generative AI systems, a thorough understanding of how task urgency shapes user trust is essential. Measures should be taken to optimize system response speed, enhance performance under varying levels of urgency, and simultaneously improve system transparency and user education. These are critical for building and maintaining trust in AI.

4. Differences in Task Contexts: Variations in Error Tolerance between Everyday and Professional Settings

The nature of task scenarios—whether in everyday life or professional contexts—plays a pivotal role in shaping users' trust in generative AI. This influence arises not only from the inherent characteristics of the tasks themselves but is also closely linked to users' psychological expectations, tolerance for errors, and anticipated performance of AI systems. In-depth exploration of this topic necessitates a multidimensional analysis, encompassing the environment of human-AI interaction, the formation of psychological expectations, and the broader socio-cultural context.

There are fundamental differences between everyday life scenarios and professional contexts in terms of purpose, complexity, and the requirements for accuracy and reliability. Everyday scenarios typically encompass a wide range of diverse tasks, such as home automation, personalized entertainment recommendations, or daily travel planning. The common feature of these tasks is their relatively low demand for accuracy, with errors generally not resulting in serious negative consequences.[1] Therefore, in these contexts, users exhibit a higher tolerance for errors generated by AI, a leniency that stems from the pursuit of convenience in daily life and a relative underestimation of associated risks.[2]

In contrast, professional contexts such as medical diagnosis, legal consultation, and financial analysis demand exceptionally high levels of expertise, accuracy, and reliability. In these scenarios, any errors generated by AI systems may result in severe consequences, including economic loss, legal liability, or even personal injury.[3] At this point, users' trust in AI systems is predicated upon rigorous evaluation of their professional competence and output quality, with an extremely low tolerance for mistakes.[4]

This distinction plays a pivotal role in shaping users' psychological expectations. In everyday life scenarios, users typically expect AI to enhance convenience and quality of life; therefore, they are more willing to accept and adapt to the limitations and occasional errors of AI systems. For example, if a smart speaker misunderstands a voice command, users may perceive this as a minor mistake that does not significantly impact their trust. In contrast, within professional contexts, users expect AI to deliver highly accurate and reliable expert advice or services. Any deviation in such

---

1 GUO, Lu, FAN, Wei. Research on personal intelligent connectivity services in everyday life scenarios[J]. Knowledge Management Forum, 2020, 5 (1): 36-46.
2 JEUNG, J. L., HUANG, J. Y. C. Correct me if I am wrong: exploring how AI outputs affect user perception and trust[C].Companion Publication of the 2023 Conference on Computer Supported Cooperative Work and Social Computing. 2023: 323-327.
3 WU, Jun, ZHANG, Di, LIU, Tao, et al. Acceptance of human trust in artificial intelligence and its neural cognitive mechanisms: an empirical and neuroscientific meta-Analysis[J]. Journal of Management Engineering, 2024, 38 (1): 60-73.
4 RIBEIRO, M. T., SINGH, S., GUESTRIN, C. "Why should I trust you?" Explaining the predictions of any classifier[C]. Proceedings of the 22nd ACM SIGKDD International Conference on Knowledge Discovery and Data Mining. 2016: 1135-1144.

settings may be deemed unacceptable and could severely undermine users' trust.

The influence of task scenarios on trust in generative AI is also shaped by sociocultural contexts and individual experiences. In certain cultures, where there is a generally high level of trust in technology, individuals may be more inclined to accept the integration of AI into everyday life and exhibit greater tolerance toward errors produced by AI systems. Conversely, in cultures that emphasize professional precision and reliability, users may demonstrate lower tolerance for AI errors, even in routine scenarios.

For example, in the applications of AI in healthcare settings, such as AI-based diagnostic support systems, even a minimal error rate can result in a sharp decline in trust from both medical professionals and patients. In such contexts, the design and development of generative AI systems must not only prioritize technical accuracy, but also thoroughly address potential ethical implications, user education, and the enhancement of transparency, in order to establish and sustain user trust.

On the other hand, when AI is employed in the creation of music, literary works, or other forms of art, even if the outputs exhibit marked differences from those of human artists, such innovation and uniqueness may precisely align with what users anticipate and appreciate. In these creative applications within everyday life, users' trust in AI is likely to be grounded more in their appreciation for novelty and creativity than in their concern with the accuracy of the outputs.

Therefore, the task context exerts a profound influence on trust in generative AI, encompassing not only direct assessments of AI's technical performance but also a comprehensive reflection of users' psychological expectations, sociocultural backgrounds, and individual experiences. Understanding and addressing these complex influences are critical for the design, development, and application of AI technologies. This necessitates that developers focus not only on technological advancement, but also gain a deeper understanding of the diversity of human societies and cultures, and how these factors shape public trust in and acceptance of technology.

Section 2 Social Context: The Role of Institutional Environment in Shaping Trust in Generative AI

The social context—including social acceptance, the comprehensiveness of relevant laws and regulations, and the standardization of industry norms—also exerts a profound influence on trust in generative AI. Social acceptance reflects the public's attitudes toward and willingness to embrace AI, which is shaped not only by perceptions of AI's potential but also by expectations regarding its societal impacts, whether positive or negative. The completeness of legal and regulatory frameworks provides the necessary legal foundation for AI development, ensuring that technological applications do not cross ethical or legal boundaries and that users' rights are protected, thereby enhancing public trust in the reliability and fairness of AI systems. Simultaneously, the standardization of industry norms ensures that the development and deployment of AI systems adhere to consistent quality and safety standards, offering objective criteria for evaluating the trustworthiness of AI technologies. Collectively, these three factors constitute the basis for the broad social acceptance of and trust in AI technologies, serving as critical supports for the healthy development and widespread application of AI. Within this framework, the advancement of AI technologies must not only pursue innovation and efficiency, but also ensure alignment with societal values, operating within legal boundaries and conforming to industry standards. This approach guarantees that technological progress garners broad social support and trust. Trust-building based on the social context is of vital significance for promoting the sustainable development of generative AI and fostering a harmonious coexistence between technology and society.

1. Foundations of Social Cognition: Factors Influencing Public Acceptance of AI Technologies

Social acceptance, as an indicator for measuring whether new technologies or innovations are widely embraced and adopted, exerts a profound influence on the level of trust in generative AI. This influence is not a straightforward, unidimensional relationship, but rather a complex, multi-layered process involving technological literacy, cultural values, ethical considerations, and socio-economic factors. To thoroughly examine how social acceptance shapes trust in generative AI, it is essential to conduct an integrated analysis from the perspectives of social psychology, communication studies, and the philosophy of technology.

First, social acceptance influences the public's fundamental understanding of and attitudes toward generative AI technologies. In a society that maintains an open attitude toward new technologies, individuals are more likely to view generative AI positively, believing that it can deliver beneficial outcomes such as enhanced productivity, the creation of new artistic forms, or improvements in quality of life. Such positive expectations directly increase users' trust in AI systems.[1] For example, if a society generally believes that autonomous vehicles can reduce traffic accidents, public trust in this technology will correspondingly increase, and more people will be willing to accept and utilize it.

In contrast, within societies that adopt a conservative or skeptical stance toward new technologies, the social acceptance of generative AI may

1 VENKATESH, V., DAVIS, F. D. A theoretical extension of the technology acceptance model: Four longitudinal field studies[J].Management Science, 2000, 46 (2): 186- 204.

remain limited, even if the technology itself has reached a high degree of maturity. This, in turn, affects public trust in such systems. Under these circumstances, individuals may express concerns about the potential risks associated with AI technologies, such as privacy violations, unemployment, or ethical and moral dilemmas, leading to a cautious or reserved attitude toward AI adoption. For instance, if there is widespread societal apprehension that AI capable of generating realistic news reports or artistic works could be misused to create disinformation or infringe upon intellectual property rights, public trust in these advanced AI systems is likely to remain low, regardless of their technical sophistication.

Second, social acceptance is closely intertwined with cultural values and ethical standards. Different cultures and societies exhibit significant variations in their receptivity to technological innovation, reflecting the trade-offs each society makes between progress, innovation, and the preservation of tradition.[1] In societies that prioritize innovation and technological advancement, the development of generative AI is likely to be encouraged and supported, resulting in higher levels of public trust in these technologies. Conversely, in cultures that place greater emphasis on traditional values and social stability, there tends to be heightened vigilance regarding the rapid development and widespread adoption of generative AI, with concerns centering on the potential disruption these technologies may pose to social structures and human values.

Furthermore, social acceptance is also influenced by economic and political factors. Driven by economic interests, certain industries may actively promote generative AI technologies to enhance efficiency and reduce costs. Such promotional activities can increase public awareness of

---

1 SONG, Yan, CHEN. Lin, LI, Qin, et al. Ethical risk perception, trust, and public engagement in artificial intelligence[J]. Studies in Science of Science, 2022, 40 (7): 1153-1162, 1171.

AI technologies, thereby affecting societal acceptance and trust. However, if the public perceives that these technologies are being promoted primarily for corporate gain while neglecting potential social and ethical concerns, this economic motivation may, conversely, lead to a decline in public trust.

In addition, government policies and regulations are also critical for the social acceptance of AI. Government support and oversight of generative AI technologies not only reflect the broader societal attitude toward these technologies but also provide a legal framework for their application. Proactive policy support and appropriate regulatory measures can enhance public trust in generative AI technologies and promote their healthy development.

Therefore, social acceptance is a complex phenomenon shaped by the interplay of multiple factors, which profoundly influences public trust in generative AI.[1] To enhance this trust, it is necessary to adopt a comprehensive approach that integrates technological innovation, cultural values, economic interests, and regulatory policies, as well as education and public engagement. Only so can the public's understandings and recognition of AI technologies be strengthened, and the potential social and ethical issues arising from technological advancement be effectively addressed. Such multidimensional efforts not only improve the social acceptance of generative AI but also constitute the key to establishing and maintaining public trust.

2. Legal Guarantee: The Role of Regulatory Comprehensiveness in Sustaining Trust in AI

The comprehensiveness of laws and regulations also plays a crucial role in building trust in generative AI technologies. Amid the rapid

1 CHOUNG, H., DAVID, P., ROSS, A. Trust in AI and its role in the acceptance of AI technologies[J]. International Journal of Human-Computer Interaction, 2023, 39 (9): 1727-1739.

advancement of AI, legal frameworks not only provide essential norms and guidance for technological applications, but also embody a society's ethical standards and value judgments regarding these technologies. A thorough exploration of how the comprehensiveness of legal and regulatory systems influences trust in generative AI requires consideration from multiple perspectives, including legal philosophy, technology ethics, social psychology, and related disciplines.

First, a comprehensive legal and regulatory framework provides clear guiding principles and operational guidelines for the development and application of generative AI. Within such a framework, developers and users can clearly identify which behaviors are permitted and which are prohibited, thereby enabling exploration and application within the boundaries of the law. For example, data privacy regulations ensure that AI systems adhere to minimum standards when processing personal data. The EU's GDPR, for instance, explicitly stipulates principles such as transparency in data processing, purpose limitation, and data minimization. These provisions enhance users' trust that their data will be handled by AI systems in a secure and lawful manner.

Second, comprehensive legal and regulatory frameworks can effectively mitigate the social risks potentially posed by generative AI. By establishing standards and restrictions, these frameworks can reduce the likelihood of AI technologies being misused, for example, by preventing the creation of fake news in opaque environments, indiscriminate surveillance, or their application in unjust decision-making processes. Such risk mitigation directly enhances public trust in AI. For instance, clearly defined liability attribution and incident response mechanisms of autonomous vehicles provide the public with clearer expectations regarding the safety and reliability of this technology, thereby strengthening their trust in it.

Furthermore, the comprehensiveness of laws and regulations also embodies society's ethical considerations and value orientations regarding technological advancement. When AI technologies potentially encroach upon ethically sensitive domains—such as bioethics, privacy rights, and fairness and justice—robust legal frameworks can provide moral guidance, ensuring that technological development does not deviate from fundamental human ethical principles. For example, legal regulations governing facial recognition technology, through strict limitations on usage scenarios, access rights, and intended purposes, reflect society's prioritization of individual privacy rights and enhance public trust in the reasonable application of such technology.

However, the absence or lag of legal and regulatory frameworks relative to technological advancement may result in a deterioration of trust. In the absence of clear legal and regulatory guidance, the development and deployment of AI can become unpredictable and difficult to govern, triggering public concern regarding the potential negative impacts of AI technologies. Consequently, individuals may adopt a cautious or even resistant stance toward such technologies. Unregulated AI applications may give rise to issues such as data misuse, algorithmic bias, and privacy breaches, thereby undermining public interests and diminishing overall societal trust in AI.

In addition, the comprehensiveness of laws and regulations must be accompanied by effective enforcement mechanisms. The mere existence of legal frameworks, without robust oversight and enforcement, is insufficient to establish public trust. Therefore, a sound legal and regulatory system must be complemented by effective supervisory measures to ensure that the application of AI not only adheres to legal principles, but also aligns with social ethics and public expectations.

In summary, the comprehensiveness of laws and regulations constitutes the cornerstone for building and maintaining trust in generative AI. Such legal frameworks not only provide normative guidance for the development of AI technologies but also embody societal considerations of technological ethics and value orientations. This, in turn, mitigates the risk of technological misuse and enhances public trust in these technologies. Consequently, as AI technologies continue to advance, the ongoing revision and refinement of relevant legal and regulatory systems to ensure fine alignment with technological progress is essential for establishing public trust in and fostering the healthy development of the technologies.

3. Industry Norms: Ethical Standards as the Baseline for Building Trust in AI

Industry standards and regulations play a central role in shaping public trust in generative AI. These standards and regulations not only provide explicit guidance for the development and application of AI technologies but also serve as critical mechanisms for ensuring technological quality, promoting information exchange, and safeguarding technological security.[1] By conducting an in-depth analysis of the formulation, implementation, and impact of industry standards and regulations on trust in generative AI, we can understand their complexity and significance from multiple perspectives, including technology ethics, social psychology, and economics.[2]

First, unified industry standards and norms directly enhance user trust in generative AI by ensuring the reliability and consistency of technological products and services. These standards typically encompass multiple dimensions, including data processing, algorithm design, user interaction, and security requirements, thereby guaranteeing consistency and comparability across different products and services with respect to key

---

1 ZHAO, Bo. Accelerating the construction of standards systems to promote the industrialization of artificial intelligence: interpretation of China's *Guidelines for the Construction of the National New Generation Artificial Intelligence Standards System*[J]. Information Technology and Standardization, 2020 (8): 4-6.

2 YAN, Mei, WANG, Yuntao, SUN, Mingjun. Coordinated utilization of standardization measures to promote the healthy development of the artificial intelligence industry[J]. Information and Communication Technology and Policy, 2019 (2): 74-77.

performance indicators. For instance, there are dedicated standards for NLP applications that assess and validate AI models' language comprehension, as well as the coherence and accuracy of generated text. Such standards enable users to compare different products within a transparent evaluative framework, thereby increasing their trust in the technology.

Second, the existence of industry standards and norms mitigates the issue of information asymmetry in the market. In the absence of unified standards, users often find it difficult to assess the actual performance and safety of AI products, which increases uncertainty in their decision-making processes. The establishment of standards and norms provides a common language and evaluation framework, enabling users to better understand product characteristics and performance differentials, thus facilitating more informed choices. This not only enhances technological transparency but also fosters user trust in AI technologies and the broader market.

Furthermore, industry standards and regulations embody the ethical considerations and value orientations of society regarding the development of AI technologies. By explicitly delineating the moral boundaries of technological development and application within these standards—such as ensuring algorithmic fairness, preventing data misuse, and safeguarding user privacy—societal trust in AI technologies is established and maintained. These standards and regulations serve not only as technical guidelines but also as manifestations of society's ethical expectations for technology deployment, thereby strengthening public confidence in the rational and responsible use of AI technologies.

However, the absence or lag of standards and regulations can result in a decline in public trust. In the rapid advancement of AI technologies, many emerging application domains have yet to establish unified industry standards. This uncertainty may result in users harboring doubts and mistrust toward new technologies.[1] For example, the rapid development of deepfake technology has attracted widespread social attention. However, in the absence of effective regulation and industry standards, the public inevitably becomes concerned about the potential misuse of this technology and its broader social implications, leading to a decrease in the trust.

Moreover, the formulation and implementation of industry standards and norms themselves have a significant impact on public trust. This process necessitates the broad participation of diverse stakeholders, including technology developers, government regulatory bodies, industry associations, and consumer representatives, to ensure the fairness, rationality, and forward-looking nature of the standards. A transparent and open standard-setting process can enhance public acceptance of these standards, thereby further strengthening their trust in generative AI.[2]

Therefore, industry standards and norms are crucial for building and maintaining public trust in generative AI. By ensuring technological reliability, reducing information asymmetry, reflecting social and ethical considerations, and fostering a transparent standard-setting process, these standards and norms provide a solid foundation for the healthy development of AI technologies. Moreover, as the technologies continue to advance and their application domains expand, the ongoing revision and enhancement of relevant industry standards and norms are essential pathways to safeguarding the technological trust and promoting their sustainable development.

---

1 AVIN, S., BELFIELD, H., BRUNDAGE, M., et al. Filling gaps in trustworthy development of AI[J]. Science, 2021, 374 (6573): 1327-1329.

2 CHEN, Bing. Legal considerations and practical framework for promoting the regulated development of generative artificial intelligence: a commentary on relevant provisions of China's Interim Measures for the Management of Generative Artificial Intelligence Services[J]. China Applied Jurisprudence, 2023 (4): 108-125.

Chapter Eight The Myth of Intelligence: Biases in Trusting Generative AI

Amid the contemporary wave of technological innovation, generative AI is reshaping our understanding of the world through its profound intelligence and expansive application prospects. Analyzing the integration and evolution of generative AI in modern society reveals a thought-provoking phenomenon: “trust bias.” This phenomenon reflects not only the public’s psychological response to cutting-edge technologies but also their ambivalent expectations regarding the future of AI—characterized by, on the one hand, an optimistic pursuit of its transformative potential, and on the other, concerns and apprehensions about its possible risks. As AI technologies rapidly advance, these trust biases converge into a widespread societal mindset—an “intelligent myth.” This mindset embodies both the boundless anticipation of generative AI’s capabilities and deep anxieties regarding its latent risks. Such bias highlights the psychological complexities people face when adopting and utilizing AI technologies, underscoring the centrality of trust-building in the dissemination of AI. Trust bias, defined as the psychological deviation between users’ expectations of AI performance and its actual outcomes, directly influences the societal acceptance and depth of AI application. Excessive trust bias may foster blind optimism toward AI capabilities, neglecting potential risks and ethical challenges, which could ultimately trigger a collapse in public trust. Conversely, insufficient trust bias may impede the societal adoption of technological innovations, restricting AI’s potential to address critical human challenges. Therefore, the “intelligent myth” is not only an obstacle to technology diffusion but also a key to understanding the future of human-AI symbiosis. It necessitates that, while enthusiastically embracing the transformative potential of AI, we should also deepen our insight into human psychological mechanisms and how these mechanisms are reconfigured in the context of emerging technologies. Unraveling the enigma of the “intelligent myth” requires interdisciplinary efforts spanning psychology, sociology, ethics, and technology studies to ensure the healthy development and social integration of generative AI. Moreover, enhancing societal understanding of AI technologies through education and public engagement, increasing transparency in AI decision-making processes, and developing more equitable and interpretable AI systems are essential pathways to dispel the “intelligent myth” and establish robust human-AI trust relationships. Only in this way can we ensure that, in the new era of AI, technological advancement and human well-being progress in tandem, jointly forging a smarter and more human-centric future.

Section 1 The Intelligent Mirror of Cognitive Bias: The Nature and Risks of Trust Bias in Generative AI

As a significant topic in the field of human-machine communication, trust bias in generative AI, manifested as the two extremes of both overtrust and undertrust, reveals the subjective errors users make when evaluating the capabilities of AI systems. This bias stems from cognitive misunderstandings regarding the technological capabilities of AI, and is also profoundly influenced by psychological expectations, emotional responses, and sociocultural contexts. At the theoretical level, the existence of trust bias challenges traditional models of trust construction, compelling scholars to re-examine how humans establish trust relationships with non-human agents. Practically, trust bias in generative AI may lead users to either over-rely on or disregard AI recommendations during critical decision-making processes, thereby introducing potential security risks, decision-making errors, and even negatively impacting the broader societal acceptance of AI technologies. Moreover, trust bias can exacerbate the information silos among users, impeding the integration and innovation of cross-disciplinary knowledge. Therefore, a thorough understanding of the nature and hazards of trust bias in generative AI is of significant theoretical and practical value for optimizing human-AI interaction design, enhancing the social adaptability of AI systems, and promoting the development of technology ethics.

1. Conceptual Analysis: Theoretical Examination of Trust Bias in Generative AI

Trust bias in generative AI refers to the phenomenon of either excessive or insufficient trust in machine-generated content. This bias not only reflects human psychological attitudes toward technology but also reveals deeper philosophical and cognitive issues. In examining the nature of trust bias in generative AI, we begin with the ways in which human processes knowledge and information, and conduct an in-depth analysis of the fundamental causes and potential impacts of this phenomenon.

Generative AI, such as text generation and image creation technologies, is capable of producing highly realistic and creative outputs. This capability significantly challenges traditional human conceptions of "creativity" and "intelligence."[1] People typically expect AI to provide objective, accurate, and unbiased information. However, the design, training processes, and outputs of AI systems are, in fact, profoundly influenced by human values, biases, and epistemic limitations. The discrepancy between these expectations and reality constitutes one of the fundamental sources of trust

---

1 KIDD, C., BIRHANE, A. How AI can distort human beliefs[J]. Science, 2023, 380 (6651): 1222-1223.

bias.[1]

Trust, as a complex psychological state, involves the assessment of the reliability of information sources and the prediction of future behaviors. Trust bias toward generative AI manifests in two extremes: on the one hand, individuals may excessively trust the capabilities of AI, perceiving AI-generated content as objective and infallible, thereby overlooking potential biases and limitations inherent in the technology; on the other hand, due to technological opacity and a lack of understanding, individuals may develop distrust toward AI, rejecting its outputs even when such outputs may be valuable in certain contexts.

Overtrust typically arises when users lack sufficient understanding of the technology while it demonstrates capabilities beyond their expectations. For instance, in the scenario of autonomous vehicles or AI-based medical diagnostics, individuals may develop excessive reliance on these systems after observing several accurate outcomes, thereby overlooking their limitations under specific conditions. Such trust bias can result in the neglect of potential risks, heightening the likelihood of misuse or abuse of the technology.

A lack of trust commonly arises when technical failures are made public or when individuals lack sufficient understanding of AI. For example, when a news-generating AI occasionally produces inaccurate or biased articles, such errors may be amplified, resulting in widespread public distrust of the entire technology, even though it performs well in most cases. This bias impedes the acceptance and effective utilization of the technology, thereby limiting the positive role AI can play in society.

---

1 TOREINI, E., AITKEN, M., COOPAMOOTOO, K., et al. The relationship between trust in AI and trustworthy machine learning technologies[C]. Proceedings of the 2020 Conference on Fairness, Accountability, and Transparency. 2020: 272-283.

The formation of trust bias is not only related to the AI technology itself, but is also closely associated with human cognitive structures and socio-cultural backgrounds.[1] Humans tend to employ simplified models to comprehend complex systems, a tendency that becomes particularly pronounced when encountering advanced technologies. Furthermore, the process of trust construction is influenced by prior experiences, social cues, and individual expectations, with these factors exhibiting significant variation across different cultural and societal contexts.

From a philosophical perspective, trust bias in generative AI touches upon the very nature of knowledge, the construction of truth, and the future of human-machine relations. As a tool for the generation and dissemination of knowledge, AI raises trust issues that fundamentally challenge the concepts of "knowledge" and "truth." In this sense, generative AI is not only a hallmark of technological advancement but also a catalyst for transformations in human cognition, ethics, and social structures.

The key to addressing trust bias in generative AI lies in enhancing transparency, improving public understanding, and establishing reasonable expectations.[2] This requires not only that technology developers focus on the explainability and ethical design of AI systems, but also that educational and societal mechanisms assist individuals in comprehending the operational principles, capability limitations, and potential impacts of AI. At the same time, promoting interdisciplinary research—integrating cognitive science, sociology, ethics, and technology studies—can provide deeper insights and help society better adapt to the challenges posed by this emerging technology.

---

1 Ibid.

2 RIBEIRO, M. T., SINGH, S., GUESTRIN, C. "Why should I trust you?" Explaining the predictions of any classifier[C]. Proceedings of the 22nd ACM SIGKDD International Conference on Knowledge Discovery and Data Mining. 2016: 1135-1144.

In summary, the connotation of trust bias in generative AI encompasses technological, psychological, and sociological dimensions. Its exploration not only reveals human attitudes and responses toward emerging technologies, but also offers new perspectives for understanding the evolving dynamics of human-machine relationships. Through in-depth analysis of this phenomenon, we can not only leverage AI technologies more effectively, but also foster a deeper understanding of ourselves and the world we inhabit.

2. Negative Effects: Risk Assessment of Trust Bias in Generative AI

The harms of trust bias in generative AI span multiple dimensions—social, psychological, and ethical. Such bias not only impedes the effective use and development of technology but also profoundly impacts human cognitive patterns, decision-making processes, and social structures. Addressing these risks requires a multidisciplinary approach, necessitating in-depth analysis from the perspectives of philosophy, cognitive science, and sociology.

First, trust bias in generative AI undermines the authenticity and reliability of information at the social level, which is one of its most direct and severe harms.[1] When public trust in AI-generated content becomes imbalanced, even factual and verified information may be questioned for its authenticity. For example, individuals who place excessive trust in AI may uncritically accept news reports or research data generated by AI without considering their sources, methodologies, or potential biases. This can lead to the rapid dissemination of misinformation, disruption of public discourse, and even negatively impact election outcomes and public policy

---

1 KIDD, C., BIRHANE, A. How AI can distort human beliefs[J]. Science, 2023, 380 (6651): 1222-1223.

formulation.[1] Conversely, distrust in AI may result in the rejection of accurate and valuable information it provides, thereby affecting individuals' health, safety, and well-being.

At the psychological level, trust bias influences individuals' cognitive and emotional states, potentially resulting in decision-making errors and psychological stress. Those who excessively trust AI may become overly reliant on technology, thereby reducing their opportunities for critical thinking and self-reflection, which is particularly hazardous in complex decision-making processes.[2] For example, in domains such as medical diagnosis and financial investment, overreliance on AI recommendations can result in the neglect of important human expertise and intuition, thereby increasing the risk of erroneous decisions.[3] Conversely, individuals who distrust AI may excessively emphasize human intuition and experience, refusing to adopt potentially more accurate or effective solutions provided by AI, thus missing opportunities to enhance decision quality.[4]

At the ethical level, trust bias in generative AI gives rise to a range of moral issues, such as accountability, fairness, and privacy rights. When AI is excessively trusted, individuals may neglect the oversight and evaluation of AI decision-making processes, resulting in ambiguous attribution of responsibility and difficulties in holding parties accountable when AI actions lead to negative outcomes. Furthermore, AI systems may

---

1 ZHU, Jiarui. Challenges and responses in regulating harmful and false information generated by generative artificial intelligence: a case study of ChatGPT[J]. Journal of Comparative Law Studies, 2023 (5): 34-54.
2 BANOVIC, N., YANG, Z., RAMESH, A., et al. Being trustworthy is not enough: how untrustworthy artificial intelligence (AI) can deceive the end-users and gain their trust[J]. Proceedings of the ACM on Human-Computer Interaction, 2023, 7 (CSCW1): 1-17.
3 MONTEITH, S., GLENN, T., GEDDES, J. R., et al. Artificial intelligence and increasing misinformation[J].The British Journal of Psychiatry, 2024, 224 (2): 33-35.
4 CHOUNG, H., DAVID, P., ROSS, A. Trust in AI and its role in the acceptance of AI technologies[J]. International Journal of Human-Computer Interaction, 2023, 39 (9): 1727-1739.

inadvertently exacerbate social injustice by reinforcing existing biases and inequalities. For instance, if AI systems are overly trusted in recruitment processes, their latent gender or racial biases may produce unfair hiring outcomes, thereby intensifying social divisions. At the same time, inappropriate trust may also result in the unintentional infringement of personal privacy. For example, individuals may place undue trust in smart home devices, overlooking the ways in which these devices collect and process personal information.

From a philosophical perspective, trust bias in generative AI touches upon the fundamental ways in which humans comprehend the world and construct knowledge. It challenges traditional notions of truth, knowledge, and wisdom, compelling us to reconsider the meaning and value of these concepts in the era of AI. The development of AI is not merely a matter of technological advancement but also a reflection of the progress of human civilization, demanding that we critically examine the relationships between humans and machines, as well as between the natural and the artificial.

Addressing the risks posed by trust bias in generative AI requires a multidimensional strategy, including enhancing AI transparency and explainability, improving public AI literacy, and establishing robust frameworks for technology ethics and regulatory mechanisms. This endeavor necessitates not only the efforts of technology developers and policymakers but also the broad participation of the public, scholars, and various sectors of society.

By thoroughly examining the risks associated with trust bias in generative AI, we are not only able to identify and address the challenges currently faced, but also gain valuable insights into understanding and shaping a future world of human-machine coexistence. This process involves not only technological advancements and policy formulation, but also a profound reflection on and reconstruction of human cognition, ethics, and social structures.

Section 2 Multiple Pathways of Bias Formation: The Origins of Trust Bias in Generative AI

The origins of trust bias in generative AI are multidimensional and complex, encompassing individual psychological traits, the intrinsic properties of AI systems, and the specific contexts of human-AI interaction. At the individual level, users' cognitive styles, prior knowledge and experience, as well as psychological predispositions toward technology, constitute the internal foundation of trust bias. These factors shape how users process information, assess risks, and make decisions, thereby influencing the development of trust in AI. Attributes of AI systems—such as transparency, explainability, and consistency of performance—also directly impact the formation of trust. Uncertainty and complexity within these systems often exacerbate users' cognitive load, fostering the emergence of trust bias. Finally, external factors in human-AI interaction contexts, including task characteristics, risk conditions, and time pressure, also play critical roles in the formation of trust bias. These elements shape the environment in which users engage with AI systems and influence the dynamic evolution of trust. In summary, the causes of trust bias in generative AI arise from the interplay of individual psychology, intelligent machine characteristics, and interactional context. In-depth exploration of these factors is not only essential for understanding the mechanisms underlying trust bias but also provides valuable guidance for designing more trustworthy AI systems.

1. Psychological Factors: The Impact of Individual Attributes on the Formation of Trust Bias

Individual factors—such as knowledge level, experience,

psychological traits, cognitive style, and emotional state—profoundly shape the formation of trust bias toward generative AI. Individuals with high levels of knowledge may employ rational analysis to more accurately assess AI capabilities, whereas those lacking knowledge may misunderstand AI, thereby generating trust bias. Personal experience, particularly direct interaction history with AI systems, forms the foundation of trust; those with rich experience tend to exhibit a more balanced attitude toward trust. Psychological traits, such as high openness, may predispose individuals to a more positive stance toward AI technologies, facilitating smoother trust development. Differences in cognitive style—such as intuitive versus analytical users—influence both the direction and degree of trust bias: intuitive users may overtrust AI based on instinct, while analytical users may require more substantial evidence. Emotional states, including anxiety or optimism, also significantly affect trust bias: anxiety may lead users to underestimate AI capabilities, while optimism may result in overtrust. Collectively, these individual factors constitute a complex network of influences on the formation of trust bias toward generative AI, revealing the personalized and multidimensional nature of trust building.

(1) Cognitive Landscape: The Role of Knowledge Structures in AI Trust Assessment

When examining how individuals' knowledge shapes trust biases toward generative AI, we must first acknowledge a fundamental proposition: the building of trust is both a psychological process of perception and one deeply rooted in the soil of knowledge and understanding. This intricate interplay is not only fascinating but also fraught with challenges. When individuals possess a profound understanding of AI's operational mechanisms and capabilities, their propensity to trust manifests as "knowledge-guided trust"—that is, trust becomes no longer blind, but is instead based on a clear recognition of the technology's potential and limitations.

The impact of individual knowledge levels on trust bias toward generative AI can be examined from two opposing dimensions: On the one hand, a higher level of knowledge facilitates the development of trust based on rational understanding and informed judgment. On the other hand, a lack of knowledge or misunderstanding may result in unfounded trust or distrust. This phenomenon is referred to in psychology as the "Dunning-Kruger effect," where individuals with lower competence tend to overestimate their own judgment. In the context of AI, this implies either an overestimation or underestimation of AI capabilities, thereby influencing the degree of trust users place in AI-generated outputs.

For example, individuals with in-depth knowledge of machine learning and NLP technologies are likely to adopt a more cautious attitude toward the textual outputs of generative AI. Their understanding of the underlying complexities and limitations of these technologies naturally leads them to consider potential biases, errors, or creative constraints when assessing the credibility of AI-generated content. This "knowledge-guided prudent trust" stands in stark contrast to the blind optimism exhibited by those who lack awareness of technical limitations and thus may place excessive trust in AI-generated content, failing to recognize potential errors or biases.

In addition, individual knowledge levels also affect how people process and interpret information provided by AI.[1] Individuals with higher levels of expertise are more likely to identify the "creative blind spots" of generative AI when handling specific tasks—that is, those domains where limitations in AI training data prevent adequate understanding or content generation. This capability enables individuals to more cautiously evaluate

1 ZHANG, Le, LI, Senlin. Knowledge, understanding, and trust: the mechanisms of individual trust in artificial intelligence[J]. Sociological Review, 2023, 11 (3): 59-83.

AI recommendations or outputs when relying on AI for decision-making or creative work, thereby mitigating risks associated with overreliance.

In contrast, individuals with lower levels of knowledge may lack an understanding of the operational mechanisms and inherent limitations of AI technologies, and thus tend to perceive AI as an "omniscient" entity and to exhibit unconditional trust in its outputs. Such trust bias not only increases the likelihood of accepting erroneous or biased information, but may also foster a sense of dependency, rendering these individuals helpless when confronted with situations that require independent thinking and judgment.

It is evident that the influence of individual knowledge on trust bias toward generative AI is multidimensional, encompassing both the accurate assessment of AI capabilities and the appropriate interpretation of AI outputs. Within this complex interaction shaped by knowledge and trust, education and information dissemination are particularly crucial. By enhancing public understanding of generative AI technologies, it is possible not only to foster a more rational and balanced construction of trust, but also to reduce trust biases arising from ignorance or misunderstanding. This, in turn, contributes to the development of healthier and more sustainable human-AI relationships in an increasingly AI-dependent world.

(2) Experience Accumulation: The Influence of Personal Experience on Trust in AI

When delving into how personal experience shapes trust biases toward generative AI, it is essential to adopt perspectives from cognitive psychology and social psychology in order to understand how individuals construct cognitive models of technology based on their own experiences. Personal experience, as an empirically grounded cognitive resource, provides a psychological framework for the formation of individual trust biases. This framework encompasses recollections of prior interactions, emotional responses, and interpretations of the significance of those interactions. The process involves not only the reconstruction of memory, but also the joint encoding of affective and cognitive elements of experience, thereby influencing individuals' propensity to trust generative AI.

The primary consideration is that personal experience indirectly shapes trust bias by influencing expectation management mechanisms. According to psychological contract theory, interactions between individuals and technology are regarded as a form of implicit contract, wherein personal experience functions as a basis for preset expectations. When the performance of generative AI aligns with expectations formed from prior experiences, trust is reinforced; conversely, misalignment may trigger a breakdown of trust. This mechanism goes in the way that individuals learn implicit rules about AI behavior through experiential learning and subsequently, seek the validation of these rules in future interactions.[1]

From the perspective of emotion regulation, emotional responses within personal experiences exert a particularly significant influence on trust bias. As a component of experience, emotional responses become associated with specific AI interaction scenarios through emotional memory, thereby shaping individuals' trust in similar contexts. Positive emotional experiences can enhance the resilience of trust, whereas negative emotional experiences may contribute to the fragility of trust.[2] This process involves the mechanism of emotional resonance in psychology, whereby individuals

---

1 SANDERS, T. L., MACARTHUR, K., VOLANTE, W., et al. Trust and prior experience in human-robot interaction[C]. Proceedings of the Human Factors and Ergonomics Society Annual Meeting. Los Angeles, CA: SAGE Publications, 2017, 61 (1): 1809-1813.

2 LEE, S. K., SUN, J. Testing a theoretical model of trust inhuman-machine communication: emotional experience and social presence[J]. Behaviour & Information Technology, 2023, 42 (16): 2754-2767.

assess current trust through the re-experiencing of emotions.

At the same time, cognitive heuristics play a crucial role in how personal experiences shape trust biases. Cognitive heuristics are psychological strategies individuals employ to simplify complex decision-making processes. In the context of generative AI, individuals often rely on the "similarity heuristic" or "availability heuristic," rapidly forming trust or distrust in AI based on situations analogous to past experiences or experiences that are easily recalled. Although this heuristic-based trust building process is efficient, it is highly susceptible to personal experiential biases, which can result in a misalignment between trust assessments of AI and its objective performance.

In addition, social comparison theory offers another perspective for understanding how individual experiences influence trust bias. Individuals form their trust in AI based on direct personal experiences, and also adjust their level of trust through comparison with the experiences of others.[1] Such comparisons may be grounded in information exchange within social networks or derived from indirect experiences obtained through media reports and public discourse. In this process, the phenomenon of social resonance—namely, individuals' identification with and imitation of prevalent experiences within a group—may exacerbate or mitigate trust bias.

Therefore, individual experience influences trust bias in generative AI through various psychological and social mechanisms, including expectation management, emotional responses, cognitive heuristics, and social comparison. These mechanisms jointly shape the trust, revealing that

---

1 RIBEIRO, M. T., SINGH, S., GUESTRIN, C. "Why should I trust you?" Explaining the predictions of any classifier[C]. Proceedings of the 22nd ACM SIGKDD International Conference on Knowledge Discovery and Data Mining. 2016: 1135-1144.

trust bias is not merely a reflection of technological performance, but also a product of individual psychological states and social interactions. Consequently, understanding and managing trust bias in generative AI requires an interdisciplinary perspective that integrates technological development with human psychology and social behavior.

(3) Personality Differences: Divergent AI Trust Shaped by Psychological Traits

Personality traits, as stable indicators of individual behavior and response patterns, also exert a profound influence on the formation of trust biases toward generative AI. These intrinsic personality dimensions—such as openness, conscientiousness, extraversion, agreeableness, and neuroticism—not only determine how individuals process information and make decisions, but also predict their propensity to accept and trust emerging technologies. Through the lens of personality traits, we can delve into the nuanced dynamics of trust relationships between individuals and generative AI, thereby uncovering the psychological mechanisms underlying trust biases.

Individuals with high levels of openness tend to approach novel phenomena with curiosity and receptivity, which predisposes them to hold positive trust assumptions toward generative AI. Their exploratory drive regarding AI technologies facilitates a deeper understanding of these systems, enabling more nuanced and comprehensive assessments of the reliability of AI-generated content. However, this openness-driven trust propensity may also give rise to trust bias; when individuals are overly optimistic about AI capabilities, they may overlook the inherent limitations and potential risks of the technology, resulting in overtrust.

In comparison, individuals with high neuroticism may exhibit a more cautious or even skeptical attitude toward generative AI due to their propensity to experience heightened anxiety and uncertainty. This psychological trait predisposes such individuals to amplify potential negative outcomes when encountering AI-generated outputs, resulting in a conservative bias in trust. In certain contexts, this bias can help mitigate risks associated with blind trust; however, it may also impede the acceptance and effective utilization of technological innovations.

Individuals with a high sense of responsibility, characterized by their attention to detail and willingness to be accountable for outcomes, may exhibit a balanced attitude in the process of building trust in AI. Such individuals tend to carefully evaluate both the benefits and risks of AI technologies, making trust decisions grounded in rational analysis. However, the degree of responsibility may also influence an individual's tolerance for AI failures, potentially leading to a more rapid erosion of trust when errors occur—a phenomenon that can be described as "personality-driven trust withdrawal."

Individuals characterized by extraversion and agreeableness, due to their heightened social tendencies and trust in others, may exhibit an instinctively positive attitude toward generative AI. Extraverted individuals are more inclined to interact with new technologies, while agreeable individuals, valuing cooperation and harmony, may be more willing to trust AI. However, this personality-based propensity for trust is equally susceptible to challenge; when the behavior of AI fails to meet these individuals' social and cooperative expectations, trust biases may rapidly emerge, manifesting as a "breakdown of prosocial trust."

By thoroughly examining how psychological traits influence the formation of trust bias in generative AI, we recognize that such bias is not merely a product of technological attributes and individual experience, but is also fundamentally shaped by underlying psychological structures. This insight suggests that, in the design and deployment of generative AI applications, it is essential to account for a wide range of personality differences. Personalized interaction design and information presentation can be leveraged to mitigate unnecessary trust biases, thereby fostering the healthy acceptance and effective utilization of the technology.

(4) Cognitive Patterns: The Influence of Cognitive Styles on the Construction of Trust in AI

Cognitive style, an individual's predisposition in processing information and solving problems, exerts a significant influence on trust bias toward generative AI. This psychological construct elucidates how individuals receive, process, and evaluate information through specific cognitive pathways, thereby informing their decision-making processes. In the context of generative AI, cognitive style not only determines how users interpret information provided by AI systems but also affects their evaluation of the reliability of such information. Consequently, variations in cognitive style play a critical role in the formation of trust bias, shaping the expectations and foundational trust individuals place in AI performance.

An important distinction in cognitive styles lies between analytical thinking and intuitive thinking. Analytical thinkers tend to process information through logical and systematic approaches. When constructing trust in generative AI, they are more likely to rely on in-depth analysis and verification of the technology's performance. This cognitive style leads individuals to exhibit a "cautious trust" toward generative AI, often maintaining reservations about its outputs until sufficient evidence is provided to substantiate its reliability. However, this analytical inclination may also result in trust bias; when individuals excessively focus on technical details, they may overlook the practical effectiveness of AI systems in broader application scenarios.

In contrast, intuitive thinkers tend to rely on intuition and personal experience when making judgments, a cognitive style that may foster "intuitive trust" or "intuitive distrust". When forming trust in generative AI, intuitive thinkers are more likely to depend on first impressions or information that aligns with their prior experiences, rather than engaging in in-depth analysis of the technical details of AI. This predisposition may result in trust biases, particularly when intuition does not align with the actual capabilities of AI technology. Consequently, individuals may form trust decisions too hastily, rather than basing them on a comprehensive assessment of AI performance.

Moreover, cognitive style is also associated with preferences in information processing, such as the distinction between detail-oriented and global-oriented approaches. Individuals with a detail-oriented cognitive style may focus more on specific elements within AI outputs, whereas those with a global-oriented style tend to grasp overall concepts and patterns. This divergence influences how individuals assess the reliability and trustworthiness of AI. A detail-oriented cognitive style may render individuals more sensitive to errors in AI, leading to a detail-based trust bias, which may result in an overemphasis on errors and limitations during AI evaluation. Conversely, global-oriented individuals may exhibit excessive trust in AI due to their tendency to overlook details, thereby neglecting the technology's specific limitations.

Another dimension of cognitive style is the preference for structured versus unstructured information processing. Individuals who favor structured information processing are more likely to rely on systematic evidence and logical reasoning when constructing trust, whereas those with a preference for unstructured processing may depend more on fragmented information and contextual cues. This distinction is critical in shaping trust biases toward generative AI, as it determines the methods and criteria individuals use to assess the reliability of AI outputs.

Therefore, cognitive styles profoundly influence the formation of individual trust biases toward generative AI by affecting information processing methods, decision-making tendencies, and preferences for evidence. These psychological dimensions highlight the necessity of considering the diversity of users' cognitive styles when designing and evaluating generative AI systems. By providing interactions and information presentation modes tailored to different cognitive styles, unnecessary trust biases can be mitigated, thereby fostering more effective acceptance and utilization of the technology.

(5) Emotional States: Emotional Fluctuations and Instability in AI Trust

Emotional states, as a critical component of human psychology, play a decisive role in the formation of trust biases toward generative AI. Emotions not only influence individuals' cognitive processes and decision-making behaviors, but also, through emotional regulation mechanisms, shape their perceptions and evaluations of technology. In examining the impact of emotional states on trust bias in generative AI, it is essential to conduct an in-depth analysis of how emotions function as modulators, affecting information processing, the accuracy of evaluations, and the construction of trust.

First, emotional states influence the allocation of cognitive resources and information processing capabilities. Positive emotional states, such as happiness or satisfaction, tend to enhance individuals' cognitive flexibility and creative thinking, prompting them to adopt a more open attitude toward new information. Within this emotional context, individuals may exhibit a trust bias toward generative AI, as positive affect fosters an optimistic evaluation of technological potential. However, such emotion-driven trust bias can lead to overreliance, especially when the actual performance of AI fails to meet inflated expectations. Conversely, negative emotional states, such as anxiety or sadness, may result in defensive thinking and heightened sensitivity to potential risks. Trust biases formed under these emotional conditions tend to overemphasize the uncertainties and limitations of AI technologies, thereby inhibiting the formation of trust.

Second, emotional states influence the formation of trust bias by affecting emotion regulation strategies. The regulatory approaches individuals adopt when facing emotional challenges—such as cognitive reappraisal or emotional suppression—can significantly shape their attitudes toward and levels of trust in generative AI. Individuals who utilize cognitive reappraisal may be more effective in managing negative emotions arising during interactions with AI, as positive cognitive restructuring mitigates the adverse impact of these emotions on trust evaluation. In contrast, those who rely on emotional suppression may encounter greater difficulties when processing information generated by AI, since the act of suppressing emotions consumes valuable cognitive resources and diminishes the accuracy of AI performance assessments, thereby potentially leading to trust biases that are not grounded in actual system performance.

Furthermore, emotional states are closely linked to individuals' risk perception and tolerance. Positive emotions are typically associated with a higher risk tolerance, making individuals more likely to accept and engage with the inherent uncertainties of generative AI. This increased tolerance may facilitate the development of trust in AI systems; however, it can also result in the neglect of genuine risks associated with AI applications, giving rise to an optimism bias. In contrast, negative emotional states may heighten individuals' risk aversion, leading to overly pessimistic assessments of AI performance, even when such pessimism is not substantiated by the actual capabilities of generative AI.

Finally, emotional states can also influence the formation of trust biases through mechanisms of social contagion. An individual's emotional state is shaped not only by personal experiences but also by the emotions of those around them. In social networks or work teams, the dissemination of positive or negative emotions can significantly affect team members' trust in generative AI. For example, a generally optimistic emotional climate within a team may lead to excessive trust in AI, whereas prevalent pessimism may result in widespread distrust. This collective emotional resonance at the group level further exacerbates the individuals' trust biases.

The above analysis demonstrates that emotional states influence trust biases toward generative AI through multiple channels, including the impact of emotions on cognitive processes, the selection of emotion regulation strategies, changes in risk perception and tolerance, as well as the contagion effect of social emotions. These mechanisms interact to form a complex emotion–cognition–trust interplay model, revealing how emotional states profoundly shape the formation of trust biases in generative AI. Therefore, understanding and managing these influences is crucial for fostering healthy human-AI interactions and establishing trust based on accurate assessments.

2. Technological Factors: The Characteristics of Intelligent Systems and Their Impact on the Formation of Trust Bias

Trust bias in generative AI is also profoundly influenced by the intrinsic characteristics of intelligent machines. Output consistency and predictability are directly linked to users' perceptions of system reliability; highly consistent and predictable outputs facilitate the establishment of trust, whereas inconsistency or unpredictability engenders doubt. The effective implementation of error transparency and feedback mechanisms enables users to receive immediate explanations and guidance when encountering problems, thereby enhancing their understanding of and trust in AI. System explainability and logical transparency reduce cognitive load and bolster user confidence in AI decision-making processes. The intuitiveness and interactivity of user interfaces reinforce usability and user experience, directly shaping the formation of trust. The degree of personalization and adaptability reflects AI systems' responsiveness to user needs; those systems that are highly personalized and adaptive are more likely to earn user trust. Rigorous enforcement of security and privacy protection measures forms the cornerstone of trust-building; the absence of such measures may result in users' reservations toward AI systems. Collectively, these factors shape the trust bias in generative AI, delineating key pathways to mitigate bias and promote healthy human-machine interaction.

(1) Stability and Predictability: The Consistency and Predictability of Outputs as Foundational Elements of Trust

Before delving into how the output consistency and predictability of generative AI influence the formation of trust bias, it is essential to clarify first of all that trust bias, as users' deviations in evaluating AI performance—whether manifesting as overtrust or undertrust, does not accurately reflect the actual capabilities of AI systems. Output consistency and predictability, as critical indicators of AI performance, directly shape users' expectation management and trust calibration processes.

Output consistency refers to the ability of AI systems to generate stable and uniform results when performing similar tasks. High output consistency not only demonstrates the reliability of the systems but also provides users with a sense of predictability, which is crucial in the process of trust formation. When an AI system exhibits a high degree of output consistency, users may develop a positive trust bias, tending to over-rely on its judgments and recommendations because they expect it to continuously deliver accurate and dependable information. However, this bias can become problematic when the AI system encounters novel scenarios or edge cases, where its performance may not meet user expectations for accuracy or reliability, potentially resulting in a breakdown of trust.[1]

Predictability pertains to the accuracy with which users can anticipate the behavior and outputs of AI systems. A highly predictable AI system enables users to accurately foresee its actions given specific inputs, a capability that is essential for building trust. When users are able to reliably predict AI behavior, they are more likely to develop trust grounded in understanding and reasonable expectations. However, discrepancies between the actual performance of AI systems and user expectations—even minor deviations—can lead to trust bias. For instance, if an AI system that typically demonstrates high predictability produces an unexpected output during a particular operation, and even if the anomalous output is itself reasonable, users may begin to question the overall reliability of the system, simply because their prediction failed on that occasion.

The emergence of such trust bias, particularly in contexts where critical decisions are AI-dependent, may result in significant consequences. Users may, due to excessive trust in AI, disregard their own judgment or other vital sources of information. Conversely, upon encountering predictive failures by AI—even when such failures are statistically acceptable—they may irrationally reduce their level of trust in AI.

To gain a deeper understanding of how output consistency and predictability influence the formation of trust bias, we can consider several practical application scenarios. In the context of AI for medical diagnosis, highly consistent and predictable outputs are crucial for earning the trust of both physicians and patients. An AI system that consistently delivers accurate diagnostic recommendations may become excessively trusted,

---

1 DHULIAWALA, S., ZOUHAR, V., EL-ASSADY, M., et al. A diachronic perspective on user trust in AI under uncertainty[J]. arXiv Preprint arXiv: 2310.13544, 2023.

potentially leading physicians to neglect necessary manual verification of AI-generated diagnoses. Conversely, if the system exhibits inconsistency in certain situations—even when such inconsistencies arise from legitimate medical uncertainties—this may significantly undermine physicians' trust in the entire system.

In the application of AI in financial services, the ability to predict market trends is a critical factor influencing users' evaluation and trust in AI systems. Highly predictive systems may induce users to over-rely on AI recommendations without fully understanding the complexities of the market or the underlying risks, thereby fostering trust bias. Conversely, when predictive failures occur—even in the event of sudden market volatility—users' trust in the AI systems may rapidly dissipate, resulting in their reluctance to rely on AI for future investment decisions.

It can thus be concluded that the consistency and predictability of generative AI outputs are critical intelligent machine factors influencing the formation of trust bias. These factors directly affect users' trust in AI systems by shaping their expectation management and trust calibration processes. Understanding how these factors contribute to the development of trust bias is essential for designing AI systems that are more reliable and more likely to be accurately understood and trusted by users.

(2) Accountability Mechanisms and Feedback Loops: The Trust Effects of Error Transparency and Response Effectiveness

In today's era of rapid technological advancement, the error transparency and feedback mechanisms of generative AI systems have become pivotal factors shaping user trust biases. Exploration in this domain concerns not only the practical utility of technology, but also the philosophical interpretation of human-machine interaction, which is conducive to unveiling the complex and dynamic relationship between technological transparency and human trust. As core components in the design of intelligent systems, error transparency and feedback mechanisms directly influence users' perceptions of AI system reliability, thereby engendering specific biases in the trust formation.

First, error transparency refers to the extent to which AI systems can disclose error information and its underlying causes to users when encountering mistakes during task execution. A highly transparent system not only identifies errors but also explains the reasons behind them and may even offer potential solutions. As such, error transparency acts as a double-edged sword: while it has the potential to enhance user trust, it may also contribute to the emergence of trust biases.[1]

On the one hand, when AI systems exhibit high error transparency, users may develop a trust attitude grounded in understanding and acceptance. This attitude stems from users' awareness of system limitations and their perception of developer integrity, enabling them to maintain a reasonable level of trust even in the face of errors and thus avoid a breakdown of trust. However, on the other hand, excessive error transparency may sometimes lead users to overly doubt the systems' capabilities, especially when they lack sufficient expertise to accurately interpret the error information. In such cases, even if AI systems' performance meets objective standards, users' trust bias may still shift toward distrust.

Furthermore, the feedback mechanism, namely, how AI systems respond to user input, including error correction and guidance for user actions, plays a decisive role in the formation of trust bias. An effective feedback mechanism can provide users with immediate and useful

1 PETKOVIC, D. It is not "Accuracy vs Explainability"—we need both for trustworthy AI systems[J]. IEEE Transactions on Technology and Society, 2023, 4 (1): 46-53.

information, assisting them in comprehending the behavior of AI systems and thereby enhancing their sense of trust. Particularly when errors occur, timely and appropriate feedback not only mitigates users' frustration but also increases their confidence in the systems' ability to handle complex situations.

For example, when a generative AI system is used for text generation, if it is able to explicitly identify errors in the outputs and provide suggestions for correction when inappropriate or inaccurate content is generated, users may be inclined to maintain or even increase their trust in the system due to its apparent "self-awareness" and capacity for improvement. However, if the feedback mechanism is limited to merely pointing out errors without offering remediation strategies or explanations, users may develop a bias perceiving the AI system as unreliable or insufficiently competent to handle complex tasks.

In this discussion, it is also necessary to recognize that the impact of error transparency and feedback mechanisms on trust bias is not static, but is influenced by a range of factors such as user expectations, task type, and usage context.[1] For certain users or specific tasks, a high degree of error transparency and effective feedback mechanisms may be crucial for building trust; whereas in other contexts, a more cautious balance between transparency and feedback provision may be required to avoid excessive trust bias.

Therefore, the error transparency and feedback mechanisms of generative AI systems play a complex and nuanced role in shaping users' trust biases. Through the ingenious design of these system attributes, developers can not only promote users' accurate understanding of and

---

1 SCHMIDT, P., BIESSMANN, F., TEUBNER, T. Transparency and trust in artificial intelligence systems[J]. Journal of Decision Systems, 2020, 29 (4): 260-278.

reasonable trust in AI, but also provide support and guidance when users encounter inevitable errors or challenges. In this way, the long-term maintenance and enhancement of the trust relationship between humans and machines can be achieved.

(3) Technological Black Box and Logical Transparency: Dual Considerations of System Explainability and Operational Visualization

In the contemporary technological landscape, the explainability and logical transparency of generative AI systems have emerged as critical determinants of their acceptance and trustworthiness. These attributes are directly linked to users' ability to comprehend the decision-making processes of AI systems, as well as the extent to which they trust the validity and fairness of such decisions. Specifically, system explainability and logical transparency play a dual role in the formation of trust biases, both alleviating overreliance and preventing unwarranted distrust.

System explainability, defined as the capability of AI systems to provide clear explanations of their operations, decision logic, and outcomes in a manner comprehensible to users, constitutes the cornerstone of user trust. Logical transparency further demands that AI systems are not only superficially explainable, but also allow users to discern their internal logic and the rationale behind their decisions. The integration of such transparency and explainability offers users a window into understanding the "thinking" processes of AI, thereby psychologically constructing a bridge that connects human comprehension with machine logic.

When delving into how system explainability and logical transparency influence the formation of trust bias in generative AI, we first recognize that the essence of trust bias lies in users' misunderstanding or misjudgment of AI system performance. When the decision-making process of AI systems operates as a "black box" to users, the lack of understanding may lead to inappropriate levels of trust—whether this manifests as overtrust or undertrust.

For example, if a generative AI system exhibits high logical transparency and is able to clearly demonstrate to users the decision-making pathways it employs to generate outputs from specific inputs, users are more likely to develop understanding-based trust. Such trust is considered more stable and reliable, as it is grounded in an authentic assessment of the system's capabilities rather than blind reliance. However, even in this context, excessive transparency may expose the system's inherent limitations or deficiencies, potentially leading users to underestimate its capabilities and resulting in trust bias.

Conversely, when a system exhibits low explainability, users may be reluctant to trust it despite its strong technical performance, due to a lack of understanding of its operational logic. Alternatively, the opacity of its "black box" mechanisms may engender irrational overtrust. In such cases, trust bias arises from information asymmetry and a deficit in comprehension; users may adopt a cautious stance because they are unable to anticipate the system's behavior in novel contexts.

Furthermore, system explainability and logical transparency also influence users' perceptions of fairness and bias in AI systems. Against the backdrop of growing attention to AI ethics and fairness, AI systems that can demonstrate unbiased decision-making processes and equitable treatment of all cases are more likely to earn users' trust. However, transparency that reveals inherent biases or unfairness in AI systems' handling of certain tasks—even if such issues are introduced unintentionally—can result in significant trust bias among users, thereby affecting their overall evaluation and acceptance of the systems.

The above analysis demonstrates that explainability and logical transparency of generative AI systems play a complex and pivotal role in shaping user trust biases. By enhancing these attributes, AI developers can not only facilitate users' understanding of the technology but also guide them toward forming reasonable trust based on AI systems' actual performance and capabilities, thereby fostering healthier and more sustainable human-machine relationships in the long term. However, this process requires careful balancing to ensure that transparency and explainability can both enhance user comprehension and prevent inadvertently triggering unnecessary trust biases.

(4) Interface Friendliness and Interaction Experience: The Potential Role of Human-AI Interaction Design in Trust Building

The intuitiveness and interactivity of user interfaces (UIs) in generative AI systems are also critical factors shaping user experience and trust. These UI characteristics not only influence users' acceptance of the technology but also profoundly affect the development of trust bias. Trust bias, defined as the deviation in users' assessment of AI system performance, may result in either overtrust or undertrust. The formation of such bias is largely contingent upon the intuitiveness and interactivity of UIs.

The intuitiveness of UIs refers to the degree to which the design of these UIs naturally aligns with users' expectations and habitual patterns of interaction, thereby enabling users to easily comprehend how to engage with AI systems. An intuitive interface reduces users' cognitive load during operation, thereby enhancing their confidence and trust in the systems. However, if this intuitiveness excessively simplifies the underlying complexity of the systems, it may result in users misunderstanding the capabilities of AI, leading to an overtrust bias. Users might erroneously assume that AI systems are capable of handling tasks more complex than they actually can, or, when errors occur, may overlook the systems' limitations due to the interfaces' apparent simplicity and intuitiveness.

Interactivity refers to the efficiency and effectiveness of communication between users and AI systems, encompassing the responsiveness to user input, the clarity of system feedback, and the smoothness of the interaction process. Highly interactive systems are capable of providing immediate feedback, enabling users to perceive them as responsive and "attentive," which can enhance user trust in them. However, if interactive design fails to appropriately guide users in understanding the systems' underlying mechanisms and decision-making processes, it may also lead to trust bias. For instance, if a system's responses to user queries are excessively rapid or overly simplified, users may mistakenly assume that the system's decision-making process is straightforward and uncomplicated, resulting in inappropriate overreliance on AI and neglecting the necessity of human judgment in certain contexts.

Furthermore, intuitiveness and interactivity play a crucial role in facilitating users' exploration and learning processes with AI systems. A well-designed interface should encourage users to explore the functionalities of an AI system while providing appropriate guidance and feedback to help them develop an accurate understanding of the system's capabilities and limitations. This incremental learning process helps mitigate trust bias, as users' trust is grounded in a nuanced comprehension of the system's actual performance. Conversely, an interface lacking effective guidance and feedback may lead users to form erroneous assumptions during use, thereby resulting in trust bias.

For example, in the application of generative AI in content creation, such as the automatic drafting of press releases, an intuitive and highly interactive interface can assist users in quickly understanding how to guide the AI system to generate content that meets their specific requirements, while appropriate feedback mechanisms reveal how the system interprets user instructions and the logic behind its content generation. Through such interactions, users are able to gradually learn about and adapt to the capabilities and limitations of AI systems, thereby establishing trust based on comprehension and empirical performance evaluation, and reducing unfounded trust biases.

The above analysis indicates that the intuitiveness and interactivity of generative AI system UIs are critical intelligent machine factors influencing the formation of trust bias. By designing interfaces that are both intuitive and highly interactive, developers can not only enhance user satisfaction but also guide users toward more accurate and rational trust judgments. This, in turn, fosters healthier and more sustainable trust relationships in human-machine interactions. However, this requires developers to carefully balance intuitiveness and interactivity in interface design, ensuring that users benefit from efficient and convenient interactions while also correctly understanding and evaluating the capabilities and limitations of AI systems.

(5) Humanization and Adaptability: The Influence of Personalization and Intelligent Flexibility on Trust Perception

Amid the current wave of technological advancement, the degree of personalization and adaptability exhibited by generative AI has become a critical benchmark for assessing its sophistication and user-friendliness. These attributes not only reflect the maturity of AI technologies but also directly influence the formation of users' trust or trust bias in AI systems. Trust bias, a subjective deviation in users' evaluation of AI performance, may arise from either overestimating or underestimating AI's capacity for personalization and adaptability. A thorough exploration of how these factors shape trust bias reveals the complex psychological dynamics inherent in human-machine interaction.

The degree of personalization refers to the extent to which AI systems can tailor their services based on the specific needs, preferences, and behavioral history of users. Highly personalized AI systems are capable of delivering content and solutions that closely align with user requirements, thereby enhancing user satisfaction and fostering a sense of trust. However, when users hold excessively high expectations regarding the personalization capabilities of AI systems, even minor mismatches or misunderstandings can result in significant trust biases. Users may question the overall effectiveness of the systems due to isolated experiences that do not meet their expectations, leading to an overly pessimistic trust bias rooted in individual incidents.

Adaptability refers to the capability of AI systems to flexibly adjust their behavior in response to changes in user behavior or varying contexts. Highly adaptive systems are able to optimize their responses based on users' interaction histories and evolving environments, thereby delivering services that are more closely aligned with their current needs. Theoretically, enhanced adaptability should serve as a catalyst for increased trust, as it demonstrates AI systems' intelligence and flexibility. However, in practical applications, if an AI system's adaptive adjustments exceed the users' scope of understanding or expectations, it may precipitate them into confusion and uncertainty, resulting in their trust bias. For instance, if a system over-adapts to a single anomalous user behavior and thereby neglects the users' long-term preferences, they may feel that the system has "misunderstood" their genuine needs, ultimately diminishing their trust in it.

The formation of trust bias reflects both users' psychological expectations regarding the personalization and adaptability of AI systems and the systems' actual capabilities to meet these expectations. In this process, clear and transparent communication becomes essential. AI systems should employ explicit interface prompts and feedback mechanisms to elucidate the logic behind their personalization and adaptive adjustments. Such communication facilitates the calibration of user expectations and mitigates trust bias arising from misunderstandings or mismatches.

For example, if the generative AI systems in online learning platforms, where they provide personalized learning resources based on students' progress and preferences, can transparently demonstrate to the students how learning resource recommendations are generated from their interaction histories, the students are more likely to comprehend and trust the process, thereby mitigating trust biases arising from mismatched expectations. Conversely, if the personalization appears random or unpredictable, the students are likely to question the systems' effectiveness.

Therefore, the degree of personalization and adaptability of generative AI plays a complex role in shaping users' trust biases. By enhancing the transparency of personalized service quality and adaptive responses, it is possible to effectively reduce unnecessary trust biases and establish a healthier and more sustainable human-machine interaction. However, this also requires developers to gain a deep understanding of users' psychological expectations and behavioral patterns when designing AI systems, as well as to determine how to meet these expectations through technical and communication strategies. In doing so, developers can enhance both the experience and the trust of the users.

(6) Security Assurance and Privacy Governance: System Security and Privacy Protection as Foundations for Trust.

In examining the security and privacy protection measures of generative AI, as well as their impact on the formation of trust bias, it is essential to develop a nuanced understanding of the nature of trust bias and its relationship with users' perceptions of AI system security and privacy safeguards. Security and privacy protection measures play a pivotal role in shaping trust bias in generative AI; these are not merely technical attributes, but also fundamentally influence users' psychological expectations and the construction of trust in technology.

Security here refers to AI systems' capability to defend against external threats, ensuring data integrity and service reliability. Privacy protection measures pertain to how AI systems handle user data, safeguarding personal information from unauthorized access or misuse. Together, these two dimensions are two of the foundations upon which users assess the trustworthiness of AI systems, directly influencing the development of trust biases.

First, the perception of security is foundational to users' trust in AI systems. When users believe that an AI system can withstand external attacks and protect itself from compromise, they are more likely to exhibit trust in the system. However, when security vulnerabilities are exposed, or when users become aware of potential security risks through media reports, industry analyses, or similar channels, trust biases may emerge due to concerns about potential threats—even if these risks have not directly affected the users themselves. In such scenarios, users may develop a precautionary distrust bias based on the precautionary principle, even though the actual security performance of AI systems may far exceed their negative expectations.

Furthermore, the transparency and effectiveness of privacy protection measures constitute another critical factor in shaping trust bias. The extent to which users understand how their data is collected, utilized, and safeguarded directly influences their level of trust in AI systems. When users perceive that an AI system implements stringent privacy safeguards, they are more likely to exhibit a higher degree of trust in the system, resulting in a positive trust bias. Conversely, if users believe that the system lacks the necessary transparency or fails to adopt adequate protective measures in handling personal data—even if such perceptions are based on misconceptions—this alone is sufficient to significantly erode trust and induce a negative trust bias.

For example, if a generative AI system such as a personalized news recommendation engine, which requires the collection of users' reading preferences and historical data to optimize content recommendations, can explicitly present its privacy protection policy to them, explain the purposes of data collection and usage, and provide them with options to control their own data, the users are likely to develop a more positive and trusting attitude toward the system due to their perception of strong privacy safeguards. Conversely, if the system's policies in these aspects are ambiguous or if the users perceive a risk of data misuse—even when the actual risk is minimal—this may lead to a sharp decline in their trust in the system.

It can thus be concluded that the security and privacy protection measures of generative AI systems play a critical role in shaping trust bias. By enhancing the systems' security features and privacy safeguards, and by employing transparent communication strategies to foster user understanding and confidence, developers can effectively manage and calibrate users' trust biases, thereby promoting a healthy and enduring human-AI trust relationship. This necessitates that developers not only focus on the technical aspects of security and privacy, but also gain a deep understanding of users' psychological expectations and the process of trust formation. Through the combined application of technical solutions and communication strategies, unnecessary trust biases can be minimized, thus facilitating the establishment of a more trustworthy and user-friendly AI ecosystem.

3. Contextual Factors: The Moderating Effect of Application Scenarios on Trust Bias

Task characteristics, time pressure, and risk conditions in human-AI interactions significantly influence trust bias toward generative AI. The complexity and criticality of tasks demand high levels of accuracy and reliability; as the importance of a task increases, users' trust in AI becomes more fragile, with minor errors or outputs that deviate from expectations readily triggering trust bias. Under time pressure, users must rapidly rely on AI for decision-making, and this sense of urgency is highly likely to amplify trust bias, prompting users to overlook careful evaluation of AI's decision-making processes and leading to either overtrust or distrust. In risk-laden conditions, the performance of AI systems carries substantial consequences for users, whose heightened sensitivity to potential failures makes their trust in AI more susceptible to erosion. These situational factors collectively construct the backdrop for user interaction with generative AI, profoundly shaping the form and degree of trust bias, and highlighting the necessity of optimizing human-AI interaction, enhancing AI system adaptability, and improving user experience.

(1) Task Complexity and Criticality: The Dynamic Evolution of Trust Bias in Different Task Scenarios

When examining task characteristics in human-AI interaction and their influence on the formation of trust biases toward generative AI, it is essential to first clarify that task characteristics encompass dimensions such as complexity, criticality, novelty, and the significance of the task for the individual user or society at large. These task attributes not only shape users' expectations regarding AI performance during interactions but also profoundly affect the psychological processes underlying their evaluation of AI capabilities, thereby generating specific biases in the construction of trust.

Task complexity refers to the number of steps required to complete a task and the inherent difficulty of the task itself. In tasks with high complexity, users may hold elevated expectations regarding the capabilities of AI, anticipating that AI systems can manage intricate data and make sophisticated decisions. When AI systems demonstrate high processing efficiency, users may develop an overtrust bias, neglecting the necessity of human oversight. Conversely, if AI systems make errors or underperform in handling these complex tasks—even when such outcomes are technically foreseeable—users' trust may decline rapidly, resulting in an undertrust bias.

Task criticality pertains to the significance of a task for users or the broader society. When performing high-criticality tasks, such as medical diagnosis or security monitoring, user trust in AI is influenced not only by the AI systems' technical performance but also by the severity of potential consequences. In such contexts, even if the AI systems demonstrate high accuracy in the majority of cases, a single failure or error can result in a substantial trust deficit, prompting the users to question the overall reliability of the systems.

Task novelty refers to the degree of alignment between a given task and the user's prior experience. When confronted with novel tasks, users may lack direct experience to evaluate AI performance, leading them to rely more heavily on information provided by the systems or external cues to establish trust. In such high-uncertainty contexts, trust biases are likely to be exacerbated by inadequate expectation management, particularly when AI systems employ new technologies or methodologies unfamiliar to users.

Moreover, the personal or societal significance of a task is a critical factor influencing the formation of trust bias. For tasks that impact individual quality of life or have broad social implications, users are likely to adopt a more cautious attitude toward trusting AI systems. In such contexts, even minor errors or performance deficiencies may be magnified, resulting in a sharp decline in trust. Conversely, if AI systems perform exceptionally well in these high-stakes tasks, users may develop an overtrust bias, neglecting the necessity for ongoing monitoring and evaluation of AI-driven decisions.

For example, in the application of AI in the field of personalized education, a domain marked by both high complexity and personal significance, AI systems that can provide customized learning plans tailored to students' learning habits and preferences are likely to be perceived as highly effective; such positive performance can, in turn, foster the building of trust. However, excessive reliance on AI-driven personalized recommendations may result in the homogenization of educational experiences, overlooking the importance of diverse learning pathways. This can give rise to a trust bias—an overreliance on AI's capabilities to fulfill all educational needs.

The above analysis demonstrates that task characteristics in human-AI interactions play a decisive role in shaping trust biases toward generative AI. By thoroughly understanding how factors such as task complexity, criticality, novelty, and individual or societal significance influence users' psychological expectations and trust formation, designers and developers of AI systems can implement strategies to optimize user interfaces, deliver timely feedback, and provide appropriate guidance. Such measures enable effective management of user trust biases and promote healthy and sustainable human-AI collaboration.

(2) Sense of Urgency and Decision-Making Pressure: Rapid Shifts in Trust Bias under Time Constraints

When investigating how time pressure influences the formation of trust bias toward generative AI, it is essential to thoroughly understand the psychological mechanisms by which time pressure, a complex psychological phenomenon, affects users' evaluation of AI system performance within specific interaction environments. Time pressure not only intensifies users' cognitive load but may also distort their perception of AI systems' decision-making processes and outcomes, thereby triggering their trust bias.

Time pressure is essentially the perceived scarcity of temporal resources, which intensifies users' demands for efficiency and responsiveness. In high time-pressure scenarios, users may place heightened expectations on AI systems' ability to deliver rapid solutions. Such expectations can result in two extreme trust biases: overtrust and undertrust.

Under time pressure, users may tend to excessively rely on AI's judgments and recommendations, as they perceive AI systems as capable of providing fast and accurate solutions. This reliance is referred to in psychology as "convenience trust," wherein users, constrained by time, overlook the necessary critical evaluation of AI-generated judgments. For example, emergency physicians, facing urgent situations, might overly depend on AI-generated diagnostic suggestions rather than investing time in comprehensive pathological analysis. Although this bias of overtrust can enhance decision-making efficiency in the short term, it also elevates the risk associated with relying on imperfect AI systems, potentially resulting in serious consequences such as misdiagnosis or missed diagnoses.

In contrast, time pressure may also lead to insufficient user trust in AI systems. In certain scenarios, users may choose to distrust or disregard AI recommendations out of concern that the systems cannot deliver high-quality outputs within a limited timeframe. This trust bias is particularly pronounced when users lack adequate understanding of AI systems' performance and efficiency. For instance, in emergency situations, a user might ignore the suggestions of a navigation AI due to skepticism about its ability to process real-time data, fearing that it may not have accounted for the latest traffic conditions.

Increased time pressure elevates users' cognitive load, constraining their capacity to process information and evaluate AI-generated recommendations. Within such contexts of limited cognitive resources, they are more likely to rely on heuristics or simplified decision rules to establish trust in AI, rather than engaging in thorough analytical assessment. This heuristic decision-making process is susceptible to pre-existing biases and prior experiences, which can result in the formation of trust bias.

To manage trust bias under time pressure, designers of AI systems need to consider how to enhance system transparency and user engagement while ensuring rapid responses. For example, by providing real-time feedback on the AI decision-making process and helping users understand the basis of AI recommendations, users' confidence in AI decisions can be strengthened, enabling trust grounded in understanding even under time constraints. Furthermore, educating users about the capabilities and limitations of AI systems, as well as how to effectively utilize AI under varying levels of time pressure, is also a key strategy in reducing unreasonable trust bias.

Therefore, time pressure—a critical factor in human-AI interaction—affects users' psychological states and decision-making processes, thereby shaping the formation of trust bias toward generative AI. A thorough understanding of this process is essential for designing more reliable and user-friendly AI systems. Such understanding aims to balance efficiency and accuracy, optimize user experience, and concurrently manage and calibrate users' trust biases, ultimately fostering healthy human-AI collaborative relationships.

(3) Risk Assessment and Loss Control: Distinct Manifestations of Trust Bias under High-Risk Conditions

When delving into how risk conditions in human-AI interaction influence the formation of trust bias toward generative AI, it is essential to recognize that risk conditions themselves constitute a complex situational backdrop, exerting psychological impacts on users that far exceed mere cognitive evaluation. Trust bias under risk conditions is not only a deviation in users' perceptions of AI system performance and reliability but also a comprehensive reflection of risk perception, coping mechanisms, and psychological adaptability within specific contexts. The emergence of such bias is closely related to how users perceive risk, assess AI systems' capability to manage risk, and their individual levels of risk tolerance.

The formation of trust bias under risk conditions is primarily related to users' subjective perceptions of risk. In high-risk human-AI interaction scenarios, users are often particularly sensitive to potential negative outcomes. This heightened sensitivity may prompt them to apply more stringent evaluations of AI systems' performance and reliability. When AI systems demonstrate superior performance in such high-risk contexts, users may develop a form of trust grounded in the demonstrated capability. However, this trust is often fragile; even minimal uncertainty or failure on the part of AI systems can lead to a rapid collapse of user trust, resulting in a pronounced undertrust.

Furthermore, trust bias under risk conditions is also related to users' evaluation of AI systems' risk management capabilities. How users assess

AI systems' response strategies, decision-making processes, and final outputs in specific risk scenarios directly influences the construction of their trust. In this process, if AI systems can provide transparent decision logic, clearly defined risk management measures, and timely feedback mechanisms, users are likely to form positive evaluations of the systems' ability to manage risk, thereby reducing unnecessary trust bias. Conversely, if AI systems' performance in risk scenarios appears ambiguous or sluggish—even when such behavior is the result of rational decisions based on complex algorithms—users may develop excessive trust bias due to a lack of understanding.

In addition, individual risk tolerance also plays a decisive role in the formation of trust biases under risk conditions. The level of a user's risk tolerance determines their psychological responses and behavioral choices when confronted with potential risks. Users with high risk tolerance are more likely to accept the application of AI systems in high-risk scenarios; even if these applications are not flawless, they may tend to trust the decisions made by AI systems, thereby developing a trust bias based on optimistic expectations toward technological advancement. Conversely, users with low risk tolerance may remain cautious even when AI systems demonstrate high performance, harboring concerns about possible failures in future risk scenarios, which leads to a preventive distrust bias.

In exploring the formation of trust bias under risk conditions, we found that effective management of users' trust bias in such contexts requires AI systems to possess not only high levels of technical performance and reliability, but also to incorporate considerations of transparency, user education, and psychological support in their design. These measures can assist users in more accurately assessing the performance of AI systems in risk scenarios, thereby fostering a more balanced and stable trust relationship and reducing unwarranted trust bias. The establishment of such trust relationships under risk conditions is particularly crucial, as it directly affects the acceptance, usage efficiency, and ultimate societal impact of AI systems.

Chapter Nine Collaborative Correction: Calibrating Trust Bias in Generative AI

The rapid advancement of generative AI technology has profoundly disrupted the cognitive landscape, information ecology, and trust relationships within human society. Leveraging vast datasets for learning, AI systems have reached unprecedented levels in both the richness and deceptiveness of content generation. However, user perceptions of such systems are sharply polarized, oscillating between blind acquiescence and deep suspicion, resulting in frequent erosion of trust foundations. This chapter, grounded in the interactive context of human-machine collaboration, centers on three dimensions: individual cognition, algorithmic models, and interaction scenarios. The aim is to elucidate the origins of trust bias in the age of AI and to outline pathways for recalibration. Specifically, the approach involves enhancing users' rational understanding of generative AI, fostering critical thinking, and explicating the operational mechanisms of AI; upgrading and optimizing algorithms to mitigate model biases and dynamically assess content credibility; and reconstructing the human-machine interaction ecosystem by clarifying task-aligned expectations and establishing diverse verification and feedback mechanisms. These measures are intended to lay a foundation of trust essential for the sustainable development of AI. The exploratory efforts of this study may also offer valuable insights for achieving reconciliation, symbiotic coexistence, and co-evolution between human society and AI.

Section 1 Focusing on Individuals: Optimizing the Trust Foundation in User-AI Interaction

Before discussing the various measures to strengthen users' rational understanding of generative AI, it is necessary to briefly review the current macro-context of AI development and application. The evolution of AI technologies, from early expert systems to the current deep learning paradigm, has witnessed the increasingly frequent and profound interactions between AI and human society. With the continuous upgrading and iteration of algorithmic models, AI systems have achieved unprecedented capabilities in perception, cognition, and decision-making. Notably, since the emergence of generative AI such as GPT-3 and DALL·E, the richness and realism of machine-generated content have become truly remarkable. However, as AI technologies accelerate their integration into social life, issues of human-machine trust have become increasingly prominent. Numerous studies indicate that users' perceptions of AI system capabilities tend to be polarized: some users blindly overestimate the intelligence of AI, while others question its reliability and safety. This cognitive imbalance reflects users' confusion and concerns regarding the prospects of AI development, and demands immediate responses from multiple dimensions such as cognition, critical thinking, and explanation.

1. Strengthening Cognition: Enhancing Users' Rational Understanding of Generative AI

The primary task in optimizing the trust foundation for user interaction with generative AI is to strengthen users' rational cognition. At present, generative AI technology is advancing so rapidly that it often leaves users astounded, which can easily foster a mentality of blind obedience. It is undeniable that generative AI demonstrates remarkable capabilities in fields such as creative generation and knowledge-based Q&A. However, its internal operational mechanisms remain a black box. Due to cognitive deficiencies, some users tend to deify AI, overlooking its limitations and placing unwarranted trust in its outputs. For instance, in the use of GPT-3, although its conversational interaction and knowledge generation abilities are impressive, issues such as bias, errors, and information distortion frequently occur.

The cultivation of rational cognition must be predicated on users' comprehensive understanding of generative AI. Communication agencies and technology providers should proactively disclose critical information such as the technical principles of AI systems, sources of training data, and the boundaries of applicable scenarios, thereby eliminating users' cognitive blind spots. At the same time, the development of AI technology should not be mystified; excessive hype and sensationalism only serve to obscure facts and exacerbate trust-related risks. Only through accessible explanations of the technology—objectively revealing both the potential and limitations of generative AI—can users be guided to form reasonable expectations.

The reinforcement of rational cognition also requires stimulating users' critical thinking. When confronted with the diverse array of AI-generated content, users must not accept information uncritically; instead, they should remain vigilant and exercise prudent judgment regarding the authenticity and reliability of information[1]. Users need to recognize an essential fact: no matter how advanced an AI system becomes, its outputs can never be guaranteed to be 100% accurate, and may even be riddled with seemingly plausible logical fallacies[2]. In this regard, platforms should provide users with skills training in information verification, imparting fundamental principles and effective strategies for discerning authenticity. At the same time, generative AI systems should offer functionalities such as text traceability and result comparison to facilitate secondary verification and enable users to independently assess the trustworthiness of AI outputs. Only

---

1 CHEN, Yongwei. Beyond ChatGPT: opportunities, risks, and challenges of generative AI[J]. Journal of Shandong University (Philosophy and Social Sciences Edition), 2023 (3):127-143.

2 XIAO, Feng. Generative artificial intelligence and the new paradigm of knowledge production: an exploration of third-order knowledge production[J]. Social Science Digest, 2024 (4):8-10.

under the guidance of critical thinking can generative AI be regarded as a cognitive tool rather than an authoritarian supplier of knowledge, thereby allowing users to maintain agency in human-machine interaction.

2. Fostering Critical Thinking: Encouraging Users to Critically Approach AI-Generated Content

In the rapid evolution of generative AI technologies, cultivating critical thinking is indispensable for users seeking to optimize their interactions with AI. Currently, AI-generated content—such as text and images—exhibits an unprecedented level of realism and richness, making it easy for users to be misled, and consequently accept such outputs as authoritative and overlook potential flaws. For instance, works produced by Midjourney often astonish viewers with their surrealist artistry; yet they frequently turn out to have numerous defects in aspects such as detail rendering and scene integration, requiring thus extensive human intervention and iterative adjustment for the intended effect. If users lack a fundamental sense of skepticism and uncritically accept all AI-generated content, they are highly likely to fall into cognitive biases and misperceptions.

The cultivation of critical thinking requires fostering users' sensitivity to AI-generated content. Admittedly, AI possesses inherent advantages over humans in processing and integrating vast amounts of information; however, this does not guarantee that its outputs are necessarily objective, impartial, or logically rigorous. When using AI generated content, users must evaluate whether the selection of evidence is representative, whether logical reasoning is free from bias, and whether the conclusions can withstand external verification. To this end, users need to master fundamental principles of logic and argumentation, develop the ability to consider alternative viewpoints and conduct multidimensional analysis, and critically examine AI-generated perspectives from a rational standpoint in order to discern any implicit value orientations.

Meanwhile, fostering critical thinking also requires enhancing users' understanding of the cognitive limitations inherent in generative AI. Although current AI systems possess a certain degree of commonsense reasoning and transfer learning capabilities, they fundamentally lack the basic cognitive architecture of humans and are thus unable to exercise holistic control from higher dimensions. As a result, the content generated by such systems often exhibits fragmentation and internal contradictions. For instance, while ChatGPT may deliver impressive performances in role-playing scenarios, even cursory probing reveals that its conversational logic typically remains context-bound, lacking coherence and consistency, and is insufficient to sustain prolonged, in-depth dialogue. If users fail to fully recognize the limitations of AI's cognitive abilities and blindly follow its viewpoints, it is tantamount to forcing a square peg into a round hole, and may even result in wrong decision-making. Therefore, users must develop a deep understanding of AI systems' operational mechanisms and intrinsic flaws, actively situate AI outputs within specific contexts for critical examination, and assess their applicability and limitations. Only in this way can one have the initiative in human-machine interaction: leveraging AI to expand cognitive horizons while retaining autonomous human judgment, thereby achieving targeted application and avoiding overreliance.

3. Mechanism Elucidation: Endowing AI Outputs with Explainability to Enhance Decision-Making Transparency

To optimize the trust foundation in user interaction with generative AI, it is critical to both cultivate individuals' critical thinking and improve the explainability of AI outputs. At present, most generative AI systems rely on deep learning algorithms, whose internal decision-making processes exhibit a typical "black box" characteristic; even technical developers often find it challenging to fully explain the reasoning pathways and evidential bases underlying AI judgments. This opacity in decision-making processes undoubtedly exacerbates users' trust anxiety and gives rise to a series of ethical concerns. For instance, in the field of autonomous driving, if an onboard AI system makes counterintuitive decisions under complex road conditions and fails to provide reasonable explanations for these actions, users' confidence in the system's safety and reliability will inevitably be undermined, potentially leading to legal disputes.

Elucidating the operational mechanisms of AI necessitates, as a first priority, the identification of key influencing factors within the decision-making process.[1] Although the decision-making pathways in generative AI systems are highly intricate, several critical nodes can typically be distilled, such as feature extraction from input data, knowledge base matching and retrieval, and the generation and filtering of candidate solutions. Centered on these pivotal stages, technology developers should endeavor to enhance system transparency by explicating the fundamental logic and principal influencing variables at each juncture to end users. For example, in the knowledge question-answering scenario, when generating responses, the system should clarify the core knowledge bases it relies upon, demonstrate the retrieval and matching procedures, and enumerate the score rankings of candidate answers. This approach assists users in comprehending how the system arrives at its final judgments. Consequently, the decision-making process of AI systems will no longer remain an imperceptible "black box"; users will thereby gain opportunities to understand the systems' strengths and limitations, and thus foster reasonable

---

1 YAN, Kunru. Explainable artificial intelligence: origins, approaches, and practices[J]. Exploration and Argumentation, 2022 (8): 102-109, 178.

expectations.

In elucidating the mechanisms of AI, both explainability and popularization are indispensable and should not be neglected. For most users, the technical implementation of AI systems is excessively specialized and obscure; without effective popularized explanation, even the most detailed technical information is of little benefit to the establishment of trust.[1] Therefore, when AI systems communicate their decision-making logic to users, they should avoid technical jargon as much as possible, adopting instead expressions that align with everyday language, and striving to concretize and visualize abstract concepts. Simultaneously, to accommodate users' varying cognitive levels, the presentation of AI system explainability should be tailored and targeted. For general users, the systems can employ intuitive formats such as information visualization to present decision processes and highlight key nodes; for expert users, more technical details and customized interactive modes can be provided to meet their needs for in-depth "dissection" of the systems. Only through such "differentiated instruction" can targeted communication be achieved, thereby paving the way for users to understand AI operations and to dispel their doubts.

Section 2 Algorithm Upgrades: Enhancing Generative AI Models to Improve Trustworthiness

The optimization and refinement of generative AI models constitute a complex and systematic endeavor, necessitating coordinated efforts across multiple dimensions such as algorithmic enhancement, model architecture, and continual learning. From the algorithmic perspective, it is essential to

---

1 RIBEIRO, M. T., SINGH, S., GUESTRIN, C. "Why should I trust you?" Explaining the predictions of any classifier[R]. Proceedings of the 22nd ACM SIGKDD International Conference on Knowledge Discovery and Data Mining, 2016: 1135-1144.

improve the diversity and inclusivity of training data, while employing techniques such as adversarial learning to dynamically mitigate potential model biases, thereby ensuring fairness in generated content. As such, the development of dedicated trust assessment models is crucial; these models should comprehensively evaluate higher-order features, including semantic coherence, factual accuracy, and logical consistency, to quantitatively assess the trustworthiness of AI outputs and provide users with intuitive references. Simultaneously, endowing models with capabilities for active learning and adaptive evolution allows for the ongoing optimization of knowledge and strategies in response to external feedback, as well as the dynamic adjustment of generated content to meet diverse user needs, thereby enhancing output reliability. Only through a multifaceted and systematic approach can the credibility of generative AI models be substantively improved, thereby laying a solid foundation for their application in content creation, knowledge services, and related domains.

1. Optimization Algorithms: Reducing Bias to Ensure Fairness and Accuracy in Generated Outcomes

The refinement and optimization of generative AI models fundamentally hinge on enhancing algorithmic fairness and accuracy to mitigate bias and ensure the credibility of generated outputs. At present, the issue of bias in AI algorithms has become a focal concern within both academia and industry. Due to limitations in training data and flaws in model design, AI systems frequently exhibit pronounced discriminatory tendencies regarding sensitive attributes such as gender, race, and geography. The content generated by these systems often contradicts prevailing societal values, thereby eliciting widespread skepticism. For example, research has revealed that the text generation process of GPT-3 demonstrates marked stereotypical perceptions of women, tending to associate women with roles such as family and childcare[1], while attributing qualities such as leadership and rationality more frequently to men. This gender-based bias not only contravenes the principle of gender equality but also exerts a detrimental influence on users' cognition and decision-making.[2]

To mitigate algorithmic bias, it is essential to address the issue at the data source by deliberately enhancing the diversity and inclusivity of training datasets.[3] Only when training data sufficiently reflects the perspectives, experiences, and value orientations of different groups can AI models achieve a comprehensive understanding of the pluralism inherent in human society, thereby avoiding the cognitive pitfalls of partiality and homogenization. Accordingly, during the data collection process, it is imperative to intentionally incorporate voices from different genders, races, and regions, with particular emphasis on representing marginalized groups and ethnic minorities, so as to balance the data ecosystem. Simultaneously, to address biases embedded in existing datasets, human intervention is required to de-bias the data by removing harmful samples that may lead to discrimination and stereotyping.[4] Only by optimizing data quality at its source can a robust foundation for model training be established.

During the model training and optimization phases, techniques such as

---

1 BOLUKBASI, T., CHANG, K. W., ZOU, J. Y., et al. Man is to computer programmer as woman is to homemaker? Debiasing word embeddings[J]. Advances in Neural Information Processing Systems, 2016, 29: 4349-4357.

2 LATIF, E., ZHAI, X., LIU, L. AI gender bias, disparities, and fairness: does training data matter?[J]. ARXIV PREPRINT ARXIV: 2312.10833, 2023.

3 SONG, Suhong, WANG, Yueqi, CHANG, Heqiuzi. The formation logic of algorithmic gender discrimination and diversified governance[J]. Contemporary Communication, 2020 (5): 95-100.

4 ZHANG, Xin, SONG, Yuxin. Typology of algorithmic gender discrimination and fair governance in the age of artificial intelligence[J]. Collection of Women's Studies, 2022 (3): 5-19.

adversarial learning and data resampling can be introduced to dynamically identify and mitigate potential biases within AI models. Specifically, sensitive attribute classifiers can be deployed to monitor, in real time, any biases that may emerge in the models' outputs. Upon detecting discriminatory tendencies, adversarial samples can be employed for targeted retraining, guiding the models to learn more equitable feature representations. For instance, in the field of machine translation, early translation models frequently exhibited gender bias, erroneously translating neutral terms such as "doctor" as male and "nurse" as female. By embedding gender adversarial networks and continuously training the models with both positive and negative examples, more neutral translation outcomes were ultimately achieved, thus effectively reducing gender bias.

2. Model Construction: Assessing the Trustworthiness of AI Outputs to Offer Users Informed Reference

To enhance the credibility of outputs generated by generative AI models, it is necessary not only to mitigate bias and improve accuracy at the algorithmic level, but also to focus on developing dedicated trust evaluation models. Such models would quantify the trustworthiness of AI-generated content, providing users with intuitive references. Currently, generative AI is increasingly applied in content creation, knowledge services, and related domains. However, due to the inherent uncertainty and potential risks associated with its outputs, users often harbor significant doubts when consulting or utilizing such content, making it difficult to fully trust the systems. To address this issue, it is imperative to explore technical approaches for embedding trust evaluation functionalities into AI systems, thereby equipping them with capabilities for self-assessment and trustworthiness labeling.

The construction of a trustworthiness assessment model fundamentally involves learning and modeling the key factors that influence credibility, thereby establishing computational methods for evaluating the trustworthiness of generated content. This process can draw upon established paradigms from fields such as NLP and image recognition. By leveraging feature engineering and deep learning techniques, it is possible to mine and analyze vast amounts of AI-generated content and corresponding feedback data, uncovering critical distinctions between trustworthy and untrustworthy content across dimensions such as semantics, logic, and style, and abstracting these distinctions into computable feature vectors. For instance, quantifiable features of conversational content generated by dialogue systems can be extracted along dimensions such as semantic coherence, logical consistency, factual accuracy, and user satisfaction. Based on large-scale, manually annotated datasets, deep neural network models can then be trained to accurately predict the trustworthiness of dialogue content.

In the process of model construction, it is essential to prioritize higher-order features that significantly impact trustworthiness. Unlike lower-order features such as simple word frequency statistics, higher-order features involving semantic understanding and commonsense reasoning can more comprehensively reflect the authenticity and rationality of content, thereby making a greater contribution to trust assessment. For instance, in fact-based question answering, it is insufficient to merely examine the overlap of keywords between the answer and the question; it is also necessary to focus on deeper features, such as the logical coherence of the answer and the authority of cited evidence, to accurately assess the professionalism and credibility of the response. To capture these higher-order features, advanced technologies such as pre-trained language models and knowledge graphs can be employed to extract implicit information—such as semantic relationships and world knowledge—embedded within massive amounts of text, image, and video data, thereby enhancing the understanding and judgment capabilities of trust assessment models.

3. Empowering Learning Capabilities: Enhancing Output Reliability through Active Learning and Adaptation

In optimizing and iterating generative AI models, it is not sufficient to merely address algorithmic bias, enhance accuracy, or construct trust evaluation frameworks. Greater emphasis should be placed on endowing these systems with intrinsic capabilities for continuous learning and adaptive adjustment. Currently, most generative AI systems employ a static training paradigm, wherein models are trained once on specific datasets, resulting in fixed knowledge bases and strategies. However, the landscape of human knowledge and societal values is in constant flux, and user preferences and feedback are increasingly diverse. If AI systems are unable to assimilate new information in a timely manner and respond to user feedback, they risk cognitive dissonance and inappropriate outputs, which in turn erode user trust. Therefore, to continuously improve the reliability of AI-generated outputs, it is imperative to explore mechanisms such as active learning and adaptive evolution, thereby infusing these systems with sustained iterative momentum.

Active learning constitutes a critical pathway for endowing AI with the capability for continuous evolution. Distinct from the passive acceptance of training on static datasets, the active learning paradigm emphasizes that AI systems should proactively identify the most informative data points—those that can most enhance their decision-making—based on their existing knowledge and strategies, and initiate targeted queries to external sources. Through the feedback obtained, the systems acquire new knowledge and optimize their models.[1] The advantage of this learning paradigm lies in its ability to sensitively delineate the boundaries of an AI system's capabilities, to concentrate resources on reinforcing weak links, and thereby to achieve more efficient cognitive iteration. For example, when confronted with queries in specialized domains such as medicine or law, intelligent question-answering systems often struggle to provide responses that satisfy user expectations. At this juncture, the systems can employ active learning mechanisms to query domain experts, acquire critical domain-specific knowledge, and subsequently adjust their own knowledge graph and reasoning strategies. Through repeated iterations of this process, AI systems will gradually attain more comprehensive and specialized knowledge, thereby enabling them to deliver more reliable responses when faced with complex problems in the future.

On the basis of active learning, the incorporation of adaptive evolutionary mechanisms is also indispensable.[2] Specifically, this refers to the capability of AI systems to autonomously adjust their generation strategies according to factors such as different users' preferences, feedback, and usage scenarios, thereby providing personalized and differentiated content and services for diverse users. This adaptive capacity not only enhances users' subjective satisfaction but also contributes to the objective reliability of the output content. For instance, users of news recommendation systems have varying preferences regarding news topics and reporting styles, and even the interests of the same user may shift over time. To accommodate such heterogeneity and dynamism, AI systems must possess adaptive capabilities—namely, the ability to dynamically adjust

---

1 LIU, B., MAZUMDER, S., ROBERTSON, E., et al. AI autonomy: self-initiation, adaptation and continual learning[J]. arXiv Preprint arXiv: 2203.08994, 2022.

2 KONG, Weiliang, HAN, Shuyun, ZHANG, Zhaoli. Construction of adaptive learning paths supported by artificial intelligence[J]. Modern Distance Education Research, 2020, 32 (3): 94-103.

news filtering and ranking strategies in response to data such as users' reading histories, click behaviors, and comment feedback, so as to promptly deliver the most relevant and reliable news content to users. This approach not only provides a more accurate and personalized user experience but also maximizes the fulfillment of users' demands for authenticity and timeliness in news information.

Section 3 Reshaping Contexts: Creating a Human-Machine Interaction Ecosystem Conducive to Trust Calibration

Reshaping human-AI interaction scenarios and fostering an ecosystem conducive to trust calibration requires a systematic optimization of human-machine collaboration models across dimensions such as goal clarification, cross-validation, and feedback loops. The goal orientation of human-machine collaborative tasks serves as the logical starting point for all processes, influencing task division, the delineation of responsibilities and authority, performance evaluation, and iterative optimization. By leveraging standardized procedures, humans and machines can collaboratively clarify goal elements and formally embed them into the operational mechanisms of AI systems, the inevitable route to ensure the alignment of objectives and consistency of expectations. Based on this, diversified cross-validation mechanisms provide an "external" perspective for verifying the credibility of AI outputs. Through seamless human-machine integration and complementary expertise from specialized and general users, AI-generated content can be contextually refined and dynamically updated to distinguish authenticity from falsehood. At the same time, a systematically designed feedback loop serves as a continuous source of innovation and improvement for AI, enabling the efficient collection of user input and the effective transmission of feedback to each stage of the optimization process. This collective effort injects sustained momentum into AI advancement. Only by integrating goal-setting, operational processes, and feedback mechanisms across the entire chain can the human-AI interaction ecosystem progressively advance toward the ideal of trustworthiness, controllability, and optimal performance.

1. Clarifying Objectives: Defining the Expected Consistency of Human-Machine Task Alignment

Reshaping human-AI interaction scenarios and fostering an ecosystem conducive to trust calibration requires, first of all, clarifying the goal of human-AI collaboration to ensure both parties share consistent expectations regarding task definition. At present, the widespread application of generative AI across various aspects of human life and work has gradually shifted its role from a mere tool to that of an intelligent collaborative partner. In this context, discrepancies in objectives and deviations in expectations between humans and AI frequently become critical triggers for misunderstandings and distrust. For example, in AI-assisted medical diagnosis, physicians may expect AI systems to deliver reliable diagnostic solutions and alleviate their workload, whereas the AI systems may be designed primarily to provide auxiliary diagnostic support and reference suggestions, without assuming ultimate diagnostic responsibility. If there is a misalignment in the understanding of goal orientation between the two parties, unnecessary disputes and crises of trust are bound to arise.

To clarify the objectives of human-AI collaboration, it is essential to achieve "four clarities" at the task level. First, clarify task positioning, that is, delineate the boundaries and focal points of human-AI division of labor. For specific tasks, it is necessary to explicitly identify which components should be led by humans and which can be assisted or even replaced by AI, and to make this division transparent throughout the interaction process.

Second, clarify process responsibilities, namely, the allocation of rights, responsibilities, and interests during human-AI collaboration. It is important to specify the respective responsibilities of humans and AI in stages such as data collection, algorithm selection, and result interpretation, and to ensure that the advancement of tasks complies with ethical and legal standards. Third, clarify delivery standards, namely, the criteria for evaluating the quality of tasks completed through human-AI collaboration. Key performance indicators must be defined, and consensus should be reached regarding the weighting and assessment methods for these indicators. This serves as a guide for optimizing collaborative workflows and enhancing task performance. Fourth, clarify the iteration mechanism, that is, the contingency plans for adjusting the division of labor in response to changing objectives. Given the inherent complexity and variability of real-world tasks, both human and AI agents should predefine the conditions that trigger goal iteration and the pathways for optimization, thereby dynamically adapting to emerging situations and new requirements.

Clarifying objectives across four dimensions necessitates the support of standardized procedures. At the outset of human-AI collaborative tasks, it is advisable for humans to take the lead by conducting goal-oriented needs analysis based on the attributes of the tasks, thereby establishing a framework encompassing key elements such as task positioning, process responsibilities, delivery standards, and iteration mechanisms. Then AI systems can be invited to participate in discussions, utilizing multi-round Q&A, feedback loops, and other forms of interaction to enable both humans and AI to refine and confirm a shared understanding of the objective elements. This process should also be documented in a standardized electronic record for future reference and accountability. Once consensus on objectives is achieved, these should be translated into a standard format that AI systems can interpret and follow, and embedded within the systems' task planning and execution workflows. Based on the cutting-edge paradigms such as "goal-oriented AI", formal representation and automated reasoning technologies can be employed to endow AI systems with the capacity to autonomously optimize their behavior in accordance with established objectives.

2. Cross-validation: Introducing a Multidimensional Verification Mechanism to Mitigate Trust Risks in AI Outputs

To foster a human-AI interaction ecosystem conducive to trust calibration, it is necessary not only to clarify objectives at the task level, but also to introduce diversified cross-validation mechanisms to mitigate potential trust risks associated with AI-generated content. Admittedly, current generative AI systems demonstrate exceptional capabilities in data processing and knowledge discovery; however, the accuracy and reliability of their outputs remain difficult to guarantee, with possibilities of bias, error, or even intentional deception.[1] If individuals accept AI outputs uncritically and without scrutiny, the consequences of erroneous decision-making could be severe. Therefore, it is imperative to embed cross-validation procedures within human-AI interaction scenarios, so as to enable multi-layered and multi-perspective examination of AI-generated content. This approach aims to clarify the authenticity, professionalism, and trustworthiness of AI outputs, ensuring targeted interventions and distinguishing truth from falsehood.

The construction of a cross-validation mechanism must adhere to the principle of multi-stakeholder participation.[2] Given the complexity of

---

1 BROWN, T., MANN, B., RYDER, N., et al. Language models are few-shot learners[J]. Advances in Neural Information Processing Systems, 2020, 33: 1877-1901.

2 ZHANG, Sheng. Research on Semantic Association Information Fusion Methods for Multimodal Intelligent Human-Computer Interaction[D]. Wuhan: Huazhong University of Science and Technology, 2021.

real-world scenarios, relying solely on a single entity to validate AI outputs inevitably leads to bias. Therefore, it is essential to aggregate diverse sources of intelligence—machines, experts, and the public—to form a synergistic and complementary validation force through mutual corroboration. For example, in AI-assisted scientific research, when scholars consult AI-generated literature reviews, they should not only utilize tools such as knowledge graphs to automatically compare the consistency of these reviews with published literature, but also invite domain experts to conduct peer reviews focusing on research context, theoretical orientation, and other relevant aspects. Simultaneously, crowdsourcing mechanisms can be leveraged to open literature content to a broad spectrum of research professionals and solicit extensive feedback through questionnaires, comments, and similar channels. Only through the interplay and complementarity of multiple stakeholders can all dimensions of AI outputs be comprehensively scrutinized, thus enabling the timely identification and correction of inherent biases.

During the process of cross-validation, it is advisable to emphasize scenario specificity and practical effectiveness. On the one hand, appropriate validation pathways and evaluation criteria should be selected based on the task type and application domain of human-AI collaboration. For example, in legal applications, the assessment of AI-generated viewpoints may prioritize dimensions such as statutory citation and logical reasoning to establish professional credibility. In the scenario of news and media, however, the primary focus should be on scrutinizing information sources and the authenticity of data. Such context-sensitive approaches allow for targeted resolution of scenario-specific challenges and enhance validation efficiency. On the other hand, the validation process must also ensure timeliness, enabling adaptability and dynamic iteration. Given the rapid pace of knowledge renewal and value evolution, rigid validation rules and standards often become obsolete. Therefore, in human-machine interaction, it is essential to continuously monitor both internal and external environmental changes, keenly identify emerging issues and novel factors that may impact the credibility of AI outputs, and promptly adjust the focal points and evaluative criteria of validation. Only in this way can the validation be aligned with current realities and have its ongoing relevance.

3. Enhancing the Feedback Loop: Establishing User Feedback Channels to Facilitate AI Iterative Optimization

To reshape the human-AI interaction ecosystem and foster an environment conducive to trust calibration, it is essential not only to clarify objectives and establish cross-validation mechanisms, but also to focus on refining the feedback loop. This involves creating effective channels for user recommendations and suggestions, thereby supporting the continuous iteration and optimization of AI systems. In increasingly intimate human-machine collaboration, user feedback has become a critical driving force for the self-renewal of AI systems. The challenges users encounter and the insights they accumulate during interactions with AI often incisively reveal latent system deficiencies and inform directions for improvement. However, in practice, these valuable perspectives are frequently lost due to the absence of effective feedback mechanisms, thus failing to be transformed into tangible momentum for AI evolution. Therefore, it is imperative to systematically design feedback frameworks and ensure unobstructed channels for users' opinions, embracing diverse perspectives and leveraging collective wisdom as the foundation for advancing AI.

The construction of feedback mechanisms should be diversity-oriented, aiming to provide personalized channels of expression for users from various backgrounds and with different needs. Given the broad and heterogeneous nature of user groups, a single, uniform feedback model is inevitably ill-suited to all contexts. Therefore, it is necessary to tailor approaches and offer a variety of options. For instance, for heavy users, in-depth feedback channels such as regular follow-up visits and dedicated customer service can be established to encourage them to share their experiences and suggestions for improvement. In contrast, for light users, the feedback process can be simplified to lower the participation threshold, utilizing lightweight forms such as ratings or buttons to enhance their willingness to provide feedback. At the same time, feedback solutions can be customized according to specific usage scenarios. For example, in the domain of intelligent finance, feedback options can focus on issues such as algorithmic fairness and privacy protection. In intelligent education contexts, emphasis should be placed on gathering user evaluations regarding learning outcomes and the structure of the knowledge system. In this way, feedback mechanisms can be more closely aligned with practical needs, directly addressing the exigencies and obtaining more targeted and constructive inputs.

The establishment of a feedback closed-loop requires not only the aggregation of users' opinions but also the development of an efficient analytical and processing mechanism to ensure that valuable suggestions are effectively implemented, thereby enhancing the quality and efficiency of AI systems. This necessitates leveraging the synergistic advantages of AI and human expertise through human-machine collaboration and the integration of qualitative and quantitative approaches to comprehensively analyze user feedback and extract critical insights. On the one hand, intelligent algorithms such as natural language processing and sentiment analysis can be employed to enable machine comprehension and automatic categorization of vast amounts of user feedback data, thereby identifying common issues and uncovering latent patterns. On the other hand, for complex feedback involving value judgments and ethical considerations, it is essential to convene an interdisciplinary adjudication committee composed of experts in technology, ethics, law, and related fields. This committee should provide professional interpretation and value-based deliberation of the feedback, synthesizing actionable recommendations from multiple perspectives. Furthermore, it is necessary to establish standardized operational procedures that clearly define the principles for handling feedback, the workflow, and time requirements. These should be supported by digital tools such as collaborative work platforms to achieve closed-loop management. Such a system ensures that user feedback is promptly communicated to every stage and participant in the AI optimization and iteration, thereby achieving a state where understanding leads to action, and knowledge is unified with practice.

PART II Intelligent Risks in the Era of Generative AI

Chapter Ten The Evolution of Risk: Natural Risks, Human-Induced Risks, and Intelligent Risks

Risks are omnipresent and perpetual, with natural, human-induced, and intelligent risks intertwining and evolving together to shape the developmental landscape of human society. In the age of generative AI, reflecting on risk necessitates not only an examination of the complex interactions between nature and technological upheaval, but also an acute awareness of the moral paradoxes inherent in ethical decision-making. Seeking certainty amidst uncertainty is the very modus vivendi of a risk society. This chapter intends to approach the subject from the historical dimension of risk evolution, addressing topics such as the multidimensional derivation of natural risks, the compounded challenges of human-induced risks, and the disruptive nature of intelligent risks. It aims to elucidate the iterative process of risk cognition, systematically review the forms of risk at various stages, and clarify the mechanisms underlying the evolution of different types of risk. On this basis, the discussion further extends to contemporary challenges in communication studies, such as the erosion and reconstruction of trust triggered by generative AI, and the proliferation of misinformation in the era of social media. The objective is to provide theoretical support for anticipating, responding to, and mitigating risks, and to contribute a communication studies perspective to the construction of digital trust and the conceptualization of intelligent risk prevention and control.

Section 1 The Historical Trajectory of Risk Evolution: From Natural Hazards to Digital Crises

Human society has witnessed a profound transformation of risks, evolving from natural risks to anthropogenic risks, and more recently to intelligent risks. Each shift in the nature of risk not only highlights the distinct stages of social development but also reflects the progressive enhancement of humanity's capacity to manage risks. The relationship among different types of risks is not a simple linear causality; rather, they are interwoven and mutually constitutive. Natural risks have shaped the fundamental conditions of human existence, while the Industrial Revolution accelerated the modernization of anthropogenic risks. The intelligent revolution, in turn, has given rise to the unique category of intelligent risks characteristic of the digital era. Risk, in relation to the development of human society, functions both as an impediment and as a catalyst; the advancement of risk management capabilities essentially signifies the progress of human civilization. Reviewing the historical trajectory of risk evolution, it is evident that human society has consistently advanced along the path of risk co-governance, strengthening social resilience through adversity and achieving advancements in civilization through effective risk management.

1. Natural Risks: The Initial Challenge to Human Civilization

Natural risks, the primordial challenge to human civilization, encompass natural disasters and anthropogenic calamities, and embody the inherent vulnerability within the dynamic interplay between humanity and nature.[1] Catastrophic events such as widespread flooding and frequent earthquakes posed direct threats to the survival of early humans, with the collapse of prehistoric civilizations often attributable to the relentless impact of natural risks. For instance, the Minoan civilization, which flourished on the island of Crete around 2000 BCE, met an abrupt end due to a tsunami triggered by a volcanic eruption. This tragic episode underscores the destructive force of natural risks and highlights the lack of adaptive capacity in early human societies.

Even after the Agricultural Revolution, natural risks have remained the Achilles' heel of human civilization. Climate change-induced challenges such as droughts and locust plagues continually threaten agricultural production, thereby impacting social stability. For example, the decline of the Mayan civilization around 1300 CE can be largely attributed to severe, prolonged droughts. The Maya were highly dependent on agriculture, and the resulting food shortages and social unrest triggered by drought accelerated the disintegration of this once-prosperous civilization. This case illustrates the destructive impact of extreme weather events, such as drought, on the sustainability of human societies.

Disease has likewise constituted a major natural risk faced by humanity since early times. The Black Death swept across Europe in the Middle Ages, claiming the lives of nearly half the population. Diseases such as smallpox and measles inflicted devastating blows on indigenous populations during the colonial era. These pandemics not only resulted in massive loss of life but also aggravated social disorder and impeded the progress of civilization. Even today, infectious diseases remain a formidable challenge for humanity. Public health risks, exemplified by SARS and the

---

1 LIANG, Biqi. Natural disasters: humanity's arch-nemesis[J]. Green China, 2005 (2): 16-20.

COVID-19 pandemic, have posed new shocks to human society in the era of globalization.

Therefore, natural risks are unavoidable challenges throughout the development of human civilization. From the collapse of prehistoric societies to the upheavals following the Agricultural Revolution, and the impact of diseases on population dynamics and social order, the perils of nature have continuously tested humanity's capacity for response. Confronting natural risks and enhancing risk governance capabilities constitute the essential pathway for the sustainable development of human society.

2. Human-Induced Risks: Social Anxiety in the Post-Industrial Revolution Era

The Industrial Revolution, as a major turning point in human society, while bringing about immense material wealth, gave rise to a series of unprecedented man-made risks, thereby triggering widespread social anxiety.[1] The invention and widespread adoption of the steam engine marked humanity's entry into the era of machine production. However, issues such as loss of control over machinery and frequent industrial accidents persistently plagued the working class. For instance, in 19th-century Britain, tragedies involving severe injury or even death caused by machinery were commonplace in industries such as textiles and mining, vividly highlighting the safety risks inherent in the process of industrialization.

Meanwhile, although the establishment of the factory system enhanced production efficiency, it also raised concerns regarding the intensification of

---

1 ZHOU, Chengfang. On the social consequences of the industrial revolution[J]. Journal of Inner Mongolia University (Philosophy and Social Sciences Edition), 1989 (1): 86-97.

labor-capital conflicts. The relentless pursuit of profit by capitalists frequently comes at the expense of workers' interests.[1] Issues such as harsh working conditions, excessive working hours, and meager wages all reflect the social contradictions that emerged after the Industrial Revolution. In Western countries during the late 19th and early 20th centuries, labor movements surged, with strikes, demonstrations, and other forms of protest occurring one after another, leading to an increasingly acute antagonism between the working class and the bourgeoisie.[2]

The rapid advancement of urbanization, driven by the process of industrialization, has resulted in a massive influx of rural populations into cities. However, the lag in the development of supporting infrastructure has exacerbated urban issues such as overcrowding, pollution, and crime.[3] For example, in historical London, the stark disparity between the rapidly expanding population and the city's carrying capacity triggered a series of public health and security risks. The harsh living conditions in slums became breeding grounds for disease and crime. The demographic dividend unleashed by the Industrial Revolution was thus transformed into factors of social instability during the process of urbanization.

Environmental pollution is another significant anthropogenic risk that emerged after the Industrial Revolution. The extensive use of coal, coupled with the unrestrained discharge of industrial emissions and wastewater, led to a dramatic decline in the quality of air, water resources, and soil. In the 19th-century London, England, persistent smog plagued the city, and the

---

1 PAN, Runhan, ZHANG, Zhizhong. The Industrial revolution and the modernization of British society[J]. Historical Research, 1983 (6): 106-120.

2 RAN, Hao. The "New Social Risks" in capitalist states: the emergence, response, and implications of the "Post-Post-Industrial Society"[J]. China Social Public Security Research Report, 2018 (1): 210-221.

3 MEI, Xueqin. A preliminary study on environmental issues in 19th-century British cities[J]. Journal of Liaoning Normal University, 2000 (3): 105-108.

direct discharge of industrial wastewater into the Thames River caused severe ecological degradation.[1] These environmental pollutions not only jeopardized human health but also undermined the prospects for sustainable social development. Economic concepts such as the tragedy of the commons and externalities precisely elucidate the profound impact of anthropogenic risks on both the environment and society.

3. Intelligent Risks: Potential Crises in the Digital Society

As a new phase in the development of human society, the intelligent revolution brings unprecedented convenience, yet it also gives rise to a series of potential intelligence-related risks. Issues such as the digital divide, algorithmic bias, privacy violations, and cyberbullying all reflect the inherent vulnerabilities of the digital society. Although the rapid iteration of intelligent technologies has enhanced social efficiency, it has also intensified inequalities in the distribution of digital resources. For example, in the application of AI, the pervasive influence of algorithmic decision-making may exacerbate existing social injustices, with disadvantaged groups facing greater barriers in areas such as education, employment, and credit, thereby making the digital divide even more pronounced.

The issue of algorithmic bias highlights the limitations and risks inherent in AI. Selective bias in training data can lead to algorithmic models exhibiting discrimination based on gender, race, and other factors, thereby undermining the fairness of decision-making processes. For example, in facial recognition technology, insufficient representation of certain ethnic groups in the training dataset may result in disparities in recognition accuracy, which in turn can produce unjust outcomes in fields such as the

1 LUO, Junguo. Examining industrialization and environmental pollution from a historical perspective[J]. Guangdong Education (Senior High Edition), 2018 (3): 39-43.

judiciary and finance. The problem of algorithmic bias challenges the myth of technological neutrality and underscores the critical importance of algorithmic ethics.

Privacy infringement represents another highly scrutinized intelligent risk in the digital society. In the era of big data, the large-scale collection and utilization of personal information, while facilitating the provision of personalized services, also give rise to issues such as data misuse and information leakage. The Cambridge Analytica incident serves as a case in point, where Facebook user data was employed for political advertising without user consent, triggering widespread public concern. The conflict between privacy protection and data utilization poses significant challenges to the institutional design of digital governance.

Issues such as cyberbullying and online abuse present formidable challenges for the digital society. In anonymous environments, cyberspace has become a breeding ground for rumors and the proliferation of extreme discourse. For instance, among adolescents, incidents of cyberbullying occur frequently and have profound negative impacts on their physical and psychological well-being. Algorithmic recommendation systems may further reinforce echo chamber effects, aggravating social fragmentation and polarization. There is an urgent need to cultivate a healthy online ecosystem, and topics such as platform responsibility and user self-regulation warrant deeper examination.

Therefore, intelligent risk constitutes a latent crisis that cannot be overlooked in the evolution of the digital society. From the digital divide to algorithmic bias, and from privacy breaches to cyberbullying, intelligent technologies, while empowering social development, simultaneously disrupt established orders in unprecedented ways. Clarifying the nature and scope of intelligent risk and exploring institutionalized pathways for digital governance are essential steps toward building a trustworthy and controllable intelligent society.

Section 2 The Connation and Extension of Natural Risks: From Natural Disasters to Pandemics

Natural risk is a complex and dynamic concept, whose connotation encompasses not only the sudden impacts of natural forces such as disasters, but also the ongoing disturbances to the ecological environment caused by human activities. With the continuous development of human society, the scope of natural risk has been expanding, extending from traditional geological and meteorological disasters to emerging domains such as ecological imbalance and public health crises. The surging tide of globalization has further intensified the breadth and depth of transnational dissemination of natural risks. In this era of ubiquitous connectivity, natural risks have long transcended the constraints of geography and national borders, becoming a critical issue that concerns the shared future of humankind. Systematic understanding and prudent management of natural risks test not only human intelligence and courage, but are also vital to realizing the harmonious coexistence between humanity and nature. Amidst the intricate and multifaceted landscape of risks, only by grounding ourselves in scientific rationality and adhering to systems thinking can we seek certainty amid uncertainty, and seize developmental opportunities amidst risk and challenge.

1. Natural and Man-Made Disasters: Typical Manifestations of Natural Risks

Natural and man-made disasters, as typical representations of natural risks, not only underscore the irresistible force of nature but also highlight the limitations of human response capabilities. Natural disasters such as earthquakes and tsunamis are often triggered by tectonic movements, leaving humanity in a passive and vulnerable position when confronted with these sudden catastrophic events. For example, the 2008 Wenchuan earthquake in China, which registered a magnitude of 8.0 on the Richter scale, resulted in significant casualties as well as substantial direct economic losses. [1] The arduous tasks of post-disaster rescue and reconstruction further posed severe challenges to the government's governance capacity.

Compared to sudden-onset disasters such as earthquakes and tsunamis, slow-onset disasters like droughts and floods, though relatively less destructive in the short term, pose enduring threats to agricultural production and social stability. For instance, the severe drought that struck Southwest China in 2010, an event of unprecedented magnitude in a century, was characterized by its prolonged duration, extensive impact, and severe losses, inflicting substantial hardship on local agricultural activities and the daily lives of residents.[2] The timeliness and effectiveness of drought relief and disaster mitigation measures critically tested the operational efficiency of the emergency management system.

In contemporary society, the impacts of meteorological disasters have become increasingly widespread and profound. The frequent occurrence of extreme weather events—such as heatwaves, torrential rains, and hurricanes—has underscored the escalating risks posed to human society. For instance, the catastrophic rainfall in Henan Province in China in 2021, a once-in-a-millennium extreme precipitation event, disclosed the vulnerability of urban infrastructure through incidents of urban flooding,

---

1 SHANG, Zhihai, LIU, Xilin. Ecological and environmental risks of natural disasters and their assessment: a case study of secondary debris flow disasters in the severely affected area of the Wenchuan Earthquake[J]. China Safety Science Journal, 2010, 20 (9): 3-8.

2 MA, Qian. Enhancing disaster prevention and mitigation capabilities in response to the changing characteristics of disasters[J]. Statistics and Management, 2014 (5): 77-78.

transportation paralysis, and communication breakdowns. These issues highlight the urgent need for enhanced disaster prevention and mitigation efforts in the context of climate change, emphasizing the importance of integrated risk management, resilient information systems, and ethical considerations in the governance of digital and physical infrastructures.

It is important to recognize that the interplay between human activities and natural risks is increasingly blurring the boundaries between natural disasters and anthropogenic catastrophes. For instance, the catastrophic mudslide in Zhouqu, Gansu Province, China in 2010, which resulted in 1,765 fatalities, was not solely attributable to extreme weather events such as torrential rainfall, but was also exacerbated by anthropogenic factors including deforestation and illegal mining activities.[1] The compounded effects of natural and human-induced risks significantly heighten the complexity and uncertainty inherent in disaster response and risk management.

It is noteworthy that with the acceleration of globalization, the transnational transmission effects of natural risks have become increasingly prominent. Issues such as breaches of transboundary rivers and widespread sandstorms highlight both the regional and global dimensions of natural risk governance. For example, in Central Asia, the rapid shrinkage of the Aral Sea has not only triggered problems such as salt dust storms and ecological degradation, but has also impacted the socioeconomic development of neighboring countries. The establishment of mechanisms for transnational natural risk governance has thus emerged as a pressing regional and even global issue.

---

1 GONGYU, Shanren. Human error behind natural disasters: a perspective on geological hazards[J]. Southern Land and Resources, 2011 (8): 1.

2. Ecological Imbalance: Natural Risks Exacerbated by Human Activities

Ecological imbalance, a natural risk intensified by human activities, not only reflects the tension in the human–nature relationship but also highlights the absence of a sustainable development paradigm. During the industrialization, the excessive exploitation and utilization of natural resources by humans have disrupted the original ecological equilibrium, triggering a series of cascading effects. For example, large-scale deforestation, while temporarily expanding arable land, has also led to frequent occurrences of soil erosion and land desertification.[1] The rapid shrinkage of the Amazon rainforest not only threatens biodiversity but also affects the trajectory of global climate change. The worsening in ecosystem services will ultimately jeopardize human well-being itself.

The imbalance in the energy structure is another significant manifestation of how human activities intensify natural risks. The large-scale utilization of fossil fuels, while driving the rapid development of human society, has also resulted in a series of ecological and environmental issues, such as greenhouse gas emissions and global warming. Coral bleaching is a case in point: the rise in ocean temperatures leads to the dissociation between corals and their symbiotic algae, subsequently triggering the collapse of coral reef ecosystems. World natural heritage sites such as the Great Barrier Reef are facing unprecedented existential crises.[2] The transformation of the energy structure and the adoption of low-carbon development strategies have become crucial pathways for managing the

---

1 WANG, Shuli, YANG, Guangwei, ZHOU, Yanyang. The impact of land desertification on ecosystem service value[J]. Science of Soil and Water Conservation in China, 2008 (5): 50-56, 70.

2 CAI, Rongshuo, HAN, Zhiqiang, YANG, Zhengxian. Changes in the ocean and their impacts, risks, and responses for ecosystems and human societies[J]. Advances in Climate Change Research, 2020, 16 (2): 182-193.

risks associated with climate change.

It is important to recognize that humanity's desire to transform and control nature has also led to the compounding of ecological and environmental risks.[1] For instance, in the water diversion projects, large-scale inter-basin water transfer may alleviate the imbalance between water supply and demand to some extent, but it also triggers a series of secondary hazards, such as disruptions to eco-hydrological processes and biological invasions. The impact of the South-to-North Water Diversion Project on the ecological environment along the eastern route has already attracted widespread attention in the academic community. A scientific understanding of natural laws and respect for the processes of natural development are critical prerequisites for the sustainable development of human society.

The dramatic transformation of land use patterns during rapid urbanization has intensified key triggers for natural risks. Issues such as landscape fragmentation and reduced habitat connectivity have directly resulted in the loss of species habitats and a sharp decline in biodiversity. For example, in wetland ecosystems, human activities such as reclamation and landfill have caused a drastic reduction in wetland areas, threatening the survival of wildlife such as birds and undermining critical ecological functions like flood retention and water regulation. Ecological restoration and biodiversity conservation in the context of urbanization have thus become crucial topics in risk governance.

The large-scale application of chemical fertilizers and pesticides in the process of agricultural modernization has also heightened the probability of

---

1 YANG, Duogui, ZHOU, Zhitian, CHEN, Shaofeng. Challenges facing the harmonious development of human–nature relations in China and strategic choices[J]. Shanghai Economic Review, 2005 (4): 6-12.

natural risks. Issues such as soil pollution and water eutrophication not only jeopardize food safety but also undermine the sustainability of agricultural production. Soil acidification is a case in point: improper fertilizer use leads to a decrease in soil pH, which not only inhibits crop growth but also exacerbates the risk of heavy metal contamination in the soil. While healthy soil serves as the foundation of agricultural production, the development philosophy of ecological agriculture can be the guideline for risk governance.

3. The Rampage of Pandemics: Public Health Risks in the Era of Globalization

The rampant spread of pandemics, a public health risk in the era of globalization, not only reflects the vulnerability of human society but also highlights the limitations of existing health governance systems. The transnational transmission of infectious diseases has rendered epidemic risk an unavoidable global issue. For example, in the 2003 SARS outbreak, the novel coronavirus infection rapidly spread to 32 countries and regions, resulting in significant numbers of infections and fatalities. The global proliferation of the pandemic has tested the responsiveness and efficiency of public health emergency management mechanisms across nations.

Although increased vaccination coverage has curbed the prevalence of traditional infectious diseases, the prevention and control of emerging and sudden epidemics remain highly challenging. For instance, in the 2014 Ebola outbreak, the severe infectious disease triggered global panic due to its high fatality rate and the lack of effective treatments. Delays in vaccine development and accelerated viral mutations have further aggravated uncertainties in epidemic control. Consequently, a prevention-oriented and all-time prepared public health strategy has become a critical pathway for managing epidemic risks.

The dramatic increase in both the frequency and scale of population mobility has further intensified the real-world challenges associated with epidemic risk. For instance, during the 2009 H1N1 influenza pandemic, the novel influenza virus swiftly spread to 214 countries and regions worldwide, a process significantly accelerated by increased transnational population movement. Modern transportation modes such as air travel have provided convenient channels for viral transmission. Thus, how to ensure the unimpeded flow of personnel across borders while minimizing the risk of epidemic spread has become an urgent issue in global health governance that demands effective solutions.

The frequent occurrence of zoonotic diseases has further highlighted their inherent risk. The continuous expansion of human activities, coupled with the ongoing degradation of the ecological environment, has increasingly blurred the boundaries between humans and animals, significantly elevating the risk of cross-species transmission of pathogens. For example, the COVID-19 pandemic in 2020 is widely believed to be closely associated with contact with wild animals. Mechanisms for risk monitoring, source tracing, and early warning of zoonotic diseases require urgent improvement. Fundamentally, the advancement of ecological civilization can reduce the probability of epidemic outbreaks at their source.

The issue of antibiotic resistance resulting from antibiotic misuse has further exacerbated the uncertainty of epidemic risks. The increased resistance of bacteria has significantly diminished the efficacy of conventional pharmaceuticals, while the emergence of multidrug-resistant strains has raised considerable concern within the medical community. For instance, the so-called "superbug" NDM-1, an Enterobacteriaceae bacterium exhibiting extensive resistance to commonly used clinical antibiotics, has been detected in over 40 countries worldwide. The establishment of robust antibiotic stewardship mechanisms has become a critical measure in curbing the problem of antimicrobial resistance.

Section 3 A Multidimensional Perspectives on Human-Induced Risks: Technology, Economy, and Society

As an inherent feature of modern society, human-induced risks pose comprehensive challenges to sustainable human development. The intricate landscape of such risks emerges from the intertwining and compounding of technological, economic, and social risks. It has become a shared mission for both academia and policymakers to analyze the internal logic and evolutionary mechanisms underlying the various types of human-induced risks and to explore institutionalized approaches to risk governance. Only by adopting multifaceted perspectives—including legal, ethical, and institutional viewpoints, strengthening risk communication and interest coordination, and respecting diversity and inclusiveness, can we lay a solid foundation for the sound functioning of human society. Nevertheless, while the landscape of the risk society is fraught with challenges, it also contains the potential to transform crises into opportunities and threats into security. In the face of the ever-emerging human-induced risks, we must maintain necessary vigilance and, more importantly, uphold the rationality and responsibility of the "risk subject." Continuous efforts are required to improve risk governance systems and optimize risk management mechanisms in the pursuit of sustainable human development.

1. Technological Risks: The Double-Edged Sword of Scientific and Technological Advancement

As a double-edged sword, technological risks not only highlight the wisdom of humanity in conquering nature but also underscore the inherent uncertainties of technological development. The advancement of nuclear technology, while paving the way for clean and efficient energy utilization, has simultaneously raised widespread societal concerns regarding its safety and risks. The 1986 Chernobyl nuclear disaster, for instance, was triggered by operational errors and resulted in the release of large amounts of radioactive material, posing severe threats to the health and lives of residents in the surrounding areas. Since then, risk management in such areas as nuclear power plant siting, operation, and waste disposal has become a critical issue for the sustainable development of the nuclear energy industry.

Similarly, although genetically modified (GM) technology has enhanced crop yield and stress resistance, its ecological risks and potential health hazards cannot be overlooked. For instance, the extensive adoption of herbicide-resistant GM crops has effectively controlled weeds, but has also led to the emergence of herbicide-resistant superweeds. Moreover, the long-term effects of GM crops on human health have triggered widespread debate across various sectors of society. How to maximize the benefits of GM technology while minimizing its negative impacts has become an urgent and complex challenge in the field of agriculture.

The rapid advancement of information technology has also given rise to a series of emerging technological risks, notably in the domain of cybersecurity. Data breach is a case in point. The large-scale exposure of personal privacy information not only infringes upon citizens' legitimate rights and interests, but also facilitates criminal activities such as financial fraud. Global ransomware incidents, such as WannaCry, have further exposed the inherent vulnerabilities of cyberspace. Effectively safeguarding personal privacy and cybersecurity, while ensuring the free flow of data, has thus become a critical issue in digital governance.

The rise of AI technologies has triggered a series of ethical risks, such as machine malfunction and algorithmic discrimination. In the case of autonomous driving accidents, when faced with trolley problem-type moral dilemmas, the decision-making logic and value orientation of driverless vehicles directly impact the dignity of human life and the realization of fairness and justice. Furthermore, biases embedded in machine learning algorithms may exacerbate systemic discrimination in areas such as employment and the judiciary. Ensuring the explainability and accountability of AI, as well as constructing a socio-technical framework for human-machine collaboration, has become a frontier issue in the relevant academic fields.

The rapid advancement of biotechnology has also given rise to ethical risks in areas such as gene editing and human organ transplantation. For example, the case or experiment of gene-edited twins ("CRISPR babies") in 2018—a controversy or a scandal triggered by concerns over "off-target" effects—demonstrated, to some extent, the technical feasibility of intervening in human embryonic development, but also breached the ethical boundaries recognized by the academic community. In the field of organ transplantation, the emergence of the so-called "red market" or illegal organ trade further highlights the human rights risks associated with the misuse of technology. Thus, how to establish robust legal and ethical safeguards while harnessing biotechnology for the benefit of humanity has become an urgent and inescapable issue in contemporary risk management, ethics, and social governance.

2. Economic Risks: Potential Threats in Financial Markets

Economic risks, as latent threats within financial markets, not only reflect the inherent uncertainty of economic operations but also underscore the complexity of financial regulation. The rapid development of financial derivatives markets, while providing more sophisticated tools for risk management, has simultaneously increased the vulnerability of the financial system due to their intrinsic leverage and complexity. The 2008 global financial crisis, which originated in the U.S. subprime mortgage market, exemplifies this dynamic: the swift transmission of risk through the chain of financial derivatives transactions escalated into a worldwide systemic crisis, exposing numerous deficiencies in financial regulatory frameworks and risk prevention mechanisms.

As a critical variable in the international financial market, exchange rate risk also tests the effectiveness of macroeconomic policies. For instance, the "abnormal fluctuations" in China's stock market in 2015, an episode of intense turbulence originating in the stock index futures market, was exacerbated by factors such as the volatility of the RMB exchange rate and capital outflows, ultimately triggering a significant correction in the equity market. The policy game inherent in the process of exchange rate reform further highlights the formidable challenges of exchange rate risk management. How to maintain exchange rate stability while promoting balance of payments equilibrium has become a key issue in an open economy.

Internal control risks arising from imbalances in corporate governance represent a significant latent threat faced by financial markets. The bankruptcy of Enron in the United States (US) serves as a paradigmatic case: this scandal, triggered by financial fraud, exposed numerous vulnerabilities in both corporate governance structures and internal control mechanisms. Problems ranged from the lack of auditor independence and distorted incentive schemes to misrepresentation in information disclosure and the failure of checks and balances. Collectively, these problems reflect the systemic risks inherent in corporate governance. Strengthening modern corporate systems and improving governance frameworks have thus become fundamental strategies for mitigating internal control risks.

The rise of financial technology has also introduced a series of emerging risks, such as technological failures and algorithmic malfunctions.

For instance, the extreme volatility of the Bitcoin market illustrates how this decentralized cryptocurrency, due to its anonymity and cross-border nature, has become a breeding ground for illegal activities such as money laundering and tax evasion. Moreover, the malfunction of high-frequency trading algorithms can trigger extreme market events such as "flash crashes." It has become a critical issue in the era of fintech to strike a balance between financial innovation and risk mitigation, and construct a regulatory framework adapted to these challenges.

The expansion of the shadow banking system has exacerbated the latent threat of systemic financial risk. For instance, P2P lending platforms, operating outside the traditional regulatory frameworks and fraught with such problems as information asymmetry and adverse selection, have lots of accumulated risks. A series of internet finance incidents, such as the "Ezubao" fraud case (Ponzi scheme), have further exposed the vulnerabilities inherent in the shadow banking system. Integrating shadow banking into the regulatory framework and improving mechanisms such as functional regulation and look-through supervision have become pressing priorities for safeguarding financial stability.

3. Social Risks: Social Tensions Exacerbated by Increasing Inequality

Social risks, triggered by social contradictions intensified by growing inequality, reflect the imbalance of social structures and underscore the formidable challenges of social governance. The widening gap in income distribution has led to increasingly severe polarization between the rich and the poor, resulting in the continuous accumulation of social tensions. For example, the Occupy Wall Street movement in the US, which originated in New York, adopted the slogan "We are the 99%," highlighting issues of social injustice arising from the unequal distribution of wealth. A range of problems—from the scarcity of educational resources and disparities in employment opportunities to unequal access to social security and the inaccessibility of healthcare services—expose the latent risks inherent in an imbalanced social structure.

The decline in social mobility has also intensified structural contradictions such as class solidification. For instance, the phenomenon of "involution" (*tangping*, or "lie down" literally)—a topic that has sparked widespread discussion in Chinese society—reflects the state of excessive competition among social members in areas such as education and employment. The academic pressure in elite schools and the workplace dilemma of the "996"[1] work schedule all underscore the narrowing channels for upward mobility. How to break down identity barriers and improve mechanisms for interest articulation has become critical for mitigating social risks.

The crisis of social identity is also a major challenge facing contemporary society. The frequent occurrence of mass incidents and the prevalence of populism both reflect the lack of social consensus. For example, the highly controversial referendum of Brexit not only fractured British society but also exposed the corrosive impact of populism on social identity. From ethnic conflicts and regional antagonism to cultural barriers and religious tensions, social divisions are continuously widening. How to reconstruct social consensus and promote the inclusion of differences has become a central issue in the governance of social risks.

The intensification of the information cocoon effect and the resulting social fragmentation warrant serious vigilance. Algorithm-driven homogeneous information overload increasingly narrows channels for

---

1 It refers to working from 9 a.m. to 9 p.m., 6 days a week.

dialogue between different groups. For example, conspiracy theories triggered by 5G technology—widespread on social media—demonstrate how misinformation can distort social cognition. The echo chamber effect further exacerbates opinion polarization and deepens societal antagonism. Strengthening the accountability of internet platforms, improving mechanisms for misinformation governance, and fostering a healthy online environment are the urgent issues in contemporary risk management.

The inadequate protection of the rights and interests of vulnerable groups is also a significant source of social risk. For instance, the migrant workers—a unique group that has emerged during China's modernization process—face a series of challenges in urbanization, including housing, children's education, and social security. Problems such as the "difficulty migrant workers face in claiming wages" further highlight the fragility of the rights and interests of vulnerable groups. Enhancing the social policy system, strengthening inclusive and fundamental social welfare, and addressing shortcomings in the provision of basic public services are the foundational projects for fostering inclusive social development.

Section 4 The Rise of Intelligent Risks: Potential Crises of AI Technology

Previous research on intelligent risk has predominantly adopted a technological lens, exploring ways to reduce the probability of intelligent systems losing control through algorithm optimization and system design. However, as AI technologies are increasingly pervasive, their ethical, legal, and social impacts are becoming ever more pronounced. This chapter analyzes the multifaceted challenges encountered in the development of AI from three dimensions: algorithmic bias, data privacy, and the loss-of-control risk. Algorithmic bias arises from machine learning models inheriting and amplifying human social prejudices, and reflects the formidable challenges of AI ethics. The large-scale collection and utilization of personal information highlight significant dilemmas in data privacy protection. The uncertainty inherent in the autonomous evolution of AI systems further exacerbates the latent risks of intelligent systems spiraling out of control. The rapid iteration of intelligent technologies stands in stark contrast to the lag in ethical regulation, legal frameworks, and social cognition, underscoring the urgent need to reshape AI governance from multiple dimensions, including technological advancement for good, embedded ethics, rule-of-law regulation, and social communication. Only through the integration of humanistic care and the pursuit of technology for good can we effectively manage the risks associated with intelligence and usher in a trustworthy and controllable future for AI.

1. Algorithmic Bias: Inherent Flaws in Machine Learning Models

Algorithmic bias, an inherent flaw in machine learning models, not only underscores the limitations of AI technologies but also accentuates the complexities of intelligent risk management. Selective bias in training data inevitably causes algorithmic models to assimilate and perpetuate various social biases during the learning process. For example, in facial recognition technology, the absence of data from certain ethnic groups in training samples—essentially a "data bias"—results in discrepancies in recognition accuracy across people of different skin tones. From gender discrimination in employment to racial bias in the justice system, a wide range of issues underscore the challenges algorithmic bias poses to social fairness and justice.

Subjective assumptions in feature engineering further exacerbate the risk of algorithmic bias. Developers' value judgments in selecting feature variables are often deeply influenced by their own social backgrounds. For example, the inclusion of variables such as “parental criminal record” in crime prediction models reflects the entrenched notion of “original sin” in human society. In the domain of personal credit scoring, the emergence of the “digital redline” phenomenon has exposed the latent crisis of discrimination embedded within algorithms. How to embed ethical considerations into the algorithm development and construct an inclusive and equitable intelligent decision-making system has become a critical issue within the industry.

The opacity of black-box models exacerbates the challenges of algorithmic bias. Due to their complexity and lack of explainability, deep learning algorithms are often regarded as “black boxes.” The absence of transparency in the decision-making process makes it difficult to trace the origins of bias. For instance, in the field of intelligent healthcare, the application of deep learning algorithms in areas such as assisted diagnosis and medication recommendation has improved the efficiency of medical services, yet the internal logic of these systems remains difficult to interpret, errors are hard to trace, and the associated risks are significant. Achieving “explainable AI” and opening the algorithmic black box has become an exigency within the industry. Furthermore, the self-reinforcing nature of bias under feedback loops constitutes a critical latent risk in intelligent systems; biased algorithmic outputs influence subsequent data collection and processing, thereby creating a vicious cycle.

For instance, in the use of search engines, feedback from users’ click behavior data can result in the excessive exposure of certain categories of information, thereby aggravating the filter bubble effect. YouTube’s recommendation algorithm, due to its tendency toward “big data authoritarianism,” has become particularly controversial. How to avoid the amplification of algorithmic bias and ensure diversity in information dissemination has emerged as a critical issue within the industry.

The emergence of meta-bias issues has made the governance of algorithmic bias increasingly challenging. Biases formed during the training process of machine learning models can subtly influence subsequent iterations and upgrades of algorithms. For example, the gender stereotypes observed in Google Translate stem precisely from implicit biases embedded within vast training datasets. The phenomenon of meta-bias—ranging from teacher bias to student bias, and from old model bias to new model bias—renders the intergenerational transmission of intelligent risks even more covert. Breaking the vicious cycle of bias and preventing its continual self-reinforcement throughout algorithmic evolution has become a significant challenge facing the industry.

2. Data Privacy: A Major Challenge in Personal Information Protection

Data privacy, as a major challenge in the protection of personal information, highlights both the vulnerability of privacy rights in the era of big data and the formidable complexity of digital governance. While the large-scale collection and utilization of personal information have greatly facilitated the provision of personalized services, they have also given rise to a series of privacy risks such as data misuse and information leakage. The Cambridge Analytica incident serves as a pertinent example: Facebook user data was employed for political advertising without consent, sparking widespread public concern. Personal privacy has become a bargaining chip for commercial exploitation, with the rights of data subjects frequently infringed upon and the prospects for effective privacy protection remaining bleak.

The challenge of balancing data utilization and privacy protection poses a significant test for policymakers. On the one hand, the circulation and sharing of data serve as essential drivers of economic development and social innovation; on the other hand, safeguarding personal privacy remains an inviolable fundamental human right. How to stimulate data vitality while simultaneously constructing a robust firewall for privacy protection has become a major legislative issue. The introduction of the GDPR has, to some extent, strengthened the rights of data subjects. However, the effective implementation of provisions such as the right to data portability and the right to erasure still faces significant obstacles. Furthermore, superficial compliance and formalistic regulatory practices have highlighted numerous shortcomings in the current privacy protection and oversight mechanisms.

The pseudo-proposition of "de-identification" in big data further exacerbates the challenges of personal privacy protection. While data masking techniques can reduce the risk of privacy breaches to some extent, the aggregation and correlation of multi-source data still enable the re-identification of individuals. In the case of taxi data, even when pick-up and drop-off locations are anonymized, data mining techniques can be employed to infer sensitive information such as passengers' residential addresses and workplaces. With the (mis)use of such techniques as re-identifying individuals within datasets, constructing detailed user profiles, analyzing trajectory data and mapping social networks, personal privacy is becoming increasingly vulnerable to exposure. Breaking the vicious cycle of "anonymity and re-identification" and achieving a balance between data utility and privacy protection has emerged as a critical and complex challenge for the industry.

The implicit "privacy tax" under the free service model further marginalizes privacy rights. Internet platforms use free services as bait, enticing users to "voluntarily" surrender their privacy while enjoying convenience. From likes and comments on social media, to search histories on search engines, and from shopping preferences on e-commerce platforms to health data on fitness apps, personal information is wantonly harvested and reduced to raw material for commercial exploitation. Behind the façade of free services lies the covert erosion of privacy rights. How to reconstruct individual control over personal data and avoid the "free lunch" trap has become a critical and urgent challenge in the domain of privacy protection.

The applications of privacy computing technologies have brought new hope for the protection of personal privacy. Emerging privacy computing paradigms such as homomorphic encryption and secure multi-party computation provide technical support for data circulation and collaboration in an encrypted state. For example, federated learning, a distributed machine learning paradigm, enables collaborative modeling and utilization of multi-party data without the need to directly share raw data. A multifaceted approach, encompassing technological empowerment, institutional frameworks, regulatory coordination, and the cultivation of a privacy-conscious culture, is required to address the challenges of data privacy protection. The awareness of individuals in managing their privacy boundaries, the commitment of enterprises to respecting user privacy, and the dedication of society to safeguarding privacy rights collectively form a robust framework for privacy protection.

3. Loss-of-Control Risk: Uncertainty in AI Systems

The loss-of-control risk, an inherent uncertainty in AI systems, not only indicates the double-edged nature of intelligent technological development but also highlights the complexity of human-machine collaborative governance. While the autonomous learning and evolutionary capabilities of machine learning algorithms have significantly expanded the application boundaries of AI, they have also given rise to unpredictable risks of losing control. For instance, when confronted with complex road conditions, the decision-making logic of autonomous driving systems is often fraught with uncertainty. Ethical dilemmas akin to the "trolley problem" further test the value judgments and trade-off capabilities of algorithms. From prioritizing the protection of in-vehicle passengers to minimizing overall casualties, and from individual interests to the public good, the boundaries of algorithmic ethics are becoming increasingly blurred.

The opacity of algorithmic self-evolution further amplifies the uncertainty associated with the loss-of-control risk. The strategies developed by deep reinforcement learning agents during the training process often surpass the anticipations of human designers.

From AlphaGo's "move of God" to OpenAI Five's unexpected maneuvers in e-sports, the creative actions of algorithms have triggered concerns about the so-called "singularity." While the "Terminator" scenario—where machines break free from human control and ultimately dominate the world—may be somewhat sensationalized, it nonetheless serves as a reminder that the risk of AI systems running amok is not entirely unfounded. Achieving effective human-machine collaboration, while preserving the innovative potential of AI and clearly delineating the boundaries of algorithmic behavior, has emerged as a critical challenge for the industry.

The endogenous loss-of-control risks of algorithmic social governance based on big data also warrant serious attention. While the widespread application of machine learning algorithms in domains such as crime prediction, financial risk control, and social credit assessment can enhance the precision and efficiency of social governance, the rigidity and biases inherent in algorithmic logic may trigger outcomes akin to "digital authoritarianism." For instance, in predictive policing, algorithms utilizing historical crime data can facilitate targeted crime prevention; however, if these algorithms embed racial biases, they may in fact, aggravate inequities in law enforcement. Under the regime of big data "dictatorship," every stage—from data collection to analytical application—harbors the risk of AI spiraling out of control.

The phenomenon of model drift, which leads to decision biases, also highlights the dynamic risks inherent in AI systems. While machine learning models excel at fitting historical data, their decision logic may become biased when confronted with new data distributions and application contexts. For instance, in the financial sector, market environments are highly volatile, and historical data can hardly encompass all future risk scenarios. During periods when "black swan" events occur frequently, over-reliance on historical information becomes a critical vulnerability for machine learning models. Therefore, the capacity for continual learning in dynamic contexts has become a pivotal factor for the robustness of AI systems.

The existence of the algorithmic principal-agent problem renders the attribution of responsibility for the risks of intelligent system failures increasingly ambiguous. As proxies for human designers' intentions, machine learning algorithms frequently generate decision-makings that cannot be entirely attributed to human subjective intent. From liability in autonomous driving accidents to the illegality of algorithmic price discrimination, the boundary between human and machine agency is becoming ever more indistinct. The awkward absence of clearly defined responsible parties further exacerbates the risks of AI running out of control. Clarifying the boundaries of human and machine responsibility, and constructing a multidimensional risk governance framework that incorporates ex-ante prevention, continuous oversight, and ex-post accountability, pose significant challenges to policymakers and legislators.

Chapter Eleven Governance Strategies: Intelligent Risk Management in the Era of Generative AI

Generative AI is rapidly reshaping the landscape of production and everyday life. However, the proliferation of algorithmic black boxes and the spillover of intelligent risks have intensified the public trust crisis, posing unprecedented challenges to the governance of intelligent communication. This chapter, grounded in the profound transformation of the communication ecosystem in the era of generative AI, seeks to explore a consistent legal logic and systematically elucidates multidimensional governance approaches, including legal regulation, ethical evaluation, technological innovation, platform self-governance, social co-governance, and international cooperation. The aim is to resolve the causal paradoxes of intelligent risks and provide institutional frameworks for rebuilding digital trust and ensuring the steady and sustainable progress of the intelligent revolution. Ultimately, this chapter aspires to offer a systematic theoretical exposition of innovative concepts, methodologies, and pathways for the governance of intelligent communication, thereby contributing new disciplinary knowledge from communication studies and proposing Chinese solutions for reconstructing digital order in intelligent societies.

Section 1 Legal Regulation: Building the Legal Foundation for Generative AI Governance

The rapid advancement of generative AI technology creates numerous opportunities for social progress, while simultaneously challenging existing legal frameworks. Traditional legal rules are often insufficient to address the ethical risks and rights-related challenges arising from generative AI, which necessitates urgent innovation and improvement of current governance mechanisms. It is thus timely to construct a comprehensive, nuanced, and dynamic legal regulatory system. Such a system should be grounded in a clear understanding of the technological essence, balance the incentives for innovation with risk prevention, integrate the rigidity of legal norms with the flexibility of ethical considerations, and seek equilibrium between the protection of rights and the promotion of development. Only in this way can we establish a fundamental framework for the orderly development of generative AI, thereby upholding the rule of law and promoting justice in the age of intelligence. Legal regulation serves as the cornerstone of generative AI governance, and its construction requires the collective participation of legislators, law enforcement, the judiciary, and the broader public. On the one hand, legislation should embody foresight, specificity, and inclusiveness, leaving space for technological innovation. On the other hand, judicial practice should actively respond to contemporary demands, reflecting the ethical core of the law in case adjudication. Through persistent efforts, a sound legal ecosystem for generative AI can be cultivated to ensure its steady and far-reaching development in service of human well-being.

1. Legislation as a Priority: Establishing Regulatory Frameworks for Generative AI to Delineate Rights and Responsibilities

Generative AI, as an emerging technology, is developing rapidly and being widely applied, thereby posing new challenges and requirements for existing legal systems.[1] The formulation of regulatory frameworks specifically targeting generative AI has become an urgent priority in the

---

1 CHENG, Le. Legal regulation of generative artificial intelligence: a perspective centered on ChatGPT[J]. Journal of Political Science and Law, 2023 (4): 69-80.

legal development of various countries. Such legislation must be grounded in a clear understanding of the technical characteristics of generative AI, with a primary focus on delineating the rights and responsibilities, while also balancing the diverse imperatives of fostering innovation, mitigating risks, and safeguarding users' rights and interests.

Specifically, the regulation and legislation of generative AI should focus on the following aspects. First, the legal status and responsibility for generative AI systems should be clarified. Given the autonomy, unpredictability, and creativity exhibited by generative AI, it is necessary to re-examine the adequacy of the "instrumental theory" in regulating such systems and to explore the possibility of conferring quasi-legal subject status upon them.[1] For infringements arising from algorithmically generated content, developers and operators should bear corresponding liabilities.[2] Second, the development and use of relevant data and computational resources should be regulated and strictly limited. Compliance reviews of training data for LLMs such as ChatGPT should be strengthened to curb the widespread misuse of data and the infringement of personal information.[3] Necessary restrictions should be imposed to prevent monopolization of computational resources.[4] Third, the intellectual property regime should be improved. The current intellectual property system lacks adequate protection for AI-generated content. There is an

---

1 LIU, Zhenyu. Legal regulation of generative artificial intelligence: recognition or redistribution[J]. Local Legislation Studies, 2023, 8(4): 36-52.
2 ZHOU, Xiaomei, CHEN, Yanxia. Copyright protection of AI-generated content: a perspective based on the tool attribute of artificial intelligence[J]. Communication and Copyright, 2021 (11): 112-117.
3 ZHANG, Ping. Breakthrough innovation in generative artificial intelligence requires sound laws and good governance: taking the legality of data training as an example[J]. New Economy Guide, 2023 (8): 26-28.
4 GHOSH, A., LAKSHMI, D. Dual governance: the intersection of centralized regulation and crowdsourced safety mechanisms for generative AI[J]. arXiv Preprint arXiv: 2308.04448, 2023.

urgent need to clarify the rules regarding the attribution of rights for AI-generated content and to refine standards for creativity and copyrightability. It is worth drawing on the amendments to Japan's Copyright Act and adopting a "deemed authorship" model for rights protection. Fourth, the mechanism for regulatory coordination should be improved. Given the inherent complexity and global impact of generative AI technologies, it is difficult for any single department to oversee them comprehensively and effectively. Legislative efforts should be directed toward establishing an inclusive and prudent multi-agency collaborative regulatory mechanism. Contingency plans should also be formulated to address issues such as cross-border data flows and legal conflicts.

Internationally, generative AI regulatory legislation, exemplified by the EU's Artificial Intelligence Act and the US's Algorithmic Accountability Act, has already commenced. Although the specific content of these regulations varies in emphasis, they all demonstrate a pragmatic, prudent, and balanced approach. China's legislation on generative AI can draw upon valuable international experience, while also being grounded in its domestic legal context, to address contemporary challenges, and establish a robust legal foundation to ensure the orderly development of the generative AI industry.

2. Rights Protection: Safeguarding Citizens' Legal Rights in the AI Era and Improving Infringement Remediation Mechanisms

The rapid development of generative AI technologies has provided new avenues for the realization of citizens' rights in the digital age; but at the same time, it has also engendered numerous risks of infringement. The large-scale collection and utilization of personal data during the training of foundational models such as ChatGPT may violate individuals' rights to privacy and data sovereignty. Algorithmically generated content may infringe upon citizens' personality rights such as reputation and portrait rights. Furthermore, the ambiguous attribution of intellectual property rights in AI-generated works may undermine the economic interests of original creators. Confronted with such complex forms of infringement, it is imperative to establish and refine remedial mechanisms aimed at protecting citizens' legitimate rights and interests.

Procedurally, existing regulations such as GDPR can serve as references to establish mechanisms for prior consent and post hoc remedies that cover all stages of data collection, processing, storage, and use. In response to privacy infringements in algorithmic decision-making, procedural rights such as the "right to explanation" and the "right to object" should be established, thereby strengthening judicial review of issues like algorithmic discrimination and algorithmic violence. Substantively, the attribution principles and evaluation criteria of traditional tort liability should be reconstructed in light of the specific characteristics of generative AI technologies. The Civil Code of the People's Republic of China and its judicial interpretations can serve as the bases to redefine both developers and deployment operators as tort liability subjects, and to refine rules concerning fault determination, causality assessment, and grounds for exemption from liability.[1] At the same time, a punitive damages regime may be instituted to increase the cost of violations. Regarding intellectual property disputes arising from AI-generated content, it is advisable to balance incentives for innovation with the promotion of dissemination, and take into account the interests of all stakeholders. The regulatory approaches for deepfake technologies can be drawn on to develop a comprehensive regime encompassing ex ante review, ongoing monitoring,

---

1 LU, Binghong. On the Copyright Protection of Artificial Intelligence-Generated Works[D]. Changchun: Jilin University, 2021.

and ex post accountability.[1]

In terms of remedies, apart from judicial avenues, the advantages of non-litigation dispute resolution mechanisms such as arbitration and mediation can be leveraged to provide parties with more flexible and efficient redress. For example, the United Kingdom (UK) has established an independent arbitration tribunal specifically for handling tort disputes arising from social media and other internet platforms. In China, it is feasible to develop a specialized online dispute resolution mechanism for generative AI-related cases based on the existing framework of internet courts. Additionally, given the current public's limited awareness of the risks associated with AI technologies, it is necessary to intensify science communication efforts, promote awareness of data rights protection, and enhance individuals' capacity for self-advocacy. Lowering the cost of rights protection is essential to forming a virtuous cycle of effective governance.

Therefore, the protection of citizens' legitimate rights and interests constitutes an essential element in establishing the legal foundation for the governance of generative AI. Only by addressing the root causes of risk, strengthening ex-ante prevention, and improving ex-post remedies can an institutional balance be achieved between fostering innovation and safeguarding rights. This, in turn, will ensure the well-being of citizens in the era of intelligent technology.

3. Ethical Reflection: Integrating Ethical Considerations into the Legal Framework to Establish Value Orientation for Generative AI

As a disruptive technology, generative AI should not be driven solely

---

1 LEE, K., COOPER, A. F., GRIMMELMANN, J. Talking about AI generation: copyright and the generative-AI supply chain (The short version)[C]. Proceedings of the Symposium on Computer Science and Law. 2024: 48-63.

by utilitarian motivations in its development and application; rather, its value orientation must be clearly defined by ethical boundaries. Admittedly, ethics and law belong to different domains, yet they ultimately share the fundamental objective of upholding human dignity and promoting social justice. Integrating ethical considerations into the legal framework governing generative AI not only strengthens its normative function but also facilitates the alignment and unification of legal values with moral ideals.

Specifically, legislation on generative AI governance should address the following ethical issues. First, the problem of "algorithmic bias." Currently, language models such as GPT-3 exhibit biases in training data selection related to gender, race, and other factors, which may lead to the model generating discriminatory statements.[1] In this regard, legislation should strengthen ethical review of model training and data selection, incorporating anti-discrimination as a fundamental requirement in algorithm design. Second, the issue of "algorithmic discrimination." AI systems may aggravate the digital divide and undermine fairness and justice by making differentiated decisions about individuals based on user profiling and other mechanisms.[2] Therefore, legislation should clearly delineate the boundary between reasonable differential treatment and algorithmic discrimination, and establish the principle of equality protection. Furthermore, the protection of privacy rights is a critical concern. While technical measures such as de-identification and other forms of data anonymization are important, it is even more essential from the ethical perspective to clarify the definition and boundaries of personal information, as well as the

1 MENG, Lingyu. From algorithmic bias to algorithmic discrimination: an inquiry into the responsibility issues of algorithmic discrimination[J]. Journal of Northeastern University (Social Science Edition), 2022, 24 (1): 1-9.
2 LI, Zhiying. The two faces of algorithmic discrimination and its legal regulation[J]. Jiaoda Law Review, 2024 (1): 148-161.

legitimacy conditions for its collection and use.[1] At the same time, it is necessary to guard against the risks of "individual profiling" and "surveillance" inherent in automated decision-making processes. In the domain of content generation, the concerns raised by ChatGPT regarding "content rewriting" and "fake news" also demand an urgent legislative response. Content authenticity review can be incorporated into platform responsibilities, curbing the abuse of technologies such as deepfakes while encouraging innovation.[2]

It is undeniable that, due to the complexity of technology and the plurality of ethical perspectives, the integration of ethical considerations into generative AI legislation cannot be achieved overnight. As a feasible approach, the concept of "ethics by design" can serve as the basis for embedding ethical principles such as privacy protection, fairness and non-discrimination, and transparency and controllability in throughout the entire lifecycle of AI system development, deployment, and application. At the same time, the ethical impact assessment mechanism, modeled after environmental impact assessments, can be employed to strengthen ex-ante review of generative AI projects. For decisions involving significant public interest, a stakeholder participation mechanism can be incorporated to address diverse demands. Furthermore, in adjudicating individual cases, ethical considerations should also be emphasized, balancing case-specific justice with legal certainty.

Looking ahead, ethical reflection and technological innovation should advance in tandem, jointly driving the construction of an inclusive and prudent governance framework for generative AI. Law, as the cornerstone

---

1 SONG, Weixue. Research on Raising Ethical Requirements for Generative Artificial Intelligence [J]. Management and Administration, 2024 (6): 1-11.

2 HEALY, M. Approaches to generative artificial intelligence: a social justice perspective[J]. arXiv Preprint arXiv: 2309.12331, 2023.

of social norms, ought to address proactively ethical considerations to guide the sustainable and responsible development of generative AI for the benefit of humanity. Only in this way can the dialectical unity of rule of law and moral governance be realized, collectively shaping a promising vision for the intelligent era.

Section 2 Technological Innovation: Advancing Generative AI Risk Management through Innovative Approaches

While generative AI technologies are unleashing digital productivity and stimulating innovation, their potential safety and security risks and ethical dilemmas have become increasingly prominent. Issues such as algorithmic opacity, data bias, and uncontrolled content, if left unchecked, may not only erode fairness and justice but also undermine the very foundations of technological development. Therefore, innovating risk prevention and control of generative AI and proactively addressing the multifaceted challenges posed by technological advancement have become a shared consensus and responsibility across sectors. Only by systematically enhancing its algorithms, safety, security, and traceability, strengthening its explainability and robustness, and building a comprehensive closed-loop accountability framework, can we cultivate a fertile ground for the sustainable development of generative AI. This is not only crucial for the future of the digital economy, but also for the trajectory of human civilization.

1. Algorithm Optimization: Developing Safe, Secure and Controllable Algorithms to Enhance Generative AI Robustness

Algorithmic optimization serves as the critical engine propelling generative AI toward safety, security and controllability. Indeed, from

EleutherAI's GPT-Neo to OpenAI's ChatGPT, contemporary generative AI algorithms have made significant advancements. Nevertheless, in the face of increasingly salient safety and security risks and ethical dilemmas, it is imperative to address these challenges through algorithmic optimization. This approach aims to overcome the "black box" problem inherent in deep learning, elucidate causal inference mechanisms, and enhance robustness and explainability, ultimately achieving a "transparent box" that is amenable to prudent oversight and regulatory governance.

In terms of specific approaches, the adversarial machine learning can be utilized to enhance AI models' robustness against interference by introducing adversarial examples and similar techniques, thereby improving their stability when confronted with unknown environments and malicious inputs. For example, the Invariant Risk Minimization algorithm mitigates AI models' overfitting to highly variable environments by constructing loss functions under different conditions. Data augmentation techniques can increase the diversity of training data, thus enhancing the models' generalization capabilities. In the training of GPT-3.5, OpenAI adopted the Self-Instruct dialogue data to expand the range of task scenarios while ensuring data quality.

In addition, we must focus on enhancing the causal reasoning capabilities of algorithms. Unlike current large models such as GPT-3, which primarily rely on correlation-based predictions, causal language models are able to uncover causal dependencies among variables, thereby enabling reliable predictions even in small-sample scenarios. This is of significant importance for improving model robustness and strengthening explainability, and to some extent, it also helps prevent models from making biased decisions based on erroneous data associations. The Constitutional AI framework recently proposed by Anthropic aims to endow AI models with causal reasoning and ethical deliberation abilities, and the

Claude model trained under this framework has preliminarily demonstrated encouraging "moral guidelines."

Furthermore, by optimizing model training paradigms and adopting privacy-preserving technologies such as federated learning and privacy computing, it is possible to mitigate the risk of the Matthew Effect to a certain extent. This approach provides equal opportunities for small and medium-sized enterprises as well as startup teams to participate, thereby stimulating grassroots innovation. Additionally, exploring the application of blockchain technology in model training and lifecycle management can enhance end-to-end traceability. Moreover, strengthening mechanisms for algorithmic iteration and updates, and establishing comprehensive systems for algorithm registration, filing, and review, thereby leveraging external regulation to enforce intrinsic security, are also critical components for optimizing these processes.

The optimization of generative AI algorithms is by no means an overnight achievement; it requires collaborative efforts from industry, academia, and research communities to overcome complex challenges. While pursuing technological innovation, equal attention must be paid to ethical values, regulatory frameworks, and societal needs to establish a governance model for generative AI that is autonomous, controllable, safe, secure, and trustworthy. This, in turn, will lay a solid foundation for the development of digital civilization. Looking ahead, algorithmic innovation should steadfastly adhere to the core principle of human-centricity, acting as both a driver of responsible technology and a catalyst for advancing human well-being.

2. Safety and Security Protection: Building a Multi-layered AI Safety & Security Protection Framework to Strengthen Systemic Immunity

The safety and security protection of generative AI systems constitutes a complex challenge, necessitating a multi-layered approach that encompasses data, algorithms, hardware, and applications to construct a robust and resilient security framework. At present, with the iterative evolution of technologies such as NLP and computer vision, generative AI models exhibit new characteristics, including massive parameter scales, high data demands, and concentrated computational resources. These developments introduce significant safety and security risks that warrant serious attention. Biases inherent in training data may cause models to inherit prejudices and produce harmful outputs; the inherent vulnerabilities of models may be exploited by malicious actors to conduct adversarial attacks; and latent defects in hardware systems can result in severe consequences such as chip backdoors and supply chain contamination.[1] As such, it is imperative to adhere to the principles of "proactive immunity and precise prevention and control," and to establish a multi-dimensional safety and security protection system characterized by defense-in-depth, dynamic situational awareness, and real-time response.

At the data layer, safety and security audits should be reinforced throughout the processes of training data collection, cleaning, and processing. Techniques such as differential privacy and homomorphic encryption can be employed to achieve data usability without visibility,

---

1 NEUPANE, S., FERNANDEZ, I. A, MITTAL, S., et al. Impacts and risk of generative AI technology on cyber defense[J]. arXiv Preprint arXiv: 2306.13033, 2023.

thereby maximizing the protection of privacy.[1] By leveraging technologies such as Trusted Execution Environments (TEE) and federated learning to construct privacy-preserving sandboxes, collaborative modeling can be achieved without requiring data to leave its local environment. Additionally, it is necessary to establish data provenance mechanisms and utilize technologies such as blockchain and digital watermarking to record the traceability of data flows, and facilitate subsequent audits. At the algorithmic layer, formal verification and fuzz testing can be utilized to specifically detect and remediate algorithmic vulnerabilities, thereby enhancing robustness. The introduction of adversarial examples can further strengthen AI models' resilience to perturbations. Techniques such as model encryption and secure multi-party computation can prevent model theft and tampering. Furthermore, it is essential to intensify algorithmic ethical reviews to prevent the models from learning or amplifying erroneous value systems.

At the hardware level, it is essential to strengthen the autonomous controllability of key components such as chips and to improve a trustworthy supply chain system. Technologies such as reconfigurable computing and homomorphic encryption should be leveraged to achieve privacy protection and safety and security governance through cloud-edge-end collaboration. In anticipation of the cryptographic security challenges that may arise from quantum computing, proactive measures must also be taken. At the application level, it is necessary to implement scenario-specific policies and conduct specialized safety and security assessments for typical applications such as content generation, decision support, and interactive responses, in order to prevent potential risks. For

---

1 TANG, Fengyi, LIU, Jian, WANG, Huimei, et al. A deep learning training data generation scheme for data privacy protection[J]. Computer Applications and Research, 2021, 38 (7): 2009-2012.

example, ChatGPT has previously generated inappropriate content involving violence and pornography due to the lack of effective content moderation mechanisms. To mitigate similar risks, a human-machine collaborative review process can be adopted, supplemented by clearly defined boundaries of applicability and disclaimers. Furthermore, establishing a hierarchical and categorized application safety and security management system and enhancing end-to-end traceability are also important measures to prevent misuse and abuse.

Overall, there is no local optimum in generative AI safety and security; only a global optimum can be achieved. It is essential to advance technological innovation and institutional design in tandem. While it is necessary to strengthen defenses by "mitigating" risks, it is equally important to stimulate vitality by "facilitating" responsible use. Only through collective wisdom and concerted efforts from all sectors, and by advancing prudently within an open and inclusive environment, can we attain a dynamic balance between development, safety and security, thereby establishing a trustworthy and controllable safety and security assurance system for generative AI. This will, in turn, safeguard the high-quality development of the digital economy. Looking to the future, the path to AI security remains long and challenging, demanding our resolve and courage to forge ahead, and to chart a new course for digital civilization guided by the principle of "technology for good."

3. End-to-End Traceability Mechanism: Establishing a Comprehensive Traceability Framework for Generative AI to Enhance Accountability and Facilitate Risk Mitigation

Establishing a comprehensive traceability mechanism throughout the entire generative AI lifecycle is a critical safeguard for achieving holistic risk prevention and precise accountability. Admittedly, given the high degree of autonomy, large parameter scale, and numerous training stages inherent to generative AI systems, implementing end-to-end traceability is no easy task. Nevertheless, in the face of phenomena such as uncontrolled content generation and rampant model misappropriation, only by integrating each stage—data acquisition, model training, content generation, and application deployment—into a closed-loop management system that ensures "traceable origins and accountable destinations," can effective governance be realized. This approach is essential to ensuring that generative AI develops in a safe, secure and healthy manner under transparent oversight.

In the selection of provenance tracing pathways, blockchain technology stands out as a powerful tool. By leveraging blockchain's immutable and traceable sequential database, it is possible to construct an "AI genealogy" system that encompasses key elements such as algorithmic models, training data, and generated content, thereby recording the entire lifecycle footprint and clarifying the attribution of rights and responsibilities. For example, by deploying smart contracts to delineate the boundaries of responsibility among participating entities and embedding necessary auditing interfaces, an integrated framework for process supervision and post hoc accountability can be established. During the data acquisition phase, technologies such as digital watermarking and privacy-preserving computation can be employed to "label" data, ensuring transparency of data provenance and traceability of data flows. In the model training phase, the iterative process of algorithms can be securely recorded and solidified to prevent unauthorized tampering. Regarding content generation, critical information such as the time of creation and the identity of the producer can be documented using trusted timestamps and electronic signatures. In application scenarios, the introduction of trusted execution environments can further clarify the responsibilities of all parties involved. Should issues such as model misuse or illegal content arise, the responsible entity can be rapidly identified and dealt with in accordance with laws and regulations.

It is not difficult to discern that the successful implementation of blockchain-based provenance solutions relies on the synergistic integration of cryptographic technologies such as trusted timestamps, multi-party computation, and TEE. This also necessitates the organic incorporation of mechanisms including autonomous consensus, incentive-compatible game theory, and Sybil attack resistance. At the same time, it is essential to fully consider the differentiated demands of various scenarios, striving to maximize data value while safeguarding model intellectual property, and to foster innovation while ensuring content moderation and compliance. Moreover, the development of standards and regulations in the domain of AI provenance remains lagging; there is an urgent need to formulate unified norms, drawing on existing achievements in software provenance and tailoring them to the unique characteristics of AI systems, so as to provide a foundational regulatory framework for cross-sectoral collaboration.

From a holistic perspective, as the digital ecosystem rapidly evolves, generative AI holds immense potential to transform both production and daily life, while simultaneously introducing new regulatory challenges and safety and security risks. By establishing robust end-to-end traceability mechanisms and embedding a "safety and security DNA," it is possible to achieve a dialectical balance between innovation and risk management. The journey toward comprehensive AI traceability remains arduous and demands collaborative efforts across government, industry, academia, and research sectors to foster co-construction, co-governance, and shared benefits. The surge of generative AI is not only a challenge but also an opportunity. We should therefore leverage traceability as a pathway to unlock new drivers of the digital economy and compose a new chapter in the advancement of human civilization.

Section 3 Platform Autonomy: Empowering Platforms to Implement Intelligent Risk Management

1. Guideline Development: Independent Formulation of Standards by Platforms for the Creation and Dissemination of Generative AI Content

As pivotal hubs for intelligent content creation and dissemination, generative AI platforms play a critical role amid the current wave of technological innovation. Their autonomous formulation of content guidelines is not only a matter of corporate reputation and social responsibility but also fundamental to the healthy evolution of the industry ecosystem. Indeed, with the rapid iteration of generative AI tools—exemplified by ChatGPT—traditional content moderation mechanisms are encountering significant challenges. The exponential surge in intelligent content production has rendered manual review increasingly inadequate, while cross-modal and cross-domain content generation has outpaced the capacity of existing regulatory frameworks. As such, platforms must respond decisively and adaptively to the new situation, leveraging their unique capabilities and aligning with prevailing trends to explore and establish content production and dissemination standards that are ethically sound and attuned to the developmental realities. By doing so, platforms can set a precedent for regulatory compliance and self-discipline, thereby fostering a demonstrative effect that contributes to the orderly operation of the generative AI sector as a whole.

The formulation of guidelines must be explicitly oriented and operationalized with detailed pathways. On the one hand, platforms should internalize the core social values and manifest them in practice, positioning the cultivation of a civilized digital ethos as a guiding principle. They must take a clear stance against harmful content such as misinformation, pornography, and violence, as well as resolutely oppose behaviors like algorithmic abuse and model theft. Simultaneously, they are encouraged to actively promote the generation of positive content that is closely linked to public welfare and real-world issues, leveraging AI to interpret and embody contemporary values. On the other hand, platforms need to fully consider the unique characteristics of AI-generated content. Building upon the strengths of traditional regulatory frameworks, they should adapt and enrich the guidelines with a developmental perspective and innovative thinking. For example, given the tendency of AI-generated content to be broad but lacking depth, it is advisable to increase the weighting of indicators such as "empathy." In response to the proliferation of cross-modal deepfakes, requirements for intelligent watermarking and source identification can be refined for different modalities, including text, audio, and video. To address risks associated with falsification, deception, theft, and copyright infringement in generative content, the delineation of rights and responsibilities among platforms, developers, and users should be clarified.

The implementation of guidelines requires systematic design and enhanced overall coordination. It is essential to integrate technological governance with humanistic care, and to give equal emphasis to both rigid regulations and flexible guidance. In the research and development phase, a knowledge base of content guideline can be established by leveraging large model parameter-sharing platforms to provide a foundational resource for compliant content generation. During the training phase, guideline requirements should be embedded into the optimization functions of training objectives to enable simultaneous identification of harmful content and optimization of generation strategies. In the application phase, the advantages of human-machine collaboration should be fully utilized by adopting a spiral escalation pathway of "early warning tagging, manual review, and iterative feedback," thereby forming a more precise and dynamic closed-loop intelligent review system. At the same time, comprehensive assessment, evaluation, and accountability mechanisms should be established and refined, incorporating content compliance as a key performance indicator for platforms and developers to enforce implementation through reverse pressure.

It is undeniable that, in the complex and multifaceted digital era, the autonomous formulation of generative AI content guidelines by platforms cannot be achieved overnight. Only by anchoring these efforts in digital humanities, with ethics as the "core" and good governance as the "imperative," can we forge ahead in the dynamic landscape of human-machine interaction and sustain progress along the continuum of algorithmic ethics. The vessel of generative AI has already set sail, calling for collective action and harnessing innovation to activate new dynamics in information dissemination, and shape the evolving landscape of digital civilization. We should unite to embark on this new journey of intelligent communication and collaboratively forge a promising future for the digital age.

2. Human Intervention: Establishing a Human-Machine Collaborative Review Mechanism to Curb the Spread of Harmful Information

While generative AI platforms reap the dividends of intelligence, they simultaneously face the severe challenge of the proliferation of harmful information. The massive volume of synthetic content generated by large models such as ChatGPT has bred new grounds for illicit activities such as rumor-mongering, gambling, and fraud. Once disseminated through these platforms, such harmful information can spread exponentially and erode the foundational values of society. In response, platforms must take proactive and anticipatory measures, assuming responsibility and leveraging the dynamics of the AI era. It is imperative to explore intelligent content moderation mechanisms characterized by human-machine collaboration and dynamic evolution, in order to promptly detect and curb the dissemination of harmful information and resolutely safeguard the ideological security frontier.

The development of a human-machine collaborative review mechanism should be grounded in the contextual scenarios of generative AI, building upon traditional content moderation experience while leveraging the advantages of AI technologies and adapting to local conditions and evolving trends. On the one hand, iterative advances in cutting-edge technologies such as machine learning and knowledge graphs provide new avenues for the training and optimization of intelligent moderation models. Platforms can employ algorithms from NLP and computer vision to achieve precise identification and real-time interception of cross-modal harmful information. For instance, constructing multi-dimensional text representations using contrastive learning algorithms can effectively detect highly covert harmful content such as "soft pornography" and "implicit gambling." On the other hand, in response to limitations such as algorithmic bias and the "black box" nature of intelligent moderation, platforms should establish mechanisms for human intervention, including pre-emptive warnings, real-time review, and post-event handling. Through human-AI interaction and iterative feedback, the accuracy of content moderation can be continuously improved. For example, dedicated human review teams can be established to re-examine content flagged as potentially harmful by machines, thereby forming an upward spiral process of "early warning and reporting, human judgment, and feedback optimization."

The implementation of human-machine collaborative review requires the integrated consideration of legal, rational, and emotional dimensions, and the adoption of multidimensional strategies. It is essential to uphold a bottom-line mindset by strictly handling illegal and harmful information—such as rumors, defamation, pornography, and violence—in accordance with laws and regulations. At the same time, it is necessary to dialectically address issues such as algorithmic false positives and excessive intervention, seeking a balance between maintaining public order and good customs and safeguarding legitimate freedom of expression. For identified harmful information, corresponding measures should be taken based on the severity of the risk. For minor infractions, preliminary interventions such as warnings or interviews may be conducted to prompt self-correction and internal review. For egregious violations, decisive actions—including post deletion, account suspension, and referral to law enforcement agencies—should be implemented. The advantages of intelligent technologies should be proactively leveraged to ensure timely evidence preservation and digital archiving, thereby providing a robust digital evidence chain for administrative and judicial proceedings. Simultaneously, platforms must effectively enhance their technological governance capabilities by embedding harmful content identification mechanisms into key processes such as human-machine dialogue and content recommendation. By optimizing algorithmic models and decentralizing management focus, a more robust and comprehensive technological barrier against harmful information can be established.

From a holistic perspective, human-machine collaborative review is an essential component of intelligent governance and cannot be achieved overnight. Only by grounding efforts in the current stage of development and attuning them to the prevailing trends, and striking a dynamic balance between encouraging innovation and exercising prudent inclusivity, can we both empower generative AI to reach its full potential and implement the necessary safeguards to ensure its safety and security. As we enter a new era of intelligent communication, platforms bear an inescapable responsibility. We must leverage the opportunities presented by human-machine collaboration to uphold core values, promote the rule of law, and forge ahead amidst challenges. Through effective governance and principled innovation, we can pave a broad and promising path for the advancement of digital civilization.

3. User Empowerment: Enhancing User Risk Awareness Education and Fostering a Collaborative and Trustworthy Digital Ecosystem

While generative AI empowers intelligent communication, it simultaneously imposes higher demands on users' media literacy. Admittedly, intelligent tools such as ChatGPT offer the public unprecedented convenience in participating in content creation. However, the proliferation of counterfeit information and the rampant spread of algorithmic biases have become a "Sword of Damocles" hanging over users. In response, platforms, while practicing self-governance, should also assume the responsibility of empowering users and promoting their risk awareness, thereby fostering a healthy digital ecosystem characterized by mutual trust, collaboration, and co-governance.

User empowerment should adhere to a needs-oriented approach, implementing targeted strategies for specific user groups and delivering precise interventions. For digital natives, risk prevention skills can be embedded into immersive and interactive experiences through innovative media channels such as short videos and virtual influencers, thereby integrating education with entertainment. For middle-aged and elderly users, empathetic design—such as features that allow adult children to authenticate on behalf of their parents—can provide appropriate protection while respecting privacy. For adolescents, the focus should be on value-driven guidance, leveraging the exemplary role of positive models and conducting diverse forms of peer education. Furthermore, differentiated demands across user groups should be addressed by offering personalized risk alerts and safety and security services tailored to individual needs, thereby enhancing users' sense of empowerment and satisfaction.

User empowerment requires collaborative efforts to establish a diversified co-governance framework. Digital platforms should proactively engage in cross-sectoral cooperation, forming synergies with government agencies, educational institutions, and parents to jointly foster a clean and upright cyberspace. For instance, platforms can collaborate with educational authorities to develop "Generative AI Literacy" curricula, integrating risk awareness education into the information technology syllabus at primary and secondary school levels. Additionally, they can initiate "AI for Good" parent training camps, providing guardians with empowerment toolkits. At the same time, it is essential to explore flexible and interactive educational approaches, such as showcasing exemplary cases and sharing real-world examples, to enhance the appeal and impact of educational initiatives. Furthermore, platforms should establish both online and offline interactive communities, encouraging users to participate in experience sharing and feedback, thereby facilitating the precise alignment of supply and demand.

User empowerment is by no means an overnight process; it urgently requires the stimulation of intrinsic motivation for self-governance. The transition from external regulation to self-discipline hinges on the establishment of institutionalized channels for user participation. Platforms should further refine community guidelines, clearly delineating the boundaries of user rights and responsibilities, innovate incentive and penalty mechanisms to encourage lawful and self-disciplined behavior, and improve appeals processes to safeguard users' legitimate rights and interests. At the same time, it is essential to enhance the transparency of information disclosure—by providing feedback on user behavioral preferences and algorithmic recommendation outcomes—to strengthen users' autonomy over their actions. In response to potential risks, timely push notifications should be delivered to raise users' risk awareness. Furthermore, an open and inclusive environment should be fostered, providing space for personalized user expression and achieving co-creation and sharing through respect for diversity.

Building a clean and healthy cyberspace is a collective responsibility, and empowering users plays a crucial role in achieving this goal. In the era of generative AI, collaborative action across sectors is essential. Good governance should serve as the "rudder," and rule of law as the "compass," so as to activate positive momentum through iterative advancement, and forge new communication paradigms through mutual trust and co-governance. We should embrace empowerment as the foundation of our actions, and education as the key to enlightenment, thus pooling collective strength to advance digital civilization and sustain the modernization of cyberspace governance. As we dispel the fog of AI, the future grows ever more promising. User empowerment will catalyze a transformation in information dissemination, bringing the vision of a digital utopia within reach.

Section 4 Social Co-Governance: Harnessing Collective Efforts across Sectors to Build Synergistic Management

Platform self-governance, a crucial pathway for intelligent risk management, has empowered the field of generative AI to soar to new heights. This emerging concept embodies profound significance and practical value. It originates from the broader transformation of digital space governance structures and is anchored in the value proposition of platform accountability. As pivotal arenas for the production and dissemination of intelligent content, generative AI platforms bear the responsibility of guiding the healthy development of the industry. Only by leveraging their intrinsic strengths and proactively driving institutional innovation can these platforms strengthen their ethical foundations amid the uncertainties of algorithmic ethics, thereby fulfilling their responsibilities for effective governance in the pursuit of multi-stakeholder co-governance. Platform self-governance calls for adaptive institutional frameworks, dynamic human-machine collaboration, and user-centered empowerment practices, thereby continuously fostering a new paradigm of intelligent communication characterized by co-construction, shared benefits, mutual trust, and collaborative governance.

1. Multi-stakeholder Participation: Encouraging Broad Involvement of the Public, Media, Experts, and Other Stakeholders in Generative AI Governance

Governance of generative AI, a disruptive technological paradigm, is far from a solo performance by a single actor; rather, it resembles a symphony involving the collective participation of the entire society. While governments and platforms bear inescapable responsibilities, it is the broad engagement of diverse stakeholders—including the public, media, and academia—that constitutes the crucial fulcrum for enabling effective governance. Such pluralistic participation not only helps clarify stakeholder interests and build a foundation of shared consensus, but also facilitates the aggregation of collective intelligence and resources, thereby inaugurating a new era of collaborative social governance.

Public participation is the wellspring of good governance. As both direct beneficiaries and potential victims of generative AI technologies, the public is entitled to legitimate channels for expressing their concerns and participating in decision-making. For instance, in the regulatory formulation, public opinion can be widely solicited through legislative hearings and public consultations. In risk assessment, the public can be mobilized for reporting and oversight, facilitating the timely identification of issues such as algorithmic bias and privacy infringements. In educational outreach, interactive approaches such as scenario simulations and sandbox exercises can vividly illustrate the essentials of safe AI usage. At the same time, both online and offline platforms should be established to encourage public engagement in dialogue, negotiation, complaints, and rights protection, fostering routine and sustained interaction. Furthermore, inclusive and equitable participation opportunities should be provided for vulnerable groups, ensuring that the dividends of intelligence benefit everyone.

Media participation serves as the authoritative voice in promoting good governance. As a vital bridge connecting the government and the public, the media bears an indispensable social responsibility in guiding public opinion and disseminating knowledge. On the one hand, the media should exercise its agenda-setting function by focusing on pressing issues such as algorithmic failures and model misuse, thereby urging relevant stakeholders to conduct governance in accordance with laws and regulations. On the other hand, the media should fully leverage the advantages of integrated media communication, enhancing audience engagement and sense of participation through immersive reporting and interactive Q&A formats. Furthermore, the media must adhere to professional ethics, employing rigorous and meticulous investigative methods to uncover the truth, and guiding social expectations with rational and composed discourse. In the complex and dynamic digital era, the media should champion mainstream values and foster the dissemination of positive information.

Academic participation serves as a vital source of intellectual inspiration for good governance. Academic institutions such as universities and think tanks can bring together experts and scholars from diverse fields, forming a core force for advancing interdisciplinary collaboration and innovation. Scholars in the humanities and social sciences—including philosophy, law, ethics, and psychology—can provide intellectual support for the governance of generative AI from a macro perspective, addressing issues such as social impact and ethical risks. Meanwhile, scholars in science and engineering disciplines—such as computer science and cybernetics—can focus on technical dimensions such as model optimization and security evaluation, to diagnose and manage intelligent risks. For example, dedicated AI ethics research centers could be established to systematically explore interdisciplinary theoretical frameworks. Cross-disciplinary expert advisory panels could be formed to offer recommendations for decision-making and policy evaluation. Regular academic conferences and the publication of advisory reports would further facilitate the translation and application of research outcomes.

There are no bystanders in collaborative social governance; every sector serves as a vital driving force. Only when diverse actors unite and form a synergistic alliance can endogenous motivation be activated, thus pioneering a new paradigm of co-construction, co-governance, and shared benefits. This participatory governance is, in essence, a process of reinvention characterized by legally defined rights and responsibilities, as well as coordinated efficiency. The government should innovate institutional mechanisms and further broaden channels for social participation. Digital platforms must cultivate a strong sense of responsibility and earn public trust through openness and transparency. Meanwhile, the public should actively exercise their rights and fulfill their obligations, fostering social cohesion and promoting public rationality through active participation. By drawing upon collective intelligence and strength, we can address the challenges posed by intelligent risks, and collaboratively shape a promising future for digital civilization through collaborative governance.

2. Educational Guidance: Enhancing Public AI Literacy and Competence in Intelligent Risk Identification

As a transformative force shaping the future, the sound governance of generative AI fundamentally depends on the overall enhancement of digital literacy across society. Indeed, in the face of burgeoning intelligent risks such as algorithmic bias and content loss-of-control, rigid institutional frameworks alone are insufficient for establishing effective, long-term regulation. Only by fostering a sense of participation throughout society, strengthening the public's capacity to identify and withstand intelligent risks, and systematically building a resilient foundation, can we maintain the proper course amidst the rapid technological advancements—proactively steering and leading progress, rather than passively and blindly following the uncertain tides of change.

AI literacy education should be adapted based on "intelligence," with educational content precisely designed according to the cognitive foundations and application contexts of different groups. For primary and secondary school students, gamified learning tools can be employed to popularize fundamental AI knowledge in an engaging and enjoyable manner, while also fostering awareness of responsible AI use and the risks associated with addiction. For the elderly, the focus should be on practical applications such as eldercare and intelligent assistants, with hands-on demonstrations to teach techniques for avoiding potential pitfalls. For media professionals, it is essential to strengthen their ability to identify risks specific to their field, such as deepfakes and automated content generation, thereby reinforcing the firewall of professional gatekeeping. Simultaneously, educational approaches should be diversified according to different environments, expanding the reach of AI literacy both online and offline. Online immersive courses can be developed through MOOCs and live streaming platforms; offline activities, such as visits to science and technology museums and participation in training camps, can seamlessly blend education with entertainment, promoting learning through engaging and enjoyable experiences.

AI literacy education must be strategically aligned with prevailing trends, attuned to the pulse of contemporary societal and technological development, and designed to foster sustained learner engagement through continual innovation. For instance, by leveraging the strengths of internet platforms, algorithm-driven personalized educational resources can be disseminated, thereby cultivating an omnipresent learning environment that is accessible anytime and anywhere. The integration of emerging technologies such as virtual reality and augmented reality can facilitate immersive risk simulation scenarios, reinforcing muscle memory for risk awareness and avoidance. Collaborations with authoritative experts and scholars to produce micro-lecture videos can embed cutting-edge theoretical concepts within accessible case studies, enhancing both the relevance and approachability of knowledge acquisition. Furthermore, it is essential to emphasize the cultivation of emotional and ethical values by employing narrative techniques to recount the developmental history of AI, thereby inspiring patriotism and a spirit of scientific inquiry. Showcasing exemplary AI enterprises that embody responsible innovation, ethical conduct, and societal contribution can further highlight the ethical imperatives and social responsibilities incumbent upon major technological actors.

AI literacy education is a complex and systematic undertaking that urgently requires an open and integrated ecosystem of collaboration. Government agencies should enhance strategic planning by incorporating AI literacy education into the top-level design of the national education system, improving supporting measures such as curriculum standards and textbook development. Enterprises must shoulder social responsibility, not only emphasizing digital inclusion but also establishing open platforms for public engagement in discussions on AI ethics. Schools can collaborate with institutions such as science and technology museums and libraries to promote mutual teaching and learning as well as resource sharing. Meanwhile, the media should fully leverage its immense potential to shape public opinion, awakening public awareness of risks through topic selection and in-depth reporting, and dispelling algorithmic myths with rational discourse.

The mission of AI literacy education remains formidable and will inevitably undergo continuous iteration and enhancement as the intelligence revolution deepens. Establishing a sustainable, education-led mechanism hinges on a human-centered approach that stimulates broad engagement across society, on integrating knowledge with action, thereby reinforcing the synergy between classroom instruction and practical cultivation, and on maintaining inclusivity and prudence, allowing ample space for differentiated exploration. It is imperative for us, with a commitment to both integrity and innovation, to promote the qualitative and effective advancement of AI literacy education. By steering technology toward the good, we can infuse the development of digital civilization with the transformative power of education, collaboratively shaping a shared vision for the intelligent era, and confidently advancing toward a future of harmonious human-machine coexistence.

3. Collaborative Synergy: Establishing Cross-Sector and Cross-Domain Governance Mechanisms to Achieve Collaborative Governance across Government, Industry, Academia, and Research Institutions

The governance of generative AI is akin to a polyphonic symphony of diverse stakeholder dynamics, where government, industry, academia, and the public each play distinct instrumental roles. Only through coordinated collaboration and precise alignment can we orchestrate the governance of intelligence in the digital era. At present, discourse surrounding generative AI models such as ChatGPT remains fragmented, characterized by divergent perceptions and imbalanced standards. There is an urgent need to build consensus through synergistic engagement, leveraging collective intelligence to facilitate cross-sectoral and cross-disciplinary institutional innovation.

The construction of cross-sector and cross-domain governance mechanisms must adhere to a problem-oriented approach and platform empowerment, leveraging an open and collaborative new national system to address the challenges posed by intelligent technologies. On the one hand, it is essential to fully utilize the government's capacity for overall coordination by establishing deliberative and consultative platforms encompassing government, industry, academia, and research institutions, particularly to address critical issues such as model spillover and content moderation. Through joint meetings, roundtable forums, and similar formats, stakeholders can regularly assess the situation, share information, and collaboratively develop response strategies. On the other hand, the proactive application of emerging technologies such as big data and blockchain—utilizing carriers like digital twins and intelligent cognitive systems—can enable the interconnection and interoperability of multi-source information and facilitate real-time monitoring and early warning. This, in turn, provides high-quality decision support for the effective implementation of policies.

Cross-sector and cross-domain governance requires a strengthened sense of mission and improved institutional support to achieve co-construction and shared benefits under the rule of law. For instance, it is advisable to draw on the experience of the Guangdong-Hong Kong-Macao Greater Bay Area in China in facilitating cross-border data flows to establish and refine mechanisms for cross-domain data sharing, thereby removing barriers to efficient government-enterprise collaboration and joint risk prevention and control. At the same time, it is essential to actively leverage industry self-regulation by formulating group standards that comply with ethical norms, using contractual linkages along the industrial value chain to compel platforms to fulfill their social responsibilities. Furthermore, regulatory sandbox approaches and third-party evaluation of innovative products should be fully utilized as inclusive and prudent regulatory tools, to create policy "green channels" to support technological breakthroughs and the commercialization of research outcomes.

The key to collaborative governance lies in accurately defining roles and clarifying boundaries, thereby enabling division of labor and complementary advantages within a dynamic equilibrium. The government should focus on rule-making to delineate the fundamental rights and responsibilities for all stakeholders, uphold value-driven principles to guide enterprises and society in harnessing technology for the greater good, and act as a catalyst by leveraging institutional innovation to foster synergistic interaction among diverse actors. Enterprises must assume responsibility by internalizing ethics throughout the entire lifecycle of algorithm design and model optimization, and proactively embrace openness by establishing transparent accountability mechanisms and accepting oversight from all sectors of society. Academia should be mission-driven, strengthening interdisciplinary collaboration and innovation to promote the integration of AI, neuroscience, psychology, and related disciplines, thereby addressing the "AI black box" challenge and expediting the translation of research findings into systematic solutions that ensure the safe deployment of generative AI. The public should actively engage in the governance, cultivate a scientifically informed understanding of intelligent technologies, and consciously resist inappropriate practices such as algorithmic abuse and excessive data extraction.

From a holistic perspective, collaborative governance is the fundamental strategy for ensuring the long-term stability and sustainable development of generative AI. Only by further breaking down the barriers of fragmented management, strengthening vertical integration and horizontal coordination, and stimulating the governance vitality of grassroots innovation and societal participation, can we accurately identify and address critical issues within the complex web of stakeholder interests, thereby crafting a compelling blueprint for pluralistic co-governance. Standing at the crossroads of the digital era, we must both ground our approach in local realities and adopt a global outlook, seeking the greatest common ground for global governance through dialogue and mutual learning. We can illuminate the path of AI for the benefit of humanity through collaborative symbiosis, and shape a promising future for digital civilization by steadfastly advancing technology for good. There is no need to fear distant goals; continued progress will bring them within reach. The dynamic and youthful vigor will undoubtedly open a new chapter of leapfrog development through tireless dedication and effort.

Section 5 International Cooperation: Active Participation in the Global Governance of Generative AI

The governance of generative AI is a global endeavor that transcends national borders, and its rapid evolution and widespread application pose significant challenges to existing governance frameworks. Differences in countries' levels of development, legal systems, and regulatory philosophies create numerous obstacles for the formulation and implementation of governance rules. Nevertheless, the cross-jurisdictional deployment of AI systems and the spillover effects of associated risks call for the international community to embrace a shared future for humanity, to build consensus beyond divisions, and to construct a multilateral, inclusive, and equitable global governance architecture. As a responsible major country, China should, at this new stage of development, participate actively in the global governance with an open and inclusive mindset. It is expected to demonstrate leadership in facilitating dialogue and exchange, seeking mutual recognition of regulatory standards, and deepening collaborative governance, thereby contributing China's wisdom to the healthy development of the global generative AI ecosystem.

1. Mutual Exchange and Learning: Strengthening International Dialogue in AI Governance

The governance of generative AI is a global issue that transcends national borders. The cross-domain applications of large models such as ChatGPT reflect the era's defining characteristics: technology knows no boundaries, and risks are equally borderless. No single nation can comprehensively chart a roadmap for AI governance on its own. It is thus imperative to uphold a cooperative philosophy grounded in mutual benefit and shared success, to strengthen strategic dialogue and pragmatic exchanges internationally in the field of AI governance, and to build consensus through comparative learning. Only with a sense of shared responsibility for humanity's collective future can we open a new chapter in the global governance of AI.

In choosing pathways for mutual exchange and learning, it is essential to uphold multilateralism and seek points of converging interests and opportunities for cooperative development through equal consultation. On the one hand, specialized dialogues on AI governance can be conducted within multilateral frameworks such as the G20, BRICS, and the Shanghai Cooperation Organization, allowing for the sharing of conceptual explorations and practical experiences in such aspects as algorithmic fairness, data security, and privacy protection. On the other hand, high-level platforms for international exchange can be established under the auspices of the United Nations, such as a global "AI for Good" summit or an international AI governance research center, leveraging "minilateral" mechanisms to catalyze broader cooperation. At the same time, it is crucial to adopt the perspective of developing countries by actively promoting China's approaches to intelligent public welfare and bridging the digital divide, in order to foster greater understanding and support from the broader developing world and to amplify the voice of "digital justice" on the international stage.

It is essential to grasp the substantive connotations of mutual exchange and learning, innovating modes of cooperation and expanding areas of collaboration through seeking common ground while reserving differences. Efforts can be concentrated on issues of shared global concern, such as the international order in cyberspace and the cross-border flow of data elements. On the basis of broad-based dialogue, a set of universally applicable AI governance principles can be distilled, thereby laying a value foundation for global governance. For example, a comparison of AI governance documents from China, the US, and Europe reveals that, despite differences in regulatory philosophies and legal systems, there is convergence on overarching visions such as safeguarding human rights and advancing human well-being. These shared aspirations can serve as the "greatest common denominator" for dialogue and exchange. Building on this foundation and guided by a spirit of rational pragmatism, pilot cooperation on AI governance can be carried out in key areas such as pandemic prevention and control, poverty alleviation and support for vulnerable groups, and climate change mitigation. By addressing major challenges through targeted, incremental breakthroughs, it is possible to make substantive progress.

It is important to emphasize that mutual exchange and learning should not be equated with blind imitation, nor with abandoning principles or seeking superficial harmony. Upholding independence and respecting national differences are essential prerequisites for conducting equal dialogue. While we should embrace the intellectual achievements of other countries with an open and inclusive mindset, we must also base our approach on the national context and pursue a path of AI governance that aligns with our own stage of development. We should adopt what is compatible and discard what is not. On matters of principle that concern core national interests, we must take a clear and uncompromising stance. If certain countries politicize or weaponize AI governance, maliciously slander other nations, or frequently erect "glass doors" and "spring doors," we must be prepared to respond decisively, use reason to persuade, and resolutely defend national sovereignty and dignity.

The world today is undergoing unprecedented changes not seen in a century, with AI emerging as the most dynamic and potentially transformative force. The governance of generative AI is pivotal to the advancement of human civilization and requires collaborative engagement from all nations. We should embrace an inclusive mindset, enhancing strategic mutual trust through principles of equality and mutual benefit, adopt an open and integrative approach to jointly address governance challenges, and demonstrate pioneering courage to lead the construction of a shared future for humanity. We should approach these endeavors with composure and confidence, fostering collective strength through candid dialogue, and, with a spirit of openness for global consultation and shared benefit, together craft a magnificent blueprint for global governance.

2. Mutual Recognition of Rules: Establishing an International Governance Framework for Generative AI to Facilitate the Mutual Recognition of Regulatory Standards

The establishment of a governance framework for generative AI is a critical issue in global technology governance. Admittedly, differences in legal foundations and regulatory philosophies among countries have resulted in varying levels of compliance barriers for generative AI platforms such as ChatGPT. However, given the extensive range of application scenarios and the potential for risk spillover, governance rules formulated by a single nation are unlikely to achieve comprehensive protection or control. Therefore, it is imperative to pursue mutual recognition of rules and harmonization of standards at the international level. Only by adhering to a rule-of-law framework can the wings of legal certainty and ethical oversight be attached to the innovation of generative AI, thereby ensuring its sustainable and responsible advancement.

The core of mutual recognition of rules lies in the integration of values, thereby enabling the interactive embedding of interests and normative logic through the assimilation of diverse strengths. This necessitates a foundation centered on the well-being of all humanity, guiding rule-making with a philosophy of cooperation and mutual benefit, so that AI governance frameworks can embody the "greatest common denominator" of all stakeholders' interests and reflect a broad collective consensus. Adhering to the principle of mutual benefit, we can, through broad-based dialogue, distill universally recognized foundational concepts—such as responsibility, inclusiveness, and human-centricity—and elevate them as guiding principles for international AI governance. At the same time, it is essential to fully respect national sovereignty, reserving space within international regulatory frameworks for differentiated approaches, and encouraging the development of context-specific implementation standards tailored to national circumstances, thus avoiding a one-size-fits-all model.

Mutual recognition of regulations should remain problem-oriented, addressing global challenges such as cross-border data flows and algorithmic bias, and achieving breakthroughs through targeted, incremental approaches. For example, by drawing on the negotiation model of digital tax reform, special consultations could be conducted on the cross-border movement of data elements, with enhanced coordination in the formulation of rules for data classification, grading, and security assessments, thereby reducing redundant verification processes. To address potential disputes related to copyright and privacy arising from generative AI models, the international intellectual property treaties can serve as references to explore the establishment of new property rights protection frameworks covering algorithms, data, and models. Furthermore, attention should be directed toward the application of generative AI in key sectors such as education, healthcare, and transportation, with the development of unified technical standards and ethical norms to create conditions conducive to transnational mutual recognition.

Currently, the competition and cooperation among countries over the governance frameworks for AI are intensifying. The EU's AI Act and the US's Algorithmic Accountability Act have both been prominently introduced, signaling strong intentions to shape and lead the development of international regulatory standards. In response, China should position itself at this new stage of development to actively participate in and guide the formulation of relevant global rules. Throughout extensive dialogue and negotiation processes, it is essential to maintain a rational and open stance, leveraging initiatives such as the Belt and Road Initiative and the Global Data Security Initiative to promote the transformation of Chinese approaches into international consensus. Building on legislative foundations such as the Personal Information Protection Law and the Data Security Law, China should strive to elevate its domestic experience into universal regulatory norms. At the same time, it is important to candidly acknowledge the imbalances and inadequacies in China's own developmental context, to learn modestly from beneficial international practices, and to achieve self-renewal and transcendence through integrating the strengths of diverse approaches.

Amidst unprecedented transformations unseen in a century, generative AI is reshaping the global landscape at an extraordinary pace. The international community must uphold the concept of a shared future for humanity, transcend prejudice and preconceptions, and draw upon inclusive wisdom to forge the broadest possible consensus for cooperation. Only by establishing equitable and inclusive governance frameworks through dialogue and negotiation can we unlock the full potential of the intelligence revolution and continuously inject new momentum into global innovation and development. We should join hands and leverage collective wisdom and courage to bridge regulatory divides, foster mutually beneficial global partnerships, and collectively create a promising future of human-machine collaboration and symbiosis.

3. Global Collaborative Governance: Active Participation in the International Governance of Generative AI and Contribution of Chinese Perspectives and Solutions

The governance of generative AI is a global undertaking that profoundly impacts the future of humanity, and no single nation can remain unaffected or act in isolation. As a permanent member of the United Nations Security Council and a responsible major country, China should actively engage in the global technological governance, leverage the leadership of multilateral platforms such as the United Nations, contribute Chinese insights with the vision of a shared future for mankind, and, with an inclusive approach to the common good, help usher in a new era of global co-governance of AI.

Global collaborative governance requires foresight and a broad strategic vision, identifying the key leverage points in top-level design. It is advisable to incorporate AI global governance into the United Nations 2030 Agenda for Sustainable Development to build broad-based political consensus. The establishment of a dedicated UN Committee on AI Governance could be initiated to facilitate the systematic organization of governance issues. Additionally, efforts should be made to draft a Charter for Global AI Governance to establish fundamental principles and bottom-line standards within the framework of international soft law. At the same time, China should leverage its new stage of development to become deeply embedded within existing international organizational structures, striving to play a more prominent role in specialized agencies such as the International Telecommunication Union and the International Organization for Standardization, and to advance governance agendas that address the demands of the current era.

Global governance should also be problem-oriented and refine its pathways, leveraging the bridging and linking functions of multilateral platforms. Given the differentiated applications of generative AI across various domains and contexts, governance strategies should be tailored to specific scenarios and advanced in parallel. For instance, in the education sector, a collaborative network for “AI + Education” projects could be established under the auspices of UNESCO to facilitate exchanges in teacher training and curriculum development. In the healthcare sector, the World Health Organization’s professional expertise could be harnessed to lead the formulation of ethical guidelines for smart healthcare, standardizing critical processes such as data collection and model training. At the same time, it is essential to focus on universal human values such as fairness and justice, and to actively promote AI for Social Good initiatives, thereby harnessing technology for the betterment of humanity and safeguarding the core achievements of civilization.

At present, global AI governance stands at a critical juncture marked by profound transformations. China should, in alignment with the new era and its evolving mission, embrace a spirit of openness and inclusivity to fulfill its responsibilities as a major country, contributing more Chinese solutions to the global governance. On the one hand, it is essential to actively disseminate and promote the “Chinese experiences” in building internet civilization, advancing the transformation of initiatives such as the Beijing AI Principles and the G20 Digital Economy Development and Cooperation Initiative into international guidelines for action. On the other hand, China should leverage its position as a responsible major country to collaborate with a broad range of developing countries, jointly steering the AI governance agenda toward addressing pressing livelihood concerns such as poverty alleviation and pandemic response, thereby constructing a "digital bridge" that facilitates North-South dialogue.

It is encouraging to note that China's influence in the global digital governance has grown significantly. Initiatives such as the Digital Silk Road and the Community of Shared Future for Mankind have emerged as value benchmarks guiding the intelligent era, providing direction for the modernization of global governance. Looking ahead, we should further demonstrate institutional confidence by elevating China's explorations in generative AI governance to the level of global consensus. Together with countries around the world, we should steadfastly advance the vision of a shared future, jointly building a community of shared future in cyberspace, and allowing the light of intelligence to illuminate the path of human progress.

Amidst a multitude of competing vessels, those who strive forward take the lead. The surge of generative AI is sweeping across the globe, heralding the advent of a new era in global governance. We thus should embrace openness and connectivity, positioning ourselves at the forefront of international rule-making in the digital domain. With a commitment to the greater good, we should exemplify the responsibilities of a major country in multilateral affairs. In this grand march of our times, by unwaveringly adhering to the path of peaceful development and advancing the construction of a shared future for humanity, we are poised to usher in a magnificent chapter characterized by human-machine symbiosis and the mutual enrichment of civilizations.

Chapter Twelve Relational Challenges: The Crisis of Human-Machine Trust in the Era of Generative AI

The rise of generative AI heralds the dawn of a cognitive revolution for humanity. Amidst the sweeping tide of digitalization, AI's extraordinary content generation capabilities have disrupted our traditional understanding of the principles governing information production and dissemination. While this transformation significantly enhances the efficiency of information processing, it simultaneously precipitates an unprecedented crisis of trust. The authenticity, rationality, and traceability of machine-generated content face formidable challenges; the boundaries of responsibility and accountability in human-machine interactions are becoming increasingly blurred. An era of "illusory mirages" in information is unfolding, where virtuality and reality are intertwined, and the distinction between truth and fabrication grows ever more elusive. As AI attains an unparalleled capacity to imitate, surpass, and even supplant human cognition, the urgent tasks before us are to reconstruct the foundations of mutual trust between humans and machines, clarify the ethical and social norms governing algorithms, and strike a balance between technological advancement and broader humanistic concerns. These are now imperative for maintaining the order of communication. This chapter takes generative AI as a focal point and, through the multiple lenses of information ethics, legal norms, and related frameworks, seeks to investigate the root causes of fissures in digital trust. The aim is to provide a theoretical reference for building a credible vision of human-machine symbiosis. Only in this way can we harness the momentum of "intelligence," ensuring that technology genuinely serves the pursuit of human values and, amid the ravages of the trust crisis, foster a new, inclusive, and trustworthy ecosystem of communication.

Section 1 Cognitive Gap: The Rapid Advancement of AI Capabilities and the Lag in Human Cognition

With the rapid and ever-evolving advancement of AI technologies, the pace and scope of their development have far surpassed the capacity of human society to adapt to such transformative changes. While AI capabilities are experiencing exponential growth, human cognition remains constrained by the limitations of linear thinking, resulting in an ever-widening gap between the two—a phenomenon that can be described as a cognitive fissure. This fissure manifests not only at the technical level but also permeates the domains of social psychology and ethics. The extraordinary performance of AI systems in areas such as go and natural language generation has exceeded human imagination and expectations, leading to heightened anxiety and unease regarding our own cognitive limitations. Simultaneously, the "black box" nature of AI technologies exacerbates public confusion and skepticism about their internal operational mechanisms and gives rise to cognitive dissonance. This has led to polarized perceptions: some individuals excessively mythologize AI's omnipotence, while others unduly diminish the uniqueness of human intelligence. Such cognitive biases are eroding the foundational trust between humans and machines. There is an urgent need to take proactive measures to bridge this divide. Only by adopting an open yet prudent stance, enhancing public education and ethical awareness, and elevating AI literacy across society—while simultaneously improving the transparency and explainability of AI systems—can we build a foundation of trust between humans and machines before the cognitive fissure further widens. This, in turn, will pave the way for a collaborative and trustworthy future in the era of intelligent technologies.

1. The Technological Singularity: Exponential Growth of AI Intelligence and the Limitations of Linear Human Thinking

The exponential growth of AI intelligence is reshaping every aspect of human society at an unprecedented pace. The speed and scale of this growth far exceed the expectations and imagination rooted in human linear thinking. The concept of the technological singularity aptly characterizes this phenomenon: the rapid and discontinuous advancement of AI capabilities leads to orders-of-magnitude improvements within a short timeframe, resulting in a cognitive gap as human cognition struggles to keep pace with these developments.

For instance, AlphaGo, underpinned by the successful application of deep learning algorithms, has demonstrated capabilities in go playing that surpass those of top human experts.[1] The advent of AlphaGo marks a significant breakthrough in AI's capacity for solving complex problems, highlighting the exponential growth potential of AI intelligence.[2] Even more astonishing is that AlphaGo's upgraded version, AlphaGo Zero, achieved overwhelming victories against its predecessor, with the speed of self-iteration and upgrading in AI intelligence far outpacing that of human go players.[3]

The emergence of the GPT-3 language model, with its massive parameter scale and exceptional language generation capabilities, has once again redefined public perceptions of AI. GPT-3 is capable of producing

---

1 AN, Bo. Artificial intelligence and game theory—starting from AlphaGo[J]. China Development Observation, 2016 (6): 13, 17.
2 HUANG, Qian. Insights from AlphaGo for the development of smart cities and a preliminary discussion on the spatiotemporal intelligence framework[J]. Beijing Planning and Construction, 2016 (6): 23-27.
3 ZHAO, Aopei. The Logic of Neural Cognition from the Perspective of AlphaGo[D]. Guiyang: Guizhou University, 2018.

text that is virtually indistinguishable from that written by humans, spanning a broad array of domains from creative writing to programming code. This development signifies that AI now possesses a certain degree of creativity and logical reasoning—competencies that were previously regarded as the exclusive province of human intelligence.[1] While GPT-3's expressive power is remarkable, the underlying mechanisms driving its performance are difficult to interpret through human intuition and experience, thereby exacerbating the cognitive gap.

In fact, the limitations of human linear thinking make it difficult for us to fully grasp the exponential growth trajectory and impact of AI intelligence. Humans tend to predict the future based on their own cognitive experiences, yet the development of AI often transcends such linear extrapolation. The advent of the technological singularity signifies that the growth curve of AI intelligence will become increasingly steep, whereas the curve of human cognitive advancement remains relatively gradual. This cognitive dissonance may result in misjudgments regarding AI capabilities—either overestimating or underestimating them—which in turn affects the foundation of trust in human-machine interactions.

Therefore, bridging the cognitive gap and constructing a future vision of human-machine symbiosis requires a prudent assessment of the current state and developmental trends of AI, an objective understanding of the limitations inherent in human cognition, and an active exploration of pathways for human-machine collaboration. Only in this way can we achieve complementary advancement and mutual progress between human and machine intelligence at the advent of the technological singularity, rather than falling into the predicament of cognitive dissonance.

---

1 RUAN, Xiaodong. Observing the future of artificial intelligence from AlphaGo's victory[J]. New Economy Review, 2016 (6): 69-74.

2. Cognitive Dissonance: Public Misconceptions of AI Capabilities and the Emergence of Trust Crisis

The widening gap between the rapid advancement of AI capabilities and the lagging public understanding is giving rise to a phenomenon of cognitive dissonance. This dissonance is manifested in the public's misconceptions about AI, ranging from exaggerated idealization to undue underestimation. Such cognitive biases are eroding the foundational trust in AI and brewing a potential crisis of trust.

For example, in NLP scenarios, when chatbots accurately comprehend semantics and engage in fluent conversations, some individuals may perceive them as omnipotent "universal assistants," leading to unrealistic expectations. They might request chatbots to solve problems beyond their technical capabilities or become excessively reliant on the advice provided, thereby overlooking the inherent limitations and potential risks of AI systems. When chatbots fail to meet these inflated expectations, disappointment and a sense of distrust are likely to ensue.

On the other hand, in the face of increasingly advanced AI-generated art technologies, some artists and designers may perceive their professional skills as being threatened. They may underestimate the uniqueness of human creativity while overestimating the likelihood of AI replacing humans. This cognitive dissonance can lead to resistance toward AI, subsequently affecting their willingness and efficiency in collaborating with AI systems.

The root cause of cognitive dissonance lies in the public's insufficient awareness and understanding of AI capabilities. Many individuals perceive AI as a "black box," possessing little knowledge of its internal operational mechanisms. This knowledge gap readily breeds suspicion and misunderstanding. For instance, when people are unable to explain the decision-making outcomes of facial recognition systems, they may question the fairness and accuracy of these systems, ultimately leading to a loss of trust.

At the same time, media coverage of AI may exacerbate cognitive dissonance. Some media outlets tend to sensationalize the "miraculous" aspects of AI while neglecting its limitations and potential risks. This imbalanced dissemination of information can mislead the public, fostering unrealistic expectations regarding AI capabilities and thereby sowing the seeds for a potential trust crisis.

Bridging cognitive dissonance and rebuilding public trust in AI requires us to strengthen science communication and enhance AI literacy across society. This entails not only disseminating accurate and objective knowledge about AI to the public, but also reinforcing education in ethics and morality to guide individuals toward a proper understanding of AI's role. At the same time, AI enterprises should proactively assume responsibility for information disclosure, increasing the transparency and explainability of AI systems to alleviate public concerns. Only through concerted efforts from multiple stakeholders can we overcome cognitive dissonance, build a bridge of trust between humans and machines, and collaboratively create a promising future in the era of intelligence.

Section 2 Ethical Dilemmas: Moral Risks and Ethical Challenges Posed by Generative AI

The rapid advancement of generative AI, while bringing significant convenience to human life, has simultaneously triggered a series of ethical issues. These concerns encompass multiple dimensions, including the value orientation of AI-generated content and the attribution of responsibility, reflecting the inherent tensions between AI and the normative frameworks of human society. AI systems are trained on massive datasets, and although the content they generate may appear objective and neutral, it is, in reality, inextricably influenced by human subjective values. When AI-generated content approaches the boundaries of ethical and moral standards, conflicts between machine logic and human values inevitably come to the fore. Manifestations of such conflicts include algorithmic bias in news reporting, copyright disputes in artistic creation, and the malicious fabrication of misinformation. At the same time, while AI-generated content enhances efficiency, it also blurs the boundaries of responsibility among various stakeholders. Traditional causal attribution frameworks are difficult to directly apply in AI contexts, which creates significant obstacles for the identification and sanctioning of unlawful or non-compliant behaviors. Clarifying the complexities of responsibility in an era of human-machine symbiosis and establishing innovative governance frameworks and ethical norms present urgent and formidable challenges. This not only tests the trajectory of technological development but also concerns the reconstruction of social order. We must adopt a prudent yet proactive approach, striving to find a balance between technological progress and ethical constraints, in order to realize the promising vision of AI serving the betterment of humanity.

1. Value Conflicts: The Collision between the Value-Neutrality of AI-Generated Content and Human Ethical Standards

The ethical dilemmas brought about by generative AI are primarily manifested in the conflict between the value-neutrality of AI-generated content and human moral standards. AI systems operate according to the logic of machine learning, generating seemingly objective and neutral content based on massive datasets. However, this neutrality is rooted in the optimization objectives of algorithms rather than human value judgments. When AI-generated content approaches the boundaries of ethics and morality, the collision between these two sets of values becomes inevitable.

Algorithms generating news reports, for example, may prioritize content tailored to users' reading preferences, thereby potentially compromising journalistic authenticity and objectivity. Such "algorithmic recommendation" practices can exacerbate the filter bubble effect, resulting in users being exposed to biased or even false information. From the perspective of human moral standards, this undoubtedly constitutes a deviation from journalistic ethics.[1]

For instance, the creation of AI-generated artworks may involve the imitation and appropriation of existing works. While consistent with the logic of machine learning, this practice may infringe upon intellectual property rights and trigger copyright disputes.[2] From the perspective of human moral values, such practices lack respect for the labor and achievements of original creators and run counter to the principles of fairness and justice.

Even more concerning is that when AI is employed to generate disinformation or deepfakes, its value-neutrality can be maliciously exploited, turning it into a tool that harms society. For instance, AI-generated false political propaganda may mislead voters and disrupt democratic processes; AI-synthesized fabricated evidence could influence judicial decisions, resulting in wrongful convictions. Such practices not only violate fundamental human ethical standards but also underscore the urgent need for robust AI ethics governance.

---

1 YE, Tongrui, LIU, Mingyang. Technological penetration of generative AI and ethical reflections in journalism[J]. Youth Journalist, 2023 (16): 89-91.
2 DAI, Hongduo. Ethical reflections on artificial intelligence-generated art: a case study of AI painting[J]. Studies in Dialectics of Nature, 2023, 39 (10): 142-144.

In fact, the value neutrality of AI-generated content is only a relative concept. In a certain sense, AI systems themselves serve as carriers of human values, as their training data and algorithmic designs are inevitably shaped by human subjectivity. Therefore, we cannot expect AI-generated content to be entirely independent of human value orientations. On the contrary, we should strengthen AI ethical guidelines and embed human moral standards into the design and application of AI systems.

This necessitates a reassessment of the value orientation of AI-generated content to ensure its alignment with the ethical and moral standards of human society.[1] For instance, in algorithm design, we can incorporate considerations of diversity and inclusivity to mitigate algorithmic bias; during content generation, we can establish ethical boundaries to prevent AI from producing content that is illegal, non-compliant, or contrary to public order and good customs; and in terms of application scenarios, we can enhance human-machine collaboration by implementing human intervention and review mechanisms to promptly rectify deviations in AI-generated content. Only by addressing both technological and institutional dimensions can we resolve the value conflicts brought about by AI-generated content and realize the desirable vision of human-machine symbiosis.

2. Attribution of Responsibility: The Lack of Responsibility Attribution and Accountability Mechanisms for AI-Generated Content

Generative AI, while creating content, also introduces challenges regarding the attribution of responsibility. When AI-generated content

---

1 SUN, Weiping, LI, Yang. On the ethical principles of artificial intelligence development[J]. Philosophical Analysis, 2022, 13 (1): 3-14, 196.

contains errors, biases, or even violates laws and regulations, the question arises: who should ultimately be held accountable? This issue is increasingly becoming a focal point in AI ethics. The ambiguity in defining responsibility and the absence of robust accountability mechanisms have led to significant difficulties in the governance of AI-generated content.

For instance, in journalism, when AI-generated news reports contain inaccurate information, the attribution of responsibility becomes ambiguous and complex. Should the news organizations that provide the training data be held accountable, or is the responsibility borne by the technical teams who design the algorithms, or perhaps by the platforms that ultimately publish the content? The responsibilities among these different stakeholders are often difficult to define. This ambiguity in responsibility may lead to mutual shirking and buck-passing, ultimately undermining the public interest.

Similarly, in the field of autonomous driving, determining liability when an unmanned vehicle is involved in a traffic accident presents significant challenges. Should the responsibility lie with the vehicle manufacturer, the algorithm designer, or the vehicle owner? Existing legal frameworks lack clear stipulations on this matter. This vacuum of accountability not only complicates the enforcement of compensation for accidents but may also undermine the risk awareness and sense of responsibility among all stakeholders.

The absence of accountability mechanisms further exacerbates the dilemma of attributing responsibility. In many domains, robust accountability frameworks for AI-generated content have yet to be established. This implies that even if we can identify responsible parties, there is a lack of effective means to hold them accountable. For instance, the malicious creation and dissemination of AI-generated fake videos can easily result in reputational or economic harm to the individuals involved. Under the current legal framework, it is both costly and difficult for victims to seek redress, and it remains challenging to promptly prevent and penalize such behavior.

At its root, the difficulty in attributing responsibility for AI-generated content arises from its disruption of traditional causal attribution logic. In human society, responsibility is typically defined based on the agent's subjective intent and objective behavior. However, AI systems themselves lack autonomous consciousness, and the content they generate is often the outcome of probabilistic statistical processes. As a result, it becomes challenging to apply conventional frameworks of responsibility attribution to determine accountability for AI.

Therefore, clarifying the attribution of responsibility for AI-generated content urgently requires the establishment of innovative governance models and legal frameworks. This endeavor may necessitate a multidimensional approach: first, it is essential to define the legal status of AI systems, granting them appropriate rights and obligations; second, a liability-sharing mechanism tailored to AI should be established to reasonably delineate the boundaries of responsibility among stakeholders; third, the accountability mechanisms for AI governance must be improved, with enhanced sanctions for violations of laws and regulations; and finally, the promotion of AI ethics education should be strengthened to raise the sense of responsibility across society. Only through coordinated efforts across legal, institutional, and ethical dimensions can we dispel the ambiguity surrounding responsibility for AI-generated content and construct a trustworthy and reliable order of human-machine symbiosis.

Section 3 Information Distortion: The Impact and Implications of Generative AI on the Information Ecosystem

The rapid development of generative AI technologies has brought unprecedented opportunities and challenges to the information ecosystem. On the one hand, the increasing realism of AI-generated content is blurring the boundaries between AI and human cognition, posing severe challenges to the authenticity of information. When fabricated content is indistinguishable from reality and proliferates across digital platforms, the public is prone to cognitive biases, which in turn undermine the construction of social trust. On the other hand, while personalized recommendation algorithms enhance the precision of information dissemination, they may also confine users within information cocoons, thereby reducing their exposure to diverse perspectives. The homogenizing effect of algorithmic recommendation mechanisms undoubtedly intensifies social polarization and antagonism, and may further erode the public's capacity for critical thinking.

The impact of AI-generated content on the authenticity of information fundamentally stems from its "simulation" capabilities, which are built upon vast amounts of real data. Meanwhile, the information cocoon effect caused by personalized recommendation algorithms originates from their tendency to prioritize commercial interests at the expense of valuing information diversity. The various distortions introduced into the information ecosystem by generative AI reflect the complex tension between technological progress and societal development. This necessitates a prudent reflection on the trajectory of AI, as well as targeted efforts across multiple dimensions—including technological innovation, social governance, and individual cultivation—to construct a firewall for the information ecosystem in the AI era. Only by doing so can we maximize the potential of AI while minimizing its adverse effects, thereby achieving the vision of human-machine symbiosis and co-creating a better future.

1. Authenticity Dilemma: The Challenge of Information Veracity in AI-Generated Content

The rapid iteration of generative AI technologies is reshaping our perception of information authenticity. The realism of AI-generated content has reached a point where it is virtually indistinguishable from the reality or the one created by human, thereby exerting an unprecedented impact on the information ecosystem. As the boundaries between AI and human intelligence become increasingly blurred, discerning the veracity of information and safeguarding objectivity and public trust in information have emerged as urgent challenges requiring immediate attention.

For instance, LLMs such as GPT-3 have already acquired the capability to produce text that closely resembles human writing. These AI-generated articles are virtually flawless in grammar, semantics, and logic, making it extremely difficult to identify them as machine-written. When such AI-generated content proliferates throughout cyberspace, individuals can easily be misled by its surface appearance, subsequently accepting and disseminating fabricated information as fact. This undoubtedly poses a significant challenge to the authenticity of information.

For example, certain malicious actors exploit AI's text generation capabilities to mass-produce pseudo-original material, intermixing it with authentic information in pursuit of illicit gains. These pseudo-original texts often evade traditional plagiarism detection methods through techniques such as synonym substitution and syntactic transformation. The embedded false information can mislead public perception, thereby undermining the foundational integrity of the information ecosystem. In the visual domain, AI-generated content is even more striking. From StyleGAN to StableDiffusion and other AI models, it is now possible to generate hyper-realistic portraits, landscapes, and even artworks. Some forgers leverage these tools to fabricate false evidence, deceive public opinion, and even threaten social security.[1] For instance, there have been cases where malicious actors utilized AI synthesis technologies to create fake pornographic videos of celebrities for the purpose of extortion. Such acts of deepfake not only violate individuals' rights to image and privacy, but also pose a serious threat to social trust.

The fundamental reason why AI-generated content poses a threat to information authenticity lies in its verisimilitude capability, which is built upon vast amounts of real data. This capability endows AI-generated false information with an unprecedented level of deceptiveness, making it easy to mislead individuals into forming erroneous perceptions. In the post-truth era, AI technologies have undoubtedly provided new grounds for information distortion.

To address the authenticity challenges posed by AI-generated content, we must reconstruct the firewall of the information ecosystem.[2] This requires simultaneous efforts on both the technological and institutional fronts. On the technological level, we need to accelerate the development of tools and algorithms for identifying AI-generated content, thereby enhancing our capacity for the detection and traceability of disinformation.

---

1 KHOO, B., PHAN, R. C. W., LIM, C. H. Deepfake attribution: on the source identification of artificially generated images[J].Wiley interdisciplinary reviews: data mining and knowledge discovery, 2022, 12 (3): e1438.

2 DENG, Shengli, WANG, Fan, WANG, Haowei. A study on methods for identifying AI-generated content in online communities[J]. Library and Information Knowledge, 2024, 41 (2): 28-38, 149.

On the institutional level, it is imperative to improve the legal and regulatory frameworks for information governance, intensify crackdowns on fraudulent activities, and strengthen the content moderation responsibilities of information platforms. Meanwhile, we must also enhance public media literacy education to improve people's ability to critically evaluate information, thereby fostering their rational skepticism and independent thinking. Only in this way can we safeguard the authenticity of information and construct a trustworthy information ecosystem in the age of AI.

2. Information Cocoon: The Erosion of Information Diversity by Personalized Recommendation Algorithms

The information distortion brought about by generative AI is manifested not only in the erosion of content authenticity but also in the weakening of informational diversity. AI technologies, exemplified by personalized recommendation algorithms, are exerting a subtle yet profound influence on the information ecosystem. While algorithmic recommendations enhance the precision of information dissemination, they may also confine users within information cocoons, thereby restricting their exposure to diverse perspectives.[1]

The original intention of personalized recommendation algorithms is to provide users with tailored information services. By mining and analyzing user behavior data, these algorithms can infer their interests and preferences, thereby delivering highly relevant content. This "one-to-one" recommendation mechanism to some extent fulfills users' individualized needs. However, when the algorithms' objectives become overly focused on maximizing user engagement and retention, the quality of

---

1 LIU, Jianguo, ZHOU, Tao, WANG, Binghong. Research progress on personalized recommendation systems[J]. Progress in Natural Science, 2009, 19 (1): 1-15.

recommendations may be compromised.[1]

Algorithmic recommendation systems often adhere to the principle of "homophily," that is, recommending content aligned with users' previous interests. Over time, this can lead them to become trapped in an information cocoon, where the range of perspectives they are exposed to becomes increasingly narrow, and viewpoints that diverge from their own cognitive framework are gradually filtered out. In such a state, the users find it difficult to access diverse and heterogeneous information, which in turn constrains their comprehensive understanding of the world.

For instance, in social media, when algorithms detect that users are interested in a particular type of political discourse, they continuously push similar content to those users. Over time, this easily leads to the formation of an "echo chamber effect," where the information environment surrounding the users becomes saturated with homogeneous viewpoints, while dissenting voices are marginalized. Undoubtedly, this exacerbates social fragmentation and polarization, and may also undermine the quality of democratic decision-making.

The information cocoon effect may also undermine the public's capacity for critical thinking. When individuals are immersed for extended periods in information environments that align with their own perspectives, their abilities to discern and critically evaluate information gradually deteriorate. In such circumstances, certain seemingly plausible yet misleading viewpoints may be accepted as "truth," thereby impairing judgment. This, in turn, undoubtedly heightens the risk of the spread of online rumors and extremist ideologies.

---

1 LV, Wei, YANG, Ying, ZHANG, Yanbing. The impact of perceived personalization on consumers' click intentions in AI-driven personalized recommendation systems[J]. Management Science, 2020, 33 (5): 44-57.

The fundamental reason why personalized recommendation algorithms give rise to the information cocoon effect lies in their orientation toward serving commercial interests rather than the public good. [1] For many Internet platforms, attracting user attention and increasing advertising revenue constitute the core objectives. Consequently, these platforms often employ algorithmic recommendations to cater to user preferences, while neglecting the value of information diversity.

To break free from the information cocoon and escape the "enchantment" of algorithms, it is imperative to reconstruct the value orientation of personalized recommendation systems. This requires internet platforms to prioritize social responsibility over commercial interests by incorporating considerations of diversity and inclusivity into their algorithmic design.[2] At the same time, it is essential to improve the explainability and transparency of algorithms, thus granting users greater rights to information and autonomy of choice. On the individual level, it is important to proactively cultivate individuals' awareness of "breaking out of echo chambers," encouraging them to approach issues from multiple perspectives and to embrace the diversity and divergence of viewpoints. Only through a multi-pronged approach can we preserve the diversity of the information ecosystem in the algorithmic era and advance our self-cognition.

---

1 ZHANG, Sheng, CAI, Yongtao. Research on the formation mechanism of the "information cocoon" in the Algorithmic Era[J]. Information Theory and Practice, 2023, 46 (4): 67-73.

2 ZHANG, Pengfei, WANG, Yigui, ZHANG, Zhijun. Research on personalized recommendation algorithms integrating tags and multidimensional information[J]. Computer Engineering and Applications, 2019, 55 (5): 159-165.

Section 4 Privacy Breaches: Threats to Personal Privacy Posed by Generative AI

While generative AI technologies bring significant convenience to human society, they simultaneously pose new challenges to the protection of individual privacy. As AI algorithms continuously "learn" from and mine vast amounts of data, information that was previously regarded as personal privacy has now become the "nourishment" for algorithmic models. Although this data-driven technological logic enhances the intelligence of AI systems, it inevitably exacerbates the risk of personal privacy breaches. The boundaries of data subject rights are increasingly blurred, and the scope for individual informational self-determination is continually eroded. Driven by profit motives, some AI enterprises disregard data ethics, engaging in excessive or even illegal collection and utilization of user data, thereby subjecting personal privacy protection in the digital age to unprecedented challenges. At the same time, the misuse of AI-generated content technologies further exposes the imbalance between technological advancement and ethical regulation. The emergence of deepfakes, voice cloning, and similar technologies has revolutionized digital content production, yet has also provided malicious actors with tools to impersonate others for fraudulent purposes. The resulting identity leakage not only infringes upon individuals' rights to image and reputation but also poses latent threats to social order and public security. These novel privacy infringements underscore the urgency and necessity of robust AI governance. It is imperative to reassess the impact of AI on individual rights from both legal and ethical perspectives, and to strike an appropriate balance between technological innovation and privacy protection. Only in this way can we construct a firewall for personal privacy in the digital era.

1. Data Utilization: Excessive Collection and Unauthorized Use of User Data

Although the development of generative AI has opened up new frontiers in information processing and content creation, it has also posed unprecedented threats to personal privacy. The most immediate manifestation of this threat lies in the excessive collection and unlawful use of user data. In the data-driven era of AI, user data has become the raw material for algorithmic models. In pursuit of maximizing model performance, some AI enterprises have resorted to risky practices, excessively collecting or even illegally acquiring user data, which has triggered a series of privacy breaches.

For instance, OpenAI, the developer of ChatGPT, has been exposed for using publicly available user information from the internet to train its language models without obtaining consent. Among this data are instances containing sensitive personal information, such as individual logs and private conversation records. Such unauthorized data collection practices undoubtedly infringe upon users' rights to privacy. What is even more concerning is that, due to the "black box" nature of AI models, users find it exceedingly difficult to ascertain how their private data is actually being utilized.

In the field of voice assistants, companies such as Amazon and Google have been accused of using users' voice data to train their AI algorithms. Some voice assistants have even been found to "eavesdrop" on users' daily conversations without their knowledge, thereby exposing private information such as daily routines and interpersonal relationships. For users, this creates a predicament akin to becoming a "transparent person"—in the era of AI and big data, personal privacy is rendered impossible to remain undetected.

The illegal use of user data is also a cause for concern. Some AI enterprises utilize user data for commercial purposes—such as targeted advertising and user profiling—without obtaining explicit user consent. This practice undoubtedly infringes upon users' data sovereignty. Even more troubling, certain malicious actors exploit AI algorithms to trade illegally obtained user data on the black market, engaging in criminal activities such as extortion and blackmail.

The frequent occurrence of data security incidents highlights the AI industry's shortcomings in privacy protection. Many AI enterprises exhibit a weak awareness of safeguarding data subjects' rights and demonstrate inadequate adherence to data ethics. Driven by profit motives, they often prioritize the benefits of data collection while neglecting the adverse consequences of insufficient privacy protection. This inversion of priorities undoubtedly exacerbates the risk of personal privacy breaches.

The root cause of privacy breaches lies in the ambiguous boundaries of individual data rights. In the era of AI, digitized personal information has emerged as a novel factor of production and possesses strong public attributes. Striking a balance between data utilization and privacy protection presents a significant challenge. To address this, it is imperative to establish a robust legal framework for personal data rights, clarifying the boundaries of data collection, usage, and circulation, and standardizing the data practices of AI enterprises. At the same time, society must strengthen data ethics education to enhance public awareness and capacity for safeguarding data sovereignty. Only by addressing privacy breaches from both legal and ethical perspectives can we defend privacy rights, the "moat" of personality rights, in the digital age.

2. Identity Exposure: Potential Risks of AI Synthesis Technologies to Personal Identity Protection

The rapid advancement of AI synthesis technologies, while

empowering digital content creation, also poses potential threats to personal identity protection. These threats are primarily manifested in the risks of identity leakage associated with technologies such as AI-based face swapping and voice cloning. At present, it is possible to use AI algorithms to generate highly realistic virtual representations. Some malicious actors exploit these technologies to forge others' digital identities, thereby engaging in fraudulent, defamatory, and other illegal activities. This undoubtedly presents unprecedented challenges to the security of personal identity.

Deepfake technology represents a significant "trump card" in AI-generated synthesis. Leveraging algorithms such as Generative Adversarial Networks (GANs), the technology enables the transplantation of a target individual's facial features onto another person's face, producing highly realistic synthetic videos that are difficult to distinguish from authentic footage. Since its inception, this technology has attracted widespread attention and sparked considerable controversy. Certain malicious actors have exploited deepfake technology to fabricate pornographic videos featuring celebrities, subsequently engaging in extortion and blackmail. Others have used this technology to create falsified evidence intended to mislead judicial proceedings. Undoubtedly, these actions constitute serious violations of individuals' rights to their images and reputation.

Speech synthesis technology also raises significant concerns. By learning from target individuals' voice data, AI algorithms can mimic their speech characteristics and generate synthetic voices that are virtually indistinguishable from the original. Malicious actors may exploit this technology to forge others' voice commands, enabling them to steal bank accounts or perpetrate telecommunications fraud. On social media platforms, some ill-intentioned users might use cloned voices to disseminate false statements, thereby misleading public opinion. Such activities pose risks not only to individual reputations but also to social order as a whole.

It is important to remain vigilant, as the emergence of concepts such as the metaverse may further facilitate the exploitation of AI-generated technologies for identity theft. In virtual environments, users often exist in the form of digital avatars. Once these virtual representations are misappropriated by malicious actors, the boundary between users' identities in the physical world and digital space becomes increasingly blurred. This convergence poses heightened risks to personal privacy and asset security.

The abuse of AI synthesis technologies has largely become possible due to the imbalance between technological advancement and ethical norms. Amidst the wave of innovation, some enterprises have underestimated the negative impacts of these technologies and lack the necessary precautions and regulatory measures. At the same time, the current legal framework for characterizing and regulating AI-generated content remains ambiguous, making it difficult to establish effective deterrence. This regulatory vacuum provides opportunities for malicious actors to exploit the technologies for fraudulent purposes.

The issue of identity leakage serves as a warning that, while embracing AI-generated technologies, we must also carefully consider the ethical risks they entail. This necessitates the integration of personal identity protection into the broader framework of AI governance, with clear legal boundaries for AI-generated content established at the legislative level and improved measures for addressing infringements and enforcing penalties. At the same time, it is imperative to accelerate the development of a trustworthy digital identity authentication system and to strengthen end-to-end protection of users' identity information. On the individual level, we must also enhance public risk awareness and encourage caution regarding the disclosure of identity information online.

Only by striking a balance between technological innovation and ethical regulations can we effectively safeguard the "firewall" of personal identity security in the age of AI.

Section 5 Employment Impact: The Displacement Effect of Generative AI on Traditional Occupations

The rapid advancement of generative AI technologies is fundamentally reshaping the landscape of content production. As intelligent algorithms demonstrate exceptional capabilities in areas such as copywriting, visual design, and music composition, traditional content creation professions are facing unprecedented disruption. Leveraging advantages of efficiency, low cost, and scalability, AI is increasingly exhibiting a substitution effect on human practitioners. This "intelligent substitution" stems from machines' distinctive strengths in pattern recognition and large-scale data processing. For creative tasks characterized by high degrees of repetitiveness and regularity, AI systems can swiftly learn creative patterns from historical data and mass-produce content. Under a competitive logic that prioritizes quantity, the comparative advantage of human creators is being progressively eroded. The impact of intelligent substitution is both complex and profound. It may intensify occupational competition and trigger structural unemployment; yet, it may also give rise to new professional roles, such as AI system trainers. For content professionals, the key lies in their ability to identify their positioning within human-machine collaboration and to foster core competencies for the AI era through continual knowledge and skill upgrades. Content creation has always symbolized human intelligence. The rise of AI in this domain not only sows the seeds of transformation but also provokes humanistic reflection. As participants in this paradigm shift, we must respond with keen insight and prudent attitudes. This issue concerns not only individual career choices, but also the future trajectory of human creativity.

1. Intelligent Substitution: Advantages of AI in Content Creation and the Displacement of Human Roles

With its advantages of high efficiency, low cost, and scalability, generative AI is reshaping the landscape of content creation. The remarkable capabilities demonstrated by AI in copywriting, visual design, music production, and other domains have already begun to exert a displacement effect on human professionals. This trend of intelligent substitution is not only transforming the methods of content production but also triggering profound changes in the labor market. The rise of AI presents human creators with unprecedented opportunities and challenges.

For instance, in news writing, the emergence of automated writing software is reshaping the newsroom ecosystem. Powered by AI algorithms, these applications are capable of automatically generating highly structured news content, such as financial reports and sports coverage. Compared to manual writing, AI-generated articles demonstrate significant advantages in terms of speed and accuracy. Media outlets like The Guardian have already begun experimenting with AI-assisted news production. Against this backdrop, certain traditional journalism positions are at risk of becoming obsolete.

Turning to the design industry, the rise of AI-powered design tools is transforming the production of visual content. For instance, Adobe's Sensei platform leverages machine learning algorithms to automatically process images and generate design solutions. Designers can simply input basic textual descriptions, and the AI is capable of returning multiple creative designs. This undoubtedly enhances the efficiency of design production. However, in light of this trend, certain entry-level design positions may be at risk of displacement or automation.

The application of AI in the field of music is equally remarkable. AI composition systems such as FlowMachines are capable of learning the creative styles of human musicians and autonomously generating professional-grade musical works. Google's Magenta project has even attempted to commercialize AI-generated music. Compared to human composers, AI can engage in large-scale music creation tirelessly, with its productivity advantages being self-evident. However, with the rise of AI-generated music, the creative space available to some human musicians is likely to be encroached upon.

The emergence of intelligent substitution stems from AI's distinctive advantages in pattern recognition and data processing. For creative tasks characterized by high repetitiveness and regularity, AI systems can learn creative patterns from vast historical datasets and automatically generate content. This capability to "win by volume" is difficult for human creators to match. From the economic perspective, AI is eroding the comparative advantage that humans have traditionally held in the field of content creation.

It is important to recognize that the impact of intelligent automation on the labor market is both complex and profound. It may intensify occupational competition and trigger structural unemployment; however, it can also give rise to new forms of employment, such as AI system trainers and data annotators. The crux lies in whether humans can accurately identify their own positioning and demonstrate unique value within human-machine collaboration. This necessitates the upgrading of knowledge and skills, as well as the cultivation of core competencies essential for the AI era.

Content creation has always been a hallmark of human intelligence. The rise of AI in this domain presents both opportunities and latent risks. As participants in this evolving landscape, we must maintain acute insight and respond with prudence. This is not only pertinent to individual career trajectories, but also to the future of human creativity itself. With the integration of AI, content production paradigms are bound to be restructured; nevertheless, the brilliance of human imagination will remain the most captivating foundation of our era. We should approach this transformation with openness, and together, in the symphony of human-machine collaboration, compose the defining narrative of our times.

2. Skill Obsolescence: The Iterative Advancement of AI Technologies and the Accelerated Depreciation of Human Professional Competencies

The rapid iteration of AI technologies is reshaping the landscape of professional skills. With the continuous advancement of intelligent algorithms, the specialized competencies required for many traditional occupations are at significant risk of rapid obsolescence. This phenomenon of skill redundancy is not limited to content creation but also permeates sectors such as finance, healthcare, and law. Driven by the pervasive influence of AI, human labor is undergoing an unprecedented transformation in professional skill requirements.

For example, in the sector of financial accounting, the emergence of intelligent financial and tax robots is disrupting traditional accounting practices. Leveraging technologies such as NLP and knowledge graphs, these robots can autonomously perform complex tasks such as invoice processing and financial reconciliation. Compared to manual operations, intelligent financial and tax solutions offer superior efficiency and accuracy. In light of this trend, traditional accounting skills are under increasing pressure to rapidly evolve. Practitioners unable to keep pace with intelligent automation may face uncertain career prospects.

In the healthcare sector, AI is reshaping the competency framework for medical imaging diagnostics. From IBM Watson to Google DeepMind, AI has demonstrated capabilities in medical image analysis that surpass those of human physicians. These systems can automatically detect anomalies in medical images such as CT and MRI scans, identifying subtle signals that are often imperceptible to the human eye. As imaging AI continues to mature, the diagnostic skill set of traditional radiologists may face significant challenges and require substantial upgrades.

The legal field has likewise not been immune. The emergence of AI judges is challenging the traditional professional roles of lawyers. For instance, Seoul, South Korea, has already implemented an AI judge system to assist in handling straightforward cases. These systems can rapidly retrieve case information and offer judgment recommendations, significantly enhancing judicial efficiency. With the advancement of technologies such as case-based reasoning, AI may eventually replace lawyers in performing a broader range of legal tasks. Traditional legal practitioners, especially junior lawyers, are facing the risk of devaluation of their case-handling skills.

The root cause of skill obsolescence lies in AI's simulation and surpassing of human cognitive abilities. The traditionally high skill requirements in professional fields have largely stemmed from inherent cognitive limitations. However, with advancements in technologies such as machine learning, AI has begun to demonstrate advanced cognitive capabilities, including pattern recognition and logical reasoning. In performing structured tasks, machines often surpass human brains in terms of efficiency and stability. This fundamentally undermines the scarcity value that has long underpinned many traditional skills.

It is important to remain vigilant regarding the risk of skill obsolescence, as it may exacerbate the polarization of the labor market. High-end professionals equipped with interdisciplinary skills and innovative capabilities are likely to enjoy more promising career prospects, whereas entry-level workers engaged in repetitive tasks may face a higher risk of unemployment. This Matthew Effect is likely to intensify socioeconomic disparities. In response, it is essential to strengthen vocational and skills education to enhance workers' digital literacy and competence in intelligent systems. Simultaneously, the social security system should be improved to provide necessary support and buffers for workers undergoing occupational transitions.

It is worth noting that although AI is encroaching upon the traditional domains of human expertise, its very development is also generating new skill demands. Emerging roles such as data annotation and algorithm optimization are creating fresh growth opportunities within the job market. The crux lies in whether humans can attune themselves to the pulse of the times and accurately position themselves within the paradigm of human-machine collaboration. This necessitates a commitment to lifelong learning, embracing change with an open mindset, and continuously iterating one's own repertoire of knowledge and skills.

Amidst the torrent of transformation, our only viable response is to embrace intelligence with openness and inclusivity. This is inevitably a process fraught with challenges, yet it is also replete with boundless possibilities. Within the symphony of human-machine collaboration, every individual should become the tuner of their own destiny. Let us move forward together with integrity and sincerity to compose the resounding anthem of our era. While the landscape of skills continues to evolve, the enduring brilliance of human nature remains unchanged. With unwavering determination and innovative spirit, we can inscribe unique chapters of our lives in this era of rapid transformation.

PART III Reconstructing Digital Trust from the Perspective of Intelligent Risk

Chapter Thirteen Technological Construction: The Hard Trust Building Mechanisms of Digital Trust in the Era of Generative AI

With the ongoing digitalization and the rapid emergence of generative AI technologies, human society is entering a new era of intelligence. The decentralized and highly ubiquitous human-machine relational networks shaped by generative AI are continuously disrupting the traditional communication ecosystem and profoundly reconstructing the landscape of social interaction for individuals, organizations, and even nation-states. However, while technological empowerment enhances the effectiveness of information dissemination, latent risks such as algorithmic opacity, model fragility, and systemic uncontrollability have rendered the foundations of digital trust increasingly precarious. Therefore, this chapter adopts a technological perspective, using the reliability, robustness, and transparency of generative AI systems as key entry points to explore the connotations, underlying logic, and developmental pathways of digital trust. Through a systematic analysis of technical mechanisms such as algorithmic optimization, security protection, and privacy safeguarding, this study aims to elucidate the critical elements of hard trust construction. Furthermore, by positioning digital trust as a bridge, it aims to investigate regulatory approaches to managing generative AI-related technological risks, thereby offering theoretical insights and academic support for the reconfiguration of communication order in the intelligent era.

Section 1 Algorithm Optimization: Enhancing the Reliability and Robustness of Generative AI Systems

Optimizing the reliability and robustness of generative AI systems is a complex systems engineering task that requires coordinated optimization across multiple dimensions, including algorithms, data, and evaluation methodologies. The algorithm forms the core of generative AI, and its performance enhancement depends on meticulous design and iterative optimization in aspects such as model architecture, training paradigms, and objective functions. High-quality training data serves as the foundation for algorithmic performance, necessitating rigorous processes in data collection, cleansing, augmentation, and annotation to ensure data authenticity, representativeness, and accuracy. At the same time, the establishment of a scientific and comprehensive evaluation framework is crucial for controlling algorithmic performance. This approach integrates automated and human evaluations with the development of fine-grained, task-specific metrics, thus enabling a holistic assessment of an algorithm's effectiveness, robustness, and generalization capabilities in real-world scenarios. Only through a multi-pronged, system-level optimization approach can the reliability and robustness of generative AI systems be maximized, thereby facilitating their seamless integration into domains such as intelligent healthcare, smart finance, and intelligent education.

1. Data Quality Control: Ensuring the Authenticity, Accuracy, and Representativeness of Training Data

Data quality control is the cornerstone of the reliability and robustness of generative AI systems. The authenticity, accuracy, and representativeness of training data directly affect a model's generalization capacity and predictive performance. For instance, GPT-3's training data comprises massive amounts of web text spanning diverse domains of knowledge. However, information on the internet is highly heterogeneous, with rumors and misinformation frequently encountered. If the training data are contaminated with substantial amounts of inaccurate information, the model may be misled during learning, resulting in erroneous knowledge associations. Therefore, it is necessary to denoise and validate the data, removing false and incorrect information to ensure data integrity and reliability. At the same time, training data must possess broad representativeness, comprehensively covering the data distributions relevant to application scenarios. For instance, in the domain of intelligent healthcare, if training data are limited to medical records from specific demographic groups, the resulting model will likely struggle to adapt to the diverse characteristics of patients, thereby significantly compromising its diagnostic and predictive accuracy. Thus, it is essential to collect large-scale medical data from various regions and populations to enhance data representativeness and diversity. Furthermore, the accuracy of data annotation is also critical. Annotation biases and errors directly degrade model performance. It is necessary to establish rigorous annotation standards and quality control procedures, conducting multiple rounds of validation on annotation outcomes to ensure labeling quality. In summary, data quality control should encompass key dimensions such as authenticity, representativeness, and accuracy. By leveraging techniques such as data cleansing, anomaly detection, and data augmentation, the overall data quality can be comprehensively improved, and a robust data foundation for the reliable operation of generative AI systems can be established.

2. Model Iteration and Upgrade: Enhancing Algorithm Robustness, Generalization Capability, and Adaptability

Model iteration and upgrading are key pathways for enhancing the performance of generative AI systems, with a focus on strengthening algorithmic robustness, generalization capability, and adaptability. For example, ChatGPT's underlying language model, GPT-3.5, has undergone multiple rounds of iterative optimization, resulting in a marked improvement in model robustness. By incorporating techniques such as adversarial training and data augmentation, it is better equipped to handle anomalous inputs, including grammatical errors and ambiguous expressions, thereby generating more robust and reliable responses. At the same time, the model's generalization ability has been significantly enhanced. During training, ChatGPT integrates vast amounts of cross-domain knowledge, forming extensive semantic understanding and knowledge association capabilities. This enables it to flexibly address diverse conversational scenarios and provide insightful responses. Moreover, adaptability is also a primary focus in model iteration and upgrading. Traditional static models struggle to accommodate continuously evolving user needs and application environments. The introduction of online learning and incremental learning technologies allows AI models to dynamically adjust themselves based on feedback and enable ongoing self-improvement. For instance, Meta's Blenderbot continuously evolves its conversational abilities by interacting with users and assimilating new knowledge. Effective model iteration and upgrading require a profound understanding of the intrinsic mechanisms of algorithms, taking into account model architecture, loss functions, and optimization strategies for systematic optimization design. Only by continuously overcoming algorithmic bottlenecks and enhancing model performance can generative AI systems maintain the momentum necessary for reliable application in real-world contexts.

3. Performance Metrics Evaluation: Establishing a Scientific Assessment Framework for Comprehensive Measurement of Algorithm Performance

Performance metric evaluation is a critical component in diagnosing the performance of generative AI systems, serving to establish a scientific assessment framework that comprehensively measures the effectiveness, accuracy, and reliability of algorithms. Currently, evaluation methodologies for generative AI remain underdeveloped. For instance, in the scenarios of text generation, traditional metrics such as BLEU and ROUGE focus primarily on assessing n-gram overlap between generated text and reference answers, which makes it difficult to capture the fluency, coherence, and semantic relevance of the generated content in a holistic manner. Therefore, there is an urgent need to develop more refined evaluation metrics that integrate multiple dimensions—such as grammar, semantics, and logic—to comprehensively assess the quality of generated text. Additionally, it is necessary to combine human and automated evaluation methods to balance accuracy and efficiency in assessment. In the domain of image generation, metrics like FID (Fréchet Inception Distance) and IS (Inception Score) can quantitatively evaluate the realism and diversity of generated images, yet they still fall short in fully capturing the aesthetic value and subjective perception of images. The introduction of human scoring mechanisms, such as expert reviews and crowdsourced annotations, enables the acquisition of more comprehensive and granular evaluation results, thereby providing reliable feedback for algorithmic optimization. Moreover, the establishment of an evaluation framework must take into account the specific requirements of different application scenarios. For instance, in intelligent healthcare, model explainability and fairness are particularly critical. It is necessary to design targeted evaluation metrics to measure the transparency of model decision-making processes and to assess whether models exhibit bias or discrimination. In intelligent finance, the focus of evaluation lies in model stability and risk control capabilities. This necessitates the construction of stress-testing scenarios to evaluate model performance under extreme market conditions and to verify its risk resilience. Performance metric evaluation provides an essential foundation for optimizing generative AI systems. By constructing a comprehensive and scientific evaluation framework, it becomes possible to accurately assess algorithmic performance, identify performance bottlenecks, and guide iterative optimization of algorithms, thereby continuously enhancing the reliability and robustness of generative AI systems.

Section 2 Security Protection: Building a Robust Fortress for Generative AI Systems

The security protection of generative AI systems is a complex and pressing issue that requires the construction of a comprehensive and multidimensional security defense framework, encompassing identity authentication, data encryption, and real-time monitoring. This endeavor not only demands the innovative application of cutting-edge technologies, but also necessitates the internalization of security concepts, fostering a security-conscious culture in which all stakeholders contribute to a shared security ecosystem. Establishing security assessment frameworks and standardized regulations for generative AI, strengthening foundational security infrastructure, reinforcing security auditing and regulatory oversight, and cultivating interdisciplinary security professionals are all critical measures for effectively implementing and sustaining this system. Only through a coordinated approach that integrates technical, managerial, and institutional dimensions can we safeguard the healthy development of generative AI systems, and ensure that their benefits to humanity are realized without compromising security, thereby enabling sustainable and trustworthy progress.

1. Identity Authentication Mechanism: Preventing Impersonation and Unauthorized Access with Multi-Factor Authentication

The identity authentication mechanism is a critical component in constructing the security defenses of generative AI systems, with its core lying in the adoption of multi-factor authentication to prevent impersonation and unauthorized access. Currently, generative AI systems face numerous security challenges, such as identity spoofing and information leakage. Relying solely on single-factor password authentication is insufficient to withstand increasingly sophisticated attacks. Therefore, it is imperative to introduce multi-factor authentication mechanisms, which enhance the reliability of identity verification through multiple layers of validation. For example, facial recognition leverages cameras to capture users' facial features, utilizing algorithms such as liveness detection and feature extraction to achieve rapid and accurate identity verification. Integrating additional biometric modalities, such as voiceprint and fingerprint recognition, can further bolster authentication security. Moreover, the incorporation of external authentication elements, such as hardware tokens and digital certificates, provides additional layers of assurance for identity verification. For sensitive operations, authentication strategies can be dynamically adjusted, adopting different combinations of authentication factors according to the assessed risk level to achieve adaptive authentication strength. For instance, high-risk activities like fund transfers may require simultaneous facial recognition, hardware tokens, and SMS verification codes, thereby establishing multiple lines of defense; whereas for routine information browsing, the authentication process can be streamlined to enhance user experience.[1]

In addition, continuous authentication is a crucial method for ensuring system security. Traditional authentication approaches typically verify identity only once at the beginning of a session, making it difficult to detect identity tampering or impersonation during subsequent

---

1 ALBALAWI, S., ALSHAHRANI, L., ALBALAWI, N., et al. A comprehensive overview on biometric authentication systems using artificial intelligence techniques[J]. International Journal of Advanced Computer Science and Applications, 2022, 13 (4): 1-11.

interactions. Continuous authentication mechanisms facilitate real-time, multidimensional analysis of user behavior and interaction patterns, and enable dynamic assessment of the authenticity of the current session. Upon detecting anomalies, these mechanisms can immediately implement corresponding defensive measures to block unauthorized access in a timely manner. The development of multi-factor authentication mechanisms must be grounded in a comprehensive risk assessment of generative AI systems, taking into full account factors such as technological maturity, user acceptance, and cost-effectiveness. The goal is to design authentication solutions that are secure, trustworthy, and user-friendly, thereby providing a robust safeguard for the secure operation of the systems.

2. Encrypted Data Storage: Ensuring the Security of Stored Data with Robust Encryption Algorithms

Encrypted data storage constitutes a critical component in the security framework of generative AI systems, whose key is the application of robust encryption algorithms to the comprehensive safeguarding of data storage security. Generative AI systems typically process vast amounts of user data, which often contains sensitive information; any leakage of such data poses serious threats to user privacy and system security. Therefore, it is indispensable to employ advanced encryption algorithms for encrypted data storage to ensure data confidentiality and integrity. Homomorphic encryption, for example, features unique ciphertext computation properties that allow for direct processing and analysis of encrypted data without the need for decryption, enabling analytical results to be obtained while maintaining encryption.[1] The application of this technology to generative AI systems enables data sharing and collaborative computation while simultaneously protecting data privacy, thereby substantially reducing the risk of data breaches.[2] Attribute-based encryption technology, on the other hand, binds access policies to ciphertext, enabling fine-grained access control. Data owners can flexibly define data access rules according to different users' attributes and permissions, thereby preventing unauthorized parties from stealing or abusing data. Furthermore, the design of encryption schemes must balance both performance and security. Traditional encryption algorithms often involve high computational complexity, making it difficult to meet real-time processing requirements. Thus, algorithm selection requires comprehensive trade-offs, incorporating novel encryption techniques such as lightweight encryption and searchable encryption to improve encryption and decryption efficiency and minimize system performance impact while maintaining security. Encrypted data storage is a systematic endeavor that must address every stage of the data lifecycle—generation, transmission, storage, and processing—to construct an end-to-end security defense. At the data generation stage, sensitive data should be encrypted and promptly transmitted to secure storage locations. During data processing, technologies such as secure multi-party computation and trusted execution environments should be employed to ensure the confidentiality of intermediate computational results. Only by implementing rigorous data security protection measures at every phase of the data lifecycle can a robust security network be established, thereby guaranteeing the secure

1 LAUTER, K. Private AI: Machine Learning on Encrypted Data[M]. Recent advances in industrial and applied mathematics. Cham: Springer International Publishing, 2022: 97-113.

2 LIU, Beishui, GAO, Rui, LI, Dan, et al. Research on data storage encryption technology[J]. Electronic Product Reliability and Environmental Testing, 2020, 38 (4): 44-47.

operation of generative AI systems.

3. Real-time Monitoring and Early Warning: Promptly Detecting Potential Threats with Intelligent Monitoring Systems

Real-time monitoring and early warning constitute a critical line of defense in constructing a robust security framework for generative AI systems. The core of this approach lies in deploying intelligent monitoring systems capable of promptly detecting and responding to potential security threats. At present, generative AI systems face numerous security challenges, such as data poisoning and adversarial attacks. Traditional post-hoc detection and passive defense mechanisms are inadequate to counter increasingly sophisticated attack vectors; thus, it is imperative to establish real-time, proactive security monitoring and early warning mechanisms.[1] For example, in adversarial attacks, attackers can craft adversarial samples that deliberately induce the models to make erroneous decisions, resulting in significant security risks. Intelligent monitoring systems, however, can conduct real-time analysis of input data to promptly identify potential adversarial samples. By integrating techniques such as anomaly detection and few-shot learning, these systems can rapidly adapt and recalibrate detection models even in the face of novel attack modalities, thereby enabling real-time discovery and warning of emerging threats.[2] Meanwhile, heterogeneous data correlation analysis based on graph neural networks can deeply mine multi-source heterogeneous data

---

1 WANG, B. X., CHEN, J. L., YU, C. L. An AI-powered network threat detection system[J]. IEEE Access, 2022, 10: 54029-54037.

2 AMARASINGHE, A., WIJESINGHE, W., NIRMANA, D. L. A., et al. AI based cyberthreats and vulnerability detection, prevention and prediction system[C]. 2019 International Conference on Advancements in Computing (ICAC). IEEE, 2019: 363-368.

generated during system operation, uncovering the intrinsic relationships among various security incidents, predicting attackers' intentions and behavioral patterns, and achieving early threat detection and warning. Concurrently, it is essential to establish rapid response mechanisms to promptly intercept and mitigate security threats. Intelligent security orchestration and automated response technologies can dynamically adjust system defense strategies and security configurations based on early warning intelligence, achieving rapid isolation and handling of threats. For example, in the event of a data poisoning attack, a system equipped with such technologies can automatically detect, cleanse and repair contaminated data and retrain the model, thereby minimizing the impact of the attack to the greatest extent possible.

In addition, the introduction of blockchain technology offers new approaches for the traceability and auditing of security incidents. By storing critical monitoring data and response actions on-chain, it creates immutable records of security events, providing reliable evidence for post-incident analysis and accountability. The realization of real-time monitoring and early warning relies on the efficient processing and intelligent analysis of massive, heterogeneous data. The adoption of distributed computing frameworks and stream data processing technologies can significantly enhance the real-time and parallel processing capabilities of data. Meanwhile, the application of AI technologies such as machine learning and knowledge graphs endows monitoring systems with more advanced analytical and decision-making capabilities. This enables the precise identification and prediction of security threats in complex and dynamic environments, thereby providing a solid foundation for the long-term security and stability of generative AI systems.

Section 3 Privacy Protection: Safeguarding User Privacy Rights in Generative AI Interactions

The rapid development of generative AI technologies has injected new momentum into the digital economy, while simultaneously giving rise to unprecedented challenges in privacy protection. During the training and inference phases of generative AI models, the collection, circulation, and utilization of vast amounts of user privacy data can easily lead to a series of privacy breaches, such as excessive collection of sensitive information, unauthorized access, and data misuse. These issues not only undermine users' legitimate rights and interests but also cast a shadow over the sustainable development of generative AI applications. Consequently, how to construct user-centric privacy protection mechanisms, strike a balance between individual privacy and data utilization, and uphold ethical standards in the digital era has become a critical issue in the age of generative AI.

1. Data Access Control: Implementing Stringent Management of Data Access Permissions

Data access control is a critical measure for safeguarding users' privacy rights in generative AI interactions, whose essence rests in the implementation of stringent data access permission management to ensure the confidentiality and privacy of user data.[1] Generative AI systems typically involve the collection, storage, and processing of vast amounts of user data, which often contains sensitive user information. If maliciously exploited, such data could inflict irreparable harm to user privacy. Therefore, it is imperative to establish fine-grained data access control

1 BELLETTINI, C. BERTINO, E., FERRARI, E. Role based access control models[J]. Information Security Technical Report, 2001, 6 (2): 21-29.

mechanisms to rigorously regulate data access and usage. Role-Based Access Control (RBAC) models can dynamically configure data access policies according to users' identities and responsibilities. By categorizing users into different roles and granting each role corresponding data access permissions, refined management of data access can be achieved. For example, in generative AI applications within the healthcare sector, differentiated electronic medical record access rules can be established based on roles such as physicians, nurses, and hospital administrators: ordinary medical staff may only access the medical data of patients under their care, while hospital administrators may be authorized to access aggregated, de-identified statistical information. This approach simultaneously fulfills diverse data needs and minimizes the risk of privacy breaches.

In addition, the establishment of independent access control domains tailored to different data assets has proven to be an effective approach to strengthening privacy protection. By partitioning sensitive data—such as users' identity information, behavioral logs, and biometric features—into discrete access control domains, and implementing separate authentication and authorization mechanisms for each domain, it is possible to prevent unauthorized access and cross-correlation of sensitive data, thereby mitigating the privacy risks associated with data aggregation. Simultaneously, the adoption of data lineage analysis technologies enables the tracking of data throughout its entire lifecycle, from generation to application, illuminating the context of data access and utilization, and facilitating the timely detection and interruption of unauthorized data access. The effective implementation of data access control is inseparable from reliable identity authentication and authorization mechanisms. For instance, in the federated learning scenario, collaborative model training among multiple parties must be achieved while safeguarding the data sovereignty of all participants. To this end, cryptographic technologies such as trusted execution environments and secure multi-party computation are employed to verify the identities of participants and assign data access permissions based on authorization credentials, all without exposing raw data. This ensures both the normal progression of model training and the security of each party's data assets. Only by addressing data access control at its source, and building a robust defense based on cryptographic and access control technologies, can the inviolability of user privacy be fundamentally safeguarded in generative AI applications.

2. Privacy-Preserving Algorithms: Application of Advanced Privacy-Preserving Technologies such as Differential Privacy and Homomorphic Encryption

Privacy-preserving algorithms serve as a critical technological foundation for safeguarding users' privacy rights in generative AI interactions. The core of these algorithms is the implementation of advanced privacy-preserving technologies such as differential privacy and homomorphic encryption, which provide comprehensive protection for user privacy throughout the entire data lifecycle. In both the training and inference phases of generative AI systems, it is inevitable that substantial volumes of user-sensitive data are accessed. If such private data are directly utilized for model training, there exists a significant risk of privacy breaches. Differential privacy introduces random noise into the data, thereby preserving the statistical properties of datasets while preventing the disclosure of sensitive information.[1] For instance, in news recommendation scenarios that leverage users' browsing histories, original

1 DWORK, C., ROTH, A. The algorithmic foundations of differential privacy[J]. Foundations and Trends in Theoretical Computer Science, 2014, 9 (3/4): 211-407.

browsing records can be processed with differential privacy to generate privacy-protected aggregate statistical data, which are then used to train recommendation models. This approach both enhances the predictive performance of the models and prevents the direct exposure of users' private information. In collaborative scenarios such as smart healthcare, where multi-party data integration is involved, the adoption of homomorphic encryption provides a novel paradigm for achieving a win-win balance between privacy protection and data utility.[1] Hospitals and research institutions can locally train homomorphically encrypted local models using raw patient medical data. Through encrypted gradient aggregation, federated learning can be realized, enabling global model performance improvements without sharing raw private data, thereby achieving collaborative modeling under true data isolation.

In addition, hardware-based trusted execution environments (TEEs) constitute a critical approach to implementing privacy-preserving algorithms. Technologies such as Intel SGX can establish a secure enclave within the processor, where code and data are accessible only inside this isolated region. Deploying privacy-preserving algorithms within a TEE can prevent malicious eavesdropping and tampering with both data and computational processes, thereby further enhancing the reliability of privacy protection.

It is noteworthy that while privacy-preserving algorithms facilitate data utilization, they also introduce new security vulnerabilities. Although techniques such as differential privacy can safeguard individual privacy, the risk of group privacy breaches persists. Therefore, the design and implementation of privacy-preserving algorithms must be grounded in

---

1 MITTAL, S., SHARMA, S., RAMKUMAR, K. R. A matrix-based homomorphic encryption for preserving privacy in clouds[J]. ECS Transactions, 2022, 107 (1): 5441.

comprehensive privacy risk assessments. Rigorous validation of the privacy protection capabilities of these algorithms should be conducted through mathematical proofs and formal verification methods. Furthermore, privacy protection strategies should be tailored to specific application scenarios to achieve an optimal balance between data utility and privacy preservation, thereby reinforcing the foundational safeguards for personal privacy in the era of generative AI.

3. Data De-identification: Mitigating the Risk of Privacy Breaches by De-identification Techniques

Data de-identification, or data masking, is a critical component of privacy protection in generative AI systems. Its primary objective is to sanitize sensitive data by employing techniques such as de-identification and pseudonymization, thereby attenuating the association between data and individual identities and mitigating the risk of privacy breaches.[1] During the data collection phase, it is essential to de-identify identifiable information, such as users' identity data and biometric features, converting them into irreversible anonymous identifiers to sever any direct linkage between the data and real-world identities. In addition, the numerical transformation and normalization of sensitive data attributes can obfuscate the original semantic meaning of attribute values, preventing the inference of personal identity through direct numerical comparison.

Moreover, adopting a flexible and diversified approach to data de-identification technologies, tailored to different data attributes and application scenarios, is an essential pathway to enhancing the

---

1 CHEN, Tianying, CHEN, Jianfeng. Intelligent data masking system in the context of big data[J]. Communication Technology, 2016, 49 (7): 915-922.

effectiveness of privacy protection.[1] For example, in the de-identification of geolocation data, spatial encryption techniques can be employed to encrypt and transform location coordinates. This ensures that the de-identified location data retains its spatial characteristics, thereby supporting operations such as range queries and proximity searches. In this way, privacy is robustly protected while the application value of location data is maximally preserved. In contrast, for data involving social relationship networks, graph data anonymization algorithms can be utilized. By randomizing node identities and sensitive attributes while maintaining the topological structure of the graph, these methods reduce the risk of privacy leakage and simultaneously support graph-based data mining and analysis.

Data de-identification should not be regarded as a one-off process. In the face of increasingly complex data forms and evolving privacy threats, data de-identification strategies must dynamically evolve in tandem with the data lifecycle. Different levels of de-identification intensity can be applied based on the temporal sensitivity of data. For example, for online inference data that requires high real-time responsiveness, a lower granularity of de-identification may be appropriate, providing the minimum necessary privacy protection while ensuring inference performance. In contrast, historical data intended for long-term storage should undergo the most stringent de-identification procedures to thoroughly eliminate traceability. Furthermore, as new privacy threats such as data linkage attacks continue to emerge, de-identification strategies must also keep pace with these developments. This entails regularly assessing and updating de-identification algorithms to address

---

1 BIAN, Chaoyi, ZHU, Shaomin, ZHOU, Tao. Implementation and evaluation of a big data desensitization system based on format-preserving encryption[J]. Telecommunication Science, 2017, 33 (3): 119-125.

potential privacy vulnerabilities and to build a privacy protection framework that evolves in response to the changing threat landscape.

Section 4 Enhancing Explainability: Improving the Transparency and Comprehensibility of Generative AI Systems

The explainability of generative AI systems is a critical prerequisite for their widespread adoption in real-world applications. Enhancing explainability not only facilitates users' understanding and trust in AI-driven decisions, but also serves as the cornerstone for AI systems' self-optimization and effective human-AI collaboration. Strengthening explainability requires systematic design across multiple dimensions, including model architecture, visualization, and user interaction. This can be achieved by employing inherently explainable algorithmic models, intuitively presenting AI systems' decision-making processes, and providing accessible natural language explanations. Such approaches help construct a transparent, auditable, and mutually trustworthy environment for human-AI cooperation, enabling a transition from perceptual intelligence to cognitive intelligence, and from one-way service provision to bidirectional collaboration. Only by making AI's reasoning patterns and behavioral logic accessible to human insight, and leveraging technology to bridge the gap between humans and machines, can the application of AI break free from the constraints of the "algorithmic black box" and deliver benefits to humanity across a broader range of fields.

1. Design of Explainable Models: Employing Algorithmic Models with Explainability

The design of explainable models is a critical pathway for enhancing the transparency and comprehensibility of generative AI systems. Its core lies in employing algorithmic models with inherent explainability, endowing the models with the intrinsic capability to self-explain and elucidate the rationale behind their decisions. Although traditional deep learning models have achieved remarkable success in domains such as image and speech processing, their internal operational mechanisms remain akin to a "black box," making it challenging to understand the underlying logic driving specific model decisions. [1] In contrast, explainable models explicitly model the relationships between data features and decision outcomes, rendering the decision-making processes transparent and traceable. This enables users to comprehend the basis of the models' judgments and to assess the reasonableness of their decision outcomes.

For instance, in image classification tasks, traditional convolutional neural networks, while efficient at recognizing image content, struggle to explain which specific features of the image ultimately lead to the classification outcome. In contrast, explainable image classification models are capable of learning explicit correspondences between features and categories. These models can intuitively present the regions of an image that most influence the classification result by visualizing heatmaps. This allows users to determine which key features the models focus on, thereby facilitating the understanding and validation of the classification rationality. For instance, in medical image diagnosis, explainable models can not only provide localization results for lesions but also clearly indicate the critical features within the lesion area, thus assisting physicians in diagnostic validation and etiological analysis.

In addition to feature-association-based explainable models,

---

1 WU, Fei, LIAO, Binbing, HAN, Yahong. Explainability of deep learning[J]. Aeronautical Weapons, 2019, 26 (1): 39-46.

generative models that incorporate prior knowledge represent another significant approach to enhancing model explainability. Traditional generative models predominantly rely on massive datasets to learn data distributions; however, the latent space representations they acquire often fail to align with human intuitive cognition. In contrast, generative models that integrate prior knowledge—such as Bayesian Rule Lists—can explicitly model the logical rules between data features and generated outcomes, enabling the models' outputs to be explained through straightforward logical rules. For example, in NLP, generated texts must not only adhere to grammatical norms but also conform to common-sense semantic logic as understood by humans. Text generation models that embed prior knowledge can incorporate grammatical rules, causal logic, and other forms of human knowledge into the generation process, ensuring that the outputs are not only fluent and natural but also exhibit coherent causality and logic, thereby facilitating human understanding and interpretation.[1]

2. Visualization of Decision-Making: Facilitating User Interpretation by Intuitive Representation of AI Decision-Making

Visualization of decision-making is a crucial approach for enhancing the transparency and explainability of generative AI systems. Its primary aim is to intuitively present the systems' decision-making processes, thereby making the underlying logic explicit and facilitating user interpretation and scrutiny. Traditional AI systems typically operate as end-to-end black boxes, where decisions are formed through multiple

---

1 ZENG, Chunyan, YAN, Kang, WANG, Zhifeng, et al. A review of research on the explainability of deep learning models[J]. Computer Engineering and Applications, 2021, 57 (8): 1-9.

layers of complex data transformation and feature abstraction, resulting in the rationale for decisions being obscured within vast numbers of parameters and inaccessible to users. In contrast, decision-making visualization seeks to deconstruct the decision-making processes layer by layer. By leveraging visual tools such as infographics and flowcharts, it concretely represents the flow of data through each layer of the models, making the intricate processes of decision reasoning transparent and observable.

For example, in the task of text classification in NLP, traditional deep learning classifiers typically map text into a high-dimensional semantic space and perform classification through complex nonlinear transformations. The semantic extraction and reasoning processes involved are often difficult for laypersons to comprehend. In contrast, classifiers employing visualization of decision-making can intuitively demonstrate the contribution of different words and phrases to the classification outcome by presenting steps such as "bag-of-words" feature extraction and co-occurrence statistics. Furthermore, visualizing the classification process in the form of a decision tree renders the classification rationale more accessible and explainable. This enables users to discern whether the models' understanding of textual semantics is accurate and whether their sensitivity to keywords is reasonable, thereby facilitating the interpretation and critical evaluation of the reliability of classification decisions.

In the field of computer vision, decision-making visualization is increasingly becoming a critical aid for tasks such as image classification and object detection. For instance, in medical imaging diagnosis, the process by which a model arrives at a diagnostic conclusion often involves multiple stages, including lesion localization, extraction of key features, and inferential reasoning linking features to disease states. By visualizing, layer by layer, the lesion region "heatmaps," the extracted textural and morphological features, as well as the decision chain underlying disease classification, clinicians are better able to interpret the diagnostic reasoning process, assess the credibility of the model's diagnostic recommendations, and, when necessary, provide feedback to optimize the model's feature extraction and reasoning strategies. This fosters a virtuous cycle of human-AI collaborative diagnosis and iterative optimization.

3. Natural Language Explanation: Enhancing Human-Machine Trust by Clear and Accessible Natural Language

Natural language explanations represent another crucial approach to enhancing the transparency and explainability of generative AI systems. Their primary objective is to provide accessible, comprehensible textual justifications for system decisions, thereby translating complex reasoning processes into plain language. This narrows the gap between technology and the humanities and fosters greater trust between humans and machines. While traditional AI systems are capable of producing task-oriented computational outputs, they often obscure their underlying logic; users are frequently confronted with abstruse mathematical expressions and technical jargon and thus difficult to grasp the true rationale behind system behaviors. In contrast, natural language explanations aim to reconstruct machine reasoning in human terms. By articulating the basis for decisions and the logic of inference in written language, these explanations demystify system decision-making, rendering it more approachable and integrating it into the broader public discourse.

For instance, in knowledge graph-based question answering systems, traditional approaches based on graph embedding and neural networks are capable of achieving precise query matching; however, they often lack the ability to provide convincing explanations for the selection of specific answers. In contrast, question answering systems that integrate natural language explanations are able to offer readable explanations of the candidate answer ranking mechanisms. Such systems not only present the final answer but can also generate explanatory texts such as, “A was chosen over B because A has a shorter relational path to the query in the knowledge graph, and the types of relationships are a better match.” This enables users to understand the knowledge basis and logical rationale underlying the systems’ decision-making, thereby offering a more intuitive sense of the answer’s reliability.

Section 5 Security Protection: Building a Defense-in-Depth Framework for Generative AI Systems

The security protection of generative AI systems presents a complex and formidable challenge, requiring a comprehensive, multi-faceted approach that integrates software, hardware, and network components to collaboratively construct a defense-in-depth architecture. Secure coding standards are powerful tools for mitigating software vulnerabilities; by adopting rigorous coding standards and adhering to security best practices from the outset, the resilience of AI systems against code-level attacks can be significantly enhanced. Simultaneously, the integration of hardware security technologies such as trusted computing and security chips aims to establish a secure execution environment for AI systems, rooted in hardware-based trust, thereby defending against chip-level attacks and data breaches. As the critical conduit connecting distributed AI systems, network security is equally indispensable. The deployment of emerging concepts and technologies—such as intrusion detection and zero trust—enables effective identification of network threats and enforces rigorous authentication and authorization for every access attempt. Only by integrating both software and hardware safeguards, and addressing security at the levels of code, hardware, and networks, can a robust security barrier be established for generative AI systems, thereby ensuring their steady progress on a compliant and controllable trajectory.

1. Software Security Hardening: Enhancing Software Resilience against Attacks with Secure Coding Standards

Software security hardening serves as the cornerstone for constructing a defense-in-depth architecture in generative AI systems. Its core lies in the adoption of secure coding standards, thereby enhancing software resilience against attacks at the source. Currently, most AI systems are rapidly developed based on open-source frameworks and components, which themselves may harbor numerous security vulnerabilities. Adversaries can exploit these weaknesses through techniques such as code injection and buffer overflow, enabling them to implant malicious payloads or even gain full control over the AI systems. Therefore, it is imperative to address security from the source code level by employing stringent secure coding practices, minimizing security vulnerabilities, and strengthening the systems' inherent defensive capabilities.

For example, the root cause of buffer overflow vulnerabilities originates in improper validation of user input and flawed memory operations. Attackers can craft excessively long strings to overwrite the program's return address, thereby executing malicious code. However, AI systems developed with secure coding standards can implement multiple layers of defense during user input validation and processing. Measures such as input length restriction and special character escaping can effectively mitigate the risks posed by illegal input to memory space. In terms of memory management, employing compiler-based security hardening techniques such as Address Space Layout Randomization (ASLR) and Data Execution Prevention (DEP) can further reduce the risk of memory corruption during code execution.

In addition, AI systems should adhere to the principle of least privilege, rigorously restricting the influence of external data on core components. By adopting a modular and microservices-based system architecture, AI systems can be decoupled into independent functional units. Utilizing containerization technologies enables access control and resource isolation across modules, thereby minimizing the cascading effects when a single component is compromised. Furthermore, implementing differentiated security reinforcement strategies tailored to specific modules allows for precise deployment of protective measures while simultaneously accommodating performance requirements.

2. Hardware Security Protection: Application of Hardware Security Technologies such as Trusted Computing and Security Chips

Hardware security protection is a crucial component in constructing a layered defense system for generative AI. Its objective is to leverage hardware security technologies—such as trusted computing and security chips—to provide AI systems with secure and trustworthy computing environments. Currently, while the computational power of AI chips is advancing rapidly, their security protection capabilities remain underdeveloped. Malicious actors can exploit potential vulnerabilities such as side channels and backdoors within chips to exfiltrate sensitive information or even take control of AI systems. Therefore, it is imperative to fortify the foundation of AI security at the hardware level, starting from components such as chips and firmware.

The introduction of trusted computing technologies can establish a secure and reliable execution environment for AI systems. Through the use of a Trusted Platform Module (TPM) chip, critical system components can be measured and verified, ensuring the integrity of both hardware and software remains uncompromised. Mechanisms such as memory encryption and key protection safeguard the confidentiality of sensitive information such as AI model parameters and user private data. Even if an attacker gains physical access, it remains difficult to exfiltrate sensitive data from memory. The application of Trusted Execution Environment (TEE) technologies to AI chips can further isolate security-sensitive operations from general applications, preventing malicious programs from spying on or tampering with critical data.

With the increasing complexity of AI systems, traditional central processing units (CPUs) are no longer able to meet their performance requirements. Custom AI chips, such as application-specific integrated circuits (ASICs) and field-programmable gate arrays (FPGAs), have thus emerged. However, the security verification of custom chips faces numerous challenges. The chip supply chain is highly intricate, providing opportunities for malicious actors to implant hardware backdoors during the design or manufacturing stages, or even alter the physical structures of the chips. Consequently, it is imperative to employ technologies such as formal verification and trusted manufacturing to embed security assurance measures throughout all phases of chip design and production. By applying formal modeling and verification to chip layouts and circuits, potential security vulnerabilities can be identified during the design stage. Furthermore, trusted manufacturing platforms, leveraging hardware roots of trust, enable comprehensive monitoring and auditing of the entire chip production process, thereby facilitating the timely detection and removal of suspicious components.

3. Cybersecurity Protection: Deploying Cybersecurity Measures such as Intrusion Detection Systems and Firewalls

Cybersecurity protection also constitutes a critical component in establishing a layered defense system for generative AI architectures. Its primary objective is to deploy cybersecurity measures such as intrusion detection systems and firewalls, thereby fortifying the network security perimeter of AI systems. At present, most AI systems utilize cloud computing and distributed architectures, resulting in the transmission of large volumes of sensitive data and computational tasks across networks. However, the increasing frequency of cyberattacks indicates that significant vulnerabilities persist in the network security of AI systems. Techniques such as Distributed Denial of Service (DDoS) attacks and packet sniffing can lead to service disruptions, leakage of sensitive information, and even catastrophic consequences. Consequently, cybersecurity protection has become an urgent requirement to ensure the stable and secure operation of AI systems.

The introduction of Intrusion Detection Systems (IDS) can establish a comprehensive surveillance and inescapable protective barrier for AI systems. Anomaly detection algorithms based on machine learning are capable of identifying suspicious activities from massive volumes of network traffic, enabling the timely detection of potential intrusion attempts. By conducting real-time analysis of system logs and resource utilization, IDS can also accurately trace the activities of intruders, providing robust support for security incident investigations and accountability. Furthermore, IDS can be integrated with threat intelligence platforms, leveraging globally distributed honeypot networks to capture the latest attack techniques and characteristics. This facilitates the continuous updating of detection models, ensuring that the security of AI systems evolves in step with emerging threats.

The rise of Zero Trust security architecture has introduced new concepts and practices to the cybersecurity of AI systems. Traditional perimeter-based security defenses are increasingly inadequate for the decentralized and diverse network structures characteristic of AI systems. In contrast, Zero Trust security adheres to the principle of "never trust, always verify," enforcing rigorous identity authentication and authorization for every network access attempt. By implementing granular controls over devices, users, and applications, the attack surface of AI systems can be minimized. The integration of technologies such as encrypted micro-tunnels and software-defined perimeters into AI systems enables the construction of a globally pervasive, flexible, and controllable security network, thereby safeguarding the execution of distributed AI tasks.

Section 6 Fault Tolerance Mechanisms: Enhancing the Robustness and Resilience of Generative AI Systems

The fault tolerance of generative AI systems is a crucial guarantee of their reliability and practical utility. In the face of increasingly complex application scenarios and massive volumes of data, enhancing system robustness and resilience has become a pressing challenge that demands immediate attention. Technical approaches such as anomaly detection and response, fault recovery mechanisms, and multi-node redundancy offer a wealth of strategies for improving the fault tolerance of generative AI systems. By leveraging real-time monitoring, intelligent diagnostics, redundant backups, and dynamic scheduling, these systems can establish comprehensive fault-tolerant defenses at multiple levels, thereby minimizing and mitigating the impact of failures to the greatest extent possible and ensuring service continuity and data integrity. This section will focus on the application patterns and implementation mechanisms of these three major technical initiatives in strengthening the fault tolerance of generative AI systems, aiming to provide systematic methodological guidance for the development of highly robust and resilient generative AI systems.

1. Anomaly Detection and Response: Real-time Monitoring of Anomalies and Implementation of Emergency Response Measures

Anomaly detection and management are critical measures for enhancing the robustness and resilience of generative AI systems. The core of this approach lies in the real-time monitoring of anomalies during system operations and the implementation of timely and effective contingency responses to minimize the impact of these anomalies on system performance and user experience. Currently, generative AI systems are highly complex, encompassing multiple stages such as data preprocessing, model training, and inference services. Anomalies in any of these stages can trigger cascading effects, resulting in significant performance degradation or even catastrophic outcomes. Therefore, comprehensive and real-time anomaly detection and management have become an urgent requirement to ensure the stable operation of generative AI systems.

Anomaly detection algorithms based on machine learning can serve as an “intelligent defense line” for generative AI systems. By conducting real-time analysis of system performance metrics and log data, anomaly detection models can promptly identify abnormal changes in system behavior and automatically trigger corresponding alert and response processes according to the severity and scope of the anomalies. For example, when the system of a chatbot detects sudden spikes in response latency or error rates, the anomaly detection model can automatically diagnose issues in language model inference and dynamically adjust load balancing strategies in real time, routing requests to backup nodes to ensure service quality remains unaffected. Furthermore, the model can perform in-depth analysis to identify the root causes of anomalies—such as data source contamination or algorithmic drift—thereby providing precise decision support for subsequent remediation and optimization efforts.

The effectiveness of anomaly detection is inseparable from comprehensive, multi-dimensional monitoring across the entire stack of generative AI systems. It is essential to deploy dedicated monitoring probes at every stage, including data acquisition, feature engineering, model training, and online inference, to collect operational state data systematically. Particularly for end-to-end generative AI pipelines, it is imperative to adhere to the principle of "seamless integration and interconnection," breaking down data silos between different stages and constructing a holistic monitoring framework throughout the entire process. This approach enables the timely identification and localization of complex anomaly sources. Furthermore, the correlation analysis of heterogeneous data can reveal the intrinsic relationships between performance metrics and business indicators, thereby facilitating the transition from "anomaly detection" to "insight discovery."

2. Fault Recovery Mechanism: Minimizing Losses to the Greatest Extent Possible

Fault recovery mechanisms are a critical pillar in enhancing the robustness and resilience of generative AI systems. Their primary objective is to establish effective protocols that minimize losses in system availability and data integrity resulting from failures. Generative AI systems are inherently complex, involving vast amounts of data and numerous parameters. The failure of any software or hardware module can trigger cascading effects, potentially leading to prolonged system downtime or even irreversible data loss. Consequently, comprehensive and automated fault recovery mechanisms are essential to ensure the reliable operation of generative AI systems.

Disaster recovery and backup constitute the first line of defense in fault recovery. By implementing geographically distributed and multi-media redundant backups of critical components and data within generative AI systems, users can enable rapid failover to standby resources in the event of a malfunction, thereby minimizing system downtime. For instance, large-scale language model training often spans several days or even weeks; any interruption can potentially render all prior efforts futile. The adoption of distributed training frameworks addresses this risk by periodically saving model checkpoints and training metadata, thus ensuring the persistence of training states. If a node failure occurs, the system can automatically transfer training tasks to alternative nodes and resume from the most recent checkpoint, thereby significantly reducing the temporal and computational costs associated with system failures.

The development of disaggregated compute-storage architecture has also introduced new approaches to fault recovery in generative AI systems. In traditional tightly coupled architectures, compute and storage resources are co-located, so any failure interrupts both data access and computational tasks. In contrast, disaggregated compute-storage architecture decouples data storage from computational resources, enabling flexible resource orchestration via high-speed networks. When faults occur, the systems can dynamically reallocate computational resources, rapidly reconstruct failed nodes, and recover data from distributed storage, thereby significantly enhancing system recoverability.

3. Multi-node Backup: Enhancing the Disaster Recovery Capability with a Distributed Architecture

Multi-node backup is a critical measure for enhancing the robustness and resilience of generative AI systems. Its core rests in adopting a distributed architecture that leverages redundant backups and load balancing to improve disaster recovery capabilities and scalability. Generative AI systems typically employ cloud-native and microservices-based architectures, encompassing modules such as data acquisition, feature engineering, model training, and online inference. A failure in any single module can trigger a cascade effect, potentially rendering the entire service unavailable. This risk is exacerbated in single-point deployment architectures, where a malfunction at a key node can paralyze the entire system. Consequently, the adoption of a multi-node distributed architecture has become an indispensable approach to ensuring high availability and reliable operation of generative AI systems.

Microservices architecture serves as the cornerstone for achieving multi-node redundancy. By decoupling a generative AI system into independent microservices, with each service responsible for a specific function, the impact scope of single points of failure can be significantly reduced. The introduction of container orchestration platforms such as Kubernetes further enables automated deployment, scheduling, and scaling of services. The system can dynamically adjust the number of service instances based on workload and automatically reschedule services to healthy nodes in the event of node failures, thereby achieving seamless service migration and recovery. For instance, in model inference services, the system can deploy multiple instances and distribute requests across different instances via load balancing. Should any instance fail, the load balancer can automatically reroute requests to other instances, ensuring uninterrupted service delivery from the user's perspective. Furthermore, the evolution of multi-cloud architectures offers new paradigms for multi-node redundancy in generative AI systems. Traditional single-cloud deployments face risks such as vendor lock-in and availability zone outages. In contrast, a multi-cloud architecture enables redundant deployment of services across different cloud platforms, significantly enhancing the systems' disaster recovery and resilience capabilities.

Chapter Fourteen Social Cultivation: The Soft Trust Building Mechanisms of Digital Trust in the Era of Generative AI

The rapid evolution of generative AI technologies is reshaping both the connotation and extension of digital trust. The latent proliferation of intelligent risks, such as algorithmic opacity and machine bias, poses severe challenges to the soft infrastructure underpinning digital trust. Soft trust, the socio-emotional foundation of digital trust, serves as a flexible adhesive within the trust landscape of digital society. Exploring the mechanisms underlying the construction of soft trust is of significant importance for pioneering a novel paradigm of symbiotic human-machine trust. This chapter focuses on the diverse pathways for cultivating soft trust in the era of generative AI. It distills the key mechanisms for building soft trust from the perspectives of institutional ethics, cultural values, media ecology, and educational empowerment, with the aim of providing both theoretical nourishment and practical guidance for the reconstruction of trust and communicative order in intelligent societies. By navigating the complexities of rapid AI advancement and confronting the critical and multifaceted challenges of human-machine trust, this chapter endeavors to carve out a lucid framework for strengthening the soft foundations of digital trust through the logical trajectories of cognitive trust reconstruction, ethical responsibility clarification, and environmental mechanism optimization.

Section 1 Reshaping Social Cognition: The Evolution of AI Technology and the Transformation of Trust Concepts

The rapid advancement of AI technology is profoundly reshaping both the connotation and extension of social trust. The mechanisms underlying the generation, maintenance, and dissemination of trust are undergoing unprecedented transformation. The trust ecosystem, empowered by technology, is now characterized by diversified actors, heterogeneous sources, and dynamic construction models. Trust is evolving from a purely interpersonal attribute to a complex property arising from the symbiotic integration of human-machine interactions, social systems, and technological systems. This profound shift in the context and production of trust brings both opportunities and challenges, and exerts a significant impact on traditional cognitive frameworks and governance paradigms of trust. The reconstruction of social trust urgently requires a synergy between technological rationality and humanistic care, as well as a dual drive of innovative development and ethical regulation. Only through prudent exploration of the path toward beneficial technology can we reconstruct a symbiotic vision of human-machine trust and usher in a new era for intelligent society.

1. Contextual Shift of Trust: From Interpersonal Interaction to Human-AI Interaction

The rapid development of AI technology is profoundly transforming the trust landscape in human society. Traditional notions of trust are grounded in interpersonal interactions, emphasizing face-to-face emotional exchanges and the gradual development.[1] However, the rise of AI has extended the scope of trust beyond interpersonal relationships to encompass human-machine interactions. The construction of trust is no longer confined to human-to-human relationships; issues of trust between humans and intelligent machines are becoming increasingly prominent.

The migration of trust to human-machine contexts engenders a series of cognitive challenges. People are accustomed to placing trust in flesh-and-blood individuals endowed with wisdom and rationality; however, AI systems, as intangible algorithmic black boxes, possess decision-making processes that are inherently opaque, thereby undermining human trust in these systems.[2] Cognitive disparities exist between humans and machines, making it difficult to establish reciprocal and intersubjective trust relationships. Moreover, AI may exhibit unpredictable behaviors, resulting in unmet human expectations of trust. For instance, incidents involving autonomous vehicles and inappropriate responses from intelligent customer service systems have exposed the fragility of trust in human-machine interactions.

Resolving the dilemma of human-machine trust necessitates a reshaping of social cognition. Technocentrism must yield to a human-centered paradigm for constructing trust. It is imperative to move beyond a reductionist view that equates trust solely with technological reliability, and instead conceptualize it as a dynamic game involving humans, machines, and their environments. In the digital era characterized by human-machine symbiosis, trust should not be dictated by algorithms;

1 MCKNIGHT, D. H., CARTER, M., THATCHER, J. B., et al. Trust in a specific technology[J]. ACM Transactions on Management Information Systems, 2011, 2 (2): 1-25.

2 RIBEIRO, M. T., SINGH, S., GUESTRIN, C. "Why should I trust you?" Explaining the predictions of any classifier[C]. Proceedings of the 22nd ACM SIGKDD International Conference on Knowledge Discovery and Data Mining. 2016: 1135-1144.

rather, it must be grounded in human-centered values to foster greater synergy and resonance between humans and machines.[1] Cultivating rational cognition and mutual trust between people and AI is an essential component in the co-construction of human-machine trust. Only by approaching and applying AI technologies with inclusiveness, humility, and responsibility can we transcend cognitive pitfalls associated with human-machine trust and open up new vistas for mutually beneficial development.

2. Expansion of Trust Agents: AI as an Emerging Object of Trust

The accelerated proliferation of AI technologies is transforming the dynamics of social trust; AI is evolving from a mere instrument for facilitating trust into an autonomous agent of trust, thus establishing itself as a novel object of trust alongside humans and organizations. This transformation is far from a simple substitution of roles; rather, it signifies a profound expansion of the trust ecosystem. Individuals are increasingly placing high expectations on AI systems, anticipating their competence in handling complex tasks within specialized domains and making unbiased, high-quality decisions. In the financial sector, AI-powered robo-advisors are already capable of providing professional financial planning services and earning the favor of investors. In the education sector, intelligent tutoring systems deliver personalized instruction, facilitating remarkable academic progress and gaining the trust of both students and parents. In the judicial sector, AI-assisted adjudication systems are enhancing the efficiency and fairness of rulings and gradually securing societal

---

1 CHEN, Q. Q., PARK, H. J. How anthropomorphism affects trust in intelligent personal assistants[J]. Industrial Management & Data Systems, 2021, 121 (12): 2722-2737.

recognition.

However, the emergence of AI as a trust agent is by no means a smooth journey. Unlike interpersonal trust, which largely relies on emotional factors, AI must demonstrate superiority in areas such as technical reliability, ethical standards, and behavioral transparency to earn trust. This imposes comprehensive requirements on the research, development, and deployment of AI systems. First, at the technical level, emphasis must be placed on safety, security and explainability to ensure the systems are efficient, stable, transparent, and controllable. Second, at the algorithmic level, anti-discrimination mechanisms should be strengthened to guarantee fairness and justice in decision-making, with particular attention to the interests of vulnerable groups. Third, at the ethical level, moral values should be embedded into the coding logic, endowing AI with the capacity for moral reasoning and value judgment. Finally, at the application level, a human-centered approach should be maintained, with careful delineation of the boundaries of AI trustworthiness within the framework of human-machine collaboration. All these aspects call for a dual impetus of technological innovation and ethical regulation, as well as a virtuous interaction between legal oversight and public participation. Only by striking an effective balance between encouraging exploration and upholding fundamental principles can the role of AI as a trustworthy agent be substantially advanced, thus paving the way for a new paradigm of symbiotic trust between humans and machines.

3. Transformation of Trust Formation: The Shift toward a Technology-driven Model of Trust-Building

The rapid advancement of AI technology is reshaping the mechanisms through which social trust is formed. Traditionally, trust has primarily stemmed from interpersonal emotional bonds and institutional safeguards; however, technological factors are now emerging as a new driving force in the construction of trust. This transformation toward a technology-driven model of trust building is profoundly influencing both the conceptual nature and the scope of social trust.

On the one hand, the rise of blockchain technology has opened up a new decentralized pathway for the building of trust. Leveraging cryptographic principles and consensus mechanisms, blockchain enables trustworthy interactions and collaborations among multiple parties without the need for third-party intermediaries. For instance, the underlying blockchain network of Bitcoin utilizes mathematical algorithms and distributed ledger technology to effectively ensure the security and immutability of transactions, thereby establishing trust relationships among previously unacquainted nodes. This technology-enabled model of trust building offers advantages such as low cost, high efficiency, and security with transparency, injecting new momentum into the construction of trust.

On the other hand, the development of AI technology is reshaping the logic by which trust is established. Traditionally, trust judgments have relied primarily on subjective human experience and bounded rationality. In contrast, AI systems are capable of conducting more comprehensive and objective assessments of trust targets based on massive datasets and machine learning algorithms. For instance, in the domain of credit evaluation, Ant Financial's AI Credit Scoring system integrates multidimensional data such as users' consumption behaviors and social relationships to generate precise assessments of creditworthiness. This effectively reduces the risks associated with information asymmetry and enhances the scientific rigor of trust determination. Similarly, in the field of talent recruitment, intelligent interview systems can conduct in-depth analyses of candidates' speech, facial expressions, and body language and provide a holistic evaluation of their professional qualities and competencies. This offers employers more reliable references for decision-making. Such AI-driven mechanisms for trust building shift trust judgments from experiential to empirical, and from intuitive to rational, thereby providing scientific guidance for trust-related decision-making.

Of course, the technology-driven model of trust building is not a panacea. While it empowers the construction of trust, it also introduces new trust risks such as technological monopolies, privacy infringements, and algorithmic bias. In response, it is imperative to strengthen the collaborative governance of technological innovation and ethical regulation to ensure fairness and justice within trust building mechanisms. On the one hand, data collection and usage practices must be standardized, with enhanced privacy protection to prevent information misuse. On the other hand, it is necessary to improve AI governance frameworks, reinforce algorithmic auditing, and enhance system transparency and explainability. Only by striking a balance between development and regulation can the optimization and upgrading of trust building mechanisms be achieved.

Section 2 Institutional Ethics as Guidelines: Developing a Normative Framework for Building Trust in AI

AI is reshaping the landscape of social trust at an unprecedented pace; however, legal regulation alone is insufficient to provide comprehensive safeguards for the construction of trust in this domain. As a form of social norm that is more flexible yet possesses greater penetrative power, ethical standards bear an unshirkable responsibility in guiding the reconstruction of AI trust. In the face of numerous potential trust risks throughout the AI lifecycle, the formulation of AI ethical norms should be grounded in the promotion of human well-being, with a focus on establishing a moral foundation for AI development centered on benevolence, justice, and integrity. It is essential to clarify the boundaries of responsibility among various stakeholders: technology developers must ensure algorithmic transparency and fairness; enterprises should adhere to ethical bottom lines; governments need to improve the legal framework; and the public ought to enhance their literacy and actively participate in the governance. Only by opening the door to ethical governance and fostering a virtuous pattern of collaborative co-governance among diverse actors can a solid foundation be laid for the building of trust in AI.

1. Optimization of Institutional Supply: Improving the Legal and Regulatory Framework for AI Governance

Institutions are the cornerstone of social trust, and optimizing institutional provisions is crucial for the reconstruction of trust in the context of AI-driven transformations. At present, the legal and regulatory framework for AI governance remains inadequate, making it difficult to provide robust institutional guarantees for building trust in AI. Therefore, it is imperative to develop a scientifically sound and practically feasible legal framework for AI governance by advancing legislative concepts, refining rule design, and clarifying implementation pathways.

From the perspective of legislative philosophy, it is essential to foster an "AI trust co-construction" mindset and to strike a balance between encouraging innovation and mitigating risks. On the one hand, it is necessary to support the development of AI technologies with an open and inclusive attitude, thereby creating a favorable institutional environment. On the other hand, a forward-looking approach should be adopted to anticipate potential trust risks arising from AI development, and to provide necessary legal definitions regarding the boundaries of rights and the attribution of responsibilities. For instance, legislation addressing algorithmic discrimination should refrain from imposing absolute, blanket prohibitions. Instead, it should articulate the fundamental principle of equal opportunity while allowing for reasonable exceptions for enterprises, seeking a balance between promoting technological innovation and safeguarding the rights and interests of vulnerable populations.[1] Only in this way can institutional support be provided for the healthy evolution of the AI trust ecosystem.

From the perspective of regulatory design, it is essential to adhere to the "trust-centric" principle, integrating trustworthy and empathetic values into the rules governing AI. Compared with the rigid approach of "external regulation," AI governance requires more guidance from "self-regulation" rooted in values. This necessitates the internalization and externalization of foundational values such as integrity, fairness, and justice in the formulation of AI governance rules, transforming them into behavioral norms that must be followed throughout the research, development, deployment, and application of AI systems. For example, in the scenario of smart contracts, targeted trust principles for smart contracts can be formulated, explicitly stipulating that the coding process must be open and transparent, the execution outcomes fair and reasonable, and dispute resolution responsive to all legitimate requests, thereby effectively safeguarding the legal rights and interests of all parties and consolidating the trust foundation of smart contracts.[2]

From the perspective of implementation pathways, it is imperative to

---

1 WANG, Qinghua. Legal regulation pathways for artificial intelligence: a framework [J]. Modern Law Science, 2019, 41 (2): 54-63.
2 LI, B., QI, P., LIU, B., et al. Trustworthy AI: from principles to practices[J]. ACM Computing Surveys, 2023, 55 (9): 1-46.

uphold multi-stakeholder co-governance, forming a collaborative governance synergy among government, enterprises, the public, and other diverse actors. AI trust governance is far from being the sole responsibility of the government; rather, it requires the concerted participation and coordinated efforts of multiple societal actors. This calls for a substantive shift in AI governance—from the traditional government-led, top-down approach to a paradigm characterized by multi-stakeholder co-governance and interactive collaboration.[1] For instance, with AI ethics committees, it is possible to integrate the perspectives of enterprises, academia, and the public into the co-governance processes, thereby enabling more comprehensive identification and assessment of potential risks in AI systems through multi-party deliberation. At the same time, mechanisms such as public hearings and social consultations can be introduced, allowing for appropriate public participation to promote both procedural and substantive justice in AI governance. Only by forging social consensus through multi-stakeholder interaction can a solid foundation be laid for the effective implementation of institutional trust in AI.

2. Ethical Norms as Guidelines: Establishing the Moral Foundation for AI Development

The rapid advancement of AI is reshaping the landscape of social trust; however, relying solely on legal regulations cannot provide comprehensive normative guidance for the building of trust in AI. As a more flexible yet deeply influential form of social norm, ethical standards hold significant potential in guiding the development of AI trust. Anchored in the ultimate concern for human well-being, AI ethical norms should

---

1 JIA, Ting, CHEN, Qiang. Research on enhancing the quality and efficiency of institutional supply for AI technology governance under a triple logic framework[J]. Studies in Science of Science, 2024 (6): 1-16.

focus on establishing a moral foundation for the development of AI and embedding a "trust gene" within its systems.

Specifically, the construction of AI ethical norms should be guided by the lifecycle of AI, implementing comprehensive and precise moral regulation of trust-related risks that may arise at each stage, including R&D, deployment, and iteration. For example, during the autonomous driving R&D, safety and reliability should be established as the primary values in system design, resolutely avoiding short-sighted practices that prioritize functional innovation at the expense of human life and safety. In the application phase, a human-centered approach should be maintained to grant humans greater agency in delineating the boundaries of rights and responsibilities between humans and machines, thereby safeguarding human dignity and rights. During the iteration and upgrading phase, ongoing safety must remain a top priority, with systematic assessment of potential uncertainty-related risks and exploration of dynamic, collaborative risk management mechanisms between humans and machines, thus providing robust protection for passengers' trust in autonomous mobility.

In terms of value, AI ethical guidelines should emphasize fundamental principles of trust such as benevolence, justice, and integrity, striving to achieve an intrinsic alignment between the utilitarian objectives of AI development and broader social ethics. For example, in the design of intelligent diagnostic support systems, it is essential not only to endow these systems with technical attributes of precision and efficiency, but also to integrate values of equality and compassion into their decision-making processes. This ensures that every patient receives equitable medical services, and prevents systemic discrimination against vulnerable patient groups due to data bias. At the same time, it is crucial to safeguard patients' data sovereignty and strictly prevent the unlawful collection and misuse of information, thereby genuinely upholding patients' privacy trust in intelligent diagnostic technologies.

In terms of implementation pathways, the effective application of AI ethical norms requires collaborative construction and shared responsibility among multiple stakeholders. This necessitates the promotion of a co-governance framework, wherein diverse actors—including government, industry, academia, research institutions, and end-users—jointly participate in the development of AI ethics. For example, in the formulation of AI ethical guidelines, reliance solely on the academic community is insufficient. Instead, it is essential to incorporate the perspectives of governments, enterprises, the general public, and other stakeholders. Through extensive and in-depth deliberative dialogues, a consensus on core values can be forged and subsequently translated into behavioral norms that are broadly recognized and conscientiously observed by all parties. Only by embracing inclusive ethical governance and stimulating the active engagement of diverse stakeholders can we establish the broadest possible common ground to guide AI development, thereby laying a robust social foundation for building trust in AI.

3. Clarification of Trust Responsibilities: Defining the Obligations of All AI Stakeholders

Against the backdrop of rapid advancements in generative AI technologies, clarifying the trust responsibilities has become a pivotal element in constructing a reliable AI ecosystem. The delineation of responsibilities among various stakeholders in the development and application of AI must be clearly defined to ensure both the credibility of the technology and its acceptance by society.

Technology developers occupy a central position within the AI trust and responsibility framework. Developers are not only required to ensure the functionality and security of technologies but are also responsible for algorithmic transparency and fairness. For instance, in the autonomous driving sector, Tesla has drawn significant attention due to accidents related to its self-driving features. These incidents highlight the necessity for developers to consider potential risks during the research and development phase and to implement corresponding preventive measures, such as enhancing system reliability through more rigorous testing and validation processes. Additionally, developers should disclose the decision-making mechanisms of algorithms to the public in order to strengthen users' understanding and trust in the technology, thereby avoiding trust crises caused by the "black box" effect.

As users of AI technologies, enterprises bear a critical responsibility in fostering trust, an obligation that cannot be overlooked. While leveraging AI to enhance operational efficiency and service quality, organizations must ensure that their technological applications comply with ethical and legal standards. For instance, Amazon faced criticism over algorithmic discrimination in its recruitment system, highlighting that enterprises are accountable for upholding fairness and justice in AI deployment, and for preventing discriminatory outcomes stemming from data bias. Furthermore, companies are required to establish robust data privacy protection mechanisms to safeguard user data security and prevent breaches or misuse that could undermine user trust.

Governments and regulatory authorities play regulatory and supervisory roles within the framework of AI trust and responsibility. Governments are required to formulate and refine laws and regulations related to AI, establishing clear regulatory frameworks to ensure that technology operates within the bounds of legality. For example, the EU's GDPR imposes stringent requirements on data privacy protection and stipulates the responsibilities and obligations of enterprises when processing personal data, thereby setting a global benchmark for AI governance. Furthermore, governments should promote the establishment of mechanisms for international cooperation to collectively address the global challenges posed by AI technologies, ensuring that technological advancement aligns with the protection of public interests.

As the ultimate end-users of AI technologies, the public also bears an indispensable responsibility for fostering trust. It is essential for the public to possess fundamental AI literacy, having an understanding of both the capabilities and limitations of such technologies, and to maintain rationality and caution throughout the usage. For instance, when engaging with content generated by generative AI, users should enhance their ability to discern misinformation, refrain from credulity, and avoid disseminating unverified information, thereby mitigating the risks associated with the malicious exploitation of AI technologies. Furthermore, the public should actively participate in ethical discussions surrounding technology, articulating their expectations and concerns regarding its applications, so as to promote the development of a more democratic and inclusive model of AI governance.

Multistakeholder collaboration is key to clarifying AI trust and accountability. Throughout the development of AI, it is essential for various stakeholders to establish effective communication mechanisms and cooperative platforms to jointly discuss and address ethical and legal issues arising from technological applications. For instance, collaborative research among academia, industry, and government can yield more comprehensive and in-depth insights, thereby facilitating the formulation of more reasonable and effective governance policies. Furthermore, cross-sector cooperation can promote the harmonization of technical standards and ethical norms, mitigating trust dilemmas caused by divergent standards and ensuring the healthy development of AI technologies on a global scale.

Section 3 Cultural Values as Guidelines: Fostering a Social Climate of Trust to Support AI Development

With the rapid advancement of AI, the guiding role of cultural values in fostering a socially trustworthy environment supportive of AI development has become increasingly prominent. Cultural values shape patterns of thinking and behavioral habits, subtly influencing both the trajectory of AI technology and the degree of societal acceptance. Cultural concepts such as equality and mutual trust, inclusivity and innovation, as well as collaborative governance, serve as critical nutrients for the progressive and incremental strengthening of AI. In the absence of guidance and direction from cultural values, technological innovation inevitably becomes rootless and erratic. Only by constructing social trust in AI development from the perspective of cultural values can cutting-edge technologies truly take root in the hearts and minds of the public.

1. Principle of Equality and Mutual Trust: Bridging the Digital Divide and Promoting Inclusive Benefits of AI for the Public

As AI reshapes the landscape of social trust, the guidance of cultural values is becoming increasingly significant. As an intangible yet powerful social orientation system, cultural values subtly influence the trajectory of AI development and the degree of societal acceptance by shaping individuals' cognitive patterns and behavioral norms. Among the various cultural values, equality and mutual trust are particularly significant. The promotion of digital inclusion and equal opportunity advocated by these values is fundamental to fostering a social climate of trust that supports the advancement of AI.

At present, the digital divide is becoming increasingly prominent in the field of AI. For instance, in the field of digital health, despite the rapid advancement of AI-driven medical technologies, disparities in digital literacy prevent many residents in remote areas from fully benefiting from intelligent diagnostic and treatment services, making it difficult for them to develop even a basic understanding and trust in AI healthcare.[1] The solution to alleviating this contradiction lies in advancing digital empowerment, thereby ensuring that AI truly benefits the general public. For instance, leveraging the momentum of digital rural development, increasing investment in AI-driven public welfare initiatives, equipping primary healthcare institutions with intelligent decision-support systems, and providing AI literacy training for both grassroots medical staff and local residents can enhance the capacity of people in remote areas to utilize AI healthcare. These measures help to dispel feelings of unfamiliarity and skepticism toward new technologies, thereby fostering genuine acceptance and identification with AI healthcare.

Meanwhile, the principle of equality and mutual trust also requires a human-centered and opportunity-equal approach to the development of AI. On the one hand, it is essential to ensure the primacy of humans in human-machine collaboration, and to prevent the reduction of individuals to mere appendages of machines. For example, in intelligent manufacturing, efforts should be made to improve mechanisms for worker participation, providing frontline employees with ample channels to engage in the design of human-machine interfaces and the optimization of work processes. Participatory design should be leveraged to foster a sense

---

1 FISK, R. P., GALLAN, A. S., JOUBERT, A. M., et al. Healing the digital divide with digital inclusion: enabling human capabilities[J]. Journal of Service Research, 2023, 26 (4): 542-559.

of ownership among employees toward intelligent systems, thereby transforming human-machine collaboration from a "control and compliance" model to one based on "equality and mutual trust." On the other hand, it is also crucial to effectively prevent digital barriers and discriminatory phenomena in AI applications. For instance, in AI-powered video interviews, vigilance is required regarding system biases against individuals with specific regional accents or skin colors. Technical measures such as algorithm optimization and the expansion of data samples should be employed to minimize bias, while protective mechanisms such as manual review should be established to ensure that every job applicant has an equitable opportunity to demonstrate their talents.

Of course, disseminating the principle of equality and mutual trust requires the concerted efforts of the entire society. This necessitates fully leveraging the promotional and guiding functions of various cultural platforms to foster a societal culture that encourages innovation, tolerates failure, and pursues excellence, thereby securing the broadest and most enduring public trust in AI development. For instance, for AI popularization, diverse AI experience activities can be conducted through social media and public cultural institutions. These activities, which integrate education with entertainment, can enhance public understanding of AI technologies, mitigate fears and resistance stemming from cognitive biases, and consequently stimulate widespread public support and enthusiastic participation in AI development.[1]

---

1 FU, Qianqian. Social and cultural development in the age of artificial intelligence: opportunities, challenges, and responses[J]. Xinjiang Social Sciences, 2021 (1): 117-126, 170.

2. Embracing Inclusive Innovation: Encouraging Exploration and Tolerating Imperfections in Early-Stage AI Applications

The rapid development of AI is inseparable from the cultivation of an innovative environment. An inclusive mindset toward innovation serves as a crucial foundation for fostering a trust-based ecosystem that is essential to the advancement of AI. The cultural values it promotes—tolerance of failure and encouragement of exploration—function as a protective mechanism for the gradual and incremental strengthening of AI technologies. Only by establishing an open and integrative culture of innovation across society can we build the most robust social foundation for the sustainable development of AI.

From the perspective of developmental patterns, the maturation of any emerging technology necessarily undergoes a process in which quantitative changes accumulate and ultimately result in qualitative transformations. AI is no exception. In its early stages of application, issues such as insufficient accuracy and suboptimal stability are inevitable. In response, we should maintain an open yet prudent stance and exercise appropriate tolerance, thereby affording AI the necessary latitude for experimentation and iterative improvement. For example, although autonomous driving is still in its nascent phase, road tests have already been conducted in multiple cities. Unsurprisingly, there are occasional imperfect behaviors, such as sudden braking or abrupt lane changes. If society lacks tolerance and understanding, it will inevitably exacerbate the public's trust crisis regarding autonomous vehicles, thereby impeding the technological advancement. It is important to recognize that technological maturity inherently requires repeated refinement and iteration. Only by adopting an inclusive perspective toward the advancement of new technologies and acknowledging the challenges encountered during their development can we foster the necessary conditions for autonomous driving to evolve from inception to maturity, and from initial limitations to robust capability.

Meanwhile, embracing inclusive innovation also entails encouraging bold exploration in the field of AI. At present, AI is rapidly pushing the frontiers of human cognition, driven by an ambition as boundless as the universe. In this context, it is even more critical that we safeguard innovative exploration with the courage to "embrace the unknown." For instance, in the scenario of generative AI art, while its current creative output may not yet rival that of human artists in terms of quality, the technology has already demonstrated tremendous potential in creativity and inspiration. If we hastily reject it simply because it differs from traditional artistic paradigms, it would be tantamount to undermining the very foundation of this emerging form of art, stifling its potential for growth. Conversely, if we can appreciate its alternative aesthetics with an open and inclusive mindset, and create a supportive environment that allows diverse forms of expression to flourish, we will enable AI to shine more brilliantly in artistic creation and usher in a new chapter of art through human-machine collaboration.

Of course, fostering a climate of trust that encourages innovation does not equate to unprincipled indulgence. While it is essential to create space for the development of AI, we must also remain vigilant regarding the potential risks and latent hazards that may arise during its evolution. This necessitates a dialectical approach to AI innovation, seeking a balance between proactive encouragement and support on the one hand, and prudent risk management grounded in bottom-line thinking on the other. For example, with emerging but still immature technologies such as AI-based face swapping, we should adopt an inclusive and open-minded attitude to welcome their new developments, thereby providing fertile ground for innovation. At the same time, we must proactively anticipate the risks of misuse through precautionary bottom-line thinking, establishing necessary firewalls around issues such as privacy protection, ethics, and morality. Only by striking an appropriate balance between tolerating failure and mitigating risks can we effectively safeguard the healthy development of AI.

3. Awareness of Collaborative Governance: Harnessing Collective Intelligence for Synergistic Human-Machine Co-Prosperity

The healthy development of AI relies on the collaborative governance of diverse stakeholders. With AI reshaping the landscape of social trust, cultivating an awareness of collaborative governance is essential. The cultural ethos it promotes—multi-party cooperation and mutually beneficial outcomes—is precisely the key to forging a broad social consensus in support of AI development and achieving harmonious coexistence between humans and machines. Only by fostering a societal climate of solidarity and collective action can we lay the broad and resilient public foundation necessary for building trust in AI.

Specifically, the cultivation of collaborative co-governance awareness should focus on establishing a synergistic platform that enables the participation of diverse stakeholders. This implies that the development of AI should not be a "solo performance" by a handful of enterprises or research institutions, but rather a "chorus" involving government, industry, academia, and end-users from various sectors.[1] For example, in the context of AI ethics governance, it is difficult for any

1 CHOUNG, H., DAVID, P., SEBERGER, J. S. A multilevel framework for AI governance[J]. arXiv Preprint arXiv: 2307.03198, 2023.

single stakeholder to independently clarify the complex boundaries of rights and responsibilities. Conversely, if regulatory authorities, industry organizations, technology companies, academic institutions, and the public can pool their strengths and build ethical consensus through broad-based deliberation, it will undoubtedly broaden the social foundation for AI ethical governance, thereby laying the groundwork for human-machine trust.[1] In this regard, we should strive to improve mechanisms for pluralistic participation, welcome diverse perspectives with an open and inclusive mindset, resolve conflicts of interest through consultation and dialogue, and achieve sound and effective AI governance by fostering consensus.

Meanwhile, the awareness of collaborative governance also highlights the developmental philosophy of synergistic human-machine advancement. Fundamentally, the evolution of AI has never been a simple substitution of humans by machines; rather, it is a vivid illustration of human-machine complementarity and mutual empowerment.[2] As such, it is imperative to uphold a human-centered ethos, ensuring that the division of labor between humans and machines preserves a meaningful role for human agency, and thus achieving both technological empowerment and the safeguarding of human dignity. For example, in the application of AI in education, while intelligent teaching assistants have significantly improved instructional efficiency in lesson preparation and assignment grading, they cannot replace the essential role of teachers in guiding students' value formation and facilitating affective communication between teachers and students. Therefore, we should focus on optimizing

---

1 LI, Zhenzhen, YAN, Yu, MENG, Tianguang. Ethical concerns and governance pathways of artificial intelligence[J]. Journal of the Central Institute of Socialism, 2022 (5): 139-150.

2 LI, Yi, YU, Liangru, QIU, Dong. A review of human-artificial intelligence collaboration models[J]. Journal of Information, 2020, 39 (10): 137-143.

human-machine collaborative scenarios in education, enabling AI to fully unleash its empowering and efficiency-boosting potential, while simultaneously creating conditions for teachers to exercise their pedagogical expertise. Only by implementing a division of labor that leverages human-machine complementarity can we establish a new paradigm for AI development, one characterized by collaborative creation, shared benefits, and mutual advancement.

However, collaborative governance is not achieved overnight; rather, it is a gradual and progressive process. This necessitates adopting a developmental perspective on the evolution of human-machine relationships. From a historical standpoint, the evolution of AI has progressed from perceptual intelligence to cognitive intelligence, and is now advancing toward collaborative intelligence. As machines acquire vast amounts of knowledge through deep learning and other technologies, they are transitioning from mere assistants in human decision-making to becoming partners. Looking ahead, human-machine collaboration is expected to further intensify. In an increasing number of domains, AI will work hand-in-hand with humans, leveraging complementary strengths to jointly address challenges and create value. In this context, we must adopt a forward-looking and strategic vision: fully recognizing the irreversible trend of human-machine collaboration, while also maintaining a clear understanding of the complexity and difficulty inherent in the division of labor between humans and machines. Through steady and prudent advancement, we can continuously optimize human-machine relationships, ultimately achieving a dynamic equilibrium that evolves from competition to cooperation.

Section 4 Optimizing Media Environment: Strategies for Cultivating Soft Trust in the Communication Ecosystem

Against the backdrop of rapid advancements in AI technologies, optimizing the media ecosystem is crucial for fostering the public's soft trust in AI. As the nexus between technology and society, the media bears significant responsibilities in guiding public opinion and shaping collective cognition. As such, it should prioritize salient issues that impact the broader trajectory of AI development in its agenda-setting, employing open and objective reporting perspectives to steer rational discourse and build social consensus. In science popularization and public education, it ought to adopt targeted communication strategies, using accessible language to elucidate AI concepts and enhance the public's cognitive understanding. Through exemplary reporting, it should uncover demonstrative cases where AI benefits society and improves human well-being, and employ "immersive" storytelling techniques to narrate heartwarming stories about AI and stimulate public identification with AI. In the governance of deviant information dissemination, it must strengthen cross-sectoral collaboration, refine technological ethics regulations, and curb the proliferation of AI-related misinformation. Only by making concerted efforts across multiple dimensions—committed to constructing a clean online environment and fostering a healthy public discourse—can the media lay a robust social foundation for AI development and provide a solid guarantee for cultivating the public's soft trust in AI.

1. Agenda Setting as Guidance: Focusing on AI-related Topics to Foster Rational Discussion

As a vital conduit connecting society and the public, the media assumes a pivotal role in fostering trust in AI by guiding public opinion and shaping collective cognition. Specifically, from the perspective of agenda-setting, the media should adopt a transparent and open approach to reporting on AI-related topics, steering rational discourse and subtly cultivating a favorable public opinion for building AI trust.[1] Only by positioning AI issues at the center of social debate and presenting the trajectory of AI development through diverse and objective lenses can the media facilitate a broad social consensus in support of AI advancement.

From the perspective of agenda-setting, the media should uphold a broad and strategic vision that serves the greater good, prioritizing coverage of major issues that are pivotal to the overall development of AI and the well-being of society.[2] For instance, in the application of AI in education, in the face of significant challenges posed by educational transformation in the era of intelligence, the media should take a proactive role, focusing on exploring both the prospects and challenges of AI-empowered education. This requires it to transcend the limitations of a purely technological perspective and instead approach the topic from diverse angles such as educational equity and innovation in pedagogical models, thereby stimulating multi-dimensional social reflection on the application of AI in education.[3] For instance, when reporting on AI's contribution to rural education, it is essential not only to highlight its role in providing high-quality educational resources to students in remote areas, but also to critically assess concerns such as the potential exacerbation of standardized education and the weakening of individualized instruction.

---

1 TSFATI, Y., ARIELY, G. Individual and contextual correlates of trust in media across 44 countries[J]. Communication Research, 2014, 41 (6): 760-782.

2 OUCHCHY, L., COIN, A., DUBLJEVIC, V. AI in the headlines: the portrayal of the ethical issues of artificial intelligence in the media[J]. AI & Society, 2020, 35: 927-936.

3 SONG, J., LIN, H. Exploring the effect of artificial intelligence intellect on consumer decision delegation: The role of trust, task objectivity, and anthropomorphism[J]. Journal of consumer behaviour, 2024, 23 (2): 727-747.

Only by addressing the multifaceted impacts of AI in education through agenda-setting and guiding public discourse with an open yet prudent reporting tone, can the media facilitate the formation of an inclusive social consensus.

Meanwhile, agenda-setting also entails fostering a rational and constructive discursive environment for AI development. Confronted with the proliferation of AI-related topics, the media should strive to balance technological optimism with ethical apprehensions within the public sphere, guiding discussions from an objective and rational standpoint to consolidate positive social momentum for AI development. For instance, while it revolutionizes the creation of synthetic content, AI-based face-swapping technology also raises numerous controversies related to ethical misconduct and privacy violations. In this context, media coverage must avoid using simplistic labels such as "demonization" or "de-demonization." Instead, it should facilitate rational debate with openness and inclusivity, presenting diverse viewpoints in a comprehensive manner. This necessitates that the media act as a "microscope" for AI face-swapping technology—objectively demonstrating its technological value and application prospects through case analysis, while also using in-depth reporting to reveal underlying risks in ethical and legal domains. Only by maintaining an objective and rational stance in agenda-setting, and by incorporating diverse voices through critical listening, can the media cultivate a robust social foundation for the sustainable development of AI.

2. Strengthening AI Popular Science Education and Outreach: Enhancing Public Awareness and Understanding of AI

AI popular science education and outreach serve as crucial pathways for enhancing public cognitive understanding and fostering societal trust in the technology. As a bridge connecting technological advancement and the general populace, the media is expected to play a leading role in science communication by articulating AI concepts in accessible language and illustrating AI applications through vivid, real-world examples. Through such gradual and pervasive educational efforts, public perception and comprehension of AI can be elevated. Only by empowering AI to transcend the confines of the "ivory tower" and become seamlessly integrated into everyday life—illuminating cognitive uncertainties with the light of knowledge—can we build a strong foundation of public support for AI development across society.

In terms of specific approaches, AI popular science education and outreach should be grounded in the needs of the target audience, and employ differentiated strategies tailored to distinct groups. For technology enthusiasts, in-depth analyses of cutting-edge AI technologies can be conducted through technical seminars and interviews. For adolescents, partnerships with schools to offer AI literacy courses and interactive teaching methods can stimulate curiosity and engagement.[1] For the elderly population, AI experience activities can be organized in public squares and community centers to foster emotional resonance through participatory interaction. For example, in the popularization of AI-assisted diagnosis, communications targeting medical professionals may involve inviting authoritative experts to author academic papers that systematically elucidate technical principles and recent advancements. For the general public, accessible formats such as comics and short videos can be utilized to convey the sense of empowerment that AI-assisted diagnosis

---

1 GUO, Yeming. The practice and exploration of popular science activities on artificial intelligence for adolescents: a case study of Zhejiang Province[J]. Science and Technology Bulletin, 2019, 35 (8): 231-235.

brings to patients. Only by adapting to the specific characteristics of each audience and prescribing targeted science communication "remedies" can AI public education and outreach achieve subtle yet profound influence.[1]

Meanwhile, AI popular science education and outreach must also focus on cognitive blind spots, utilizing a scientific perspective that distinguishes fact from fiction to dispel misconceptions about AI. At present, cognitive fallacies about AI still find acceptance among the public. In response, the media should wield the "sword of truth," using empirical evidence to dispel the fog of misunderstanding. For example, regarding AI bias, many people mistakenly believe that "AI decision-making is absolutely objective."[2] To address this, the media should take a proactive stance by conducting in-depth reporting on issues such as algorithmic bias and data discrimination, employing detailed case studies to reveal the origins and risks of AI bias, and fostering a rational understanding that "AI is neither omniscient nor omnipotent." It must be recognized that AI systems are merely inductive mappings of experiential knowledge, not embodiments of a priori truth. Only by clarifying the limitations of AI and adopting a prudent approach to its applications can genuine cognitive advancement be achieved through the discernment of truth from falsehood.

3. Exemplary Demonstration as Guidance: Exploring and Reporting Positive Cases of AI Development

The cultivation of trust in AI is inseparable from the exemplary guidance provided by vivid case studies. As an "amplifier" of typical cases,

---

1 ZHAO, Shuying. Exploration of the application of artificial intelligence technology in science and technology communication[J]. Robotics Technology and Application, 2014 (1): 38-41.

2 XIA, Haibo. Public Communication and Social Evaluation of Artificial Intelligence Technology in China[D]. Hangzhou: Zhejiang University of Technology, 2017.

the media ought to take the responsibility of uncovering and reporting positive examples of AI development, using the specific to illuminate the general and leading by example. Through nuanced and pervasive coverage, public confidence in AI development can be enhanced. Only by integrating the achievements of AI into the everyday lives of ordinary people and by employing immersive reporting to vividly illustrate the transformative impact of AI, can society be mobilized to form a powerful support for AI advancement.

In selecting cases, the media should adhere to a pragmatic and effective value orientation, prioritizing the coverage of AI application cases in the realm of public well-being. For cases that enhance social welfare, a comprehensive multimedia approach should be adopted, utilizing text, images, audio, and video to vividly portray the tangible benefits AI brings to people's lives. For cases that contribute to high-quality economic development, in-depth reporting should be employed to analyze their innovativeness and leadership, and thus highlight their exemplary role. For example, in reporting AI-assisted support for people with disabilities, the media can focus on heartwarming stories where intelligent prosthetics offer new beginnings to individuals with disabilities, recreating moments of regained freedom and happiness through immersive reporting methods such as VR/AR. Similarly, the development and application of AI-based navigation systems for the visually impaired can be showcased through on-site experiences and expert interviews, demonstrating the confidence and empowerment these technologies provide to the visually impaired community. Only by highlighting illustrative cases that are rooted in public relevance, and by employing immersive reporting techniques that evoke emotional resonance, can a broad consensus be fostered on the ethical, pro-social, and beneficial values of AI.

At the same time, exemplary reporting should adopt a long-term perspective, incorporating cases where AI addresses challenges faced by humanity as a whole. For cases that highlight AI's potential to benefit all of humankind, it is essential to conduct in-depth, multi-part analyses that elucidate their global significance, interpreting their profound value from the perspective of a community with a shared future for mankind. For cases that demonstrate human-AI collaboration and mutual benefit, reporting should adopt a forward-looking approach to envision the promising prospects of human-machine synergy and outline a developmental blueprint for human-AI symbiosis. For instance, when reporting global pandemic prevention and control, media outlets can engage in transnational coverage focusing on exemplary applications of AI in vaccine development and viral tracing, using the narrative of "AI fighting the pandemic" to tell compelling stories of global cooperation against COVID-19. In the case of the milestone achievement of AlphaFold in deciphering the mysteries of protein structures, its far-reaching significance can be interpreted from the perspective of advancing human health on a global scale. Only by examining exemplary cases of AI development within a global framework, and situating AI within the grand narrative of humanity's future, can we inspire a sense of mission and responsibility toward AI in society.

4. Rectifying Anomic Communication: Curbing AI-Related False and Misleading Information

The cultivation of trust in AI requires a healthy and upright communication ecosystem. As a "disinfector" of misinformation, the media should more proactively shoulder its social responsibility by resolutely eliminating falsehoods and upholding truth, thereby curbing the dissemination of inaccurate or misleading AI-related information and safeguarding a transparent environment for AI development through the power of factuality. Only by maintaining a high level of vigilance against the irregular spread of AI information—and by adopting a multi-pronged approach that includes rumor clarification, source tracing, and platform governance—can we create a public discourse environment that eliminates rumors, preserves truth, and encourages rational expression. This, in turn, lays a solid communicative foundation for fostering robust social trust in the advancement of AI.

From a micro-level perspective, the media should fulfill its gatekeeping role by promptly identifying and curbing AI-related misinformation. Currently, rumors such as "pseudo-AI incompetence" and "AI out of control" are frequently encountered. In response, the media must heighten its awareness of debunking falsehoods, intervening rapidly and precisely to counteract misinformation. For instance, in the case of ChatGPT, some social media platforms have recently disseminated unfounded claims such as "it poses political risks" or "it may be forcibly taken offline." In response, authoritative media outlets have swiftly implemented fact-checking protocols, engaging recognized experts to offer evidence-based rebuttals to dispel false and misleading information and alleviate public concerns. Additionally, leveraging big data analytics enables real-time monitoring of online public opinion, facilitating the intelligent identification and precise tracing of AI-related rumors, thereby maximizing control over their dissemination. Only by establishing a rapid-response and coordinated rumor-refutation mechanism can cognitive biases among the public be mitigated through clarification of the facts, thus fostering a sound and ethical public discourse environment conducive to the development of AI.

From a meso-level perspective, the media should also serve as a guiding force, strengthening collaborative interactions with platform enterprises and research institutions. Together, they should co-develop and share resources for debunking misinformation, thereby forming a synergistic governance mechanism to curb the proliferation of AI-generated disinformation.

At present, China is accelerating the establishment of a nationwide collaborative mechanism for rumor debunking anchored in the Internet Information Rumor Debunking Platform. Against this backdrop, traditional media should deepen cross-sectoral collaboration with emerging media, share debunking resources, and enhance governance effectiveness by leveraging synergies that enable the whole to exceed the sum of its parts through increased interconnectedness. For example, the "Rumor Crusher" initiative, launched by Science Popularization China, collaborates with over 300 authoritative media outlets, including People's Daily and Xinhua News Agency, and partners with renowned enterprises such as Qingbo Big Data and Alibaba Security. Leveraging technological tools like big data analytics and knowledge graphs, this initiative aggregates a vast repository of rumor-debunking cases. Such an innovative paradigm of collaborative rumor management offers a reference model for traditional and new media to jointly curb AI-generated misinformation. It is foreseeable that as media convergence deepens, cross-sectoral rumor debunking will become the norm, and the media ecosystem, through multidimensional synergy, will form the most robust "firewall" against the proliferation of aberrant AI-generated information.

From a macro perspective, media organizations should adopt a long-term vision by optimizing algorithmic mechanisms and enhancing platform governance to safeguard the AI public opinion ecosystem. Currently, persistent challenges such as algorithmic recommendation and the absence of platform accountability continue to facilitate the proliferation of AI-related misinformation. In response, the media should play a constructive role by promoting the institutionalization of technical ethics in algorithms and platforms, thereby establishing a robust firewall for AI information dissemination. There have been some valuable initiatives that media organizations can draw upon. For example, the EU's Digital Services Act explicitly requires the "de-blackboxing" of algorithmic recommendations, which helps minimize the risk of algorithms amplifying rumors. Similarly, China's Provisions on the Administration of Internet Information Service Algorithmic Recommendations focus on building a comprehensive regulatory mechanism centered on algorithmic filing, and offer institutional support to curb the spread of false information. Media organizations should adopt a proactive approach by actively participating in relevant policy-making processes to provide insights and suggestions for system improvement, and by strengthening communication and collaboration with internet platforms to foster a virtuous cycle between technological governance and regulatory frameworks. Ultimately, this approach aims to establish a comprehensive governance system grounded in technology, rule of law, and ethics, thereby consolidating the foundation of trust in AI.

Section 5 Empowerment through Education and Training: Enhancing Public AI Literacy and Trust-Building Capacity

Building trust in AI is a complex and systemic endeavor that requires a multidimensional approach to establish a comprehensive and integrated capacity-building framework. As a pivotal instrument for enhancing public AI literacy and fostering social trust, education and training are expected to play an increasingly significant role in the contemporary practice of AI governance. Refining a curriculum system for AI trust across all educational stages, conducting immersive AI experiences and ethical practice simulations, and supporting the continuous improvement of AI application capabilities among members of society constitute the three principal pathways through which education and training can contribute to the construction of AI trust. Only by prioritizing the foundational cultivation of talent and by integrating knowledge with practice to elevate the core AI literacy of the entire populace can we nurture a fertile ground for trust, thus providing a solid foundation and talent pool essential for societal development in the AI era. The integration of education and training with AI trust-building in the new era not only demonstrates a proactive and forward-looking commitment but also reflects a sense of responsibility to serve the nation and contribute to society. From the strategic perspective of building a community with a shared future for mankind, accelerating the empowerment of AI trust through education and training represents a distinctive contribution of Chinese wisdom and solutions to global technology governance and the construction of an AI community with a shared future. Looking ahead, the field of education and training must further strengthen its sense of mission, continuously optimize top-level design in line with contemporary technological advancements, innovate operational mechanisms, and broaden as well as deepen efforts of building trust in AI. In cultivating a new generation for the times, education will thereby manifest its contemporary value by providing intellectual support and a reliable talent pool for both national modernization and building a community with a shared future for mankind.

1. Comprehensive Curriculum System: Integrating AI Trust into All Educational Stages

The foundation of building trust in AI lies in enhancing the digital literacy of the entire population. As a fundamental enterprise that shapes and influences individuals, education should assume greater responsibility in fostering public capacity for AI trust. Integrating AI trust education into curricula across all educational stages and establishing a comprehensive developmental paradigm from primary to higher education constitute a critical pathway for empowering AI trust-building in the new era. Only by cultivating a fertile environment for AI trust within educational institutions, systematically designing trust-oriented courses, and nurturing students' core competencies to address AI-related risks and actively participate in AI development, can we foster a robust foundation for AI trust among the younger generation.

In terms of curriculum objectives, AI trust education should be grounded in the demands of the current era, emphasizing the cultivation of AI literacy as the central theme, while also taking into account the cognitive characteristics of students at different educational stages. The cultivation objectives should be systematically designed in a progressive manner across the dimensions of knowledge, competence, and values. At the primary and secondary school levels, the focus should be on developing students' basic skills in utilizing AI and fostering an awareness of trust in AI applications. For example, the integration of an "AI Little Assistant" project into primary school information technology courses can guide students to experience the joys of human-AI interaction while understanding the benefits of AI in learning and daily life. In junior high school comprehensive practice courses, a thematic module such as "AI: I Trust You" can be established, leading students to investigate AI applications in their surroundings and enhancing their identification with AI-enabled development. At the higher education level, emphasis should be placed on cultivating key competencies for AI trust, and shaping students' professional literacy to address complex AI scenarios and participate in AI governance practices. For instance, offering a course on AI ethics can systematically elucidate key issues in AI governance such as machine bias and privacy protection, thereby inspiring students to engage in in-depth critical reflection on AI trust issues. Similarly, the inclusion of an "Explainable AI" project in computer science curricula can involve students in optimizing the explainability of AI algorithms, thereby enhancing their practical capabilities to improve AI transparency and mitigate the "black box" problem.

In terms of curriculum design, AI trust education should align with the characteristics of the intelligent era by actively innovating pedagogical formats and enhancing educational effectiveness through multiple approaches such as classroom instruction, experiential learning, and inter-school collaboration. For example, integrating interactive technologies like VR/AR into classroom teaching can enable students to engage in immersive simulations of ethical dilemmas in AI governance, thereby fostering rational reflection on issues of AI trust. Furthermore, leveraging the advanced resources of universities, a series of "AI Lab Exploration" activities can be organized for primary and secondary school students, allowing them to experience first-hand the development of AI systems based on principles of explainability and verifiability, and thus strengthening their identification with responsible AI. Additionally, schools at different educational levels and from various regions can be encouraged to participate in "AI Trust Partnership Programs," establishing cross-school exchange platforms through collaborative research and remote interaction, thereby deepening students' understanding of AI trust through mutual learning and exchange.

In terms of course evaluation, AI trust education should adopt an open and progressive assessment philosophy, shifting the focus from outcomes to processes and from static examinations to dynamic assessments, thereby constructing a scientifically sound and comprehensive course evaluation system that accurately measures students' holistic competence in AI trust. For classroom instruction, formative assessment can be introduced to emphasize students' performance in classroom discussions and group assignments, internalizing AI trust awareness into daily habits. In the practical activity modules, project-based evaluation can be employed by designing open-ended tasks such as "AI in My Eyes" or "How AI Changes Life," assessing students' abilities to analyze problems and apply hands-on skills in the context of AI trust. For inter-school exchange units, peer assessment can be piloted to enhance students' agency and deepen their understanding of AI trust through mutual evaluation. Furthermore, it is advisable to explore linking evaluation results to credits, scholarships, and other incentives to stimulate intrinsic motivation for learning and facilitate the effective implementation of AI trust education.

2. Practical Training Expansion: Conducting AI Experience and Ethical Practice Drills

The enhancement of AI literacy is inseparable from the expansion and deepening of practical training. As an extension of theoretical instruction, engaging in AI experiential activities and ethical practice exercises constitutes an effective approach to improving public understanding of AI and strengthening trust awareness. Only by moving beyond the classroom and embedding AI trust education into everyday life scenarios, thereby enabling the public to elevate their perception through immersive experiences and internalize trust through hands-on practice, can a genuine transformation in AI trust capabilities be achieved.

The implementation of AI experiential activities should be grounded in public needs and tailored to diverse audiences. For primary and secondary school students, technologies such as VR and AR can be leveraged to develop immersive, AI-driven interactive learning environments. Within gamified scenarios, students can appreciate the enjoyment of human-machine collaboration, and through role-playing, they can internalize the principles of responsible AI. For example, a project titled “I Am an AI Expert” could be designed for primary school students, where they interact with a simulated AI assistant in a household environment to experience firsthand the convenience that AI applications bring to daily life. Similarly, for secondary school students, an activity such as “The Making of an AI Content Moderator” could be organized, allowing participants to identify and flag harmful information on a virtual content review platform, thereby fostering a sense of responsibility for AI-assisted content governance. For the general public, public cultural institutions such as science and technology museums and libraries can serve as platforms for “Exploring AI” and “Experiencing AI” series of activities. For instance, citizens could be invited to visit NLP laboratories to observe, up close, the operational workflows of intelligent customer service and simultaneous interpretation systems, thereby deepening their trust and understanding of the safety and reliability of such technologies. Additionally, “AI Ethics Salons” could be held, focusing on cutting-edge issues such as algorithmic bias and privacy protection. Through interactive formats such as brainstorming sessions and roundtable forums, these events can foster consensus and enhance public capacity for participation in AI governance.

The implementation of ethical practices should adopt a forward-looking and leading perspective, providing the public with scenario-based simulations for engaging in complex AI applications. The specific approach can be divided into two main components. First, based on real-world scenarios, AI ethical dilemmas should be designed to guide the public in strengthening their awareness of trust through navigating conflicting choices. For example, by introducing the “trolley problem” in autonomous driving contexts, participants can assume the role of passengers in self-driving vehicles and face the dilemma of "hitting a pedestrian or swerving into a tree." Through experiential simulation, participants deepen their rational understanding of the potential risks associated with autonomous driving and develop the ability to manage such risks. Second, in virtual environments, immersive metaverse spaces can be constructed to simulate AI governance scenarios, enabling the public to participate in the entire process of policy formulation and standards development, thereby enhancing their trust in AI through systematic practice. For instance, the development of an "AI Governance Metaverse" project could provide the public with virtual parliaments and technical committees for participating in AI legislation and standards-setting. By involving the public in agenda-setting, rule deliberation, and decision-making processes, these collaborative exercises in the metaverse foster skills in building trust for real-world AI scenarios.

It is worth noting that AI practical training is by no means a simple "gamified" experience; rather, it should embody a rigorous and meticulous scientific attitude. This necessitates a holistic perspective on the entire process of experiential activities and hands-on projects, strengthening top-level planning and refining training mechanisms to safeguard the practice of AI trust. For example, during the project planning phase, comprehensive research and argumentation should be conducted, with careful topic selection centered on societal challenges and public needs. In the activity organization phase, emphasis should be placed on collaboration with universities and research institutes, leveraging cutting-edge academic expertise for guidance and quality assurance, thereby infusing scientific rigor into practical training. In the phase of outcome transformation, it is essential to distill and summarize practical paradigms that are replicable and adaptable, forming a dynamically evolving knowledge base for AI trust practices. Only by approaching AI practical training with holistic integration and system design, and by continuously developing exemplary projects through iterative advancement, can public engagement be stimulated and the enhancement of AI trust literacy across society be effectively empowered.

3. Promoting Lifelong Learning: Facilitating the Ongoing Development of Public Competencies in AI Applications

Building trust in AI is a long-term and formidable systemic endeavor. Given the rapid pace of technological iteration and the extensive range of application scenarios, relying solely on formal education within schools is no longer sustainable. There is an urgent need to establish a paradigm for enhancing AI literacy through lifelong learning accessible to the entire population. Facilitating the continuous improvement of AI application competencies among all members of society and constructing dynamic, readily accessible lifelong learning platforms are essential responses to the evolution of AI technologies and the cultivation of public trust in AI. Only by fostering a fertile environment for lifelong learning across society and creating an educational ecosystem where everyone can learn at any time can we provide a steady and robust foundation for building trust in AI.

In terms of specific approaches, facilitating lifelong AI learning should first be grounded in a needs-based approach, with the development of targeted learning platforms designed for diverse social groups. For students, it is essential to maintain an integrated approach to in-class and extracurricular training, encouraging them to utilize MOOCs, AI training platforms, and other resources to form a synergistic complement to classroom instruction, thereby strengthening their AI application skills through the integration of theory and practice. For instance, leveraging intelligent education platforms, universities can construct interdisciplinary

"AI+X" learning spaces, guiding students to apply AI technologies to solve real-world problems and enhance their cross-disciplinary integration abilities through project-based learning. For professionals, the primary role of industry and enterprises should be emphasized by establishing an on-the-job training system that integrates industry and education and supporting employees in keeping their AI skills current. For example, internet companies can be encouraged to offer AI literacy enhancement courses for their employees, incorporating cutting-edge technologies such as machine learning and human-AI interaction into employee training, thus fostering a culture of learning organizations. For community residents, it is necessary to innovate forms of community education by transforming communities into accessible AI literacy classrooms. This can be achieved by leveraging the functions of community hubs such as New Era Civilization Practice Centers[1] to regularly organize AI literacy lectures, hands-on workshops, and other activities, thereby extending the reach of lifelong learning resources to grassroots communities.

At the same time, lifelong AI learning should also emphasize supply-side innovation, proactively leveraging new technologies and models to expand learning pathways. On the one hand, AI technologies should be utilized to empower personalized learning, streamlining the learning process through intelligent recommendations, virtual assistants, and similar tools to enhance the sense of achievement in lifelong learning. For example, constructing AI learning companion systems can generate precise learner profiles based on individual characteristics and behavioral data, thereby matching learners with personalized educational resources

---

1 Comprehensive community hubs in China integrating grassroots public service resources such as cultural stations, Party (CPC) and mass service centers, and rural libraries, and serving as multifunctional platforms for theoretical lectures, cultural promotion, volunteer services, and the cultivation of civilized conduct.

and creating immersive learning experiences. On the other hand, it is essential to actively explore diverse learning scenarios and embed AI literacy cultivation into everyday contexts, enabling lifelong learning to be accessible anytime and anywhere. For instance, implementing AI experience projects in museums and science centers can foster public engagement through immersive interactions; integrating AI science communication elements into films and variety shows can stimulate public interest in a popular and approachable manner; and establishing AI science communication accounts on social media platforms can promote active learning among audiences through real-time interactions, bullet comments, and other participatory features.

Made in United States
Troutdale, OR
11/03/2026

56845411R00239